Rural China Today

Frank Leeming

Rural China Today

Longman
London and New York

Longman Group Limited
Longman House, Burnt Mill, Harlow
Essex CM20 2JE, England
Associated companies throughout the world

*Published in the United States of America
by Longman Inc., New York*

First published 1985

British Library Cataloguing in Publication Data

Leeming, Frank
 Rural China today.
 1. China – Rural conditions   2. China
 Economic conditions
 I. Title
 330.951′058   HC427.92

ISBN 0-582-30144-0

Library of Congress Cataloging in Publication Data

Leeming, Frank.
 Rural China today.

 Bibliography: p.
 Includes index.
 1. Rural development – China. 2. China – Rural
 conditions. 3. Regional planning – China.
 I. Title
HN740.Z9C64   1985   307.7′2′0951   83-25617
ISBN 0-582-30144-0

Set in 9½/11 pt. Linotron 202 Palatino
Printed in Singapore by
Selector Printing Co (Pte) Ltd

Contents

List of plates

ix

Units and equivalents

In principle the People's Republic uses the metric system of measures, but in practice a number of traditional units, now defined in terms of metric equivalents, are also used. These are so intimately related to Chinese usage that it is difficult to discard them, and they have been retained in this book. The most distinctive is the *mou*, (or *mu*) a measure of area which is very small (667 sq m, or one-fifteenth of a hectare; approximately one-sixth of the English acre). Crop outputs per unit area are usually expressed in *jin* per *mou* – the *jin* is a half-kilogram. The following table converts *jin* per *mou* (used in this book) to metric tons per hectare (ha):

Jin per *mou*	Metric tons per hectare
100	0.75
500	3.75
1,000	7.5
1,500	11.25
2,000	15.0

Throughout this text, 'tons' indicates metric tons of 1,000 kg.

The Chinese unit of currency is the *yuan*, whose official rates of exchange in 1980–83 were approximately 3.4 *yuan* to the pound sterling and 1.5 *yuan* to the United States dollar.

Pronunciation of Chinese names

In this study the official *pinyin* system of romanisation of Chinese names is used. Pronunciation of *pinyin* is broadly self-explanatory for English speakers, with the following exceptions – *pinyin c* is pronounced *ts*; *pinyin q* is pronounced *ch*; *pinyin zh* is pronounced *j*; *pinyin x* represents a sound close to *sh*. However, names of Chinese authors which appeared in print before the general adoption of the *pinyin* system in 1979 are generally given in the form in which they then appeared.

Abbreviations

Abbreviations used in the text in relation to source materials are explained on page 187, at the beginning of the References list.

Acknowledgements

In writing this book, many of my specific debts of gratitude are to institutions rather than to individuals – to the University of Leeds which partly supported my three very dissimilar visits to China in 1970, 1977 and 1982; to a number of institutions in China which welcomed me during the most recent, and by far the least depressing, of these visits; to the then Social Science Research Council which supported a research project on localities in China in 1974–6; and to the library of the School of Oriental and African Studies in London for hospitality. Few of these debts take visible form in the book, but they are nevertheless real in terms of my understanding of Chinese affairs. In language I owe debts, also invisible but real, to the Beijing Foreign Languages Institute for their *Hanying Cidian* dictionary of 1978, and also to May Huang Man-hui, my research assistant during 1974–6.

Many of my debts to individuals are much more visible – especially those to other researchers, most of them in China, who have also studied Chinese rural problems. These are acknowledged in the list of references. The maps were drawn by Tim Hadwin. Here too, however, I owe many invisible and untraceable debts to colleagues, students and friends in geography and various branches of Chinese study, and to my wife, for insight and understanding at many points. *Rural China Today* is dedicated, in affection and respect, to those who contributed to its making.

Frank Leeming
School of Geography
University of Leeds
Autumn 1983

China since Mao

China has experienced rapid change since the death of Chairman Mao, and changes in the media have been still more rapid. There is more real information to be had about the Chinese community now than at any time since 1949, and in some ways more than at any previous time in history. It is now possible to gain a realistic perspective view of the achievements and limitations of the Maoist decade which ran from the start of the Cultural Revolution in 1966 until after Mao's death in 1976, to analyse the main currents of change since 1976, and to understand in some depth various problems about which policy discussions in China are revolving. Discussion in China may not yet be free, but it is not necessarily debarred from tackling fundamentals such as the continued existence and organisation of the commune system in the countryside, the functions and status of state-owned industries, the disastrous shortage of small and varied enterprises of all kinds, the problems created by surplus rural labour, and many others. Reaction against the Maoist mental strait-jacket, conjoined with partial recognition of many kinds of stagnation, waste and depression in Maoist China, has stimulated a very varied crop of analyses, criticisms and proposals on a wide range of topics in economic and community management.

In these discussions, the leadership insists upon some principles as sacrosanct – continued public ownership of the means of production is the most important – but beyond them, social, political and management discussions range very widely, at least in some phases of time and some walks of life. It may range similarly in imaginative literature, as W J F Jenner has shown. Given the unhappy experience of the academic and professional communities under the Maoists, it is not surprising that the professional journals in the economic and social studies fields (such as *Economic Research*) are content to remain in the rearguard of the new freedoms. So, broadly speaking, do the provincial newspapers of which a number have been available in the West since 1980, though these contain much detail and for that reason must figure increasingly in regional research in the future. Paradoxically, the vanguard of the new intellectual freedoms is dominated by organs of opinion closer to political power, particularly the *People's Daily*, and for that reason the *People's Daily* has been particularly useful to the present study. The same may be said of *Red Flag* and some journals which interest themselves in management, particularly *Economic Management* and *Problems of Agricultural Economics*. All publication and broadcasting in China are still in some sense official, and phases of rigidity and relaxation come and go in the media, but published commentary particularly on rural affairs is now relatively free and open, and discussion in groups in China (for instance in the universities) is still more so.

The material upon which the present studies are based represents the countryside under the Maoist system and since, as far as possible at local level – at the level of the counties, the communes and the villages; and it has been assembled without the help of fixed preconceptions. China is immense, and truth in China is at least as many-sided as truth elsewhere. All or almost all of the material gathered is from official sources, but it displays a good deal of diversity nevertheless, and between the Maoist phase and the present, differences in outlook and approach which are fundamental and fascinating.

To gather and interpret materials on the experience of the countrysides at regional and local level during the past twenty years, and to draw from them insights about regional and local schemes of development, is of course an ambitious plan. Like all such enterprises it stands under perpetual threat from the march of time – material of this kind necessarily takes time to synthesise and produce, and inevitably it loses some degree of topicality as it does so. In these conditions it is the business of the writer to seek out materials whose significance is more than topical, and ideas which are versatile and penetrating as well as relevant to the times. Fortunately the present is a time of relatively strong consistency and continuity in policy, as well as of relative abundance of materials. Indeed, from the point of view of the existence of detailed local material, as from most other points of view, the Chinese countryside is exceptional. Since Liberation, and even before, an immense amount of detailed local survey material of various kinds has appeared in the national and regional media. Material of this kind is usually – perhaps always – corrupted in some degree by politically motivated writers and editors, and should be used critically; but the total amount of local material is very large by the standards of most communities outside the West – the Soviet Union, India or Southern Africa, for instance. It is this material, appearing in broadcasts, newspapers and periodicals, crop and management manuals, literature on models for self-improvement and so forth, which has been drawn upon in these studies. Most of it has been taken directly from the Chinese media and has not previously appeared in any form in English, though use has been made of the translation series (which themselves have a useful regional dimension) at many points. In this way, a view of change and stagnation in China may be had from the inside; and by taking up topics of discussion or exhortation in the media, we may build up a picture of current preoccupations in China as seen by the Chinese community. Ever since 1949, there has been in Chinese community management a powerful strain of populism to which Mao himself contributed a great deal and and from which in turn he drew great strength. This strain of populism and its management have had mixed effects in the media, but it is clear that in recent years the government has considered it realistic to accept its implications and to open the columns of journals and newspapers to quite wide-ranging discussions of most parts of the official system and its achievements and shortcomings during the past generation. In terms of factual materials, this freedom reached its apogee during 1979–81 and has fallen off since; but in terms of discussion much remains, especially in rural affairs. All these materials are of interest as representing a *Chinese* commentary upon the experiences of the community.

The Maoist scheme of development received a good press in the West (Committee of Concerned Asian Scholars; Milton, D, Milton, N and Schurmann; Robinson 1969; Burchett; FAO Study Mission). Accounts of it were being published coevally with the ecology movement, the energy crisis and Western disillusionment with the boom philosophy of the 1960s; and the notion of a practical scheme of development on a very big scale, which made its achievements through low or intermediate technology and whose use of scarce resources was quite limited, made widespread appeal. Less attention was paid to the very low standards of personal and collective consumption in China, the growing backwardness of the technological foundations of the Chinese economy, the extent of social coercion exerted by the system among the people, and problems of depression, waste and stagnation. But problems of all these kinds did arise within the Maoist system, and shadowy evidences of them were appearing in the Chinese media from the early 1970s onwards.

There were obvious discontinuities between the Dazhai (Tachai) model of development and the opportunities and needs of rural communities in parts of China distant from highland Shanxi. Problems obviously arose in the deployment of enterprise and labour in particular rural development contexts, and not all of these could be solved (as they were supposed to be) by a proper analysis of the situation in terms of Mao's delphic slogan, 'Take grain as the key link, promote all-round development' – though some heroic efforts went into print. Most fundamental of all, it was far from clear, during the Cultural Revolution and the Maoist decade, what socialism in China was *for*. What it was not for, evidently, was the enrichment of the working class in the short run and on the local scale – that aim was often criticised, as leading to revisionism and in the end back to capitalism. In the words of one rural production brigade, published in *Red Flag*: 'The revolutionary aim of the proletariat is not to feed and clothe oneself well, but to gradually reduce and wipe out the three major differences [between town and country, industry and agriculture, physical and mental labour], rid the world of exploitation of man by man, realise communism, and liberate the whole of mankind.' (Hsiaohsiang production brigade: 35) The average loyal and hard-working countryman might be forgiven for finding the links between the proclaimed aims of the system, and his own working and family life, unclear – and nowhere more than in Yushu county to which Hsiaohsiang (Xiaoxiang) brigade belongs, where years of hard work in the service of the Maoist state led to chronic indebtedness (Ch. 11). Ambiguity about ultimate aims led to ambiguity about intermediate and local aims and methods and to increasing reliance on the routine and bureaucratic side of the system, not least in the media; and hence to disillusionment, cynicism and apathy.

Since the death of Chairman Mao in September 1976 and the almost immediate denunciation and imprisonment of his close followers and intellectual heirs the Gang of Four, the government of China has been headed by the victors in the political struggles of 1976, the changing and developing group centred around Vice-Premier Deng Xiaoping (Fontana; Feuchtwang and Hussain). Under this regime, a number of important changes have been made in Chinese policy, as well as in ideology. Some of these changes affect the foundations of the state, particularly the

beginnings of a reconstruction of the legal system and important changes in the machinery of administration. Revolutionary committees, the nominated organs of community management during the Cultural Revolution, have been replaced by local and provincial people's congresses, with direct elections for those at county level and below. Other parallel changes are of less formal importance, but nevertheless deeply affect the practical lives of many millions of people – the dropping of the Maoist policy of enforced rustication of young people from the cities, the uneasy restoration of free rural and urban marketing, the rises in urban wages and rural farm prices, the introduction of a varied range of group and individual 'responsibility' systems in agricultural production and various policies designed to stimulate local economies.

Above all, enrichment of the people, especially the working class, is now a proclaimed aim of the Chinese system. Enterprise and success in collective production, formerly rewarded (in selected politically praiseworthy cases only) mainly by political pats on the back, now receive material reward as well as praise in the media; and the same applies to private enterprise at the level of the individual household. Bureaucratic tyranny, privilege and incompetence are sometimes exposed, especially where they can be linked with extravagant Maoist political attitudes and denounced as part of the Gang of Four system. To some extent, perhaps, we have here a reversal of political fortunes such as may take place at a Western election; the incoming party hastens to demolish the most offensive features of its predecessors' institutions, and to hunt out inadequacies, especially those which have ideological roots. This process can be satisfying in itself in the West, and may well be much more so in China. But far beyond this, the Chinese community is being pressed to recognise new goals and to adopt new methods to reach them. The changes of the present are quite as fundamental as those of the Cultural Revolution in their time (Burton and Bettelheim; Feuchtwang and Hussain).

The signal for the high tide of relatively free (and hence constructive) comment in the Chinese media was the third plenary session of the eleventh meeting of the Central Committee of the Chinese Communist Party in December 1978, often called the Third Plenum (Wang Hongmo). From this time the criticism of Maoist rural policy, which had already enjoyed some exceptional

历史的垃圾

The Gang of Four and their six principal accomplices slide into the rubbish-tip of history. But who is the skeleton in the overcoat? *Source: People's Daily*, 24 Nov. 1980. The artist is Miao Di.

ventilation in the press during the summer of 1978, became a main preoccupation in the official media. Criticism, which began with type examples of exploitation of junior units by senior units in the rural collective system, moved on to the frequent humiliating shortages (of soap, consumer goods, protein foods, vegetables, housing) in the countryside, and in due course to the problems of collective decision-taking involving the fundamentals of the commune system itself on the one hand, and the imperative needs of the state plan and state grain surplus procurement systems on the other.

During 1979 and 1980 radical modifications of policy were already being proposed, notably the diversification and renewed commercialisation of production, the widespread reintroduction of rural markets, and responsibility and contract arrangements for production within the collective system; and from 1980 onwards these proposals were progressively brought to reality on the ground. Prosperity, now a proclaimed aim of the

system, has certainly increased. No doubt a further crop of rural problems is already on the way, arising out of prosperity as well as the new management system. Realistically, it is not too much to say that the Chinese community is now gleefully entering the Third World; but we need not suppose that in this position it will be protected from characteristic Third-World evils.

Hence the present is a time of exceptional interest in China. It is also a time when the media materials are exceptionally revealing. The changes introduced by the present administration are not extravagantly revolutionary like those of the Cultural Revolution in 1966, but they are nevertheless quite radical. Because the government wishes to carry the people along in support of its policy for more local orientations leading (hopefully) to more economic growth and more local prosperity, plentiful local discussion materials have appeared in the media, especially on local development. These are full of interest, and of course contrast with those of the past decade in many ways – as the universal rural model of the Cultural Revolution phase, Dazhai, has been superseded by other models which represent peasant prosperity and devote little space to socialist piety. There are also increasing signs of the people taking the development process into their own hands. Regional differences are tremendous, and changes in outlook of this order have implications for these vastly differing regions. In retrospect, important regional differences of level, style and priorities of development under the Maoists are becoming apparent – differences which never reached the public in the Maoist phase, or reached them only through the language of political motivation and socialist achievement. But the regional differences which are now developing, under the pressures of economic opportunity in the best areas and inflexible poverty of resource in the worst, are very much greater.

China is immense. The total extent of the territory of the People's Republic is almost 10 million sq km, an area much larger than Western Europe or the United States mainland. It is necessary first to recall that nearly half the country – the western half, in Xinjiang, Tibet and Qinghai, together with parts of Gansu and Sichuan (see Fig. 1.1) comprises a vast system of basins, plateaux and deserts extending far into central Asia, with a total population less than 5% of that of the whole, and much less than that

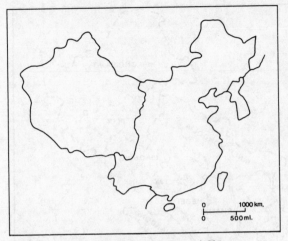

Fig. 1.1. The two geographical halves of China.

centred. It is not easy to do this kind of work well. Field-work in any real sense is not permitted to foreigners. Visits are exciting but superficial – a few hours spent in a commune of 20,000 or even 50,000 people. The literature is relatively plentiful, but its quality is uneven and can be very low due to political obsessions, amateurish statistical approaches, pussy-footing of various kinds and discontinuity over time – it is generally much better now than formerly, partly because there is now discussion of priorities and alternatives, but it still consists mainly of general media material, intended rather to explain and popularise official policy, or to raise morale and confidence, or to air specific grievances, than to supply Chinese or Western commentators with solid or comprehensive data. It is particularly difficult to make useful comparisons between materials produced in different policy phases, because the criteria of selection of materials differ so dramatically from phase to phase that comparison may well be literally impossible.

All this means that Chinese study above the most superficial level continues to present exceptional difficulties along with some surprising opportunities. But whatever the difficulties, the continued development of Chinese counties, with populations numbered in the hundreds of thousands, and of smaller local units such as the tens of thousands of people's communes, cannot fail to arouse continued interest – not least because most of them now have populations approaching double those of 1949. Chinese localities go on developing, and however simple their methods of survival and banal the materials which explain them, we cannot be indifferent to their progress through our own generation of time. In fact, as we can show, the methods by which survival is assured and prosperity approached in many villages and communes in China are far from simple.

Finally, it is worth drawing attention to some obvious, but revealing and important, parallels relating to the scale of Chinese communities and the size of provinces and counties (Fig. 1.2). An 'average' Chinese province such as Hubei has about 45 million people and surface area around 180,000 sq km, rather larger than England and Wales but with slightly fewer people; rather larger than Illinois but with four times the population. Guangdong, a province of more than average size, is slightly smaller than Great Britain or New York–New Jersey–Pennsylvania, and has a similar

proportion of total production. Central Asian China has its own environments, its own history, its own geographical and ecological relationships and its own peoples whose languages and cultures are not Chinese; its problems and opportunities differ radically from those of homeland China to the south and east. The studies in this book relate only incidentally to the central Asian half of China. But even the eastern half of China is immense, smaller by about one-quarter than the United States mainland, but still much bigger than western Europe. It is also remarkably varied, stretching through 36 degrees of latitude from north to south, and rising through more than 3,000 m elevation.

In this vast and varied area live almost the whole of a total population now around 1,000 million, still almost one-quarter of the rapidly increasing human family. While examining the problems which arise in Chinese community and resource management, and in productive relationships in many fields, the magnitude of the achievement of the community in maintaining its vast numbers in peace and decency should not be forgotten or underestimated – it may almost be taken for granted today, but could not so be taken in the century before 1949. The secret of their maintenance has of course to be sought in the localities where they live and have their subsistence; and it may be that the secret of the structure of the Chinese community itself should be sought in the same places. In China, local studies are of necessity of exceptional interest.

It is upon such localities, in the heartlands of eastern China, that the studies in this book are

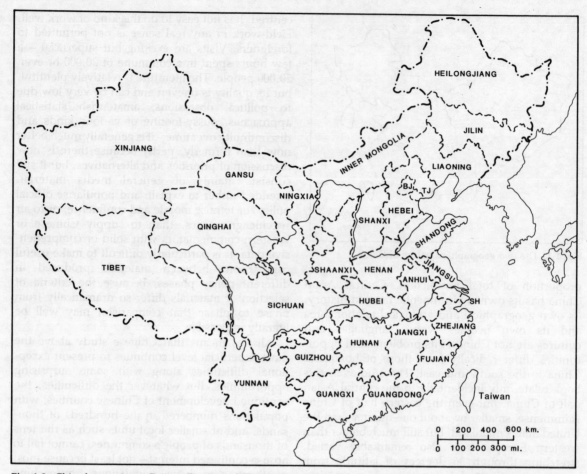

Fig. 1.2. China by provinces. Beijing, Tianjin and Shanghai (BJ, TJ, SH) have the rank of provinces. A typical province has about 70 rural counties grouped into about 8 prefectures.

population (around 53 millions) to Great Britain, but about 50% more than New York–New Jersey–Pennsylvania. Compared with all Japan, Guangdong is about 40 per cent smaller in area, and has about one-half the population. In broad terms, Chinese provinces are of the same order of size and population as European states. (Much the same is true of the larger states of India, such as Bihar.) An average Chinese rural county, for instance in Hubei, covers about 2,500 sq km and has around 500,000 people – this would be comparable with Northamptonshire in England, and similar in population to the State of Delaware but with only about one-half the area.

Where governments and official management systems are dealing with basic units of the order of size of the Chinese provinces, it is not surprising that these units differ considerably in regional terms (because nowhere are regional conditions uniform over areas of this order of size, for instance in respect of climate), and also in social terms (because even without powerful traditions of separatism, local spoken languages, forms of subsistence and historic preconceptions necessarily differ over such large areas). From this standpoint, what is surprising is not that China (specifically, the eastern half of China) contains so much diversity in management, some of which might be called inconsistency, but that it contains so little of either diversity or inconsistency.

South and north

The vast size of China naturally finds expression in a wide range of rural environments. Some of the kinds of landscape which provide subsistence to the Chinese rural community (now numbering upwards of 800 million people) are reasonably familiar to the Western observer, especially the paddy plains and valleys of the south, with irrigated soils and fringing bamboo groves – and, for those who have read the Dazhai literature, the dry plateau of the inland north, with its gullies and terraces. Other Chinese landscapes are less familiar – the limitless and almost featureless dusty landscapes of the north China plain and the north-east (the old Manchuria), the forested mountains of the centre and south, the rubber plantations of Hainan island or the pinewoods of the north-eastern mountain fringes. Some brief introductory distinctions among the regional environments of China will be helpful in clarifying development problems and possibilities, and in indicating the parameters of regional and local differences which may well be critical on the ground. They will also serve to introduce more extended treatment of Chinese environments by other writers (Institute of Geography, USSR Academy of Sciences; Pannell and Ma).

The most important regional distinctions which arise in the maritime eastern half of China are those of climate, and of these the most important are the incidence of winter cold and the amount and reliability of summer rain. Owing to the great size of the Eurasian continent in global terms, the cooling of the continental interior of Asia in winter is exceptionally severe. Most places in China are very cold in winter by the standards of places elsewhere in the same latitudes, particularly those located on the western margins of the continents, as is shown by the intense winter cold of Mohe in northern Heilongjiang (−31 °C in January) compared with standard January temperatures in Liverpool (+4 °C) at the same latitude. Land masses located in middle latitudes on the eastern margins of the continents typically received little rain in winter, but in northern China, for a group of reasons not clearly understood, the incidence of rain in summer is less generous and less reliable than might be expected. Taken together, the effects of these two peculiarities suggest a regional distinction in the maritime eastern half of China between a dry north with cold winters, and a moist south with relatively

7

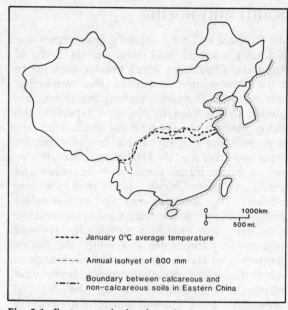

- - - - - January 0°C average temperature

- - - - Annual isohyet of 800 mm

-..-..- Boundary between calcareous and
non-calcareous soils in Eastern China

Fig. 2.1. Features of the boundary zone separating southern and northern China. *Source: Qingnian dituce*: 58–9, 62–3.

warm winters. The transition zone between these is conventionally recognised as that which follows the Qin Ling in southern Shaanxi and Funiu Shan in northern Henan, passing eastwards through the plain around the latitude of Xuzhou and reaching the sea south of the Shandong peninsula, and which is marked by the annual isohyet of 800 mm and the January isotherm of 0 °C (Fig. 2.1). The same transition zone represents a year with about 210 frost-free days, and also the break between the leached acid soils of the south and the calcareous brown soils of the north. John Lossing Buck recognised the same environmental transition in his distinction between a 'rice region' to the south and a 'wheat region' to the north. To the north of this transition zone water is often scarce, because potential evapotranspiration exceeds precipitation, though not in the north-east; but to the south the reverse is true, and drought is relatively rare. To the north, environments often suffer stress in spring and summer due to drought, and always suffer stress in winter due to cold. To the south, the environments suffer such stresses to a much reduced degree, though southern China may well be bleak in winter, with frost possible everywhere except in the extreme south; and the south-eastern coast is subject to typhoons in summer and autumn which may cause serious destruction.

Throughout eastern China in summer, whether north or south, exceptional rainfall or exceptional lack of it may create regional flooding or drought, on a scale which may be destructive or even disastrous to agriculture in whole provinces.

Topography is the most important differentiating feature of Chinese environments after climate; and it operates generally more abruptly and on a rather smaller scale. The north China plain, one of the largest densely occupied topographical regions on earth, lies across the climatic transition zone separating north from south, and must be treated as a whole. It comprises the provinces of Henan, Hebei and Shandong with parts of Anhui and Jiangsu. Inland at the Taihang scarp, elevations rise abruptly from the plain to upwards of 1,000 m. Above is broadly the loess plateau of Shanxi, Shaanxi and eastern Gansu, extending westwards and northwards through progressively worsening conditions of winter cold and risk of drought to the Great Wall and beyond, into Inner Mongolia and towards the Gobi. This may be called the Great Wall frontier. North-eastwards from Tianjin, on the other hand, the north China plain leads on, beyond the barrier of the Yan Shan where the Great Wall reaches the sea, to the vast north-eastern extension of the plain in Liaoning, Jilin and Heilongjiang, with peripheral mountain chains east and west, the Da Xingan Ling and the Changbai Shan. Unlike the loess plateau and the north China plain, which have been the homelands of the Chinese people since prehistoric times, the north-east has been colonised virtually only within the past century.

To the south of the regional transition zone between north and south lie the southern regions, which have also experienced Chinese colonisation, though over much longer periods – since before the time of Christ in the case of the Yangzi provinces such as Sichuan, Hubei and Anhui.

Topographically, southern China, with its smaller plains, mixed topography and marked mountain interfluves, is very different from northern China with its simple and dramatic distinction between plain and plateau. Many southern provinces, such as Sichuan, Hunan, Jiangxi and Guangdong, occupy plains each based on a simple or complex river system with boundaries on the watersheds. In terms of broad regional distinctions, Sichuan is usually linked with Guizhou and Yunnan as the south-west; Guangdong with Guangxi and Fujian (and Taiwan) as the south; and the three provinces of the middle Yangzi, Hubei, Hunan and Jiangxi as a vast mixed region of the inland south. The area of southern Jiangsu and northern Zhejiang, together with Shanghai, may also be reckoned a region in its own right, both by reason of its concentration upon Shanghai itself, and by reason of its advanced levels of development in various respects. In the south, climatic stress is less marked than in the north, and environmental differences are generally on a smaller scale. Owing to the widespread availability of transport by river, access is generally better than in the north. There is evidence that these differences are sufficient to give southern China a degree of environmental advantage over the north which is reflected in rural incomes and living standards, and which perhaps will always be so reflected, though, as will be shown, other features of the southern environments, particularly local diversities of all kinds, also play a part in supporting these advantages.

The environments of northern China are not only harsher than those of the south; on the whole they are also more fragile, and have suffered more severely over the centuries of human occupation than those of the south. Ever since 1949, the People's Government has tended to lay its main emphasis in regional development upon reconstruction in the north, and the south has been relied on to promote its own welfare. In part this distinction appears to have arisen out of direct physical need in the north, in such forms as the rehabilitation of the water and soil resources of the Yellow River basin (both plateau and plain), together with the Hai and Huai river systems in the north China plain. In part, particularly through the role played by Mao himself, it appears to have arisen from a sense that the south was less tolerant of egalitarian and centralising policies than the north – the Dazhai movement was based on the northern plateau, and rather little trouble was taken at any time to defuse the obvious limitations to 'learning from Dazhai' in southern countrysides already far in advance of Dazhai. Yet the south has rather more than half of the Chinese population and certainly more than the same proportion of rural outputs.

Official policy on the land

Chinese official rural policy since Liberation in 1949 has been marked by sharp changes of direction at intervals of a few years – through land reform in 1950–52, the cooperative movement in 1952–56, collectivisation in 1956–57, the commune movement and Great Leap Forward effort in 1958–59, the Cultural Revolution beginning in 1966 and the Dazhai campaigns in 1970, the last finally ebbing away only after 1976; to give place to the present complex of schemes moving towards professional collective management on the one hand, and household self-management on the other. These movements were of the highest importance in their time, and so were many of the circumstances surrounding them (Walker 1965: 3–19; Donnithorne 1967: 31–91; Domes 1980). This is not the place to review them in detail, but some basic issues should be noticed.

From 1949 to about 1962, rural policy had a powerful component which related directly to tenure of the land. This need occasion no surprise. Questions of land tenure dominated study of the Chinese countryside, especially among Left-wing intellectuals, for some decades prior to 1949; and the land reform of the first years after Liberation did not solve all problems of landholding in China whether theoretical or practical. On the one hand, in crowded areas, the extent of arable land was insufficient to maintain individual family farming for all rural households at the then level of technique; and on the other, powerful currents of opinion in the Communist Party looked for collective modes of production as a matter of principle. In 1954 and 1955 cooperative arrangements of various kinds were being widely adopted in the countryside – these were consolidated as the 'lower-stage cooperatives', and typically involved individual ownership but collective use of land and other means of production such as draught animals. In 1956 these arrangements were broadened and deepened under central leadership, with the introduction of collective ownership of land and other means of production. The new ownership and management units were the 'higher-stage collectives'.

Finally in 1958 the commune system was inaugurated, specifically under Mao's protection if not his direction. This system, which has endured to the present, is discussed in Chapter 3. It preserved the comprehensive collective ownership of the means of production previously adopted. In addition it provided a hierarchical structure of authority through its three levels (commune, brigades and production teams), which proved central to the management of the rural planning system; and it united social organisation and (until 1982) local government with the functions of farm production.

Partly because of their ambitious scope, the communes encountered many problems at first, but by 1962 may be considered broadly stabilised. To that extent, the underlying problems of land tenure in China were by that time solved, at least for a generation of time; there have been no fundamental changes subsequently though the institutional level at which rights of land ownership are exercised has not always been clear; and at various times up to the present, official policy on land ownership has been equivocal. Broadly, the commune system continues to provide a framework for the organisation of rural production which both local communities and the state find tolerable.

After 1962 policy turned much rather to questions of the management of the system – who shall control the rural production system, by what means, and with what objectives? – and it is these discussions which are continuing up to the present. Broadly it is the developments of the years between about 1960 and the death of Mao in 1976 which form the foundation of experience, policy and controversy in the present phase in rural China. Most of the developments which have taken place in rural China since Liberation have suffered some degree of discontinuity; they have taken place under powerful pressures from political factions and the planning system; over the years they have registered some important successes but they have also introduced serious distortions into many local rural production systems, as various examples will show.

The most powerful body of pressure in rural policy and experience between 1958 and 1978 was certainly that of Mao Zedong and his followers. Above all, in the years of the Cultural Revolution and its aftermath (1966–76), Maoist policy in its various forms went virtually unchallenged in the media, and challenged only with difficulty on the ground.

The heart of Maoist rural policy was class struggle. As late as 1976 we read in *Red Flag*: 'Although some comrades pay lip-service to class struggle, in actual work they bury themselves in production, thinking that as long as the collective economy is developed, capitalism will be discredited. This idea is wrong . . . Chairman Mao pointed out recently, "Class struggle is the key

link, and everything else hinges on it."' (Hsiang Hui: 86) 'Although basic victory was won in the socialist transformation of the means of production in the countryside, the remnants of the individual economy still exist, and their transformation is still a drawn-out task.' (Hsiang Hui: 87) This is the task of the leadership and the masses through the continuing class struggle.

From this standpoint, it is easy to understand the Maoists' uncompromising insistence upon collective production and distribution in the countryside, and their refusal to acknowledge production or distribution, no matter how valuable, which was not collective in form and intention. Poverty without individual production was totally and unconditionally preferable to prosperity with it. Opposition arose in practice because despite endless political pressure through the media, many peasant families resented collective production methods on the land and egalitarian distribution both within and among local units; because low state prices and gross inadequacy in the state commercial monopolies led to very low cash incomes and low standards of consumption; and because the Maoist authorities insisted not only upon the suppression of production which was not collective, but the limitation of collective production to very few crops, often little more than grain (together with potatoes) and cotton. These are all far-reaching problems, but while egalitarian distribution and collective production may be thought necessary parts of a radical socialist outlook, low rural prices, poor commercial mechanisms and the suppression of varied rural outputs need not be so thought.

It cannot be said that suppression of rural outputs other than grain was a recognised arm of Maoist policy; many articles were published which praised such outputs by collective producers (*People's Daily*, 23 Jan. 1973, translated in *SCMP*, 73 (6) 80–1); and even some which criticised the suppression of family production (*People's Daily*, 22 Aug. 1975, translated in *SPRCP*, 71 (4), 245–6). But after 1978 such suppression was widely reported from the Maoist decade in terms of great bitterness, having resulted apparently either from more rigorous phases in official policy or from decisions by over-zealous local officials, or both. In Qu county in Zhejiang the people planted fruit, melons and vegetables on their private plots and marketed them themselves on foot. When in consequence they were accused of capitalism, they lost interest in the whole economy of the village; costs rose, the value of the working day fell to 0.3 or 0.4 *yuan* and incomes fell too; the villages became very depressed. In this county, where many households have domestic orange trees, these trees were collectivised in 1968, with disastrous results to orange production (*People's Daily*, 11 Feb 1979). Also in Zhejiang (a province where the extreme Left were particularly active), in Linan county, mulberry groves, some planted only a decade earlier on riverside land newly created at great expense in money and effort, were destroyed as late as 1975 in attempts (under official pressure) to reach the planned targets for increase in grainland. In one case the county authorities, who appear to have been the moving force, insisted on cutting down mulberry trees without even allowing for the maturing of the current crop of silkworms, obliging the local brigade to buy mulberry leaves elsewhere. Tea-gardens were similarly treated. These policies led to serious loss by local brigades and teams who could ill afford to lose money; as might be expected the mulberry and tea land (which is usually hilly or rocky, or otherwise unsuitable for arable fields) has often gone back to waste after the clearances (Lin Lixing). Even real land construction, the creation of fresh arable from scrub hillsides, could not attract many friends when the outputs from the new land could only be unprofitable (and often poorly suited) grain. Other versions of this kind of experience are also recorded. In Guangdong, at a production team called Chaxia, we read in 1973, 'the people are not clear about the distinction between diversification and spontaneous capitalist tendencies, and so have not dared to start diversification; they just keep to grain. As a result they are short of capital and fertiliser and their grain output does not rise' (Guangdong province Propaganda Department: i; 20). This report probably brings us close to many real experiences of the time.

The reasons for the narrowness of much rural production policy under the Maoists have not been made clear in China, though the policy has been consistently and bitterly criticised since the fall of the Gang of Four. Ostensibly the Maoists feared the reconstruction of capitalism through local trade and the small business which such production necessarily generates (Chiang Wei-Ch'ing; 14–15). A second reason may well have been egalitarianism – insistence upon policies which would maximise economic and social equality among rural communities, even at the

cost of a universal standard hardly rising above poverty. Dazhai itself, although as a village quite rich in diversification, for instance on the hillsides, was used as a model in the media to proclaim little except the basic Maoist objectives – the primacy of grain yields and grain contributions to the state, egalitarian social policy, the potential achievements of physical labour in such fields as land reconstruction, and the underlying primacy of the class struggle. A third reason may often have been over-zealous local cadres seeking to create a good impression in high places. It is now said in China that ultra-Left policies were promoted much more enthusiastically by some county committees than by others, in accordance with the the political outlook of the officials.

It is now the universal claim of the media that these 'ultra-Left' policies of insistence (through the planning system, 'learning from Dazhai', and political browbeating of non-conforming units) upon bulk arable outputs in the countryside was a disaster; since 1978 widespread and varied publicity has been given to efforts to climb out of the pit of Maoist prejudice. Many Maoist claims to achievement have been stood on their heads, as various local and regional examples will show.

Rural policy since 1978 represents a dramatic reversal of Maoist priorities. Grain output is no longer the sole objective of rural production. Diversification is actively encouraged, and the incapacity of the state trading monopoly to handle all the varied outputs of the countryside is acknowledged by the toleration of rural markets and other forms of collective and private trade. Large areas of purported official price and allocation control have been given up. The right of local units, including those at the humble village level, to take planning and business decisions is not officially recognised, though it may still be conditional upon official approval at senior level in practice. Increasingly, the same rights are being extended even to households. There are two main results of these changes in official priorities – a powerful surge in economic growth almost everywhere, but especially where natural or social conditions, or both, are favourable; and a powerful shift of real power in the countryside to villages conceived as groups of households, and to households themselves. Stability is one obvious potential casualty of these changes, but in spite of appearances the system before 1976 was itself not stable, and more stability has probably been gained by the satisfaction of popular demands than lost through the weakening of institutional control.

Growth may be thought desirable and desta-bilisation undesirable; but realistically neither can be avoided if change is to take place in a country-side where for twenty years growth has been traded for stability, but population has continued to increase. Stability combined with growth is in many ways the central issue in the Chinese coun-tryside. In the present state of affairs the new demands made on the economic system are fairly modest, but it is the nature of such demands that their satisfaction provokes their extension. It is not easy to foresee the means by which the rural (and urban) communities of China will be controlled as demands of all kinds escalate in the years to come. It was one practical merit of the Maoist system in its time that it held down consumption and expectations.

Land use and the cropping system

The maps of rural land use and agricultural

systems (Figs 2.2 and 2.3) are adapted from recent Chinese materials. In both, the transition from north to south in the zone of the Qinling and the Huai can be identified, marked in both by the practical northern limit of farm systems based on paddy – a limit which owes more to the transition to loose calcareous soils in this zone than to lower summer temperatures. The land use map (Fig. 2.2) calls to mind the greater extent of dryland arable in China than of paddy, the mixed landscapes of the south contrasted with the plains and plateaux of the north, and the vast extent of deserts in western China. The category 'meadow and prairie' is ambiguous, including exposed high plateaux with scanty soil in Tibet, the loess plateau between the north China plain and the desert, and in the south, extensive cut-over former forest land, often on steep slopes, and also usually with very poor soils. Forests are almost confined to the south-west and north-east, together with widely scattered outliers in the mountain south.

The map of agricultural systems (Fig. 2.3) distinguishes pastoral areas (basically, the north-western half of the country which has already been identified), and for the rest of the country distinguishes characteristic regional agricultural

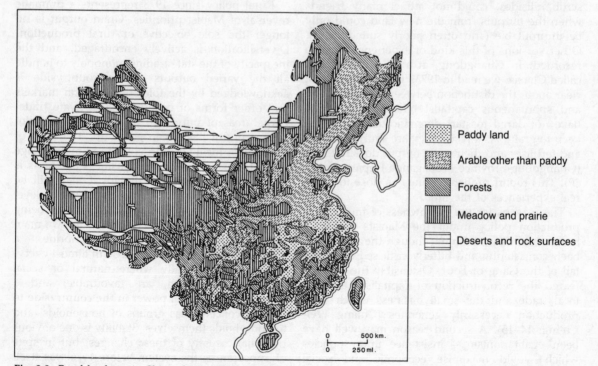

Fig. 2.2. Rural land use in China. *Source: Zhongguo dituce*: 14.

Paddy land

Arable other than paddy

Forests

Meadow and prairie

Deserts and rock surfaces

0   500 km.

0   250 ml.

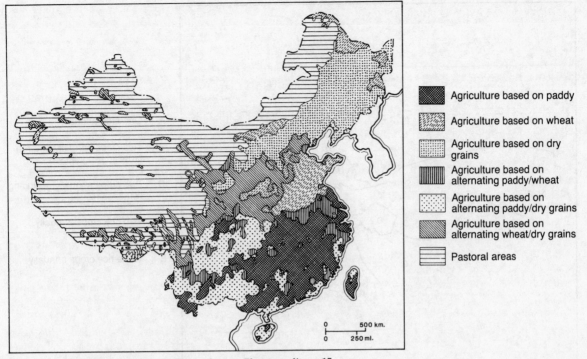

Fig. 2.3. Agricultural systems in China. *Source: Zhongguo dituce*: 15.

Legend:
- Agriculture based on paddy
- Agriculture based on wheat
- Agriculture based on dry grains
- Agriculture based on alternating paddy/wheat
- Agriculture based on alternating paddy/dry grains
- Agriculture based on alternating wheat/dry grains
- Pastoral areas

systems. Broadly, paddy systems occupy the lowland south and systems based on wheat or other dry grains occupy the lowland north and north-east. Paddy rice may be double cropped as on the south coast, or cropped in summer together with a winter crop of wheat, barley or oilseed as on the lower Yangzi in central China, or cropped alternately with maize or potatoes as in the highland south-west. In much of central China, winter wheat may be alternated with other dry grains such as maize, or with potatoes. In modern times, increasingly, Chinese agricultural systems assume the opportunities and constraints of double cropping, or of approximations to it such as three crops in two years, interplanting and so forth. In addition, triple cropping is now technically feasible in favoured areas in southern and even central China; but its wider implementation waits upon institutional and economic factors, many of which are still unfavourable to it.

Much more detail is given in the map of cropping systems (see Fig. 2.5), also adapted from a recent Chinese publication (Hou Xueyu 1979). In this map, the key speaks in large measure for itself, with the help of the key diagram (Fig. 2.4).

Figure 2.5 is based on the recent official map

of vegetation cover in China. Detail is of course much more exact in the original. For those parts of China where natural vegetation has given place to human farming, this map is in effect a map of cropping systems. It is certainly the most important document of its kind to be published since John Lossing Buck's well-known map of agricultural areas of 1937 (37), and Norton Ginsberg's revisions of it (1958: 174–5; 1966: 55). Comparison with Buck's map and the tables upon which it was based reveals differences of both method and material, particularly much more exact attention to geographical detail in the present map, greater emphasis upon degrees and forms of double cropping as the key to farming systems, and a less complex version of subsidiary cropping. It should be realised that (particularly in respect of double and triple cropping) the allocation of areas to systems on this map, and even the identification of systems, owes something to perceived potential and model practice, and is not limited to the recording of present typical practice.

Northern systems as shown on this map (groups A and B) typically support one crop per year or three crops in two years. Significantly, it is in the Qinling–Huai transition zone (B3), in the

13

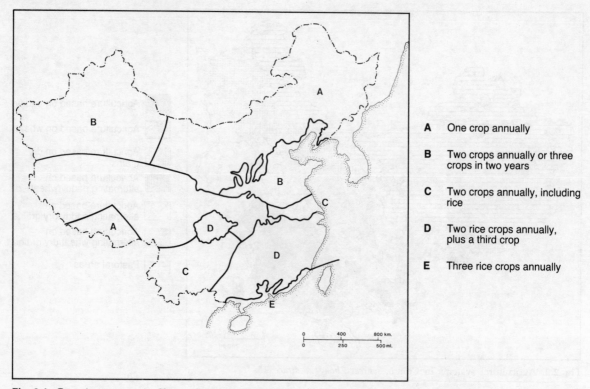

A One crop annually

B Two crops annually or three crops in two years

C Two crops annually, including rice

D Two rice crops annually, plus a third crop

E Three rice crops annually

Fig. 2.4. Cropping systems in China – key diagram (see Fig. 2.5). For regions D and E, triple cropping with two or three rice crops respectively, or by other methods, should be regarded as ideal and potential, and in places where realised exceptional, rather than typical in present conditions.

southern quarter of the north China plain and the Wei valley around Xian, that double cropping becames feasible. Southern systems support two crops annually as a rule, and in exceptionally favourable conditions or under powerful administrative or other pressures may support three. All areas have their characteristic economic crops, both field–herbaceous (sugar-beet, cotton, rapeseed) and orchard–plantation (fruit, mulberry, tea). In southern China a distinction is drawn between paddy on the one hand and upland or dryfield summer crops such as maize or peanuts on the other. All winter crops are dry crops, but some dry crops, particularly sweet potatoes, rank as summer crops in northern China but as winter crops in the far south. In the analysis adopted in the map, concepts of regional potential, as distinct from present practice, emerge in the prominence given to orchard crops, as well as the optimistic standards of double and triple cropping adopted.

Fig. 2.5. Cropping systems in China. *Source*: Hou Xueyu 1979.

Key

Group A. One crop annually, with cold-resistant economic crops.

A1 (north-east)
Spring wheat, soya beans, maize, millet, sugar-beet, flax, plums, apricots, Chinese apples.

A2 (loess)
Spring wheat, millet, potatoes, sugar-beet, flax.

A3 (Tibet)
Spring barley, spring and winter wheat, peas, potatoes, rapeseed.

Group B. Two crops annually or three crops in two years (with rice locally), with warm-temperate economic forests and deciduous orchards.

B1 (Shandong, Liaodong)
Winter wheat, soya beans (or maize) – two crops annually; peanuts, sweet potatoes, tobacco; apples, pears, grapes.

B2 (north China plain)
Winter wheat, coarse grains (kaoliang, maize, millet) – three crops in two years; soya beans, cotton; Chinese dates; apples, pears, grapes, persimmons, chestnuts, walnuts.

B3 (transition zone)
Winter wheat, coarse grains (maize, millet, sweet potatoes) – two crops annually; cotton, peanuts, soya beans; Chinese dates, apples, pears.

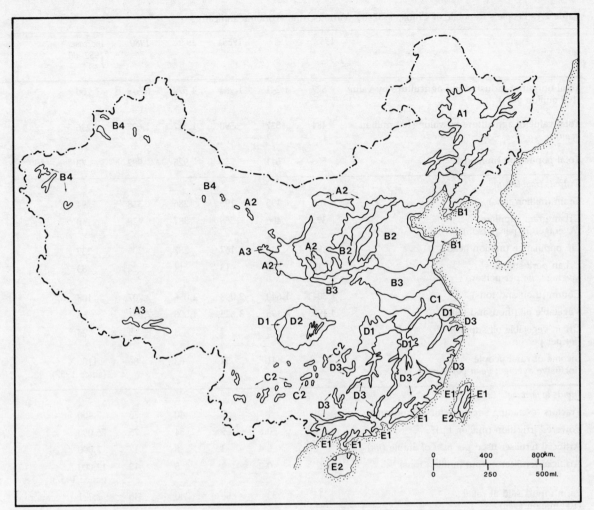

B4 (Xinjiang)
Winter (spring) wheat, maize, millet – three crops in two years or two crops annually; cotton; grapes, melons, pears, apricots.

Group C Two crops annually (rice and a dry crop), with subtropical evergreen or deciduous economic forests and orchards.
C1 (Yangzi – north)
Summer rice, winter wheat (or rapeseed) – two crops annually (double-cropping rice locally); cotton, peanuts; tea, pomegranates, peaches, pears, loquats.
C2 (south-west)
Summer rice (or maize), winter wheat, (or rapeseed) – two crops annually; potatoes, tobacco; tea, lacquer, red bayberry, walnuts, apples, pears.

Group D Double-cropping rice followed by a cold-tolerant crop annually, or three upland crops annually, with subtropical evergreen economic forests and orchards.
D1 (Yangzi – south)
Double-cropping rice followed by winter wheat (or rapeseed or green manure); cotton, ramie, mulberry, oranges.

D2 (Sichuan)
Single or double-cropping rice followed by winter wheat (or rapeseed) annually; sweet potatoes, peanuts, dry grains – five crops in two years; sugar-cane, ramie; oranges, tong-oil, mulberry, palm.
D3 (southern coasts, valleys)
Single or double-cropping rice followed by winter wheat (or rapeseed or green manure) annually; or sweet potatoes, dry grains, soya beans – three upland crops annually; ramie, jute; tea, tea-oil, red bayberry, oranges, loquats.

Group E Triple-cropping rice annually, or double-cropping rice followed by subtropical crops, with tropical evergreen economic forests and plantations.
E1 (Guangdong)
Double-cropping rice followed by sweet potatoes; double-cropping maize; sugar-cane, manioc; litchis, longans, bananas, pineapples.
E2 (Hainan)
Triple-cropping rice, winter peanuts; sugar-cane, vanilla, sisal; rubber, coconuts, coffee, oil palm.

Other areas – agriculture local and scattered, or absent.

15

Table 2.1. People's Republic of China, 1952–80. Various rural economic indicators

	1952	1957	1965	1976	1980	Increase 1952–80 (%)
Total output of industry and agriculture by value (100 million *yuan*)	827	1,241	1,984	4,579	6,619	700
Total value of agriculture by value (100 million *yuan*)	484	537	590	1,317	1,627	236
Total population (millions)	568	641	750	925	982	73
Outputs from farming						
Grain (million tons)	164	195	195	286	318	94
Urban grain supplies (Average, *jin* per person)	395	406	366	381	428	8
Pig population (million head)	90	146	167	287	305	239
Urban pork supplies (average, *jin* per person)	12	10	13	14	22	83
Cotton (thousand tons)	1,304	1,640	2,098	2,056	2,707	108
Vegetable oil (thousand tons)	4,193	4,196	3,625	4,008	7,691	83
Urban vegetable oil supplies (*jin* per person)	4	5	3	3	5	25
Income of rural people (inclusive average; *yuan* per person per year)	—	41	52	63	86	110 (since 1957)
Inputs to farming						
Tractors (excluding small tractors) (thousands)	1	1	7	40	75	7,400
Powered irrigation (million hp)	0.1	0.6	9	54	75	75,000
Artificial fertiliser used per *mou* of arable (*jin*)	0.1	0.4	3	8	17	7,000
Artificial fertiliser output (million tons)	neg	0.2	2	5	12	12,000 (since 1957)
Farm inputs sold at retail (100 million *yuan*)	14	33	80	240	346	2,371

Source: Xue Muqiao 1981a: 139–47, tables.
Population figures apart from 1980 (Xinhua, 29 April 1981) are estimates, excluding Taiwan. Figures for total outputs by value in industry and agriculture and in agriculture are not expressed in constant prices, but are comparable with each other in each year specified.

The Maoist legacy – agriculture

One important measure of progress in the countryside since Liberation is the development of physical production. Table 2.1 gives a résumé of some relevant features of the Chinese economy since 1952 in quantitative terms. The figures are recent ones from Chinese sources. A number of central features of Chinese economic experience can be identified in the table, such as the failure of grain output to grow in the period 1957–65, the outcome of the ill-fated Great Leap Forward; the fall in cotton outputs during the decade of the

Cultural Revolution (1966–76) and the marked acceleration in inputs to farming in the same phase. The table also indicates a sharpening of growth rates in practically every sphere since 1976; and of course it also documents the growth of the population from around 568 millions in 1952 to 982 millions in 1980.

Three features of Table 2.1 are of particular importance in discussion of rural development. One is the markedly better growth performance of industry than agriculture, resulting in part from a characteristic official bias which is now much criticised. A second is the generally slow rate of growth of the outputs from farming, some of them little more rapid than the growth of population. A third is the contrasted spectacular growth in inputs to farming, especially since 1957.

Why have outputs from farming risen so little since 1957, when inputs such as fertiliser have risen so much? This is a critical question for the Maoist decade (1966–76) especially, because Maoist policy laid particular emphasis on technical advances in agriculture (Aziz: 18–45) while the critics of Maoist policy lay particular emphasis on the low rates of achievement (apart from grain outputs) registered by the countryside in that phase. This apparent paradox appears to have several foundations – the relatively high levels of productivity already achieved by much Chinese farming, using traditional methods, in 1952; the still relatively low levels of artificial fertiliser use, mechanisation and powered irrigation achieved (after many previous decades of neglect) in 1976, and the widespread limitation of the additional farm inputs to the support of grain production, in accordance with the characteristic bias of Maoist rural policy. All these considerations suggest optimistic implications for the effects of further increase in such inputs in the years to come – indeed there are some such implications in the figures for 1980 in Table 2.1, which suggest rates of increase in agricultural outputs since 1976 very much higher than those before that date. Some Western commentators (Nolan and White 1982: 175–9) are impressed by China's rural performance record; others (Domes 1976; 161–2) much less so. Jack Gray and Maisie Gray (164–71) suggest an analysis which allows for both strength and weakness in several respects. In China itself, the continued increase in grain output, by more than 40% between 1965 and 1976, is considered to be the outstanding rural achievement of the Maoist decade, accompanied by others in steel, coal and oil production and in capital construction (Gao Zhiyu).

Xie Shirong (39–40) reviews a number of features of the expansion of farm inputs. Of the total arable farmland about half, 700 million *mou* or 47 million ha, is now irrigated at least in part – double the amount of 1949; and the country now has the same extent of high- and stable-yield arable land. One-third of the arable subject to flood and two-thirds of that affected by alkalinity have been improved – in varying degrees obviously. Output of artificial fertiliser rose by more than 200 times between 1952 and 1978.

Output of tractors increased by more than ten times between 1965 and 1978. Mechanical power of all kinds now available in the farm economy totals 180 million hp, which averages about 1.5 hp per ha (*People's Daily*, 5 Nov. 1980); and there are now 90,000 small hydroelectric power stations in the country, with generating capacity around 7 million kW (*People's Daily*, 24 Oct. 1980). Population in the countryside is approaching double that of 1949, but the basic livelihood of the people is secure – an achievement which should not be underestimated. At the same time, few rural communities are in any position to contemplate the modernisation of production in a Western sense, with high rates of output per unit of labour and high levels of commercial output. Indeed, because Chinese farming is labour-intensive, and has become much more so since Liberation due to population growth and the deliberate suppression and even reversal of rural–urban migration, it does not and is never likely to yield family cash incomes which are high by world standards. Nor is it ever likely to produce diets which are high in meat, in the manner of American or even European farming. These are obvious points sometimes ignored by recent Chinese writers on rural development. What may be expected of rural China is that it may continue to maintain the vast Chinese population, totally or almost totally, in basic food and clothing; and to produce in addition enough subsidiary outputs (vegetables, fish, poultry and eggs, meat, specialist outputs such as tea and silk) to provide slowly improving diets for all the community and a useful surplus for export. Present policy appears to be directed to this end. Further intensification on the land is certainly unavoidable, and will continue to be so for as long as the rural population continues to grow. Some impressive indications of the capacity of Chinese farming systems to continue to absorb labour productively are recorded in materials used in later chapters.

Realistically, there can be no way forward which ignores this central feature of the system. Moreover, it is important to realise the extent to which the progress of the past generation has been based squarely upon the foundations laid down in traditional times – the rice-based arable systems of the south and the wheat, dry grain and potato-based systems of the north; the wide range of subsidiary outputs such as vegetables and vegetable oils, pigs and poultry, fish from ponds and rivers, and those from plantations such as tea;

the slow encroachment of the arable on the hill-sides and the continuing deforestation of the accessible wasteland. Little of this was changed in essence after Liberation; probably the most dramatic change was the rejection by the Maoists, after 1966, of many kinds of subsidiary outputs. Chinese agriculture after 1949, and up to the present, has had much to learn from Western agricultural science about tactics, but in terms of basic strategy in the maintenance of very dense populations, traditional farming in China had little or nothing to learn from the West. It is true that under the People's Government the structure and performance of the Chinese rural economy have been immensely strengthened, but in broad terms, they have not been transformed.

Farm expansion in China under the People's Government has depended above all upon inten-sification, and present signs are that it will continue to do so. Intensification in this sense is increase in production per unit area. It has been achieved by the people directly, rather than by the government or by official policy, and of course it is the principal means by which the increase in population – of approximately 78% between 1949 and 1980 – has been supported. In this gigantic effort, the rural community has had little official support. In spite of intermittent Maoist enthu-siasm for mechanisation, Chinese farming has been systematically starved of investment in order to support the greedy heavy industry sector. Under the first and second five-year plans (1953–62) the ratio of investment in agriculture to that in heavy industry ranged from 1 : 6 to 1 : 4.6, and does not appear to have risen above about 1 : 4 at any time (Jiang Junchen et al.: 55). Even under the Cultural Revolution with its proclaimed rural bias, the ratio is said to have changed only 'slightly', in favour of agriculture. Meanwhile the population of the rural sector throughout has been at least four times that of the whole urban sector. This disproportion in investment relates to the proletarianisation of the rural sector in China, as will be shown. Meanwhile industry, particu-larly heavy industry, remains inward-looking – 'The long period of lopsided emphasis on the growth of heavy industry has meant that it is essentially structured to serve its own interests.' (Liang Wensen: 65)

At the same time the agricultural sector has borne an increasing burden of farm costs, which rose much more sharply than outputs during the Maoist decade and even earlier. In Jiangsu prov-ince the return on an investment of 100 *yuan* fell from 337 *yuan* in 1957 to 308 *yuan* in 1965, 272 *yuan* in 1971, and 232 *yuan* in 1980 (Du Runsheng). These figures do not indicate lack of need for investment in Jiangsu, but low prices of farm products. Motivation in these conditions, in spite of ceaseless political stimulation, flagged.

Hence it must be admitted that Maoist achieve-ments in rural production have their limitations, even when expressed in the language of grain and cotton outputs preferred by the Maoists them-selves. Per capita grain output in China in 1977 was roughly the same as in 1957, and per capita output of cotton fell after 1965. 'Between 1957 and 1977, living standards almost remained the same. The wage average was not raised, the peasants' food grain was not increased, and about one in every three peasants led a hard life' (Xue Muqiao 1981b: 176) Otherwise expressed, total output in agriculture rose by a factor of only 2.4 in the phase 1949–78, while output in light industry rose by a factor of 19, and in heavy industry by a factor of 90 (Jiang Junchen et al.: 54).

During the Maoist decade, the commonest of all parameters of rural achievement quoted in the press was the grain yield per unit area. Even up to the present and through the future, to a coun-tryside necessarily predominantly self-sufficient, this remains an important figure, though not the only one. Grain yields also help to tie discussions of policy to regional realities. Figure 2.6 shows grain yields per unit area in 1975.

Yields are usually higher in the southern half of the country, because double cropping is common and rice (which can yield very heavy crops) is suited to soil and water conditions in the south. In the National Programme for Agricultural

Table 2.2. Targets of the National Programme for Agricultural Development

Jin per mou	Average grain yields, 1956	Planned grain yields under the programme	Planned cotton yields
North of the Yellow River	150	400	60
Between the Yellow and Huai Rivers	200	500	80
South of the Huai River	400	800	100

Source: Quan guo nongye fazhan gangyao tu jie: 13.

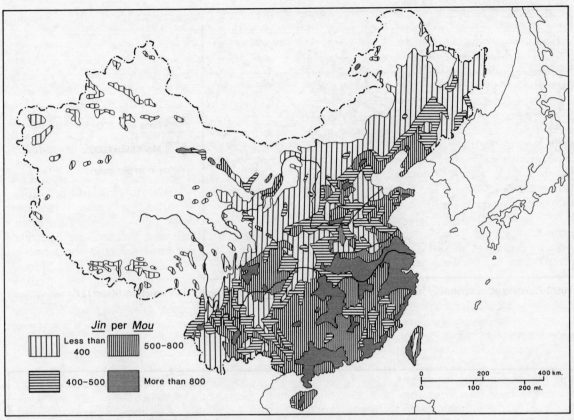

Fig. 2.6. Grain yields per unit area, 1975. *Source*: Geographical Research Institute: 121.

Development of 1956, target growth and cotton yields were proposed for 1970 as shown in Table 2.2, in a programme which had the blessing of Mao Zedong (1977a: 279–280). The figures proposed, to be fair, do not appear to represent any serious calculation of either opportunity or need; rather they appear to be naïve assessments of agronomic potential, and to that extent they need not be taken seriously. However, it appears from the map that densely populated areas in the south, though much less commonly other kinds of area, have generally reached the 800 *jin* target (parts of Sichuan and Hubei are the main exceptions), whereas for those on the north China plain, especially Hebei and Henan, the record is much more mixed. In the fifteen province-level units of northern China, two-thirds of the arable still gives yields below 300 *jin* (*People's Daily*, editorial, 28 June 1982). In addition the principal zone of weakness suggested by the map lies in a vast belt from north-east to south-west, and represents the edge of cultivation at the periphery of really difficult farm conditions – the high mountains in the south-west, the desert peripheries in the north-west and the cold fringes in the north-east.

A second map (Fig. 2.7) separates out the weakest areas in terms of grain outputs. – those with less than 200 *jin* per *mou*. They lie, predictably, mainly along the desert fringe. In places in the poorest areas, such as parts of the loess plateau, areas with excessive soil alkalinity, and red-earth mountain areas in southern China, grain yields fall further still to 100 *jin*, one-tenth or less of yields in the best areas. The strongest areas, also shown in the same map, are those with grain outputs above 1,000 *jin* per *mou*. They are all in the south, and represent rich paddy plains with dense populations and in most cases advanced farm methods.

A third map (Fig. 2.8) represents in general terms areas of surplus and deficit in grain output. This shows that over the vast majority of the eastern half of China, grain supplies are either in surplus or in balance with need. This social and physical achievement should not be underrated,

19

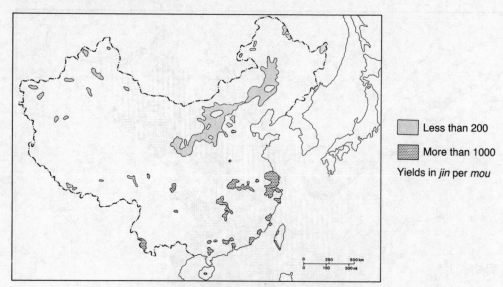

Fig. 2.7. Areas of exceptionally high and low grain yield, 1975. *Source*: Geographical Research Institute: 121.

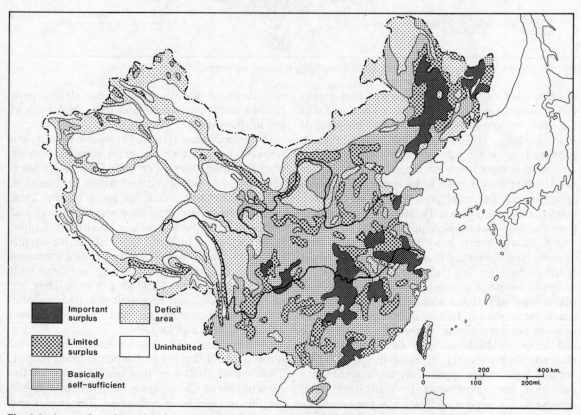

Fig. 2.8. Areas of surplus and deficit in grain output. *Source*: Geographical Research Institute: 37.

but neither should the problems represented by the subsistence of even quite small areas, with populations numbered in millions, which are not self-sufficient. The main problem area, as always, is the desert fringe. In addition, the western half of China shows considerably more deficit demand than might have been expected.

Information has also appeared which shows in summary form the main changes which have taken place in the structure of basic rural food outputs in China since 1952 (Table 2.3). These changes are one of the principal results of the body of decisions taken within the planning system during this phase. The table does not include economic crops such as oilseeds or cotton, plantation crops such as tea, vegetables in any form or green fertiliser crops – and all these are serious deficiencies. Nevertheless the table as it stands is not without interest. All figures are percentages, so that falls in the figures given do not necessarily indicate absolute falls on the ground. It shows percentage increases in sown acreages of rice, wheat, maize and potatoes, and decreases in millets and other dry grains and in soya beans. In the case of rice, the bulk of the increase is in the lower and middle Yangzi region which includes Jiangsu and Hubei; it represents partly improved irrigation, but also the introduction of double cropping of rice in these areas. The fall in the area sown to wheat in the same region is in part a result of the increase in rice area, and probably the same is true of the fall in the area sown to maize. The sharp rise in the area sown to wheat in Guangdong and Fujian indicates the introduction of winter wheat along with triple-cropping systems. There are marked rises in potato production everywhere except in the far south and Tibet, and similar rises in maize production in most regions. Maize and potatoes are both heavy-yielding crops and preferred by the planners on that account, but they are neither traditional nor popular in most Chinese diets. To some extent, to judge from Table 2.3 and also from the general literature, increases in potato and maize land have been gained by reductions in land sown to the various millets and such crops as buckwheat, which are traditional and popular items of diet, generally easy to grow and tolerant of poor husbandry. The most conspicuous single feature of this table is the fall of the share of crop-land occupied by the dryfield small grains from 30% to 15%; and this probably represents a once-for-all change, particularly in the north China

plain, the lower Yangzi area and the north-east. The almost equally marked fall registered by soya beans, on the other hand, is the outcome of the Maoist policy of depression of industrial crop outputs; it is the main reason for the vexatious shortage of beancurd, but it does not seem likely to prove permanent.

As a whole the sown area of China rose, according to these figures, by 7% between 1952 and 1978; the greatest rise was recorded in the north-east, as might be expected, but falls were recorded in Inner Mongolia–Xinjiang (due presumably to the abandonment of land on the fringes of the deserts), and the north China plain (due presumably to city and industrial growth). Much of the rise recorded in the sown area outside the north-east must be due to increased double cropping and triple cropping, since total arable area has fallen since 1952.

The Maoist legacy – the commercial system

Internal commerce has rarely occupied much space in Western analysis of Chinese development experience. This is partly no doubt because of its complexity and partly because of a general scarcity of Chinese materials, especially during the Maoist decade. On the whole, internal commerce took a low priority among Maoist authors in China, because in political terms the implications of commerce were thought to be capitalist. A writer in *Red Flag* in 1975 says:

What is most serious and brings out the most adverse influence is 'free trade' Some people seriously affected by spontaneous capitalist tendencies not only demanded the right to fully dispose of a part of the collective and household sideline products, which are not subject to state restriction, but also wanted to indefinitely ensure this right. They did not fulfil state plans nor set aside reserves but sold products at high prices through free trade channels. By so doing, they actually subjected the production plans, distribution of products and labour management to control by the law of value, providing the ground for capitalist restoration activities. Lenin pointed out: 'Freedom to trade means going back to capitalism.' This is absolutely true. (Chiang Wei-Ch'ing: 15)

In this context, other words of Lenin were often

Table 2.3. Changes in total sown area and the allocation of sown area among crops, by regions, 1952–78 (all figures are percentages)

	Increase or decrease in sown area, 1952–78	Rice			Wheat			Maize			Potatoes and sweet potatoes		
		1952	1978	Diff-erence	1952	1978	Diff-erence	1952	1978	Diff-erence	1952	1978	Diff-erence
Inner Mongolia Xinjiang, Ningxia	−3	1	3	121	18	47	159	11	14	27	4	7	66
Shaanxi, Gansu, Shanxi	6	2	2	6	33	37	12	10	20	188	5	9	84
north-east (Liaoning, Jilin, Heilongjiang)	38	3	6	115	9	14	55	18	33	107	3	3	14
Hebei, Honan, Shandong, Beijing, Tianjin	−5	2	3	81	32	40	25	11	24	121	8	13	74
Jiangsu, Shanghai, Zhejiang, Anhui, Hubei, Hunan, Jiangxi	6	42	59	41	19	16	−17	5	4	−10	6	8	36
Guangdong, Guangxi, Fujian	13	75	72	−4	2	7	196	5	6	22	14	10	−30
Sichuan, Yunnan, Guizhou	20	36	30	−18	9	19	105	22	20	−9	11	16	51
Qinghai, Tibet	92	neg	neg	—	33	43	29	neg	neg	—	9	6	−32
China	7	23	29	24	20	24	21	10	17	64	7	10	40

neg = negligible.

Source: Adapted from Geographical Research Institute: 132; Table 4.5.

quoted (from *Left-wing communism, an infantile disease*): 'Small-scale production engenders capitalism and the bourgeoisie continuously, daily, hourly, spontaneously, and on a mass scale.' (Chiang Wei-Ch'ing: 14) Not all Maoist pronouncements on local trade were as uncompromising as this, but official views of this kind , in the hands of local bureaucrats, appear to have been quite sufficient to inhibit the growth of trade outside the official system. Alternative and less militant pronunciations were packed with ambiguity –

It is wrong to think that rural fair trade is marginal and may be turned on and off as suddenly as the fancy strikes us. Such an approach would only bring the peasants inconvenience, interfere with a vigorous rural economy and even lead to the secret growth of rural capitalist spontaneous forces. Of course, it is equally wrong to think that trade fair control is optional and such trade may be allowed to take its own course. Rural fair trade has traditionally been an important position of class struggle. (Hung Ch'iao: 163)

Nevertheless, rural fair trade was often treated as marginal, and turned on and off for political reasons. Attacks were launched on rural markets in 1958, when some people were already advocating total abolition of production for markets other than the state; but local trade was already being restored in 1959 and 1960. During the Cultural Revolution, rural markets were again attacked as instruments of capitalism, and several thousands were officially closed (Tang Lunhui et al.: 16–18). It is now said that many continued to operate in secret – 'After being noisily cleared away, they were quietly restored. From being open markets, they became black markets.' Nevertheless, marketable production of items such as fruit, vegetables and cooked snacks suffered great contraction due to suppression of local marketing (Tang Lunhui et al.). The suppres-

Millets and other dry grains			Soya beans		
1952	1978	Difference	1952	1978	Difference
62	28	−55	3	1	−55
44	29	−34	5	3	−43
48	26	−46	20	17	−13
35	14	−60	14	6	−53
21	7	−67	9	5	−41
2	3	50	3	2	−8
19	13	−32	3	2	−31
58	51	−12	neg	neg	—
30	15	−50	9	6	−37

sion of local markets in both town and country was a sad loss of working-class culture in favour of political principle.

Meanwhile the official system had, and still has, its own problems. Wholesale trade in China, and a substantial sector of retail trade as well, were to all intents and purposes nationalised by a series of decrees in 1954–55 (Weiss: 651). Subsequently, with the introduction of the communes in 1958, the supply and marketing cooperatives, which were and are responsible for the great bulk of rural commerce, were transferred to commune administration. Weiss (652) also considers that some opinion existed in this phase which hoped to abolish commerce completely, an ideal of which there have been various subsequent indications. The supply and marketing cooperatives already had many and varied functions including both purchase of rural surpluses and supply of all kinds of local needs for both production and consumption. In addition the managements of

these cooperatives, although committed in principle to an ideal of service to the people, were often urban oriented and department oriented rather than village oriented, and their work was often criticised – as Weiss says, rural trade is a matter of rural welfare as well as of economic development (Weiss: 654–7). Weiss agrees that internal trade came under further attack during the Cultural Revolution (657), but offers little detail. Writers since 1979 can give much more (Huang Jichang).

In the cities, especially cities other than Beijing, fruit, vegetables, beancurd, soy sauce and other kinds of simple rural produce were scarce and very poor in quality, while at the same time villages were being refused permission to try to cater for urban demand. Restaurants began to purchase supplies upon various kinds of black market. Soap and even soda (to make soap) were very scarce in official shops – 'How can we keep clean, or even (handling manure all day) protect our health, without supplies of soap?' (People's Daily, 15 Aug. 1979) Black marketeers, however, could supply soap at fancy prices. Packaged items such as tea could be as much as 20% underweight (People's Daily, 19 Mar. 1979). What consumer goods could be obtained were old-fashioned in design. Clothing was hard to find, and tailoring workshops very few (People's Daily, 21 June 1981). Local offices of the supply and marketing cooperatives (in effect, the village shops in many cases) were said to overcharge, use false measures, and keep very poor stocks of many day-to-day items (People's Daily, 31 May 1979, 12 May 1980). Many of these problems remain up to the present.

Waste was a gross evil, exciting frequent circumstantial attacks in the media. Transport inadequacies led to bottlenecks, in spite of the limited state of enterprise and trade. In Sichuan, because of the limited state of commercial facilities including refrigeration, only 3% of fish output entered trade in 1978, but in the summer of that year, the Department of Commerce brought 10 tons of sea-fish to Chengdu from Shanghai, half of it rotten on arrival (People's Daily, 2 Nov. 1978). Wild produce such as herbs and honey, available for state purchase, was rotting in village sheds because uncollected, or in state sheds after collection (People's Daily, 17 Mar. 1979, 10 Aug. 1979). Grain was still rotting in public granaries in Anhui in 1979 and 1980 (People's Daily, 3 Jan. 1981).

Rural collective units found industrial goods

such as tools and plastic sheeting scarce, expensive and poor in quality. Too much of the new farm machinery was poor in quality, and fell apart (*People's Daily*, 29 Dec. 1978). Provinces in subsequent years have tried to force rural units to buy their own products such as farm machines, rather than well-known and successful machines manufactured elsewhere, but they have been bitterly attacked for attempting 'economic blockades' (State Council 1982). Pioneer mining and industrial workers starting new enterprises, especially in isolated parts of the country, were expected to provide themselves with necessities such as vegetables, rather than depending on official or even local supplies (Department of Commerce 1977) – a system which was confirmed by the State Council in 1981 (FBIS *Daily Report*, 19 Oct. 1981, quoting a Beijing broadcast of 15 Oct. 1981). From the point of view of the villages, probably the most serious criticism of all is that the rural supply and marketing cooperatives, which until very recently have had the official monopoly of rural commerce and who even now must be expected to handle the majority of this commerce, were ineffectual both in purchasing rural outputs and in providing rural communities with simple farm inputs and simple consumer goods (Songjiang county: 183–4). Many self-critical articles from the Department of Commerce in Maoist times confirm its frequent gross neglect of the needs of working people in the villages, and its habit of recourse in times of criticism to still more Maoist rationalisation and still more attacks on Liu Shaoqi (Department of Commerce 1972).

In addition to changes in the management of internal trade and very poor practical performance by the Department of Commerce, commerce itself was sharply constrained between 1957 and 1979. In these twenty-five years, gross national retail sales increased 6.3 times, but the total number of retail sales outlets fell by 73% from 1,010,000 to 280,000 (*People's Daily*, editorial, 8 July 1981, translated in FBIS *Daily Report*, 28 July 1981, K8-K10). In 1957 there were 790,000 collective commercial units in the cities and towns throughout the country, but in 1978 only 77,000, a fall of 90%. In Beijing between 1957 and 1979 the urban population grew from 3.41 millions to 4.95 millions, but the number of commercial service units dropped in the same period from 31,802 to 8,260 (Jian Hua: K18). Figures with a rural dimension have appeared for Jiangsu province. In 1957 Jiangsu

had 226,000 retail outlets of all kinds, around 5.4 per 1,000 people, a satisfactory ratio. After 1958, under such slogans as 'change consumer cities into producer cities', and 'production before livelihood', the family shops, small stalls and hawker parts of business were cut back; and during the Maoist decade, still more so. In 1978 compared with 1957, population had increased by 39%, and retail turnover by 25%, but shops were 68% less in number. There were now only 1.3 shops per 1,000 people (Ji Jianxin: 47).

But the importance of commerce in development is self-evident. The commercial system in rural China must be responsible for the purchase and transportation of rural surpluses and the supply (such as it is) of industrial goods for consumption and investment in the countryside. It must assemble and pay for the 45–50% of China's exports which are rural in origin (Eckstein: 252), and the 20% of grain output which the state handles, together with cotton and other industrial crops. It must establish means to manage the supply and marketing cooperatives which are more than the equivalent of village shops in rural China. In many parts of China before 1949, sophisticated commercial systems were already well established. Even though the Communist Party preferred to see local subsistence needs satisfied locally, probably rightly, obviously the broad depression of commerce could not be constructive. It cannot have benefited standards of living, the quality of life, healthy diets or personal satisfaction. Equally obviously it must have thrown out of work many people for whom alternative jobs could not readily be found, and contributed to widespread rural underemployment.

In all these respects, and many others which have been illustrated and discussed at length in the official press since the fall of the Gang of Four, the Maoist commercial system did not provide for satisfaction of the reasonable needs of the working people, even though in many cases the means for satisfaction of these needs lay directly to hand among the people themselves. It is noticeable that while the rural working class have returned (willingly it would appear) to the traditional method of increased intensification on the land to solve the problem of growing demand, the Department of Commerce has certainly not succeeded in creating a socialist commercial network which matches either the increase in numbers or the more sophisticated demand schedules of the present rural population, compared with that of 1949.

With the advantage of hindsight, it is now evident that even without direct political interference, the creation of a sound modern commercial network in rural China after 1949 would have encountered many problems. Among these must be the incomplete, discontinuous and inadequate networks for trade, particularly in non-specialist commodities and non-suburban localities, in pre-Liberation China; the great widening of the spectrum potentially available to trade, due to technical change during the past generation – farm machinery, electrical items, plastic goods, pharmaceuticals; and the effects of social change, particularly the substitution of a widespread mass market in simple consumer and producer goods for the specialised market of rich families looking for consumer goods of a generation ago. All east Asian communities have experienced these vast changes in commercial demand since the Second World War; what is sadly not apparent is that the systems of official control adopted in China have contributed very much to the effective handling of them.

Models of development and the rural communities

In rural China between 1970 and about 1977, a special place was occupied by the campaigns to 'learn from Dazhai' (Tachai). During this phase, rural development of any kind practically could not be discussed in China without reference to Dazhai, which was represented everywhere in the media as the universal exemplar, in both political and practical terms, of what rural development should be. A brief review of the Dazhai experience, and of a counter-model of the immediate post-Maoist phase in 1978–79, Xiashidang, will illustrate some features of Chinese controversy about rural development, and also serve to introduce the many local studies in the Chinese media, from which this book is in large part written, and from which virtually all indications of diversity in modern rural China are necessarily derived.

Some writers, especially in China, have laid great stress on the magnitude of the transformation of policy and experience across the divide of the Third Plenum in December 1978. Others, especially in the West, have tended to lay stress

on continuity. Both, needless to say, are right. On the one hand, where policy continues to accept the commune system of organisation and to depend upon the state plan, change is not yet fundamental. On the other, when policy accepts many features of rural practice formerly literally unthinkable, like private marketing of grain surpluses, change cannot be denied. Nor are these paradoxes confined to matters of policy. They also arise in practical experience across the divide.

Some of these features of continuity and change may be illustrated by review of models of rural development. Models are successful communities whose achievements are noteworthy and have been achieved within the framework of official policy as understood by those who proclaim the model. The abundant regional and local materials on Chinese development, whose existence sets a study of the present kind apart from most kindred studies elsewhere in the world, are generally basically model materials, suggesting emulation of successful communities by those in search of success.

The whole concept of models is one which invites corruption, whether through selective reporting of the facts (if not deliberate misrepresentation) or through distortions of materials (Travers). At the same time the publicist in rural China, with more than 2,500 counties and 5 million production teams to choose among, has in effect an infinity of experience at his disposal; it is more than likely that in any phase of policy, many cases can be found where good experience relates well to policy, and where a story can be put together which is basically true as well as edifying. Broadly, the evidence is that selective reporting, rather than distortion, has been the main tool of the propagandist in this field in China over the years.

Dazhai

The practice of propaganda through models has a long history under the Chinese communists. The most important single collection of rural model articles appeared in 1956 (CCP 1956) the time of transition from lower-stage cooperatives to higher-stage collectives, and before the communes. However, Dazhai does not appear in this collection. Dazhai made its public appearance first in 1963–64, under the patronage of Mao Zedong. It is a village in Taihang country in eastern Shanxi, with some eighty-two households and total extent around 1.5 sq km, of which about one-third is arable. Dazhai's earlier history since Liberation is one of local enthusiasm for collectivisation and egalitarian policies, with the community and its leadership united in opposition to more conservative attitudes in the senior units. Its achievements up to 1964 were partly in ideology and principle, partly in practical social cooperation, partly in land reconstruction in difficult mountain conditions, partly in improvements in farm production, and partly those of reconstruction and social resilience following disastrous floods in 1963 (Maxwell: 53–8; Zhang Lijuan and Shi Zhanao). As early as 1964, Dazhai and its able leader, Chen Yonggui, were already involved in national politics through Mao Zedong – part of the preliminary skirmishing of the Cultural Revolution (Maxwell: 57).

Dazhai appeared first in the national press in December 1963, four months after the floods, and again with much more prominence in February 1964. In fact, 1964 was a vintage year for village studies in *People's Daily*. Many of them had much in common with Dazhai; and some or all of them, presumably, were potential allies for Mao against his political rival Liu Shaoqi, who had already identified a model village at Taoyuan in Hebei, subsequently much vilified (Burchett: 127–42). Mao and Chen met in 1964, and became firm allies, apparently on the foundation of closely similar political attitudes. The Dazhai movement as it took shape in the years following 1964 became an inseparable part of the Cultural Revolution. 'From that convulsion Tachai and all it stood for emerged triumphant. Tachai was accepted as the model for rural China . . . and became the focus of a vast and continuing lay pilgrimage. Between the beginning of 1963 and the end of 1972 more than 6 million travelled to Tachai to learn from its example' – and they continued to do so by hundreds of thousands each year at least until 1976 (Maxwell: 57). Dazhai was vital to Maoist thinking and credibility at that time. It offered a clear guide to the countryside in the practical implications of Maoism, and provided the Maoism of the time with an irreproachable rural pedigree.

When in 1970 the 'great slogan', 'In agriculture, learn from Dazhai', did finally appear, the contours of the ideal Maoist village or county were taking definite shape. These contours were rather simple, as any collection of articles on

learning from Dazhai shows. Localities (brigades and communes first, later larger units such as counties) are praised for increasing grain yields first and foremost; for land construction and waterworks; for supplies contributed to the state; and finally and as the foundation of all else, for the correct political line, embracing continuing class struggle, egalitariansim including manual work for cadres, local self-reliance and total reliance on the poor and lower-middle peasants. Other kinds of progress do appear in this literature – electricity, mechanisation, double cropping, fertiliser, rural industrialisation – but these are exceptional; the staples are rising grain yields based on land construction and both arising from the proletarian political line. This is the account of Dazhai which was beatified in 1964 and canonised in 1970. The Dazhai village study of 1964 was fossilised as the universal rural model.

Several features of Dazhai's development after 1970 deserve further comment. In some ways this development represents direct continuity with the model; in some ways not.

Land reconstruction continued. Dazhai built 100 *mou* of good land in the years 1971–73, mainly by local topographical reconstruction; and Chen points out that these fields represent at least 100,000 *jin* of grain annually – enough to supply 200 people. Chen Yonggui points out that the frost-free season at Dazhai lasts only about 150 days, giving a long winter as slack season; and he insists that these slack months must be used in construction. He reckons at least 200 work-days to construct 1 *mou* of terraced fields, and argues that although the investment to make this land good in one year is quite considerable, its subsequent yield of 800 *jin* of grain per year for ever more than justifies this kind of investment (Chen Yonggui 1973: 95–6). This kind of reasoning is more convincing in highland Shanxi or on the loess plateau than in other areas where more alternatives are available, but in its own terms it remains realistic.

Dazhai also contributed some experiments and achievements in scientific farming, especially the improvement of soil quality through deep ploughing, physical mixing of soil materials and more generous use of fertiliser. The name of Dazhai was used to popularise 'sponge' or *sanbao* fields, which are those with at least a foot of fertile soil, rich in humus and bacteria and retentive of water and fertiliser. Chen Yonggui himself took particular interest in these developments (Chen

Yonggui 1972). In Dazhai itself, moreover, steps were taken to valorise the mountain land by means of plantations for timber and nuts.

There was less continuity with the foundation of Dazhai's growing prosperity. By 1974, 55% of the village's gross income, and no doubt a higher proportion of net income, was contributed by the non-farm sector (Xiyang county; 72–5), and the principal component of that sector was the procession of visitors who came to study Dazhai, and who made of it a Lourdes of Maoist piety. Neither in Dazhai nor elsewhere were rising grain contributions to the state the foundation of local prosperity.

But even apart from internal inconsistency, Dazhai presented some problems considered as a universal, rather than a regional, model. In prosperous parts of southern China, scientific farming has been practised for centuries, in environments much more generous than those of highland Shanxi. To a degree, the improvements at Dazhai consist of the adoption of southern standards and practices – garden husbandry, terracing, irrigation, intensification and diversification. In the south, intensification, water control works and land rationalisation were still going on, but broadly at a productive level above that of Dazhai. When Dazhai started double cropping, advanced areas in the south were already practising triple cropping. True, further improvements such as mechanisation or crop spraying, promoted in the name of Dazhai, were and are still to come even in prosperous areas; but clearly this is not quite the same thing as learning from Dazhai in (for instance) the rest of the Taihang countryside.

The Dazhai model also raised problems in the field of diversification, subsidiary production and production for the market.

Diversification means in practice farm production apart from grain or other bulk cereal crops such as potatoes. Under the Maoists, outputs of subsidiary crops which were marketed through the state purchasing organisations and budgeted for in the state plans generally faced no problems, though the authorities were usually reluctant to supply grain in return for commercial crops and often put pressure on producing units to become self-sufficient in grain; and state prices could be very low. But outputs which were not demanded by the purchasing organisations and not budgeted for in the state plans did face serious problems, partly because the state had (and has) little grain to sell to such units, and partly because the

Maoist state disliked unofficial commercial activity and sharply resisted any tendency to gravitation towards a money economy, fearing that small business interests would lead back to capitalism. In many places, usually but not necessarily in the south, the practice of subsidiary production and commerce was already in the early 1970s producing collective incomes of the same order of size as those dependent on grain farming. The Dazhai model had little to offer such units as these, apart from moral uplift.

After the death of Mao Zedong in 1976, the Dazhai movement was retained at first, but since 1978 the authorities have moved progressively to positions in which the Dazhai system can have no place. At first the new commentaries on the Dazhai experience took the form of criticism of such features of Dazhai practice as (it was said) the pursuit of high physical outputs at whatever costs, investments made blindly, egalitarianism (rather than proper respect for work-points) in distributing incomes, and also complacency and self-satisfaction. Other features of the Dazhai movement which are criticised include hostility to 'the capitalism within collective production', and consequent rejection of collective enterprise in industry and subsidiary production and suppression of local markets, of domestic enterprises and private plots, and blind preference for 'big' and 'public' features in various aspects of commune organisation (*People's Daily*, 14 Mar. 1979).

Subsequently, criticism was widened to embrace the experience of Xiyang county in the time of Dazhai ascendancy in its leadership. Here what is attacked is unrealistic, unsuccessful and wasteful land construction projects, particularly ambitious projects involving large-scale diversion of rivers, but also destruction of forest resources and sideline occupations, indiscriminate transfer of resources among units in the pursuit of egalitarianism, misuse of investment funds (every increase of 10 *jin* of grain production required on average a state investment of 2.8 *yuan*, but 10 *jin* of grain is worth only about 1.2 *yuan*), and overworking the people (*People's Daily*, 3 Oct. 1977; Chen Yingci). In addition, a variety of personal charges of arrogance and interference are made. A new county committee took over in Xiyang in 1979, and Chen Yonggui was dismissed (*People's Daily*, 15 Apr. 1981). On the ground, Dazhai is now represented as settling down quietly to life under the post-Maoist system.

Models after Dazhai – Xiashidang

During 1978, the outlines of a new literature on rural localities took shape. Dazhai was gradually dropped. New rural models emerged, which generally had little in common with Dazhai. The new generation of models were usually taken from southern China, in some cases from very prosperous regions; they laid much less emphasis on working-class politics than previously; they displayed diversity in resource and resource use; they proclaimed the virtues of economic enterprise, local self-management and adaptation to local conditions. They adopted rural prosperity as a central aim of the system. They continued to go out of their way, however, to stress collective enterprise and collective ownership of the means of production, and while they were much less single-minded about grain yields and grain production than the Maoists, they usually made a point of local self-sufficiency in grain and high grain yields. In a way, these encouraging images may be said to represent the carrot of rural change under the post-Mao governments, while the revelations from Xiangxiang and Xunyi, discussed in chapter 3, represent the stick. Since the fall of Dazhai, no single model or group of models has been used in ways like those which were adopted for Dazhai. Since about 1980–81, with the introduction of the responsibility systems and progressively deepening emphasis upon household self-management, community studies have occupied much less space in the media. Nevertheless, stress is still laid upon collective ownership and accounting, and inevitably local studies are still intended primarily to fortify official policy, and in that sense are still models.

One of the best of the new models after Dazhai, in terms of completeness of detail and explicitness of the issues involved, was Xiashidang, a brigade and village of Xijie commune, in Yibin county on the Yangzi River in southern Sichuan (Huang Yanjun and Yu Quanyu 1978 a,b). During the period of more than ten years up to 1978, it had several times been sharply criticised by superior units, as a 'black flag' and a 'fake Dazhai', and for travelling the capitalist road. Like Dazhai in its time, Xiashidang insisted on going its own way, but at a high price in difficulty and opposition.

The achievements of Xiashidang are reviewed under three headings – economic growth, improvement of agriculture and improvements in living standards. Economic growth includes marked improvements in both the grain economy (with sales to the state) and the miscellaneous economy. The latter took its rise around 1964 with a flour-mill, and was later extended to include a water-mill, brickworks and a transportation business on the Yangzi River, and a pig business oriented towards sale of pigs, rather than production of fertiliser as the Maoists tended to expect. During the Cultural Revolution, however, according to Xiashidang people, 'rising incomes became a crime' in China (Huang Yanjun and Yu Quanyu 1978a). Xiashidang was criticised bitterly, and also victimised by superior units. At that time (in or around 1969) Xiashidang had urgent need to buy a diesel engine to work a pump and other machinery; they found a powerful machine at a high price and paid for it, but a county cadre came up and refused to let them take delivery of it, calling the brigade a 'black flag'. Xiashidang then rented an engine from another unit at the exorbitant rate of 2 *yuan* per hour. ('But that was not called capitalism. Only taking one's own money earned by one's own sweat, to buy a diesel engine to increase production, was called capitalism.') (Huang Yanjun and Yu Quanyu 1978a)

Xiashidang was also victimised by the commune in the quotas assigned to it – more than half the grain quota of the whole commune, in one case. At that time, according to the account, slogans such as 'the poorer we are, the more revolutionary', and 'when you get rich you become revisionist' were being put out by the Maoists.

Xiashidang is represented in these accounts as loyally accepting the constructive obligations laid upon it by the state system and Maoist policy – grain sales to the state, the state plan, triple cropping of the arable, land reconstruction – although the brigade had reservations about most of these. In many ways it appears that Xiashidang has sought prosperity by performing work for cash which lay beyond the scope of the state plan to regulate (such as the transport business) at the same time as working to satisfy all the requirements of the plan.

It was pointed out at Xiashidang in 1978 that the only thing which had interested the higher authorities for many years was crop outputs and yields – as long as grain production and supplies available for state purchase were high they were satisfied, and took little or no interest in public accumulation or the value of work-points. But what interested the commune members was the level of grain supplies distributed to households and the value of the working day, because these were the fundamentals of their livelihood. Once annual grain supplies exceed 600 *jin* per person, the people's main preoccupation turns to the price put on the day's work. The Maoist scheme on development, as reported at Xiashidang, was based on the arable farming system, with its possibilities of intensification – scientific methods, new crop varieties, triple cropping and so forth. It leads to rising grain production, but it has been more apt to reduce incomes than to raise them. The alternative scheme (it is argued) is based on brigade enterprises of various kinds, in addition to grain farming. Xiashidang adopted both schemes, but profited most by the latter. During the fifteen years up to 1978, output per person in brigade subsidiary enterprises rose from 6 *yuan* per annum to 111 *yuan*, an increase of 1,750% – and this increase enabled the brigade to cover the losses resulting from arable intensification, and still to prosper.

Rural models across the policy divide

In terms of direct comparison, the Dazhai and Xiashidang models have little in common, even bearing in mind that Xiashidang was a local sketch with a short life in the media, while study of Dazhai was for some years one of the foci of Chinese intellectual effort. Obviously the two models have very different relationships to the course of time – a model like Xiashidang, newly presented in 1978, was able to rationalise its past favourably as Dazhai did in 1964, and did not remain prominent long enough to fall victim to its characteristic corruptions, whatever they may be. The weaknesses of the Xiashidang model from the Maoist point of view are of course broadly the actual foundations of post-Maoist policy. These same weaknesses were reviewed in a very late Maoist work from Guangxi (Nanning and Yulin prefectures: i, 10–20, 88–100 and elsewhere), which gives many examples of corruptions of the collective system in that province in the years before 1966 and even up to the middle 1970s – village pig-breeding enterprises in which the majority of the pigs were privately owned; a riot (in 1975 or 1976) when in the course of land construction a certain clan's hillside grave site was to be moved; influential people quietly setting up private farms and going into trade in such things

as ginger; people gathering wild products and trading in them privately; cutting timber for private profit ('eating public, spending private'); lending money at interest, employing people, speculating in commodities; even the collective arable divided up among families in one case; collective organisations and management breaking down, and class reappearing in the countryside. All these corruptions are over and above the opening of collective brickworks and other kinds of collective commercial enterprise, such as those at Xiashidang, which were also attacked in Guangxi at that time. Obviously this list relates closely to many changes in policy later adopted by the post-Maoist authorities.

A further point of difference between the Dazhai and Xiashidang materials must relate to the environments. Both villages are in rather isolated mountain areas with environments which are in regional terms moderately difficult, but there the resemblance in environment ends. The frost-free period at Dazhai is about 150 days; at Xiashidang it is about 240 days. Average rainfall at Dazhai is about 625 mm, but seasonality is high and reliability low. At Xiashidang rainfall is about 1000 mm, with much less seasonality and much better reliability. Double cropping is common-place at Xiashidang and triple cropping quite feasible, but double cropping at Dazhai normally involves intercropping routines, and is proportionately costly. Wild vegetation and wild resources generally are surely abundant at Xiashidang, but are certainly scarce at Dazhai. Isolated or not, Xiashidang can use the river to establish a transportation business. All these differences are aspects of classic geographical differences between northern China and southern, and all, of course, favour Xiashidang and the rest of the south. We may accept the Maoist contention that the physical obstacles at Dazhai throw into relief the human achievements there, but we are bound to accept the reality of achievements made in less hostile environments by more relaxed methods.

All these points made, moreover, it is clear that in terms of attitudes and priorities the two schemes of development are widely divergent. For Xiashidang collective money-making is put forward explicitly as the heart of the system; but at Dazhai the heart of the system is the proletarian line in politics. In this respect, the two systems clearly and explicitly lie at opposite ends of the Chinese political spectrum; and the accounts of the inspirations and aspirations of the people and leadership in the two places could hardly be more different.

The realities of development, however, are something else again. In this respect, differences are less marked; far from diverging, the two schemes tend to converge. Both villages are raising grain yields and hence discharging their obligations by producing grain surpluses for sale to the state. Both are improving their farmland and practising land construction. Both are keeping animals, extending the use of fertiliser, intensifying agriculture with the help of scientific methods, diversifying production, starting local workshop industries and mechanising – all sound Maoist policies. (The tourist traffic at Dazhai is the main oddity here.) Especially bearing environmental differences in mind, the two village economies differ much less than might have been expected, and very much less than the positions of the two at opposing points on the political spectrum might be expected to indicate.

Two considerations, one practical and one theoretical, seem to underline this apparent contradiction. The theoretical consideration is the insistence of the Maoists on the overriding priority of politics – for them, unless the political line was satisfactory, development could not in the nature of things (whatever appearances might indicate) go forward satisfactorily. At Xiashidang, whatever its material achievements, this prime condition was not satisfied, and the county cadre was right to call Xiashidang a 'black flag'. Other possible schemes of socialist development, including that of the present in China, would lay less emphasis on the political line. The practical consideration is that much of the development at Dazhai comprises the adoption of essentially southern Chinese practices – more intensification, better varieties and a wider range of crops, better rotations and more double cropping, water control, more use of fertiliser, diversification beyond arable farming, the introduction of animal farming and so forth. To an important extent, much of the development which has taken place in northern China since 1949 has been of this kind – the slow adaptation and spread of southern farm practice, based on generous environments, to the north where the environments are less kindly but human ingenuity can in various ways compensate. In this sense, villages like Xiashidang are the mother of much of the improvement at Dazhai.

Fundamental structures

Since its introduction in 1958 the commune system, by and large, has displayed remarkable stability, in spite of far-reaching policy changes. It has done so because it represents a range of viable practical solutions of the problem of organisation of the vast and densely peopled Chinese countrysides, and at the same time a means to harmonise the potentially competing claims of the state for taxation and purchasable supplies, the local communities for self-sufficiency, stability and progress towards prosperity and the Communist Party (whether Maoist or not) for collective ownership and social control. Out of the wide range of forms within which these competing claims are harmonised, the extent to which each is accommodated and the levels of tension involved in each local case, arises the vast diversity of experience within the commune system at any one time. Similarly, when change takes place over time, it does so within those forms and according to rationales based upon these competing claims. Instability arises when, due to change over time, or lack of it, effective competition among these various claims remains unresolved; but the system itself has an impressive tolerance of such instabilities and of disparities of all kinds. A number of authors have investigated the experience of communities managed within the commune system in terms of organisation and decision-taking (Crook) or responses to practical and theoretical movements in society (Domes 1980) or both (Prybyla 1981: 51–86). The present sketch relates particularly to the organisation of production and livelihood within the commune system.

In 1980 there were 54,183 communes in China, with an average population of 14,967 people belonging to 3,262 households (*Yearbook 1981*: 10). Normally a commune comprises a group of production brigades, and each brigade a number of production teams – on average, a commune may have about thirteen brigades and a brigade about eight teams; but marked variations occur according to local conditions such as population densities or forms of organisation or apparently, at least until 1980, various political peculiarities of organisation (*Yearbook 1981*: 10). However, there is reason to believe that the status of the natural villages in this hierarchy is what really matters. In most places, teams are natural villages; in others,

31

villages are brigades. In principle teams, brigades and the communes themselves all have specific functions within the system; but everywhere it is usual for the villages, whether as teams or brigades, to function as the foundation of the system. In the present phase of loosening hierarchical control, there is no doubt that they do so more than ever.

The form and functions of the institutions which comprise the commune system did not arise spontaneously in their final form, although Maoist publicists have sometimes written as if they did. In the early enthusiasm of 1958 for 'big and public' social forms, the people's communes were 'the logical result of the march of events' (CCP 1958: 442). Both in the higher-stage collectivisation of 1956, and in the commune movement in 1958 and subsequently, questions arose about the extent of collectivisation of property and the level at which collective ownership and management were to be exercised. After 1958 'big and public' enthusiasm fell back, and it is moderate attitudes which underlie the 'New Sixty Articles', the regulations for the communes which were issued in 1962 (CCP 1962). These regulations lay stress on the independence and rights of ownership of the production teams at the base of the system (704–5), and remained the foundation of rural management until Mao's Cultural Revolution of 1966. Nevertheless, the victory of the moderates was incomplete, particularly in respect of the rights of senior units to allocate labour, land and implements in the villages over the heads of local people, and over the heads of the nominal owners of these resources, the production teams (Lin Tian: 10–11). Throughout, the Maoists wanted more, and more complete, collectivisation, together with ownership and management at higher levels and by larger units – broadly, they aimed for collective units above the face-to-face level of the earlier cooperatives, which were usually villages. A central and characteristic feature of commune organisation, much favoured by the Maoists, was the union of local government functions with rural economic production functions at commune level. This union invested senior units within the production system with executive authority derived from the state, which was available for use or in reserve in their dealings with junior units within the same system.

During the decade of Maoist ascendancy from 1966 to 1976, a great deal of arbitrary economic management took place in the countryside upon the authority of senior units, with junior units finding their resources of labour, land and sometimes even cash, allocated to various uses against their wishes. Great resentment was caused. Two important reports from rural counties, Xiangxiang in Hunan and Xunyi in Shanxi, introduced the criticism and partial reversal of Maoist rural policy in 1978. The first (*Xiangxiang report*) revealed that very extensive reallocation of labour had taken place in Xiangxiang on the authority of the county and at the expense of the production teams. The second (*Xunyi report*) disclosed many specific cases of persecution of individuals and groups by county and commune authorities (Chen Po-Wen: 49–51). These reports were used to introduce a torrent of criticism of Maoist rural management which prepared articulate public opinion for the changes since introduced. These changes began with the return to the New Sixty Articles which were endorsed by the Central Committee of the Chinese Communist Party at the third plenary session of the eleventh party congress in 1978, when the decision was taken to distribute this document 'for discussion and trial use' to the provinces and other senior units (*Beijing Review*, 1978/52, 130). The same decision was also taken with respect to a document entitled 'Decisions of the Central Committee of the Chinese Communist Party on some questions concerning the acceleration of agricultural development (draft)' (CCP 1978). It is from the broadcast of the latter document in October 1978 that the dramatic post-Maoist change in the content of press coverage of rural issues may be dated. These two documents, and in terms of policy particularly the latter, laid the foundations for the changes which have continued up to the present. They are at one in laying stress upon the rights of the working peasant community (usually the production team) to a high degree of self-management, as well as self-responsibility, in decision-taking and the allocation of resources. The latter document, much more than the former, also lays emphasis upon the role of collective enterprise at various levels in fostering prosperity in the countryside, and the obligation of state organs to respect the rights of local communities – and it is admitted that this obligation has not always been respected. Neither has much to say about the obligations represented by the state plan – an important topic which is discussed in Chapter 4. Both documents emphasise the importance of stability in rural organisation; but stability may have many meanings. What it does not appear to mean in this field, is lack of change. Change beyond the New Sixty Articles has continued at an accelerating pace, particularly (as will be shown) in the field of contracts for production made between collective units on the one hand, and specified working groups or (more frequently) individual households on the other. This kind of contract or 'responsibility' system need involve no interference with the institutional structure of the commune, and may well (depending on the terms of the contracts) encourage prosperous individual households to emerge in the countrysides. Since 1980 a great variety of innovations in the organisation and management have made their appearance, many of which go far beyond anything foreshadowed in 1978. These changes are reviewed in Chapter 5.

In terms of the institutional structure of the communes, one important and widely demanded change was introduced in the new Constitution of 1982 – the abolition of the conjoint exercise of management with administrative responsibility at commune level (Song Dahan and Zhang Chunsheng: 17). Discussion during recent years has linked this proposal with various alternative kinds of rural organisation other than the commune system. For instance, during official experiments in Sichuan province, some communes became mixed production–commercial complexes and some production teams became agricultural producers' cooperatives (Liu Zheng and Chen Wuyuan). A number of different kinds of village freedom have been associated in media discussions with the proposed abolition of the communes – freedom from administrative control in economic affairs, freedom or partial freedom from the demands of the state plan, freedom from the burden of unrealistic levels of cadres and other unproductive ancillary employees whom the villages must support, and freedom from all kinds of arbitrary and egalitarian management practice (FBIS *Daily Report*, 26 Aug. 1981, quoting a Beijing broadcast of 25 Aug. 1981). The decisions represented by the few words given to rural organisation in the Constitution of 1982, particularly Article 17:

Collective economic organisations have decision-making power in conducting independent economic activities, on condition that they accept the guidelines of the state plan and abide by the relevant laws. Collective economic organisations practice democratic management in accordance with the law, with the entire body of their
workers electing or removing their managerial personnel and deciding on major issues concerning operation and management (Constitution 1982: 20)
must be taken as final for the present. Substitution of 'township' government for administration through the communes is now in progress throughout China, and its completion is promised for 1984 (*Economic Daily*, 26 Oct. 1983, quoted in FBIS *Daily Report*, 27 Oct. 1983, K18).

But official pronouncements are not necessarily the end of the question. At the present time it is a normal experience to be assured by commune committee members and local officials in China that rural land all belongs to the state, and that the collective has only rights of use of it, although this notion is directly contrary to the principle of collective ownership expressed in the Beidaihe Declaration of 1958 (CCP 1958: 448), to the New Sixty Articles (which exceptionally specify ownership by the production teams – CCP 1962: 704), to the Constitution of 1982 (16), and even to the left-wing Constitution of 1975 (*Current Background*, 31 Jan. 1975, 18). This might be called the left-wing side of public understanding. At the same time, there is growing evidence that the state is sometimes willing to accept rural production relationships which are not expressed through the collective units of the commune system, and exceptionally even to deal through its own agencies with individual households. This might be called the right-wing side. The suppression of local government functions of the communes has led to a body of generalised opinion in the West that the commune system itself is being dismantled. This is far from being the case. It does appear however that in this respect as in others, the present central authorities are willing to see collective institutions diminish in importance in the course of time, as a result of growth which takes place outside them.

The commune itself is often treated as the key unit in Western discussions, in accordance with Chinese precedent. This is realistic in the sense that the commune represents the level at which the local community communicates with the state system – specifically the production planning system – through one of the 2,757 counties or equivalent units including towns (*People's Daily*, 13 Jan. 1981). But in many ways it is realistic to look first at the production team. This is the unit of lowest rank in the system, the basic unit of accounting and management, and the level at which the system is directly represented among the people. It is also the level at which the tensions of policy and practice outlined above take their most local and fragmented, but also their most immediate and operational, forms.

Production teams

A production team is a working group of households, responsible for a particular body of production. Typically, a team is allocated an area of land, within which all land and other resources (except those managed by the state or senior units) are at the year-to-year disposal of the team for purposes of production. In Mao Zedong's time, work animals, farm implements and small farm machinery were always collectively owned, but in recent years families may also own such items themselves. The team's main functions are of two kinds – production and distribution. Under the first heading comes the day-to-day management of whatever collective farm production now takes place on the team's land, together with the season-to-season organisation of household production and other production under contract. Under the second comes the management of collective accounting for all production in the team's area (other than that on households' private plots), the distribution of food and cash to member households of the team, and the satisfaction of the demands of senior units (mainly representing the state plan) for the year. All these functions are now discharged through an elected committee of members, with a team leader, who are responsible to the general meeting of the team members and to the brigade – the nominated 'revolutionary committees' of the Cultural Revolution disappeared in 1980. The production team is the social and economic unit within which the great majority of Chinese people do their work and find their subsistence; and the teams are also the units within which the vast Chinese rural community as a whole is in the last resort maintained. There were 5.4 million teams in 1980 (Zhan Wu 1982: 13). On average, a team has about 150 people, including 50–60 workers, belonging to about 31 households, and cultivates about 300 *mou* of land. Provincial figures (using 1980 data – *Yearbook 1981*: 10) diverge somewhat from the averages, from 27 households per team in densely populated southern provinces such as Fujian to 63 households in Heilongjiang, and local

figures no doubt diverge much more. Rural houses belong to individual families within the team, and new houses are built by families themselves with help from relatives and friends; sites are provided by the team, and remain in collective ownership.

The working time of team members is usually taken up in farming the team's land, using the usual regional crops and cropping systems, or variants upon them which have been introduced. Most places are expected to be self-sufficient in bulk starchy foods which may be either grain or potatoes. Many teams, however, have specialist functions, either as a whole as members of a brigade group of teams, or performed within the team by job groups – fishing, pig management, specialist cropping and so forth; and increasingly the relations between such groups and the team are contractual ones. Team members' subsistence is assured either through distribution of collective grain supplies to households or through household self-sufficiency within a system of collective allocation of land for cultivation. Under the Maoists and until after 1979, most units gained all or almost all of their cash incomes from the state, through the sale to the state of surplus grain or other farm products. These products are usually contracted for by the state through the planning system, but the state may also purchase outputs over and above the planned quantities. In addition, a team may have a cash income from subsidiary production marketed outside the state system, or from the contracted supply of labour to the brigade or commune for work other than farming – since 1979 this is one of the most important points of growth in the whole system. Where a team supplies the commune and state with products other than grain (cotton, for instance), so that it is not self-sufficient in food, it may be supplied with grain grown elsewhere, though it will usually be expected to achieve self-sufficiency in food.

Distribution of grain and cash is carried out according to the Chinese version of the Marxist principle – 'from each according to his ability, to each according to his work'; egalitarian and self-assessment systems, important in the early 1970s, have been given up. Collective labour is rewarded by work-points, which are recorded day by day for all workers, usually by means in which rate-fixing plays a prominent part. This is one place where contract production is fitted into the system. Working groups and households working under contract are paid in work-points, usually with contractual arrangements for bonuses and penalties; and in addition such groups are allowed to sell outputs above contract on the free market. At the end of the year, when the team's financial position is known, the cash available for distribution is distributed according to the total of work-points and the work-points earned by each individual or household. Under the Maoists, some provinces imposed ceilings on local income distribution, but these have been given up. Parts of the team's income are allocated before distribution to the reserve fund, welfare fund, tax and so forth. Taxation on farm produce was around 6% of gross output for the country as a whole in 1972 (Robinson 1976: 12), but of course nearer to 12% of net output. Quotas are another matter. These are assessed quantities of produce to be delivered to state purchasing agencies and paid for at official prices, which are low. Where the state sets its quota demands at a high or relatively high level, production teams may well find their economies squeezed between rising production costs and shortage of food for their own needs. Many complaints in this field reached the media after 1978, under the heading of 'high-output poverty'. Outputs of acceptable produce above quota may be purchased at standard or negotiated prices by the state agencies, but in negotiations of this sort, and in the fixing of the quotas themselves, the state has for many years had the whip-hand, mainly because sales except through state agencies were forbidden. Since 1981 units are permitted to sell surpluses outside the state system. Increasingly, moreover, households are encouraged to produce for the market independently.

Production costs for the forthcoming year are a special problem. A survey of 3.6 million production teams in twenty-six provinces and cities in 1979 shows that on average a production team can finance only 15% of its year's expenses of production from its own resources, and 40% of teams have basically no cash for this purpose, and depend entirely on loans from the banks and credit cooperatives (Sun Pu). This is the outcome of a variety of factors – low and slow growth in the past, a tendency for teams to over-distribute to households, rising costs, and loose control of cash which has led to a vast national network of debt among collective units amounting in total to more than 10,000 million *yuan* for these 3.6 million teams in 1979 (Sun Pu). In this network of debt

the state is also involved (J and M Gray: 170). In turn, lack of working capital on the land leads to low levels of technique, and in addition many units find themselves heavily burdened by interest charges. Some poor teams subsist almost wholly outside the cash economy, with no cash incomes to distribute and little or no capacity to purchase inputs (Sun Pu).

Private plots are another special problem, of a very different kind. Private plots are allocations of land made from team resources to individual households. Their extent and importance have varied greatly according to political pressures, and so has reporting about them. They are specifically authorised in the New Sixty Articles and in 'Decisions on some agricultural questions' (CCP. 1981); according to the former, 5–7% of a team's cultivated land may reasonably be allocated to private plots (CCP 1962: 715).

Under the Maoists, private plots disappeared in many units, either through political pressure or through manipulation by the authorities, for instance by allocating very poor land for them, so that the people lost interest. A conventional view in the late 1970s was that private plots occupied about 3–5% of the arable, and provided about 10% of total household incomes, but arrangements appear to have varied considerably according to circumstances.

In southern China, where population densities are high but land is very productive, 3% of the arable is about 100 sq m per household. (The standard British public allotment garden is about 250 sq m in extent.) To keep a pig on such an area, in addition to growing vegetables for domestic use, surely demands effort and planning; but it is quite common, fortified in many cases by additional fodder supplies, for instance from the team in return for fertiliser. The great majority of the pork which reaches the market in China is produced by commune members who raise household pigs, and this kind of enterprise is warmly encouraged, now usually under the name 'family production'. The State Council has now authorised the extension of private plots and feedlots up to 15% of total farmland in areas where contract and responsibility systems based on the household are not in use, and proposes that some 'private workers' should be allowed to concentrate on household production except during busy farming seasons (FBIS *Daily Report* 9 Apr. 1981, K10, quoting a Beijing broadcast, 5 Apr. 1981). Increasingly since 1980–81, whether by official intention or by default, emphasis on self-management by the individual household has led to blurring of the distinction between collective land allocated by contract to households, and collective land allocated as private plots. Since 1978 'eating public, spending private' is no longer attacked, and prosperous families (who usually have several working members) are given sympathetic press coverage. Increasingly, Chinese commentators express official policy in such terms as 'collective in important matters, individual in minor matters', and increasingly also, writers draw attention to exceptional achievements in private production, such as units where family production yields a higher proportion of income than collective production. All this means that private plots are now usually regarded as part of the family production side of the rural economy, and in practice often closely related to diversification policies.

Generally speaking, the production team is the basic rural accounting unit, and carries responsibility for its activities, income, costs, gains and losses in a business sense. One complaint often made against the Maoists was that they insisted upon policies which were extravagant or unprofitable, and then expected the production teams to carry the inevitable losses. As basic accounting unit, a production team must keep three books of principal accounts – cash and deposit, materials in stock and fixed assets; and also five books of classified accounts – income, expenses, team members' activities, other activities, funds. In each of these books, detailed accounts are set up as necessary – for instance, under 'expenses', separate accounts for production expenses, management expenses and other expenses. A journal of transactions is recommended as the foundation of the proper allocation of items to accounts as necessary. Manuals of rural accounting containing specimen accounts have been published by several provinces, and some are available in translation (People's Bank of China). Similar material has also been published by Nolan and White (1979: 36–8).

Obviously the management of a system of public accounts of this kind is an impressive achievement for a farming village in any community. Obviously also, it makes its contribution to the proliferation of 'unproductive' individuals whose livelihood is often treated as a standard grievance in the villages – though 'experts', teachers and 'barefoot' doctors are most often

quoted in this connection. Moreover, further developments in the production system, such as household responsibility schemes, can hardly take place without parallel further development of the accounting systems. Discussions of these issues in the press remains limited, but has tended to increase slowly. It appears to indicate that forms of practical administration of these schemes, including accounting, are still taking shape. Considerable emphasis is laid not only upon effective management, but upon the enforcement of contracts and the prevention of corruption (FBIS *Daily Report*, 8 July 1981, R14–R15, quoting *Shanxi Daily*, 20 June 1981) – but corruption seems likely to be a growing problem.

Discussion of the form and functions of the accounting systems in the communes does not fail to impress the Western observer. He may, however, be forgiven for imagining that the systems do not always function effectively or in due form, and evidence does appear from time to time which supports such a view (J and M Gray: 169). An article from Changping county in Beijing city (Shi Changjiang) points to a variety of habitual abuses in this field – ambitious purchasing and consequent overstocking, with very high ratios of working capital to outputs; extravagance and waste; poor care of tools; bad debts mounting; tolerance of trickery in registering work and awarding work-points; carelessness with cash; inadequacy and unduly rapid turnover of accounting personnel in local units, with consequent poor work. Obviously perfection cannot be achieved throughout this vast system, and equally obviously, good managers and the state will try to reduce corruption and waste. It serves to illustrate the magnitude and complexity of the rural accounting system and its problems that when the State Council proposed measures to 'streamline' the financial affairs of communes their proposals included clarifying family and collective property, overcoming chaos, plugging up loopholes, imposing rules, regulations and management (especially the management of collective property), increasing services and cutting expenditures; and the work was to be done under Communist Party committees and people's governments at all levels, in conjunction with management of the various production responsibilities including household responsibility (FBIS *Daily Report* 12 Mar. 1982, quoting a Beijing broadcast of 8 Mar. 1982). Clearly there was much to be done, and many ways of doing it.

Before 1978, little was heard of the production teams as decision-taking bodies, but since that time they have been brought into some prominence. They are now accorded the rights to determine the manner and time of planting of the crops and to decide upon production and management methods – unless these are delegated to contracted households. They also have rights to determine the internal distribution of their products and incomes, and to reject unreasonable demands from senior units – at least in principle. When complaints reached the *People's Daily* (27 June 1980) from a production team in Huitong county in south-west Hunan that the commune imposed a fine of 2 *yuan* per *mou* on production teams for paddy-fields planted at densities other than those specified, and 2 *yuan* per man-day for workers who did not turn up for work at the commune as stipulated, together with as many as a dozen other similar fines, the Editor remarked that however discreditable, this was not an isolated occurrence. However, unreasonable interference with junior units is no longer orthodox – but all units are, of course, expected to continue to accept the demands of the state plan.

Problems continue to lurk in this area. Rural production plans necessarily depend in some degree upon supervision of junior units by senior; and lines of demarcation between necessary supervision and unacceptable commandism are by no means easy to draw. Moreover, reports that 95% of local units in a province have adopted radically new systems of management within a year of their introduction, which appeared in 1980 and 1981 in the context of the responsibility systems, suggest that junior units continue to experience pressure to conform to official norms, even when these are in principle libertarian.

Production brigades

There are about 710,000 production brigades in China (*Yearbook 1981*: 10). Brigades have their own congresses and administrative committees, but in spite of this, and no doubt because they share direct Communist Party branch representation with the communes, they frequently appear to operate as local agencies of the communes, rather than as independent bodies or bodies representing groups of teams. Many brigade activities, such as processing mills, are alternative to the same functions performed at commune level; and at the same time the allocation of land by the teams inevitably separates team interests off from all others.

The functions of the brigades appear to be the least precise in the commune hierarchy. The brigades are said to direct, participate in, guide, examine and supervise the activities of the teams. They may organise joint undertakings among teams, and may initiate, construct and manage various kinds of productive enterprise, such as irrigation. Probably the key function of the brigade is the detailed supervision of rural management by the Communist Party – the brigade is the lowest unit at which party institutions are organised. Perhaps for this reason many local examples occur of backwardness and inadequacy regarded as a brigade responsibility, and also of the correction of misguided tendencies at brigade, rather than team, level. Brigades also maintain roads and canals, rural health services and primary schools, and may supervise local commercial institutions such as general stores and credit cooperatives. In production, they often process agricultural produce (oil; grain- and fibre-mills) and run equipment repair workshops. Some also manage orchards, fishponds, timber and animal-breeding farms. Labour for brigade enterprises is drawn, by arrangement, from teams, in return for payment to the teams; the individual workers are maintained within the team at team rates, and the wages of the people who work for the brigade, which are usually above team rates, go to subsidise the whole team. Brigades use their revenues above costs for further productive investment, and sometimes for welfare or productive purposes in weak teams. Typically, brigade and commune enterprises are more valuable per unit of labour than the farming done by the teams – sometimes very much more so. In this kind of case, the brigade and team may be competitive. In some areas, for instance Jiading county in Shanghai municipality, the Maoists insisted specifically upon the development and strengthening of the brigade-level economy at the expense of the team – 'to boost the production of the brigade-level collective economy is an objective demand for the rapid development of socialist revolution and construction'. Hence brigade activity in construction and mechanisation was strengthened. 'But as some production teams benefited little, and even suffered temporary losses from farmland capital construction carried out under the unified plan of the brigade, there was rather serious ideological resistance to it, and propaganda work and ideological re-education had to be undertaken.' (Jiading county, Party Investigation Group: 11)

A further aspect of the same kind of development has been the transfer of basic accounting functions from the production team to the brigade and (in rare instances) to the commune – another development favoured by the Maoists. When this is reported, it is usually said to indicate local prosperity, with little difference among teams in productivity and incomes, a strong local party organisation and a small and compact brigade area; but in some cases at least, this change was made upon orders from senior units, and has not been successful (Xue Muqiao 1981b: 65–6). In 1979, in China as a whole, 7.4% of brigades exercised these functions, and about 0.1% of communes (*Yearbook 1980*: 6); but these figures had fallen somewhat by 1980 (Zhan Wu 1982: 13). In this respect, there were dramatic differences among provinces, and between north and south, in 1979. In Shanxi (due in part perhaps to the local influence of Dazhai) as many as 35% of brigades exercised basic accounting functions; in the north China plain around 10%; but in Hunan and Jiangxi much less than 1% (*Yearbook 1980*: 6).

One of the commonest complaints about rural community management before 1978 is that far too many people, often not local people, were employed at brigade and commune level in unproductive jobs such as storekeeping and as 'experts', or in office work, rather than as labourers on the land. According to one critic, there may be as many as 300 such people in an average commune, or even as many as three such people for every dozen or two dozen peasant households (Lin Tian: 13). An even higher figure, of around one per household, is reported from Linhe brigade of Tanhe commune in Xinyang county, Henan, in 1979. By 1980, under new policies, the number of unproductive personnel had fallen by 71% in this case, and the burden of related expense by 92% (FBIS *Daily Report*, 26 Aug. 1981, Kl, quoting a Beijing broadcast of 25 Aug. 1981). Parallel problems arise, partly because of different priorities at different levels in the commune system, with unproductive work and unproductive expenses (Kaifeng prefecture and Gong county Working Group). Complaints on these points continue to reach the media (*People's Daily*, 2 Nov. 1983). No doubt the shedding of

personnel from the official service sectors of the rural economy must contribute considerably to the emerging real labour surplus in the Chinese countryside.

On the whole, the brigades have not had a good press in the course of the rewriting of rural experience which has taken place since 1978, and which of course has often adopted the standpoint of the production teams. Sometimes the brigades have been represented as the main instrument of unpopular official policies, or unpopular local vendettas which could claim support in official policy. A 'letter' from Shaanxi complains about egalitarian redistribution of the incomes of prosperous teams by transferring the accounting unit to brigade level, unfair allocation of state quotas among teams, requisitions for use or sale of animals belonging to teams, absorption of team enterprises at will by brigades, blocking of supplies at brigade level – even the non-payment of the electricity bill by a brigade, so that teams could not use their pumps (Liu Xingjie). Here there appears to be petty meanness at work, and also personal or inter-village spite. But there are other prototypes of brigade behaviour. A number of histories which have reached the media, including those of Dazhai and Xiashidang, indicate that when the people and leadership of a brigade are in agreement on a course of action which differs from standard public policy, they may be difficult to move in practice. A similar conclusion is suggested by details of various corrupt practices in rural Guangdong (Burns). No doubt the Communist Party presence at brigade level is intended to forestall such unconventional developments.

People's communes

As we climb up the hierarchy, it is noticeable that the units which we encounter have progressively less to do with management in the sense of production, and more with management in the sense of control. From 1958 until the restoration of local government by townships in 1982–84, the commune was a unit of local government as well as of economic production and management, and this was one mainstay of the 'big and public' side of the system favoured by the Maoists. But it caused trouble; people in the countryside complained that when faulty decisions were made by the commune authorities or even those lower in the system whose word also represented government, these bad decisions had to be treated as administrative decisions as well as economic. In some cases, we learn, violations of law and discipline such as beating up and abusing the masses, reducing their food ration or fining them were not isolated incidents in the rural areas (Beijing radio lectures: 6095/BII/14). The present regime is opposed to such behaviour and to the use of state power for purposes of economic management – 'the cadres of the rural people's communes should avoid using administrative methods of state organs to direct economic affairs' (Beijing radio lectures: 6095/BII/5). At the same time, we are reminded that the communes are to be run according to the principles of democratic centralism – 'This unity of democracy and centralism, of freedom and discipline, constitutes our democratic centralism.' (Beijing radio lectures: 6095/BII/13)

At commune level, local Communist Party and official hierarchies meet, and hopefully their views and interests, particularly those of the officials administering the state plan and those of the local people and the production teams to which they belong, can be brought into harmony under the supervision of the administrative and party authorities at county level. In agriculture, communes have no resources of their own, and undertake little production. In local industry, their activities may be quite varied – grain-milling, brick, cement or paper manufacture, hydroelectricity, quarrying, mining; sometimes more complex manufacturing, such as shoes. These enterprises function under parallel conditions of labour supply to those of the brigades. Communes also manage hospitals, high schools, agricultural experimentation and extension services, rural marketing and commercial supplies, credit and banking services. Some of these enterprises support farm production; some provide materials for state-owned enterprises outside the commune. Profits from commune enterprises are typically used to broaden the economic base of the commune itself, by further investments in commune enterprises.

The growth of commune and brigade enterprise is usually welcomed by both Chinese and Western commentators as a desirable development – widening rural horizons, exploiting new resources and providing subsidies to rural living standards. This is probably the right reaction. But in the study of the commune as an institution we should be aware of the extent of the change which these enterprises may produce in the relations among the three levels of organisation. Figures given by Zhang Chunqiao (5), one of the Gang of Four, for the communes of Shanghai municipality in 1973 and 1974, show that in 1974 income created at commune level was around 30% and rising, income created at brigade level was around 17% and rising, but income created at production team level was around 52% and falling rapidly – from 57% in 1973. This was the result of the growth of subsidiary enterprises, which are under brigade or commune ownership. Even more striking, in Wuxi county in Jiangsu, the showplace of rural industry, the proportion of rural output contributed at commune and brigade levels together was 23% in 1970, but by 1977 had risen to 64% – obviously with a corresponding fall in the proportion contributed at team level. It is evident from these figures that in advanced parts of China, the real economic power in the countryside, as well as the political power, is now exercised at a level above that of arable and grain agriculture. It is even argued that a kind of proletarianisation of grain agriculture has been in progress – a production team with twenty or thirty households growing grain has little income and no capital to start enterprises and cannot spare labour to do so; with its 300 or 500 *mou* of land, it cannot afford to mechanise – at the most it may have a hand tractor. Under the Maoists before 1978, what progress could such a community make? 'Learning from Dazhai' with land construction organised by the brigade took the best labour out of the team; political criticism of team enterprises cut out those few which the team might have; to start new ventures was out of the question. The rapid expansion of rural enterprises after 1975 profited the teams very little, according to this argument; the senior units simply employed team workers as cheap labour (Lin Tian: 11–12).

As a result of these processes, operating increasingly widely during the last years before 1976, as little as one-half of collective rural output in terms of value is contributed at the basic level of the production teams – this is in China as a whole, taking backward and progressive areas together. This is a profound and (in terms of the New Sixty Articles) unexpected change which already seems likely to be permanent. Reforms since 1978 have greatly strengthened the production team's rights to allocate its own labour, and have set off a variety of new developments, most of which tend to strengthen households; but they do not promise any redress of the balance within the system to the advantage of the teams as institutions. It is from this point that some writers now argue for a return to village self-management and control by the village over its own resources, which are associated with the early lower-stage cooperative period before collectivisation in 1956 (Lin Tian: 13). But realistically speaking, although this argument may be important in terms of the collective side of local economies, it is much less so in terms of their present course of development, where the bulk of new growth takes place either outside the collective economy (as family production) or tied to the collective economy only loosely at the planning and accounting stages (in the case of household responsibility systems). These new developments do not solve the problem of balance within the collective system, but they create alternatives to the search for advantage within it; and in the case of grain grown within the responsibility systems, they offer self-management and incentives to the individual which appear to go far to sweeten the pill of institutional proletarianisation.

4

Social organisation and control

From a Western point of view it is natural to ask, what is apparatus of social control in the Chinese countryside? By what means is the community managed so that taxes are paid, quotas delivered, needs satisfied and stability maintained – all in a vast countryside where population, increased by two-thirds since 1949, is now of the order of 800 millions?

By Soviet standards, the Chinese rural system has of course throughout been very localist and very populist, befitting the conditions of dense populations, complex local economies and deep-seated social trust which exist in China. Dense populations and complex local economies indicate the involvement of a number of people in most productive operations and also a multiplicity of such operations, and both of these lead towards social trust. All three lead towards the acceptance of local management of the year's work on the land, and realistically also to local ownership of resources and local self-responsibility for subsistence and surplus. In Maoist times, this social trust was openly manipulated for political ends, as in the Maoist insistence upon narrow, uniform and often destructive standards in culture and education, and narrow and depressively egalitarian methods and objectives in production and society. But in that case we need still more to ask, how is the Chinese community managed?

The answer to this question is quite complicated, and comes at several levels. The first part of it is that traditional family and community controls have experienced rather little fundamental disturbance under the communists. Family and community remain strong in China for the same reason as elsewhere in east Asia – that support and loyalty must be sought by the individual among his own people, because they cannot be expected from anyone else.

The second point is that a number of institutional controls exist – some positive, some negative – which make for stability. Among positive controls are the uniformity of published and broadcast materials, stressing central government policy and wherever possible simply ignoring issues to which the government does not wish to draw attention. School education, local militia training and so forth also lay emphasis on group solidarity. Negative controls include difficulties put in the way of people who try to migrate or seek private employment or in other ways to beat the system. The evidence is that these things can be done, but only corruptly and (at least until recent years) with considerable effort. In the countryside, where everyone knows everyone else's business, many problems face individuals who wish to act independently of the system. Since Mao's time, control at this level is probably less positive and certainly less political, but there is little reason to think it less comprehensive.

A third part of the answer is more direct, and probably covers the great majority of experiences, especially those which are institutional and collective rather than individual. This is the rural planning system. The principal reason why rural China displays stability and competence is because villages are required by the local senior units and the whole rural system to do so – to be responsible for their subsistence wherever possible and to produce reasonable surpluses where they have capacity; and because the planning machinery, with the state at its back, provides for suitable budgeting and commitment of resources year by year to do this. Competence, stability and self-sufficiency under the People's Government are in part the outcome of the same conditions as in time of peace in the historic past; in part the outcome of effective planning for precisely these objectives.

A fourth part of the answer relates to genuine social and economic progress. Security, investment, scientific insight, large-scale planning, effective accounting and intelligently conceived innovations have been brought to the Chinese countryside; direct social exploitation has been suppressed and food supplies increased through increased yields based firmly on improved farm systems. These achievements have certainly transformed society in rural China since Liberation, and provide a powerful practical justification for the rest of the rural management system.

What is of particular interest in the foregoing argument is the role of the state plan in the countryside. State plans are of course a common feature of communist and many non-communist states. Most of these plans propose national goals and sectoral and regional or local means of attaining them; they have a strong investment element and a wide field within which the organs of state power can undertake to make the plan reality by direct action. The next plan will take over where the last left off. Chinese planning since 1958 is not of this kind, except in the state-owned major industries, the oilfields, major construction projects, the mines (perhaps) and the state farms (sometimes) – and all even of these have experienced major discontinuities at various times. In the rural sector particularly, managed within the commune system, the state plan is a very different kind of apparatus. In the vast field of rural China, the state plan represents what is required of each local community by the state during the forthcoming year, and (no doubt less explicitly) what the local community may reasonably expect of the state during the same period of time. The state's demands may be exorbitant or minimal, or merely conventional, for any one or more of a wide variety of reasons. But it is an exceptional community in which the obligations imposed by the state, taken together with the obligation to provide for subsistence, do not constitute the central consideration in local planning for the work of the year.

At the same time, the local production unit is also an accounting unit, and it is required to take its obligations to the state directly into account in budgeting its various resources, whether land, labour, working capital or other resources of various kinds, however expensive or limiting these obligations may turn out to be. Given the prior need to provide for its own subsistence, the local unit is not expected to have much resource left after it has budgeted to satisfy the state plan. In this sense, the state plan is an instrument of government – people in the villages are required to lay out their time and money in particular forms of production over and above subsistence; and these productive activities dominate their lives individually and within their communities, leaving little time, energy or resource for unconventional activities. When in the heyday of the official planning system before 1976, local units did find opportunity for productive activities outside the plan, problems might well arise which could go far beyond inconsistencies in resource allocation or marketing. Cadres in senior units, whose duties included the supervision of the working of the state plan and the junior units within their jurisdiction, might well consider these problems sufficient reason in themselves to block any such opportunities. Since 1978, when the constraints of the planning system, particularly its peripheries such as official price controls, marketing monopolies, income controls, restrictions on enterprises and labour allocation and detailed local supervision of collective operations, have been relaxed, a measure of social control has necessarily been given up, though some of this control was no doubt fictional. Far-reaching innovations in rural management, particularly the responsibility system of farm production, necessarily go some way to weaken the stability side of social organisation; and the same is true of household production both individual and within the collective framework. Realistically, a degree of social self-management is being returned to the villages and peasant households, while hopefully the main framework of organisation and control need not be disturbed.

Rural production plans

The rural production system in China is based upon the local rural production plans, which are all in the last resort parts of the state production plan. These plans are backed by the authority of the state. They represent the year-to-year relationships between the local community and the rest of the nation, agreed and formalised. To all intents and purposes, they have the force of law. How do the plans work? A number of authors have published résumés of this group of processes which differ in various points of emphasis (Howe: 30–64; Eckstein: 110–20; Perkins 1977: 275–8; Nolan and White 1979: 34–5), but agree in essentials with one another and with additional evidence from the media and conversations in China.

Rural production plans begin in Beijing and start from the base of the plan and its performance record in the previous year. Provincial authorities agree upon plans in concert with the ministries in Beijing and in due course propose local plans based upon these to the counties. The counties propose farm production assignments to the communes, which then work out tentative cropping plans which are sent through the brigades to the teams which will have the work to do. Discussion has meanwhile been going on at team level; the team makes its own proposals which may or may not differ from those received from the senior levels. Discussion takes place, often at brigade level, and the principal differences of opinion are thought through, and in principle can be settled sensibly and amicably – cooperation on reasonable terms is in everyone's interests.

In Mao's time, change of all kinds made its way through the system mainly through pressure from above – for self-sufficiency in units which received commodity grain, for instance, for specific innovations such as triple cropping, or for phases of land reconstruction, afforestation and woodland clearance. It is noticeable that in the spate of popular technical literature on crop and land management which appeared in the early 1970s, there was no body of discussion whatsoever on cropping systems or the foundations of decision-taking at the level of the production plans, in spite of Maoist lip-service to consultation with the people. Thus, in the 703 pages of the *Scientific farming handbook* of 1975 (Beijing city) there is nothing at all on rotations or cropping plans. In a parallel handbook of the same year from Shanghai, *Handbook of agricultural techniques for state farms* (Agricultural Bureau), only 15 pages out of 632 are devoted to rotations. The same is true of the improvements proposed in the 'eight-point charter' for agriculture of 1956 (Kuo). This scheme gave priority to deep ploughing, heavier manuring, water conservancy (and irrigation), better seed, close planting, plant protection (against pests), repair of tools, and improved field management, but did not mention rotations or cropping plans, systems of diversification of production, the valorisation of under-used resources (such as wasteland), or even the planting of trees. The implication of this is that discussion of these issues at production team or other local level was not welcome because the authorities intended to keep for themselves the right to take decisions in these fields, through the planning system. There is evidence that cropping changes, which probably lie at the heart of changes made through the planning system, are introduced in the first place on an experimental scale, and extended in subsequent years if they have been successful.

Cropping changes or cropping innovations often involve some kind of trade-off between grain and cash crops, and in the literature up to 1976 were generally represented as successful. Cases have emerged since that time which turned out less well. In Guangxi in 1979, a sugar-producing brigade was instructed by the commune party committee, in conformity with the production plan handed down by the county revolutionary committee, to interplant 8100 *mou* of sugar with soya beans; and a loan of bean seed was arranged. But an official from the provincial office for light industry turned up at the brigade on an inspection tour and criticised the interference with sugar production; and the offending beans were pulled up (Qian Huiming). Conversely, at a production team in Sichuan, maize was interplanted with cotton according to custom, but officials from the county criticised this practice and had the maize pulled up, resulting in heavy loss (more than 100 *yuan* per *mou*) to the local unit (*People's Daily*, 7 Feb. 1970). But the counties have also been under pressure. At Yutian county in Hebei, the province insisted upon a 28% increase in cotton acreage in 1974, in spite of the fact that extension of cotton cultivation upon unsuitable land resulted in a fall in output. Even in 1979, after five years' experience and since the official acceptance of the production teams' rights to resist unreasonable demands upon their resources, the cotton acreage proposed to Yutian for the forthcoming year had not been reduced by a single *mou* (*People's Daily*, 2 Nov. 1979). Increasingly, such authoritarian behaviour by senior units is considered unorthodox and anti-social, and is attacked in the media, but it is not clear to what extent it continues up to the present.

On some other points, apparently, changes could be initiated at local level even in the Maoist phase, particularly where they were in accord with public policy as expressed in the media. Many units were praised for farmland reconstruction, improvement of irrigation systems and so forth. Nevertheless, such changes (involving investment of labour and other resources) required permission from senior units (usually the county) before they could proceed.

More important than such problem areas, however, because much more widespread, was the steady squeeze upon miscellaneous and cash crops within the planning system. Dozens of examples of this have reached the media since 1978, and a number are outlined in the regional chapters in the present work. Such squeezes might be straightforward, such as insistence upon virtual maize monoculture, or might be more complex for various reasons, including inefficiency or corruption within the system of control. One such case is Luancheng county, Hebei (He Guiting and Xu Xin: 15). When cotton was planted in Luancheng, apparently around 1965, the authorities insisted upon its interplanting with grain, ostensibly at a rate of 70% cotton and 30% grain, but realistically (in terms of the grain output required) at a 50% rate. At the same time,

typical allocations of land to vegetables were reduced from 5% in 1965 to 2% in 1978; allocations for soya beans, peanuts, rapeseed, sesame and other crops were similarly reduced to one-half or less. To rear a pig requires 300–400 *jin* of grain or equivalent, and (correspondingly) the allocation of 0.5–0.7 *mou* of land; but official land allocations for pigs were already as low as 0.3–0.5 *mou* at the county level, and at the commune and brigade levels these allocations disappeared altogether. Obviously this made it difficult to keep pigs even for the orthodox Maoist purpose of providing fertiliser for grain crops.

The heart of the rural planning system in Maoist times and basically up to the present has been local self-sufficiency in grain (or potatoes) in the vast majority of units. By any standards this is a realistic and necessary aim in the vast and densely peopled Chinese countrysides. A second central feature was the creation of marketable farm production surpluses for sale to the state at state procurement prices. These surpluses might be in grain or cotton, or in particular instances crops such as tea which have important export possibilities, or fruit or vegetables to supply the cities. To qualify for sale to the state, these outputs had to be included in the official production plans; and to get into the commercial system they had also to be acceptable to the Department of Commerce. Official procurement prices were low, and changed only at widely separated intervals. A third central feature was political, social and media pressure upon the rural communities to accept the guidance of the state plan and to undertake the obligations of the local production plans. The most characteristic vehicle of this pressure was the Maoist scale of measurement of local success in which high grain output per unit area, conjoined with plentiful surpluses delivered to the state, represented high economic achievement which was necessarily correlated with a proper grasp of the political line, understanding of the class struggle and so forth. The two were represented as joined by visible links such as land construction, fertiliser application, egalitarian social policy and political motivation. Dazhai was the universal exemplar. Media and other public pressure to make this model universal was an indispensable part of the system.

These points relate mainly to the collective arable land, which is the heart of the countryside from the point of view of the state plan. What is also of interest, however, is what might be called the peripheries of the state plan – production performed outside the requirements of the plan, production of items for sale which the state is not prepared to market, employment of labour in activities which have not been budgeted for and so forth. An individual village may find its labour force worked to capacity by the demands of the state plan, but it is not unusual to find that labour is sometimes underemployed, and that land or other resources may be found or created which lie outside the scope of the plan, either through previous failure to report or through anomalies of definition. Some units kept 'auxiliary land' in Maoist times which was cultivated but not reported, so that politically impressive high yields per unit area could be quoted (*People's Daily*, 5 Jan. 1979, 24 Feb. 1979). Some units have mineral resources or opportunities to produce saleable items from woods, lakes and rivers, bamboo stands and wild land of all kinds. Hence teams may have resources to hand which are not spoken for in the plan. Brigades or communes equally may undertake kinds of enterprise which lie outside the scope of the plan. Even in Mao's time money could be made (as at Xiashidang) by units which took up kinds of production which were not budgeted for in the plan, provided that they could find markets for their outputs. Many reports from all parts of China (*People's Daily*, 19 Jan. 1979) indicate that Maoist rural authorities actually prevented the use of these miscellaneous resources in many cases, because miscellaneous outputs must necessarily enter trade, and trade was thought to represent the re-emergence of capitalism. In other cases, production did take place, and units tried to get their outputs accepted into the state plan, and so into the commitments of the state purchasing organisations. In yet other cases, production (of bricks, for example) did take place, and was marketed outside the state plan, but under constant threat of denunciation and interference, though there were some signs of a cautious welcome for limited trade in privately produced commodities as early as 1972 (Hung Ch'iao). Policy on these points fluctuated to some extent even under the Maoists, as Domes (1976: 104–19) shows. Since 1978, and increasingly with the passage of time, all these kinds of enterprise meet with official encouragement and warm praise in the media, and outputs are disposed of through the revived local markets. Meanwhile the state plan continues, and local units are sharply reminded of the prior obligations which it repre-

sents. Relations between the planned and free economies are now it seems, symbiotic; each not only tolerates, but often depends upon, the other.

Commercial production and the production plans – some problem cases

Not only is subsistence grain (and potatoes) the main success of the Maoist decade, and production for the market the great failure; not surprisingly, the two sometimes came into more or less direct conflict, as various examples indicate. Various points of principle are involved.

Water-melons have been the subject of a number of test cases. In one standard text in English we read:

In 1972, when the commune asked the Chenkuang brigade to plant 30 mou to water-melon, the plans submitted by the production teams, however, all but doubled the quota. They obviously saw greater profits in water-melons. But this would in turn necessitate a reduction in the area sown to grain. To solve this problem, the brigade called a meeting of team cadres to study the Party's policy of taking grain as the key link while ensuring all-round development of other branches of production. As a result, the team cadres voluntarily reduced the area of their water-melon fields. This shows how the production brigade gives leadership to the teams through policy study or education by examples, instead of relying on administrative orders. (Wu Chou: 14–15)

This is a standard account from the Maoist phase.

But in later official publications, we read that the instructions which come from senior units may be too detailed and explicit, and also ill-considered. In Xiangfen county in Shanxi in 1977 instructions were received from senior units to plant a specified increased number of cotton plants to the *mou*, and to give up interplanting onions and garlic with the cotton in the early part of the summer, as had been customary. The commune members were angry, and cotton output, far from rising, actually fell. In 1978 there was a big change – the county party secretary himself proposed that local units should plant water-melons. Only 1% of the arable area was involved, and grain and cotton output were not affected; but this suggestion came at the end of

45

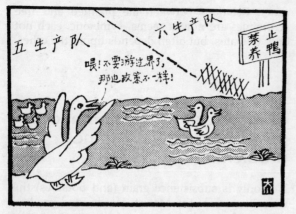

五生产队　　六生产队

喂！不要游过界了，那边政策不一样！

禁止养鸭

At the boundary between No. 5 and No. 6 production teams, a notice proclaims, 'No duck breeding here.' Mother says, 'Don't go there. Their policy isn't the same.' *Source: People's Daily*, 1 Dec. 1979. The artist is Wu Dachuan.

many years of prohibition. Two points were at issue. One was the fear that water-melon production, profitable as it is, is the thin edge of the capitalist wedge; and the other, the recognition that the state cannot necessarily make itself responsible for the marketing of a perishable, highly seasonal crop like water-melons – which presses the commune and brigade organisations back upon the unofficial 'free' markets.

This argument was brought into sharp focus in 1979 by the 'Nanzhuang melon incident'. This illustrates the problems of tension among the state plan, the villages and those who administer the relations between them to perfection, and the subsequent discussion gives valuable indications of the parameters of discussion favoured in the media (Wang Guihai et al).

Nanzhuang brigade belongs to Lincun commune in Zhengding county, Hebei. During the Cultural Revolution it had been a high-yield but nevertheless poor brigade, its production schedules kept within strict limits (grain and cotton) by the county through the production plan. Grain yield per *mou* in 1978 was 1,200 *jin*, a very respectable figure for a northern province like Hebei, but the working day was only worth 0.48 *yuan*. In the spring of 1979, the local people decided to plant 34 *mou* of melons, but the commune party committee did not agree, because of the need to maintain cotton output. The commune wanted the brigade to plant 180 *mou* of cotton, but in fact they planted 154 *mou* of cotton and 34 *mou* of melons interplanted with cotton – four or five rows of cotton to one row of melons.

The commune was not satisfied. The party committee instructed the brigade cadres to pull up the melons, and criticised the brigade for capitalist attitudes. The people and cadres at Nanzhuang were angry, and refused to pull up their melons. Visit followed visit as the melon plants grew during May and June. The commune revolutionary committee and party committee officials insisted on their authority – 'We get our instructions from the county, and you get yours from us.' It became a matter of official dignity. Finally on 21 June the deputy party secretary and a deputy chairman arrived from the commune, and announced that the Nanzhuang brigade chairman would be relieved of his post, and so would any other official who resisted the pulling up of the melons. The brigade realised that at the height of the summer, with the wheat harvest in progress and cotton to care for, it would not be possible to have further disruption of the farm-work, so the people gave in, with great bitterness; and the melons were pulled up. But their struggle was still to be successful – a month later, the county authorities announced that Nanzhuang was to be compensated for the loss of the melons at the expense of the commune. As the story appears in the *People's Daily*, the Communist Party and authorities were on the side of the melon-growing brigade throughout, and the ultimate outcome was never in doubt; neighbouring units were in an uproar, astonished at the authoritarian behaviour of the commune committee. True, it is admitted, a few poisonous influences do remain from Lin Biao and the Gang of Four, as this case illustrates. ('Take grain as the key link, and cut out everything else' as some people represent their policy.) Senior units ought to avoid adopting bullying positions and putting institutional pressures upon junior units; and the wishes of the masses and the rights of junior units (teams as well as brigades) must be given proper weight in planning and the taking of decisions. Realistically, of course, the behaviour of the commune committee in this case would have been routine even two or three years earlier – indeed the incident would never have arisen, as the Chenkuang case shows.

The public reaction to this case as subsequently reported in the *People's Daily* (20 Aug. 1979) is strongly sympathetic to the melon enterprise at Nanzhuang, and hostile to the commune authorities. This in itself is not surprising, given the climate of opinion at the time, but it is inevitably to some degree important, and it must be even more important that the flurry of comment is reported with only a very sketchy defence of the official position. Three major points are made in the discussion. The first of these relates basically to the seat, structure and exercise of authority in the countryside. Cadres, it is said, sometimes act without proper respect for the people, to whom they ought to be much more responsible – if they were elected, that would be an improvement. Quite rightly, it is pointed out that the functions of practical day-to-day management of production in the communes and the functions of local government are the responsibility of the same committee – this has been one of the fundamentals of the communes since their introduction, but it may encourage anti-social behaviour by cadres, especially when in either case real power is exercised by the local officials of the Communist Party. Reforms since 1979 have removed both of these grievances – local committees are now elected, and local government has been separated from commune administration. The second point relates to the state plan. Some senior authorities try to specify rules for junior authorities which are much too detailed, leaving the latter without any discretion. But as some people have pointed out, the commune authorities were acting quite legitimately in protection of the state plan. The third point is that the county, prefecture and province have authority to supervise the communes and their relations with other units. Not least in Hebei, this kind of supervision appears to be lax, so that bullying sometimes takes place.

Melons are a singularly apt test case; but of course the problems under discussion go far beyond the orthodoxy of the occasional melon patch, as subsequent developments have shown. Few people in the Nanzhuang melon case have a good word to say in favour of the maintenance of the rural planning system, but nobody suggests any alternative, and the fact is that as things then stood, there was none. What the *People's Daily* was arguing for was the planning system plus freedom to take decisions outside it; but that standpoint demands limits to freedom as well as to planning. To a degree, it is precisely this situation towards which the Chinese countryside has been moving since 1979. It is true that there are obvious dangers of encroachment year by year, of deals between rural suppliers and urban purchasers which may have far-reaching implications for the state-controlled part of the economy including the

supply of grain, of competition for profitable sideline markets leading to falling prices and destitution, and of favoured or successful communes and brigades cutting themselves off progressively from the state plan. It is also true that if the local production plans are the fundamental instrument of government, as well as production, in the countryside, then social control and management, as well as livelihood, are brought under threat together with the plans. In the 1980s, whether as a matter of principle or because there is thought to be no alternative, the central authorities have evidently decided to live with these problems. There is little or no sign that solutions are on the way.

The policy of encouraging – enforcing might be a better word – self-sufficiency in grain at the local level almost throughout the Chinese countryside was explicitly a Maoist one, though much of its substance remains to the present. It seems to have had three roots. The first is the recognition of the difficulties for the government in trying to service a system of widespread dependence on commodity grain in so vast and varied a countryside, with inadequate means of transport in most areas. The rationale of this may be readily accepted in general terms, though there must be many cases where total insistence on this principle would inhibit much useful and economical development. The second is the Maoist insistence on self-sufficiency for its own sake, and with this a suspicion of marketable production of any kind as leading back to capitalism. The third consideration resides in the price system. Grain in China is very cheap. It does not appear to have been possible in Maoist times for any unit to achieve prosperity through grain sales to the state, and it does not appear to be possible up to the present. Cotton has usually been more profitable than grain, but much less so than most other kinds of output, especially those marketed otherwise than through the state. In these conditions, it is necessary to maintain social and political pressure upon the peasants, if the countryside is to continue to maintain supplies. Price rises are the obvious alternative, and prices have been raised since 1978, though not enough to erase these anomalies. One underlying problem is that a policy which represents genuine national necessity (the maintenance of the rural production plans) has been corrupted during Maoist times by association with policies which represented ultra-Left prejudice (insistence upon supplies of cheap grain, egalitarianism, refusal to respect local commercial enterprise). Abandonment of the latter has inevitably led to dissatisfaction with the former. Even more fundamental is the continuing dependence of the state on the cheap grain supplies themselves.

The system which has emerged since 1978 preserves the essentials of the state plan and cheap grain supplies, but tempers its most unpopular results by encouraging miscellaneous commercial and industrial enterprise and permitting the free marketing of surpluses, including surpluses of grain. Some Chinese writers openly propose exactly this analysis (Chen Lian: 28). Fundamentally, however, these changes are palliative rather than curative. In effect they allow people to better themselves by non-Maoist means while continuing to carry Maoist burdens.

The pyramid of productivity

The central problem of Chinese rural planning is not, however, commandism and misallocation of junior units' resources by senior units acting with the support of the state. The central problem is that of widely differing levels of labour productivity, as measured by outputs in money, in various parts of the rural economy. A pyramid of productivity and profitability exists in China, whose base comprises the mass of grain-farming villages, and whose apex is occupied by state industry. This pyramid of productivity was a central feature of real economic experience under the Maoists, and it remains so up to the present.

It is a commonplace of media comment since 1978 that grain farming is not profitable. At various times during the early 1970s local units were criticised for breaking the regulations, making land available and so planting crops other than grain. These units were criticised for policies which were 'heavy on cash, light on grain', and for 'grasping cash, not grasping the line'. This kind of criticism was often applied to collective production of garden crops such as vegetables or ginger, or to fruits – all of which were very scarce in urban markets. Pig production usually escaped this kind of criticism, no doubt in part because the Maoists usually insisted that pigs represent not pork but fertiliser; and fertiliser represents grain.

Not only cash crops, but also industry, is much more profitable to local communities than grain farming. At Liuji commune in Xinzhou county, Hubei, in 1975, 15% of the labour force, employed in various subsidiary and industrial enterprises, generated 42% of the income (Xinzhou county Revolutionary Committee et al.: 22, 24). In Zhejiang province, at Shuangpai commune in Lanqi county, the 42% of the labour force engaged in subsidiary enterprises contribute 73% of total income (People's Daily, 7 Oct. 1978). At Zhoukoudian commune, Beijing, the corresponding figures are 16% and 70% (Xinhua, 8 Aug. 1978). At the model Maotian commune in Hunan, commune enterprise employs 11% of the total workforce at the three levels, and produces 40% of all earnings; and in Chiku brigade in the same commune, the 10% of all labour employed in brigade enterprises produces 40% of total output (China Pictorial, 1978(2), 27, and 1977 (12), 35). Figures from Nanhai county, Guangdong, tell the same story, 46% of labour and 72% of output (People's Daily, 26 Apr. 1979). So do others which have been collected by Western observers (Perkins 1977: 214–15). The superior profitability of industry is not only generally accepted, but is sometimes made into a propaganda point. At Xiashidang in Sichuan, it is expressly stated that a labour-day spent in producing grain is worth 1 yuan; in pig-rearing 2 yuan; and in the rural-industry sector, 5 yuan or more (Huang Yanjun and Yu Quanyu 1978a) The same point is also made in general terms by other authors in almost the same language, and an extreme case is quoted of 11% of the labour force in a rural brigade, manufacturing saws and cement, providing 70% of income (Jiang Xingwei: 75). In Suzhou prefecture, agriculturally one of the most advanced parts of China, income from grain farming fell by 9 million yuan between 1966 and 1978 at the same time as grain output rose by 1,700 million jin; the loss was made up by subsidiary rural production of various kinds, topped up in 1980 by a special cash distribution from the profits of local industry (People's Daily, 13 Nov. 1980) – an arrangement which has continued in subsequent years (Sun Ming et al.).

These examples, and in addition a good deal of comment which is not illustrated with figures, suggest that productivity of labour in subsidiary occupations in the Chinese countryside is at least double productivity in arable farming, and in most cases, particularly those involving industry, much higher. Attention has already been drawn to the part played by local enterprises in subsidising grain farming.

Additional light is thrown upon these figures by others given by Zhang Chunqiao (4–5). State-owned industry in China in 1973 employed 63% of the industrial population and produced 86% of total industrial output by value, while industry under collective ownership (by communes and brigades) employed 36% of the industrial population and contributed 14% of the output. Figures from 1978 tell a different but still discouraging story – that collectively owned industry throughout China employs one-third of all industrial workers but produces only one-fifth of industrial outputs (Liu Gang et al.: 24). These figures indicate that for whatever reason, productivity of labour employed in state-owned industry was reckoned to be at least double, and up to three and a half times, that employed in commune or other collectively owned industry. Industry at commune and brigade level, the economic aristocrat of the rural communities, is shown clearly to be the pauper of the industrial system as a whole.

The logic of this argument is inexorable – it is that field agriculture, universally acclaimed as the foundation of the state and the community, self-evidently the universal provider of food and clothing for all, and the direct economic support of at least 70% of the people, is the pauper of the whole economic system. Taken together, the figures quoted suggest that productivity per man-day in terms of cash in state-owned industry in China must be usually at least six times greater, and may be ten or more times greater, than productivity in grain farming. An average figure for this factor, representing net outputs per man-year of 2,800 and 324 *yuan* respectively, is eight and a half times (Jiang Xingwei: 75). Labour productivity is said to have risen by 75% between 1959 and 1978 in industry, but by only 15% in agriculture (Zhang Guofan: 78). It should not be thought that the farm price rises of 1979, of 20% and 50% in most cases, have altered these relationships more than marginally – in fact they represent an increase in income of only 7 *yuan* per worker on average (Liang Yan: 18). Although by 1981 as much as 60% of grain sold to the state was sold at premium prices (Wu Zhenkun), here too the effect has not been dramatic (State Statistical Bureau 1983: 10).

Recognition of these wide differences in productivity among various sectors of the economy throws light on an odd statistical mystery of Chinese development. Eckstein (228–32) shows that according to standard figuring, China's agricultural sector, still containing 70% or even 80% of the population and hence of labour input, contributes only about 20% of China's gross domestic product. Figures from China agree (80% and 25%) (Ma Hong: 2, 4). One author goes so far as to argue from these figures that 'the agricultural sector is, therefore, of diminishing significance in China's economic development, and the emphasis on the agricultural sector in the Chinese development strategy is largely from social and political factors' (Cheng: 145). Eckstein considers the service sector to be under-represented in the calculations of gross domestic product, and he believes that there are 'pricing distortions', although he does not discuss them. On the whole, Eckstein believes that the standard figures are realistic, and goes on to try to rationalise them. Evidence from the grass-roots, however, as has been shown, is that these great disparities are the outcome of great differences in labour productivity in various parts of the economy, especially when these are measured in money according to standard prices. There seems to be no doubt that these gross and presumably destructive disparities are the outcome of increasingly labour-intensive farming practices in China, together with a system of prices which holds grain very cheap. It is obvious that such a disparity, especially if it is based upon prices in an economy where the important prices are fixed by the government, must be a source of serious instability. Equally obviously, where grain production is unprofitable, local units are under constant temptation to backslide from the obligation to maximise grain production, and to take more interest, once local self-sufficiency needs have been satisfied, in profitable sidelines, industrial enterprises, whether tributary to agriculture or not, and tertiary business ventures of all kinds. As the *Han Shu* said in the first century AD, quoting a proverb already ancient, 'For the poor to seek riches, industry is better than farming, and trade is better than either.'

In a narrow sense, limited to the relations between the prices of farm outputs and farm inputs, these problems are called the 'scissors' relationship. Limited data which have appeared from time to time in the Chinese press have been assembled by Perkins (1975; 362) and Lardy (177). They show that the terms of trade between industry and agriculture have been improving (from the point of view of agriculture) ever since Liberation, but much more rapidly after 1966 than before. Some recent commentary from China, however, takes the opposite view, based on the unfavourable movement of productivity; no new figures have been produced for the movement of prices. (Hu Changnuan, 63–5) Even those in China who agree that the 'scissors' gap has not widened in recent years take the view that the 'scissors' question in a narrow sense must be distinguished from the wider productivity issue (Zhang Guofan). Figures have been published from Jiading county in Shanghai which show that Jiading's 'scissors' gap has narrowed since 1949 in terms of prices, but widened in terms of the product of the labour-day (Jiading county, Agricultural Economics Investigation Unit, 56–8). However, since the farm price rises of 1979–80 and the reduction of the priority for industrial investment in 1981, criticism has been more muted, and has broadly accepted that such differences are inevitable at present and through the foreseeable future, and must be accepted as in effect an additional farm tax. Xue Muqiao (1981b: 174) writes:

Of China's fiscal revenue, less than 10% is contributed by the peasants in taxes while more than 90% comes from industry in both taxes and profits. It looks like the workers are contributing much more to the country's accumulation fund than the peasants, but it is not so. What happens is that a large part of the value created by the peasants is transferred to industry through unequal exchange and therefore appears as part of the contribution from the workers. In fact, the peasants' contribution makes up at least a third of state revenue.

Among Western commentators, the 'scissors' relationship is treated as the central issue, and differences in productivity between agriculture and industry are then accepted as the outcome of differences in labour allocation between the two sectors. That there is still a 'scissors' gap is also accepted. 'The key issue is whether one treats as a tax the difference in price between what the farmer actually receives for his products and the higher prices he could have received in an uncontrolled market.' (Perkins 1975: 363). It would be difficult at any time for the state to put in motion a general reorganization of industrial and farm prices, not only because of the increase in general inflation which might result, but because any fall in industrial prices would represent a fall in state revenue, because most industry belongs to the state; and any rise in farm prices is a rise in state disbursements, because most foods sold are subsidised to the consumer (Jiang Xingwei: 76; Klatt: 36). In 1980, subsidies for the prices of grain and edible oil to the consumer (0.1 *yuan* and 0.8 *yuan* per jin respectively) amounted to 10,300 million *yuan*, or more than 60 *yuan* per year for each urban consumer. The total food subsidy bill was much higher, around 18,400 million *yuan* (Grain Department Research Unit: 4).

Present official policy on these problems is pragmatic. Chen Lian (26) argues that industrial price structures have been inherited from the old society; and that in the short term it is very difficult to reform the 'low farm prices, high industrial prices' structure. His view is that as agriculture diversifies (including diversification into industry), it will be liberated progressively from losses due to low prices. This view appears to be in accord with policy. Realistically, the state appears now to be relying upon the incentives and opportunities represented by the new contract and responsibility systems, conjoined with the new freedom to market surplus produce at realistic prices, to take off the sharp edge of the 'scissors' by enabling peasants to raise their incomes, if not within the planned economy, then in its peripheries. Improvement is to be achieved not through rationalisation of prices, but through the very different policy, also desirable in itself, of allowing the rural household to display individual enterprise and to exercise rather more control of the income arising from the labour of its members. The burden upon the countryside represented by the state system cannot be lifted, but it can be made more bearable by allowing the rural economies fresh opportunities for growth.

New dimensions in rural production and management

Since the Third Plenum in 1978, the Chinese countryside has been set forth upon a scheme of development which differs dramatically from that of the Maoist decade. At the very centre of this new scheme is the introduction of responsibility and contract systems for the performance of farm production. These systems are expected to restore lost motivation in work, to correct excessive egalitarianism and to increase outputs, while maintaining fundamental collective ownership and accounting structures. Beyond arable farming the new scheme seeks to promote two kinds of production – diversification of outputs and production by households. These two are not necessarily interdependent, but the course of development has allowed household production to take the lead in farm diversification in many cases, particularly where animals or poultry are involved. Successful household production systems now usually have two main components – 'responsibility' land which supplies basic food and provides the household with means to satisfy the demands of the collective unit, and 'family production' of pigs, chickens and vegetables, which represent better diets or a cash income or both. Diversification involving industry is another matter, and as various examples will show may now be the dominant partner in local production in advanced areas. In most Chinese countrysides the extent of arable land has diminished during the past generation, both relative to rural population and absolutely; and of course at the same time population has continued to grow.

Reform of the production systems has been comparatively painless, supported no doubt by the tendencies towards spontaneous capitalism to which the new economic freedoms might be thought sympathetic – or, to put it in another way, by self-help among peasant families who understand their own production systems. Rural commerce is another matter, also deeply suspect for political reasons and sharply cut back by the Maoists, but necessarily closely tied to the official bureaucracy. 'Private' marketing has been uneasily restored and the official trade system has experienced some tinkering, but internal trade remains the Achilles heel of the whole rural system. Finally, two divergent though not necessarily incompatible topics arise – the generation of prosperity within the new systems and the question of its polarisation in favoured areas, and the protection of the collective system in the face of new economic growth which usually has an uncollective dimension and whose main thrust is rarely through the collective part of the economy.

Responsibility and contract systems

The most important innovation of all in the present phase in rural China is the wide range of 'contract' and 'responsibility' systems now used in agricultural production. These were introduced in 1979 and expanded rapidly so that in 1980 20% of brigades throughout China were using them (Wu Xiang), and in 1981, 90% (CCP 1983a: K1). Some publicists are at pains to draw attention to parallel systems in use in the 1950s (Dai Qingqi and Yu Zhan). A variety of different accounts of these systems have appeared and classifications vary. Most accounts agree that a very wide range of practical arrangements has evolved in a very short space of time. The official attitude, as repre-

sented in the media, is that varied arrangements are a wholesome response to varied environmental, social and business conditions. The scheme outlined in Table 3.1 is directly official in origin and is introduced in the original with more critical and analytical comment than most. It appears to cover, in slightly more general terms, broadly the same ground as that reviewed and discussed on the basis of slightly earlier materials by J and M Gray (155–64). It is also representative of material which has appeared elsewhere in more detail (Liu Hongli and Wu Hai; Henan province).

The scheme specifies three broad types of contract system in ascending order of sophistication. The first of these represents arrangements between a team and its households, requiring each household to undertake the work involved in operating a specified cropping plan on a particular piece of communal land. This is a loose, relatively 'uncollective' system, which (no doubt for that reason) has come to be used far beyond the poor, backward and isolated units to which it

Table 3.1. Types of responsibility system in rural production

Type of system	Collective conditions retained	Responsibilities assumed by group or household	Distribution of output	Conditions in which typically applicable
'Double contract' – households contract for output and labour jointly Farm output quotas and work are assigned to each household	Collective ownership of means of production. Basic accounting at team or brigade level Collective distribution of allocated product	Household assumes responsibility for farming an area of land, either under quota agreement or with full responsibility	Quota to the state. Allocation (as contracted) to the collective Remainder is kept by household as bonus	Units at a low level of prosperity or organisation or both – especially those which rely on loans for costs of production, grain from state, and public subsidy
Labour contracts with incomes linked to output Centralised operations with limited responsibilities assigned to labourers and remuneration linked to output	As above	Labour is contracted for specified crops, phases of production and types of responsibility	Output belongs to the collective unit (which discharges obligations to the state) Fixed remuneration (in work-points) for specified outputs; bonuses for over-fulfilment and penalties for shortfalls	Relatively advanced areas with improved land, machinery, irrigation, drainage, etc.
Specialist contracts with payment by results Workers are assigned full responsibility for specified (and usually specialised) production tasks	Collective ownership of means of production	Contract represents individual's total livelihood	According to contract between worker and collective unit, with bonus and penalty provisions	Where enterprises are numerous and highly developed, so that many narrowly defined tasks are available

Source: Compiled from material in CCP 1981

was originally said to be particularly suited. Many versions of this system exist, representing various degrees of completeness of production responsibility assumed by the worker or workers of the household – whether in a situation akin to contracted labour or as producers with full responsibility; the tendency is for the latter variant to become predominant, and this tendency is the one now generally favoured by the central authorities (CCP 1983b: K1, K3). By 1982, 74% of all rural units were using some form of household responsibility system (Chen Yizi). In the second type of system, the worker becomes a kind of contracted employee of the collective unit. Payment for specified items of work is made in work-points according to the terms of the contract, and distribution of cash and food is made by the collective in the usual way, apart from bonus entitlements. The third type of system is used mainly in the advanced countrysides of the Yangzi delta and Liaoning, particularly where the production team has already been superseded and management

Advantages claimed	Limitations specified
Simple to administer. Calls fully upon household solidarity and motivation. Links work directly with income	Small-scale, tends to encourage low rates of fulfilment of public obligations (e.g. medical services, schools). May stimulate bourgeois ideology. Poor rates of birth-control
Encourages mutual aid among households	
Links work directly with income	Basically a system of labour allocation and remuneration – hence contribution to motivation is limited
Assigns responsibility for limited tasks to individuals	
	Complicated to administer
Facilitates division of labour and reaps the benefits of specialisation. Utilises human talents to advantage. Raises levels of technical skill	Definition of contract terms may be difficult – possibly problematical
Supports specialised accounting and management methods	

and accounting are already settled at brigade or commune level. Here specialist working groups contract with the collective unit for production against payment by results, and the arrangements for payment within the working group (for distribution of work-points, for example) are a matter for decision within the working group itself (Zhan Wu and Wang Guichen; Wang Guichen and Wei Daonan). The payment-by-results side of this type of system is of course quite un-Maoist; but in other respects (notably its 'big' and 'public' characteristics) the system is rather closer to Maoist ideals than might be expected. Obviously the range of possible systems is already wide, and the implication of published comment is that it may be expected to extend still further (Wu Xiang and Zhang Guangyou; Feng Zibao). By 1981, 80% of responsibility systems adopted were of kinds in which remuneration is linked directly to output, and hence involved the signing of contracts (CCP 1983a: K2).

The history of these systems is very short, but already it includes much change. One version of this history, obviously officially approved, comes from Guizhou (Yao Liwen and Xu Xiji). Here three chronological stages of development of the responsibility systems are suggested. These authors identify first an initial stage up to spring 1980, of contracts for production operated by working groups, when responsibility devolved to households was still not orthodox; second, a phase of reorientation, from summer 1980 apparently to the end of 1981, in which household contracts proliferated; and third, a phase representing fresh economic growth. A similar course of events, but up to a year earlier in time, is reported from Anhui (He Cun). The evidence is that household responsibility systems are now the characteristic form for the organisation of production in the Chinese countryside.

It is argued that as a result of these various systems, workers' motivation has risen impressively, and with it productivity, partly because people can now take significant decisions for themselves and partly because the system inhibits egalitarian redistribution of people's outputs. At the same time, waste of labour and other resources is greatly reduced; there is more realistic use of working time, and now workers can drop the pretence of working when there was nothing to do. Contracts specify (for example) allocations of labour and working capital against specified outputs, with bonus for overproduction; or they may specify allocations for labour, fertiliser, crop protection, use of machinery and so forth, in detail; and bonuses may be of more than one kind (Wu Xiang and Zhang Guangyou; J and M Gray: 155–64).

Standard forms for contracts have already been established in many fields. In Liaoning and Hubei, among other places, dozens of counties have issued their own standard outlines for contracts, which local units can adopt or modify as they see fit (*People's Daily*, 26 Oct. 1980). Norms of production costs are also being established in such fields as fertiliser, crop spraying, water, electricity, seeds, fodder, use of tools and so forth; and these lead on to standard analysis of performance by the month or the season, costs, levels of waste, depreciation, etc. There is little sign in the media either of resentment at the rate-fixing side of these contracts, or fear that in such a maze of individual and group arrangements productive motivation may be lost, or corruption grow to unacceptable levels. What has clearly disappeared is the Maoist 'single cut' policy of equality and egalitarianism in production and consumption.

It is admitted that responsibility systems have drawbacks. They tend to encourage indifference to mechanisation, to rational water management, to proper care for work animals, to pest control, soil conservation, land improvement and scientific management generally. They also tend to create difficulties for unified organisation and planning and the setting up of brigade and commune enterprises, no doubt because teams' labour is otherwise engaged; and they may make it more difficult to care for disadvantaged families, and to maintain birth-control policies (Wu Xiang; J and M Gray: 179). This list comes from Wu's article which is sympathetic to responsibility systems, but inevitably it has Maoist overtones. It is argued that proper vigilance by commune authorities and the Communist Party can handle these problems. Obviously the positive advantages of the new scheme are what interest the authorities and the people. These are listed as follows – the protection of the workers' rights to profit from their own work; the restoration of rights of self-management to workers; the suppression of systems of egalitarianism which destroyed motivation; and the adoption of rational and economical management and accounting practices on the local scale (Wu Xiang). Equally this latter list is very anti-Maoist in tone. It is revealing that simple contract systems, especially those which distribute respon-

sibility for production directly to individual households, were said in 1980 to be particularly suited to the frontier and mountain areas and poor and backward regions (*Red Flag* Editorial, 1980 (20), 10), but that in 1981, they are reported as adopted in 94% of production teams in Fujian (*People's Daily*, 13 Mar. 1981) in 60% of teams in Henan (FBIS *Daily Report*, 24 June 1981, P1, quoting a Beijing broadcast of 16 June 1981), in 54% of teams in Shandong (FBIS *Daily Report*, 7 Dec. 1981, 04, quoting a Jinan broadcast of 4 Dec. 1981), and in 95% of teams in Anhui (He Cun: 70). The figure of 74% already quoted is for all China for 1982 (Liu Xumao: 12; Chen Yizi). Increasingly the evidence is that the responsibility systems, which in principle embrace various kinds of working groups, mean in practice responsibility devolved to households and household groups, except in areas (such as the commodity grain bases) where farming is much more than subsistent.

Indeed, increasingly since 1981 this applies not only to small-scale and basically household-oriented production, hopefully with a surplus, but also to commercial and large-scale production. 'Commodity grain specialist households' have appeared. These are analogous to specialist households producing such items as pigs and poultry, discussed later in this chapter. In Shanxi grain specialist households were 6% of all households in 1982, and an enthusiastic account is given of their opportunities for mixed farming, with animals in addition to grain (*People's Daily*, 24 Nov. 1983). A specialist grain farmer in Anhui took over very unpromising land and produced a good grain crop. He sold only 28% of his grain to the state; the rest presumably on the open market, perhaps for animals or wine manufacture (*People's Daily*, 24 Nov. 1983). In parts of Shandong, we read, households themselves are now delivering their cotton quotas and surpluses to the state purchasing agency, which now deals directly with the people (*People's Daily*, 11 Nov. 1983). It is not clear that arrangements of these kinds are in any way typical, but the fact that they are given prominence in the media surely indicates that they enjoy powerful official approval. At the opposite end of the production spectrum, we read that as much as 40,000 *mou* of farmland has been abandoned in Mianyang county, Hubei, as a result of specialist households' devoting their energies to industrial or other non-farm production, to the neglect of their allotted arable plots.

Here too the media approach is sympathetic, pointing to the 'trend of the times' and a fresh round of 'contradictions' (*People's Daily*, 11 July 1983). To judge from evidences of these kinds, the central authorities are quite willing to follow the logic of the responsibility systems all the way to family self-employment as the rule in the countryside. Some kinds of self-employment are very profitable. But for self-employment by grain specialist households to be profitable, it appears that one of two conditions must be satisfied – either grain production is supported by other kinds of farm production, or a high proportion of grain produced is sold outside the state system (Ji Xijian; Fang Jianzhong et al).

There is a good deal of evidence that in addition to the merits and demerits which have been mentioned, job responsibility systems have one further important weakness – they tend to suggest the division and group occupation of parts of the land or other property of the production team, with rights which approximate to those of ownership. In cases where the job responsibility systems take the individual household as working units, arable fields may be allocated to households which are then inclined to treat them as their own property in all but name. Sometimes households have built new houses on their 'responsibility' fields, wasting arable land as well as introducing confusion between specified and unlimited rights of use. Others have insisted upon taking up fields which formerly belonged to their own families, when 'responsibility land' was being allocated. Others have thought themselves entitled to build tombs or start brick-kilns on 'responsibility' land (*People's Daily*, 21 Apr. 1981).

In many cases household responsibility has tended to lead towards division of the collective arable and its distribution among households, *de facto* if not *de jure* (*People's Daily*, 29 Nov. 1980). This is the more understandable since there are now very important, though equivocal, indications that the way towards real increased independence of individuals and households lies much less through private plots than through the job responsibility system (He Jiazheng). The social stakes in this game are high.

The official press insists that private ownership of land and individual farming are absolutely not permissible practices; indeed during 1980 and 1981 the tone of comment on this problem changed considerably, from rationalisations based mainly on the need to stimulate and harness the people's motivation, to sharply worded insistence upon the indivisibility of collective property and the absolute primacy of the socialist system (*People's Daily*, 5 Nov. 1980 and 14 Dec. 1980; *Beijing Review* 1981 (11), 16 Mar. 1981, 3–4). Stress is now laid on the express prohibition of private property in land in the Chinese constitution, in the Decisions (CCP 1978: 6) text, and in other official pronouncements. Division of land and the practice of individual farming (however defined) are, however, obvious hazards of the present course of development, and there is no reason to think that occasional denunciations will stop them. Even where the principles of public ownership of the means of production and the unified distribution of the community's output are insisted upon, individual householders naturally tend to envisage their food output as first and foremost their own food supply, and sometimes at least the authorities tacitly accept this by using a term like 'food-grain land' for land contracted to 'responsibility' production, and accepting a distinction between this and 'collective land' (FBIS *Daily Report*, 20 Aug. 1981, quoting *Shanxi Daily*, 22 July 1981). It is not to be expected that all authorities in China are always perfectly clear about the implications of rapidly developing policies. In fact, in respect of the problem of reappearance of private claims to arable land, the uncompromising positions taken up by the Maoists in defence of the collective system have been abundantly justified since 1978 as before 1966. It is one aspect of present problems in rural China that various sensible and constructive policies favoured by the Maoists are now tarred with the brush of Maoist extremism.

A further point of principle deserves comment, even if this can be little more than speculative. In favour of collectivisation it was argued a generation ago, after the land reform, that family farming could not survive in countrysides where arable land was not plentiful enough to create individual farms for all peasant households. Perhaps this argument was sometimes used disingenuously; but if it had substance at all, it must relate to the household responsibility systems, particularly in countrysides with more households and rather less arable than in the 1950s. Part of the counter-argument in this case must be that unified planning and unified accounting will preserve rational cropping (including local food supplies) and social security (including support for disadvantaged families). Part must be that 'responsibility' land is now supported by private plots which provide other kinds of food and income, in conditions where these are not now under political threat. Part must be that due to adoption of scientific practices on the land, improved irrigation, better varieties and more intensive methods, outputs per unit area are now much higher than a generation ago. Part must be that collective diversification (including industry) can now support many local rural economies through the collective accounting system, as formerly it did not. Most of these arguments would apply in advanced communities, but there are surely some, particularly perhaps in the north China plain, where they do so only weakly. These, though, are communities in which the collective systems would themselves have been weak, for the same reasons. Inevitably however, household farming must lead towards some degree of polarisation of prosperity in the countryside, with emergence of strong households even if weak households continue to receive protection. Some socialists will argue that from strong households it is only a short step to a nascent gentry class exercising widespread economic and political power.

Many – perhaps most – of the responsibility systems have one further practical implication which is probably of the highest importance, though little or nothing has been said about it in the Chinese press. This relates directly to the working life of the individual peasant. Since the introduction of the Advanced Producers' Collectives in 1956, the peasant has usually been in practice, if not in theory, an employee of the commune whose working time was organised through the brigade and team. This was as much a natural result of insistence upon collective management of production and the formidable pressures of the state plan, as of collective ownership of resources. Now, within a household responsibility scheme, the peasant individual may become in effect a self-employed farmer who leases collectively owned land, who has dues and taxes to pay and who may be obliged to work collectively at times, but who is basically his own master. In terms of the production process this change is perhaps not great, and in terms of formal ownership of the means of production minimal; but in terms of the work experience of the individual it must be tremendous. We may also suspect (the official materials do not justify any explicit conclusion) that the effect on the work

experience of the individual represents a powerful social motivation in favour of the household responsibility systems, and one which must make the proliferation of these systems, once started, difficult to resist, whatever the attitude of the Communist Party and the government. It is evident on the ground that peasants are now able to find time to go to local markets to sell produce and, incidentally, to re-create social life centred on street eating-stalls which are now reappearing. Dozens of local people now sell fruit at rural beauty spots, which in summer are usually thronged with trippers from the cities.

Diversification in the rural economy

The Maoists spoke with double tongues on the subject of subsidiary crops in the countryside, sometimes calling more loudly for taking grain as the key link, sometimes more loudly for promoting all-round development (Lu Yan). Their actions appear to have been more negative than their words, as a range of cases quoted by Croll (236–9), and many others to be found in the press, all show. Croll, who in common with many writers relates subsidiary outputs directly and explicitly to family production rather than collective enterprise, considers that Maoist hostility to these outputs was based on their association with 'individual pursuit of personal wealth and capitalist phenomena' (Croll: 237). But the evidence is that collective units were also discouraged from growing beans, oilseeds, peanuts, fruit and other kinds of subsidiary crop, and discouraged even more from marketing them. Realistically, it appears to be Maoist prejudice against trade as a foundation of business and hence of capitalism which stood most in the way of subsidiary outputs. The discouragement of diversified production is perhaps the least sensible of Maoist rural policies. In many parts of China, especially the south, it is traditional. Provided that marketing can take place and grain quotas are not affected, outputs of chickens, fish, vegetables, pigs, beans and milk will improve both consumers' diets and producers' incomes, without loss to anyone. Most subsidiary outputs are labour-intensive, and so is the implication of increased local trade; hence both may be thought good for employment. Many kinds of diversified production are at least as well suited to collective enterprise as to private plots.

As early as 1978, an interesting report on collective diversification appeared for a brigade called Dongqiao, belonging to Fengxi commune in Chaoan county, in the heart of the Chaozhou country of eastern Guangdong. Dongqiao is a big village with 1,274 households, in all 6,369 people; 2,537 *mou* of arable land; hence only 0.4 *mou* (269 sq m) per person of arable. Arable farming is based on paddy, together with sugar-cane, sweet potatoes, soya beans, jute and peanuts. There are woodland and tree-crop plantations, in all 9,650 *mou*, on the mountainside, including pine, bamboo and fir, tea, fruit orchards such as litchi, pear and the famous Chaozhou oranges, medicinal crops, chestnuts and so forth. Pigs, chickens, geese, fish, rabbits and deer are kept by the brigade. Under the Maoists, many of these enterprises were attacked. There is also a brick and tile works, a workshop for repairing farm tools, bamboo manufacturers, a pottery with clay preparation, and embroidery workshop with laundry and finishing shop – in all fifteen kinds of industrial enterprise. The embroidery business employs 600 people and the laundry and finishing shop 280 – Chaozhou embroidery is an important export specialism with markets in Hong Kong and abroad. In 1977 the brigade's total output by value was 1.8 million *yuan*, of which arable farming contributed 28% and other kinds of production 72%. Many improvements in the arable economy, including work on land and water construction, supplies of fertiliser and items of farm machinery, all depend on the brigade's income from industry and other enterprises. In 1977, grain yield rose to 1,702 *jin* per *mou*. Supplies to the state were valued at almost exactly 1 million *yuan*, indicating that at least 55% of total output entered trade. These supplies comprised 290 tons of grain, plus pigs, tea, sugar, jute, peanut oil, soya beans and fruit (*People's Daily*, 7 Dec. 1978).

Broadly speaking, the commune members prefer to work in the workshops rather than the fields, because conditions are easier and working hours shorter in the workshops. In practice, the brigade allows only one person from each household to work in the workshops at one time. These people's wages are paid as usual into the production teams' accounts for general cash distribution and the workers must also work in the fields (on pain otherwise of losing work-points) at busy times such as the spring, summer and autumn harvest and planting seasons – usually seven days' work at each.

At Dongqiao the brigade authorities lay considerable stress upon the strict and orderly system of accounting for work-points, based on five grades and twelve divisions – they call it exact, tight and rational. It was begun in 1958 and restored after the death of Mao, but during the Cultural Revolution not permitted.

Both social encouragement and material incentives are used to reward production teams which perform well in production – yields of grain above 2,000 *jin* or 1,600 *jin* per *mou*, yields of sweet potatoes above 11,000 *jin* per *mou*, yields of winter wheat above 500 *jin* per *mou*, high pig outputs and so forth. Individuals also receive incentives for high production achievements measured in terms of physical yields for particular crops for which they were responsible – foreshadowing the responsibility systems no doubt.

Public grain reserves and accumulation funds are well supplied. The brigade manages primary and lower-middle schools and provides free kindergartens and maternity clinics. Within the cooperative system operated by the brigade, medical care costs 0.15 *yuan* per person per month, and 90% of hospital charges are reimbursed to the individual. The brigade also organises sports contests, films and cultural events. In these ways the village is not too distant from the town in its forms of life. 'So they make their way on the broad road of socialism.'

This report is impressive in itself, and it also appears to represent an important transitional stage between a collectivist, grain-oriented Maoist scheme of development, and the forms of the

The commune represented on the right is labelled 'Prosperity' and 'Diversification'. That on the left is undiversified, and has already sold off its assets. *Source: People's Daily*, 15 Nov. 1980. The artist is not named.

present where the main thrust of diversification tends to be 'private' rather than collective. Dongqiao appears to suggest impressive possibilities for diversification which could be mainly collective in nature. But in practice the diversification policy appears to have developed rather slowly, in rather close association with the restored private plots and with family production generally, and with only lukewarm encouragement from the state and such state organs as the Department of Commerce.

The hesitant note is struck already by the circular on diversified rural economy issued by the central authorities in March 1981 (State Council and CCP 1981).

This document argues that China is rich in varied rural resource and also in labour, blames unrealistic grain targets for the decline in both diversified economy and family production, proclaims the primacy of grain production, and proposes various forms of intensification, such as improved rotations, on the arable. The circular links diversification of outputs in the production teams directly with the responsibility systems for specialised groups and households, and proposes a maximum of 15% of the arable as tolerable for private plots in places where output quotas are not assigned to households. Differences in household incomes which may result are not to be regarded as 'capitalist polarisation'. The state, says the circular, ought to encourage the growth of rural diversification; but the circular offers very little guidance about the best means of bringing this about.

It is surprising to find that the 1981 circular outlines the possibilities of output diversification with so little apparent enthusiasm, and with so much stress upon household participation rather than either collective enterprise (and incomes) or urban standards of living. Uneasiness about the future of commodity grain supplies in a highly commercialised countryside may underlie this. An earlier discussion from a less exalted source (Zhan Wu 1979, 13–15) laid stress upon the contribution which diversified production could make to investment on the land through increased incomes, to employment opportunities in rural units, to improved diets in town and country, to increased incomes in collective units, and to the proper utilisation of potential resources in forests, mountains and water bodies. In some respects at least, particularly the need to make better use of rural resources other than the arable, the earlier

approach seems to be more constructive than the later.

But to judge from the press, diversification continues to develop very hesitantly, and closely tied to family production. Pigs are a case in point. Production of pigs rose up to 1980, when average pork supplies to the whole population rose to 23 *jin* per year, as against 20 *jin* in 1979 (*People's Daily*, 7 Jan. 1982). Pork outputs fell sharply in 1981, but in 1982 rose to 25 *jin* per person (State Statistical Bureau 1983: 4). In 1982 the Ministry of Agriculture was pressing collective units to encourage rural households to raise pigs and sell them to the state, offering favourable marketing conditions to peasants for pigs, and stressing the need for proper maintenance of numbers of sows (FBIS *Daily Report*, 30 Mar. 1982, quoting a Beijing broadcast of 26 Mar. 1982). In fact, more than 90% of China's pigs are now bred and kept by households (*People's Daily*, 7 Jan. 1982, Editorial; the figure for 1956 was 83% – Walker 1965: 43) and even the Ministry of Agriculture does not appear to be looking to collective units to establish or develop pig farming (FBIS *Daily Report*, 30 Mar. 1982, K13–K14, quoting a Beijing broadcast of 26 Mar. 1982). One reason for this is no doubt the well-documented inadequacies of the commercial departments (Yang Yintong). Croll points out a different but related problem which she calls the 'collective and domestic tightrope'. She suggests, not unreasonably, that as a result of past experience 'the government may well have forfeited its ability to use political campaigns again as a mechanism for the adjustment of policies' (Croll: 248). Both of these are real problems. But at bottom, the reason for low collective performance in this kind of field must be the peasants' specific motivation. Collective pig production or any other kind of diversification must require positive collective decisions to diversify into pigs or other outputs, and usually also allocations of investment, labour and so forth. But in present conditions there is little positive incentive for any collective unit to take such decisions (Du Runsheng, 29). The same production can be undertaken by basically the same local families in the guise of household production, without need to reach collective investment, operating or marketing decisions, or need to share the proceeds with other families. All animal-rearing in agricultural areas (the pastoral minority regions, such as Xinjiang in the northwest, are a different matter) is subject in some degree to the rationale of this argument, and it applies equally to poultry and eggs. Hence more than 90% of Chinese pigs are privately raised, and apart from a proportion of ducks, poultry generally belong to households (China Food Corporation: 12).

Examples of successful introduction of diversified production at collective levels in recent years do appear in the press, and some are outlined in the regional chapters which follow, but they tend to be less numerous and smaller in scale than might be expected. In many cases production is delegated to specialist households, which is no doubt a realistic approach in present conditions but also suggests basic reliance on families rather than the strength of the collective economy. No doubt the adoption of 'contracted responsibility' schemes for remuneration of these households is also realistic and practical (*People's Daily*, 23 Mar. 1983, translated in FBIS *Daily Report*, 25 Mar. 1983, K4–K5) – but it does not seem likely to strengthen the collective side of these enterprises. The continuing weakness of the collective economy in these important fields (in which much potential for economic growth is contained) seems to be bad for production and very bad for the collectives; but it is hard to suggest practical alternatives.

Rural industrial enterprises

Industrial enterprises are really an aspect of the diversification side of rural policy. Chinese experience in this field has been widely studied in the West, often fairly optimistically (Sigurdson 1975; Gray). The literature up to 1978 has been reviewed by Riskin (1978: 77). However, until after 1978 information on genuine rural industry, at village and small-town levels, remained quite scarce, and much of the discussion before that time related to industry at county level, often in towns of 20,000 people or more (Eckstein: 129; Sigurdson 1979: 137–40). The American rural small-scale industry delegation of 1975 (Perkins 1977: 272–3) studied industry at both county and commune-brigade levels, but most of the latter was situated in units which were unusually large or fairly prominent as models, or both. Much of the industry at both levels was nevertheless decisively oriented to the support of agriculture (through chemical fertiliser and agricultural machinery particularly), and this role of support

for agriculture was that in which Maoist publicists invariably chose to cast local industry (Shulu County: 177; Hengyang prefecture party committee: 13; Alley: 181–6, 458–60). In fact much 'rural' industry of this kind, particularly fertiliser and steel production, was at county or even prefecture rather than local level, and much of it has been criticised since 1978 as representing very high costs (Gray, 230; *People's Daily*, 7 Aug. 1979; Zhao Ziyang 1981: K18). As Prybyla remarks (1981: 117): 'After the ascent of the modernisers to power in 1976–77, it became fashionable to stress (local) industry's problems, whereas formerly only the achievements, some of them fictional, were made public.'

At the end of 1980 there were 1.43 million commune and brigade enterprises in China, 50% more than in 1977. These local enterprises in 1980 employed 30.5 million people and produced total output of 61,400 million *yuan*, amounting to 34% of aggregate income in the rural people's communes (*People's Daily*, Editorial, 16 May 1981, translated in FBIS, *Daily Report*, 2 June 1981). Gray considers that the continued expansion of local industry owes much to continued effort in the leadership since Mao's time 'further to increase grass-roots accumulation by devolving from city to county, and from county to commune and brigade, the simpler forms of production' (Gray: 220); but in this effort they have certainly had the support of the well-known superior profitability of industry over agriculture. In fact, a prominent feature of local industry is mining. Gray comments upon this (213, 232) but does not draw attention to the inevitable problems – illegal exploitation of state-owned minerals by local units, wasteful extraction and wasteful use of energy in smelting, pollution and so forth. Particular attention is drawn to this problem in Henan in respect of gold (*People's Daily*, 7 Oct. 1981) and bauxite (*People's Daily*, Editorial, 2 Apr. 1982; Yang Yusheng and Hao Jian). Hasty development of low-grade mining is no doubt inevitable in present conditions, but it represents a very low level of industrial initiative as well as a potentially very wasteful use of resources.

The State Council issued new regulations for rural enterprises in 1981 (State Council 1981c). It is pointed out that brigade and commerce enterprises are important in creating rural jobs. They play an important part in supply of some goods in the market; they contribute to official revenues and are important in promoting general economic development. Their weaknesses are those of irrational unplanned development, poor levels of distribution of profits and, sometimes, very poor financial management.

Policy is expressed in broad terms – necessarily no doubt for a document dealing with so vast and varied a field. The state should avoid trespassing upon economic territory already occupied by these enterprises; but local enterprises without adequate technical equipment (in mining and pharmaceuticals, to take two disparate examples) should be stopped except where a special case can be made – this is because of competition for raw materials with the state schemes of production. County authorities must continue to inspect and license local enterprises, and operation without a licence is prohibited. Better integration with production teams and households from which labour is drawn is recommended, to include profit-sharing where feasible; and the health and safety of workers must be better protected. Use of land must be reasonable, and prices and qualities satisfactory. Pollution and waste are condemned. On taxation, the provisions of the directive of February 1981 (State Council 1981b) are reaffirmed. The latter document is also not without ambiguities, and gives abundant indication of a tax regime with a powerful negotiated component. Broadly, enterprises working for local consumer markets, new enterprises, and those in frontier or disaster areas may be tax-exempt. Frankly commercial enterprises and those competing with state enterprises pay tax at high rates.

These regulations indicate some underlying problems, especially those which relate to competition for scarce resources – for instance cotton-spinning factories in Henan, silk-reeling in Jiangsu, silk-weaving in Zhejiang, and wine and tobacco in many areas (*People's Daily*, 17 Nov. 1980), which compete with state industry for raw materials and produce inferior results, and which may be profitable partly because inadequately taxed. State industry is the aristocrat of the Chinese economic community, as has been shown, but it is poorly placed in many cases to withstand competition. In 1978, 24% of state-owned industrial enterprises in China were running at some degree of loss (State Statistical Bureau 1979: 27); in 1980 this figure had hardly changed at 23.3% (State Statistical Bureau 1981: 3); and in 1981 it rose to 27.1% (State Statistical Bureau 1982: 6).

Rural industry relates directly to a whole world of production and management experience in China which lies along the peripheries of the state plans (Zuo Mu 1980). In Jiangsu since 1979, frequent (almost weekly) displays of producer goods such as steel and lorries have been held, at which purchases can be freely made, even though these items have been produced within the state plan and ought in the normal course of events also to be allocated within the plan. The Nanjing Fair early in 1980 attracted buyers from almost all parts of China and offered goods worth more than 100 million *yuan*. At the same time, many items produced outside the state plan by commune and brigade industry are reckoned within the state plan when handled by the supply and marketing cooperatives. The 15 million pairs of leather shoes made by commune industry in the four prefectures of northern Jiangsu were made outside the state plan with materials part inside, part outside the plan; but when sold to the state distribution network they were wholly within the plan. Lorries are always produced within the plan, but when a few vehicles are made above the planned quota, they may be exchanged for paint, of course outside the plan. The paint, however, will be used within the plan. In this and other cases manipulations outside the plan may well be used to protect the plan's own performance. Clothing made for department stores in Shanghai and Beijing in the Jiangsu cotton county of Qidong is made outside the plan, but once they reach their destination these clothes are within the plan. Some rural units in Jiangsu make spare parts for equipment used in the Daqing oilfield – at Daqing these items are within the plan, but not in the Jiangsu communes (Zuo Mu 1980).

It is sometimes said by writers with a 'rural' bias that when there is competition between state and 'local' industry, this usually relates on the 'local' side to industry at county level rather than to genuinely rural or small-scale industry. This point is made sharply on behalf of Fujian province in an article which points out that state industry should set its sights rather higher than the problems of village competition (Yuan Ming). Here it is argued that in advanced localities, where grain supplies are abundant and farm diversification has already made progress, village industrialisation is a natural next step. Its prerequisites are surplus labour, industrial resources of some kind (often quite humble – sand, stone, farm outputs, bones or straw), capital for investment and a brisk market. Its machinery is generally elderly and its levels of technique low. But in advanced places labour has been following where profits lead in the years since 1980. In Yingqian commune, in Changle county, only 19% of labour is now employed in agriculture, against 64% in industry. Here industry now contributes 68.5% of total outputs. Yingqian has only 0.3 *mou* (200 sq m) of arable per person, and grain output has already reached 1400 *jin* per *mou* on average, suggesting broad self-sufficiency in food (Yuan Ming). The same argument is also taken up more broadly (Chen Lian). In China in 1981 there were only 600,000 industrial enterprises of all kinds (excluding, no doubt, the smallest household enterprises). Of these, only 4,072, less than 1%, may be considered large or medium; the rest are small enterprises and a high proportion must be rural in location. If 99% of enterprises are small, then small enterprises cannot but be important in supplying the needs of a developing community. Yet where supplies of materials are concerned, the state system already gets the lion's share through the planning system. In addition, runs this argument, commune and brigade industry, which employs labour which is usually surplus but which should be and can be deployed in agriculture during busy periods, is an indispensable arm of rural policy in the field of employment (Chen Lian: 28).

One further besetting problem of local industry is energy supplies (Gray: 221). Coal or other industrial fuel is difficult for local units at commune or brigade level to obtain within the state plan, and even more difficult, or impossible, outside it. However obtained, it is likely to be very expensive. Buyers have to be sent out to negotiate for diesel at 1000 *yuan* or more per ton, and coal at more than 40 *yuan* per ton, double the prices paid by state industry (Yuan Ming). This is one reason for local industry to use timber for industrial firing in boilers and brickworks, and (as will be shown) one reason for serious destruction of timber in the accessible woodlands everywhere in China. Many branches of rural industry (manufactures of reeds, timber, wine, dried foods) require little or no industrial energy, but many quite unsophisticated trades do require a significant amount (bricks, pottery, tea-curing, canning).

Of all the present developments in rural China, industry appears to be the one with the most varied range of experiences. It will be shown that in the Shanghai–Suzhou region, well-established rural industry is almost routine, at least in some counties, and that grain agriculture is routinely subsidised by it. Elsewhere in the economically advanced coastal provinces of both north and south (Guangdong, Shandong, Liaoning) various examples illustrate the potential of rural industry in a wide range of fields, but rural industry could not be called routine. Inland, however, in provinces like Hunan, Hubei or even Shanxi, with its extensive coal deposits and industrial tradition of many generations, there is little report beyond the minimum. It appears that in this respect as in many others over the years, coastal China is a different matter from the interior in terms of economic advancement. This is not really surprising, even now, when the importance of a framework of trading contacts, communications, markets and suppliers is brought to mind in the context of seedling industry.

Household production and the rural markets

The State Council's acceptance in 1981 that as much as 15% of the collective arable land of a rural unit might be allocated to private plots and animal feedlots for households is by Maoist standards generosity itself. If productivity expressed in cash is three times greater on private plots than on collective land, peasants in a freely running system of this kind could expect to provide as much as 50% of their income through private, and hopefully diversified, farming on these plots (*Shanxi Daily*, 17 June 1981, translated in FBIS *Daily Report*, 8 July 1981, R11). It has been argued that peasants will naturally prefer to build diversified local production systems on private plots rather than undertake the effort of collective cultivation and management; and allocation of resources to family use on so large a scale will leave little margin of either land or labour, beyond subsistence and the demands of the state plan, in many units.

A common scenario since 1980 appears to be that in which subsistence and the demands of the plan are met collectively but through responsibility systems, while family production is encouraged. In both fields, local advantages of resource or accessibility are important; but especially where economic opportunity is plentiful household production can lead very quickly to prosperity. According to an official survey of 15,914 rural households in 27 of the province-level units (*People's Daily*, 16 June 1981) average net income per person from household production in 1980 was 63 *yuan*, an increase of 42% on the 1979 figure of 44 *yuan* – a surprisingly high figure for an average, but one broadly supported by an earlier national estimate of '30 to 40 *yuan*' for 1979 (Xinhua, 16 June 1980). According to the survey, private plots are the principal household resource, and vegetables and livestock are the main kinds of household production; but grain and other field crops also occupy places of some importance, probably mainly as feed for poultry and pigs. An average rural household sold off one pig and four poultry in 1980, according to this survey. Another report claims that average per *mou* income for some private plots is as high as 1,000 or even 1,500 *yuan*, with costs no more than 20%. 'This economic return is many times higher than that of farmland cultivated by the collective.' (Du Runsheng)

A report of a different kind, featuring cases which are obviously exceptional, indicates the range of official ideals in this field (Chen Bijiang). It relates to families in Feicheng and Pingyin counties in western Shandong, both plains localities with limited resources and poor previous economic records. The plots of three households in Feicheng average 0.3 *mou* (200 sq m) in extent, and produce onions, garlic, Chinese yam, sweet potatoes, tree saplings and Chinese cabbage. Those of three households in Pingyin average 0.4 *mou* (267 sq m) in extent, and grow potatoes, coriander and Chinese cabbage, kohlrabi and a little grain. Gross values of output are 1,254 and 1,368 *yuan* per *mou*, against the local broad average of gross outputs on collective land of 100 *yuan* per *mou*, and local high figures at commune level of 200 *yuan*. Obviously there is no comparison between these figures. In these counties it is argued that as much as 20% of available rural labour is surplus, and that it is consequently rational to allocate these high-input, high-output plots to families. Predictably there are no complaints about triple cropping in these conditions – the possibility is welcomed. The collective farm economy is safeguarded, it is said, by the assurance that the bulk of households' fertiliser outputs will be made available to the production teams. In this case, a proportion of 12% of the arable land to be used as private plots is

suggested as a reasonable global figure.

One of the necessary adjuncts to the household responsibility systems which provide surpluses for households to sell, to private plots and to collective cropping systems which no longer produce only staple outputs marketed through state monopolies, is the revived rural markets. These markets, usually held in small rural towns, numbered 30,000 in 1979 (Zuo Ping et al.) and 37,000 in 1980 – the latter is roughly the total of such markets in 1965, before the Cultural Revolution (He Jingbei: 12), and suggests that each serves around fifteen or twenty production brigades on average. By 1982 there were nearly 45,000 such markets, handling about 15% of vegetable supplies and 25–40% of meat supplies other than pork (FBIS *Daily Report*, 24 Mar. 1983, quoting a Beijing broadcast of 23 Mar. 1983). Markets developed with remarkable rapidity after authorisation began in 1978 (*People's Daily*, 24 Sept. 1979), and received enthusiastic official encouragement, in spite of the recognition that rural markets may stimulate the revival of capitalism, discourage the fulfilment of state procurement quotas and encourage absenteeism from work. Of these, the most serious danger seems to be the revival of capitalism – not among commune members selling vegetables or chickens, but among the speculators and small traders who can find means to supply the necessities which the state networks cannot. The directive of the State Council on the control of markets and suppression of profiteering, reported in January 1981 (State Council 1981a), provides evidence of this kind of corruption in serious forms, but in spite of the severity of its language, does not guarantee effective action in this difficult field. Increased collective and private production will surely improve the supply side in terms of quantity, variety and quality, but like local markets elsewhere in the world, free markets in China are bound to provide opportunity for a proportion of cheapjacks and swindlers.

Grain sales in the free markets are an important point of principle, since they breach the state's long-cherished monopoly. After a period of partial and conditional acceptance, they are now orthodox, once state quotas have been satisfied, and appear to be increasing by a few per cent per year (FBIS *Daily Report*, 4 Nov. 1981), quoting a Beijing broadcast of 4 Nov. 1981). A national estimate of 5 million tons for grain sold in this way has been published for 1980 (Grain Department Research Unit: 13). There are some signs that markets are particularly vigorous in suburban and urban-periphery areas, as might be predicted. It was these markets which were the first to revive in 1979 or even earlier (*People's Daily*, 19 Feb. 1979).

In addition to various kinds of diversified production for the market undertaken by households in their spare time, China now has an important category of 'specialist rural households', which depend for their whole livelihood upon some phase of specialist production for the market and which are increasingly important suppliers, especially of pork and eggs (Yu Guoyao). Some of these households derive their status direct from the collective, and are really contract producers in the same way as specialist teams or job groups. Others are individual households which have moved from part-time domestic production to something much bigger and more professional. Many such households include people with special experience, training or talent. Most specialist households rear pigs or chickens, but a proportion are occupied in fishing, woodlands, craft industry and so forth. What is under discussion here is not the kind of rural household which keeps 2 or 3 pigs and 8 or 10 farmyard fowls wandering about in the village, but professional producers with 10 or 12 or up to more than 100 pigs, and between 100 and 1,000 chickens, or even more. In the average county there are now usually between 1,000 and 3,000 households of this kind. In Siping prefecture in Jilin province, the almost 10,000 specialist pig households represent 1.7% of all households but produce 14.2% of all pigs sold – most of them to the state (Yu Guoyao: 3–4). As always, new opportunities are accompanied by new needs – feeding-stuff supplies, superior strains of animals and birds, machinery, more and better scientific information and supplies, and new outlets for production in the form of food preparation factories. Both supplies of inputs and marketing of outputs are lagging behind the productive capacity of specialist households (Yu Guoyao: 4–5).

Little continues to be said about the most obvious group of opportunities for the employment of surplus labour in the countryside – the service industries, including small businesses, improved transport networks, tea-houses, restaurants and cooked-food stalls, hairdressers, photographic studios, repair workshops of all kinds, tailors and dressmakers, and a wide range of local consumer manufactures – cakes, preserved vegetables and pickles, soy sauce, soft drinks and so forth (Yang Yintong). There is virtually limitless scope for such enterprise, as the Chinese rural (and urban) community begins to furnish itself once more with the varied services typical of Asian civilisation. Skills, machinery and equipment, premises and relations with the bureaucracy, all undoubtedly present problems in these fields, particularly in the countryside and the small rural towns whose development is now being enthusiastically canvassed. The State Council's regulations on non-agricultural self-employment of 1981 authorise individuals and families to start such businesses, specifically in the fields of small handicrafts, retail sales, transportation, house repairs and other trades for which there is need but for which existing provision is inadequate. These regulations also authorise such enterprises to employ 'one or two helpers' and in cases where technical skills are involved, up to five 'apprentices' (State Council 1981e: 13). The right of individuals to employ labour is a particularly sensitive point among Chinese Marxists, but it is hard to resist the view that for adequate growth in the service industries, employment of labour will be necessary, and that in any case it is inevitable under present conditions. In 1982 reports on practice in various parts of China differed considerably. At Guangzhou private employment of labour in return for wages was already considered routine, but in Beijing it was said to be rare, and many people considered it illegal. Other places reported that private employment existed but in various, disguised forms.

'Structural reform' in the commercial system

Market trade outside the official commercial system has expanded considerably in recent years, but the official system still purchases some 87% of the farm outputs which enter trade, and must contribute at least a similar proportion of farm purchases and of rural trade in general (State Statistical Bureau 1983: 9). It has been shown that this system has been beset by problems of bureaucracy, indifference, political hostility and sharply diminished size. The rural and urban free markets have enabled the peasants with access to urban demand to create and sell surpluses, and have to some extent freed townspeople from the erratic supplies, low quality and contemptuous service of the official markets. What free markets have not done is to offer parallel improvements in trading potential to the rural communities. These communities cannot seriously attempt to solve for themselves the problems of local supply of a wide range of investment goods needed in the countryside – hand tools, small farm machines, steel, timber, plastic piping, pumps, lamps, electrical goods, building materials, wire and wire netting, etc. Nor can they make adequate progress with durable and semi-durable consumer goods, such as furniture and kitchen utensils, knives, scissors and many other articles in steel, pottery, bamboo and timber, nor with ready-made clothing (Hunan province, No. 2 Light Industry Supply Corporation). All of these, in a time of rapidly rising living standards arising partly out of rapidly growing family production, are needed more than ever. Up to the present, advanced collective units which required supplies of investment goods have usually purchased them in bulk, through catalogue lists and by telephone; but in present conditions the form of demand for such things has been revolutionised. Nor can the free markets be expected to meet the needs of rural China for increased internal trade at county level and above.

But the official system moves slowly, and each of its parts generates its own friction. One writer says, 'In China, consumer goods are handled more flexibly than the means of production' – referring to bureaucratic controls of various kinds. 'The channels of circulation are too few, the links are too many.' (Xue Muqiao 1981b: 121). Another writer says, 'Our system takes care of production, but makes light of the consumer' (Wang Xinyin, 49) – referring to the inadequacy of distributive machinery for vegetable supplies in the cities. In either case what is complained of is the inability of the official commercial system to produce supplies, not of luxury goods or imports, but of simple necessities produced in China.

The outlines of recent analyses of the rural commercial system can now be discerned (Yang Yintong; Lu Xueyi and Zhang Kaixuan). The two big practical problems are the same as ever – the poor supply, poor variety and poor quality of industrial goods supplied to the countryside, and the poor performance of the commercial organisations in taking up rural surpluses. There is still little improvement. At the same time, the coun-

tryside is now producing much more abundant and more varied surpluses, and making much more powerful demands. These changes represent genuine productive growth, and cannot be dismissed. They also represent gratifying responses to official policy.

But they represent immense problems of collection, distribution, transport and organisation. Even the banks are being overwhelmed in some places. In Dezhou prefecture in western Shandong, where the cotton harvest of 1980 brought quite unaccustomed prosperity, the banks formerly dealt mainly with 30,000 production teams together with senior units; but since 1980 they have to deal with between 1 and 2 million peasant households. Formerly most of the business was done on paper; now 80% involves cash (Lu Xueyi and Zhang Kaixuan). There is room for much increased employment here as elsewhere in the commercial system, but at a heavy cost in training recruits.

Yang Yintong argues convincingly that in China the wholesaling system, which is basically that established in the 1950s, and which remains monopolistic, bureaucratic, slow-moving and self-centred, dominates the whole trading system. There are said to be eleven stages in taking an ordinary business decision within the official trading system (Lu Xueyi and Zhang Kaixuan). It is not surprising that the system responds very poorly to change in demand or supply on the rural side. A writer in *Red Flag* (Han Jinduo) is even more emphatic. He uses Sanhe county, Hebei, as an example. The state has done its purchasing work well in Sanhe, and the free market is brisk; rural purchasing power increased by 26% and 38% in 1979 and 1980 respectively, over the previous years. In the same years, the volume of commodities made available at retail in Sanhe rose by only 10% and 6%. This means that increased supply of all kinds of goods – sugar, cigarettes, wines, apparel, clocks, soap, tobacco, chemicals, furniture – is urgently needed. Increased supply of items in intense demand, such as bicycles, transistor radios and electrical appliances must also be sought.

The Department of Commerce pleads that reliable supplies are difficult to procure from both urban and rural producers, that transportation networks are inadequate, and that both urban and rural consumers must compete with the state's enthusiasm for exports. In addition, the system of subsidies to urban consumers places heavy burdens on the official commercial networks – and these burdens are still increasing, by 22% in 1982 over 1981 (*People's Daily*, 17 Nov. 1983). These subsidies represent trading losses which are usually treated as a matter of policy, but they also conceal heavy business losses due to avoidable physical waste in the course of trade, for instance in pork and vegetables. Much of this waste takes place at county level. Meanwhile local units, also particularly at county level, do not hesitate to squeeze the commercial system for money, for instance by raising commission and other charges against them. Even the banks charge high interest rates (*People's Daily*, 17 Nov. 1983).

Since 1978 the inadequacies of the rural commercial system have been the subject of much discussion but little effective action. Given the complexity (both political and practical) of the issues involved, it is not at all surprising that reorganisation in this field has taken longer to set in motion than reorganisation of the rural production system, and that so far it appears to be much less whole-hearted. During 1982 and 1983 the officially preferred forms for 'structural reform' of the official commercial system took public shape in a number of documents. These documents are not very adventurous in thought and not always free of ambiguity; but some of the ambiguity appears to arise from the need to define a system which is suitable for the cities as well as the countryside.

The first document of the present series was the report on the Rural Work Conference of 1981 (CCP 1983a: K5–K7). The proposals of this conference are easy to accept in principle but difficult to translate into practice. Thus, the supply and marketing cooperatives, the principal organs of rural commerce, are to strengthen their organisation, their democracy and their flexibility – not a very likely body of reform to find in one package, and not one for which specific means are proposed. Experiments are proposed in the fields of collective and individual shareholding in local supply and marketing cooperatives on the one hand, and cooperation in storage and wholesaling by cooperatives belonging to collective units such as communes and brigades on the other. Meanwhile local government should coordinate, mediate and manage the various kinds of commercial channels, and ensure their respect for state policy and official regulations. The demands of the state plan must continue to be met, but local units must be encouraged in processing and manufacturing local produce, though within a planned framework. Obviously, there is much in this document which relates more directly to ideological complexity in the Communist Party than to the needs of commerce in the countryside. The heart of the proposals appears to be the experiments in local shareholding in the supply and marketing cooperatives, and thence, it is hoped, the restoration of their cooperative character. Schemes for shareholding appear in other documents in the same phase (CCP 1983b: K7–K8, and finally in new State Council regulations (State Council 1983).

Taken as a whole, the policies now adopted have five main features. The first is the restoration of cooperative form to the supply and marketing cooperatives. It is envisaged that this will help to restore democracy in management and flexibility in business dealings, and also contribute to improved worker–management relationships within rural commerce – apparently the same uneasily assorted trio as before. A second is the maintenance of state monopoly in handling some specified commodities (cotton, tobacco and wine among them), broadly the maintenance of state wholesaling of industrial goods, and of course official handling of deliveries under the state plan. A third is the liberation of wholesaling in most farm products, and the liberation of most categories of retail trade, catering and service provision from administrative restrictions, so that state, collective, cooperative and individual units may function in competition or cooperatively. A fourth is the establishment of headquarters units in the county towns, to be called county combined cooperatives. These will be responsible for the administration of the state plans in so far as they relate to the allocation and procurement of commodities, will guide local cooperatives in their work, and should themselves engage in storage, wholesaling and transportation. The fifth, rather different in kind, is the state's evident anxiety to stimulate trade everywhere, but particularly between rural and urban populations. State wholesaling units may now trade across administrative boundaries which formerly defined their territories. Trading contracts with local producers and suppliers, both rural and urban, are considered useful, and should be extended. State trading units with their new cooperative structure and (hopefully) new 'mass' character should be encouraged to serve the people by buying and selling as freely as possible (State Council 1983).

65

Obviously these decisions represent compromises between the needs of the state for procurement of commodities through the state plan and continued social control on the one hand, and the needs of the community for a greatly increased volume of local trade and business of all kinds on the other. Equally obviously, they represent a stage in the development of Communist Party management of the problems represented by local and regional trade. Various inconsistencies and anomalies are a natural consequence of both aspects of their origin. The outside observer may well feel that (not for the first time) the authorities are devoting too much of their energy to problems of organisation and ultimately political philosophy, and too little to the stimulation and encouragement of trade itself. Thus, China has only 35,000 rural supply and marketing cooperatives in all (FBIS *Daily Report*, 10 Mar. 1983, K12, quoting a Xinhua release of 8 Mar. 1983) – a number which is now smaller than the number of 'free markets', and one which compares very badly with 700,000 production brigades, or even with 54,000 communes. Everywhere in commerce, including these 'structural reforms' themselves, there are abundant indications of a system built around the bureaucracy and the state, rather than around practical social needs or the energy and opportunities in the community. Nothing in the schemes now taking shape suggests serious attention to the persistent problem of personal corruption in commerce, especially commissions and bribes of various kinds (State Council 1981d). Little or nothing in them seems designed to alleviate the problem of simple yet rigid commercial structures with too many levels, poor information flows and simplistic management practices, or that of local needs for efficient transportation and sound storage for commodities (*People's Daily*, 6 Aug. 1981, translated in FBIS *Daily Report*, 19 Aug. 1981, K6). On this showing, development in the whole field of rural commerce during the forthcoming decade will go by default to private enterprise. Yet realistically the politicians cannot be expected to act without reference to political principle, especially when most of the present trade system lies directly within official control.

Rural land

One reason for the continued intensification of rural land use may be the fall in the total arable area which is said to have taken place since 1957. The present official figure for arable land in China is about 1500 million *mou* or 100 million ha. This figure is lower by about 10.8% than that for 1957, a substantial fall which is attributed to building and other kinds of proliferating non-arable land use. As may be expected of so broad a statistic in Chinese conditions, some obscurity surrounds it. The figure for 1957 was 1,670 million *mou*, and for 1950, 1,505 million *mou*. Between 1957 and 1977, 320 million *mou* of new arable was created, but 500 million *mou* was lost, resulting in a net loss of 180 million *mou*, that is 10.8% (Zhang Zhenming; *People's Daily*, 15 Apr. 1981). A parallel account featuring slightly different figures (newly created arable, 260 million *mou*; loss of arable, 440 million *mou*; net loss of arable, 180 million *mou*) has also appeared (Yi Zhi 1981: 64). But there is also some opinion which runs counter to these estimates. Travers (483) writes: 'Study of satellite data, coupled with ground surveys . . . has convinced the Chinese that the cultivated area has been substantially under-reported by communes, probably by at least 20 per cent.' A figure of this kind (not allowed for in the figures from Yi Zhi and others quoted above) is discouraging from the standpoint of future capacity for farmland creation, but probably encouraging from the standpoint of the capacity of the farm systems to respond to further intensification measures. Walker (1981: 222) also argues that apparent loss of farmland may be due in some degree to under-reporting by collective units. Here it is the official Chinese figures which are less optimistic than unofficial and foreign estimates.

If the official estimates are accepted, the national figure for cultivated area per person fell in the period 1957–77 from 2.6 *mou* to 1.6 *mou*, a fall of 39.7% (Yi Zhi 1981: 64). In Liaoning province, where industrial demand for land is important, the cultivated area per person fell from 4.8 *mou* to less than 2 *mou* during the thirty years up to 1981 – a fall of more than 40%; but in Shaanxi province, where industrial demand for land is quite limited, the fall was almost the same. In Heilongjiang province, where arable creation has been prominent and industrialisation remains limited, the fall was 51%. Throughout the country, land has been lost, sometimes on a very big scale, due to ambitious capital construction projects (not always completed), rural and urban building and failure to rehabilitate land after natural disasters (Yi Zhi 1981: 65–7). It is now recognised that in China, in common with most countries, building usually takes place on very good land, while much of the arable newly created in outlying regions is of poor quality. Owing to the present upsurge in rural building, moreover, further losses are taking place, due in part to irresponsible though legal siting in villages, in part to new sites on 'responsibility' land occupied illegally but with the connivance of local cadres (*People's Daily*, 15 Apr. 1981), and in part to illegal and corrupt deals done by local cadres for personal profit (FBIS *Daily Report*, 19 Mar. 1982, 01, quoting a Fuzhou broadcast). In addition to rural building, the countryside has also to bear the losses of farmland which represent the urban demand for building materials – the present annual output of 140,000 million bricks represents the annual loss of 6,700 ha or 67 sq km of farmland (Li Yun: 37).

In addition to the general problem of loss of arable land in China as a whole, there is certainly a special problem of loss of land of the highest quality, adjacent to the cities and used for generations for growing vegetables, to various kinds urban use, both regular and irregular – brickworks, housing developments, urban-based factories and workshops, and various kinds of commercial enterprise such as bank branches and restaurants. This kind of occupation of vegetable land sometimes takes place by official requisition or with official permission but sometimes is basically illegal, involving sale or rent of land by rural communal units to urban users who can pay high prices. It has reached an important stage in the peripheries of Nanjing, where almost 1,000 ha of vegetable land has been lost since 1976 (Liu Zhongchun); and in a number of cities, including Wuhan and Shanghai, this loss of suburban garden land has contributed to chronic shortages of vegetables. It should be remembered also that when suburban farmland is lost, people are put out of work on the land. In 1979, on the fringe of Tianjin, 40,000 people lost their livelihood on the land and six brigades effectively ceased to exist, due to requisition of farmland for urban purposes. These people necessarily entered the urban population, contributing to the demand for urban jobs (Xia Lin and Shi Bo). Evidence of various kinds of illegal land dealing from Hangzhou (Yu Yunda) indicates frequent involvement by the banks. It is argued, however, that the People's Republic still has no land law to which people can look for guidance (*People's Daily*, 15 Apr, 1981) – an argument which must carry some weight in present conditions where opportunities and expectations have been destabilised by economic growth. By the standards of communities outside China, there is nothing very surprising about most of the problems which have been outlined in relation to land, and few of them are likely to diminish.

Surplus labour

Among Chinese commentators on the rural scene, there is no more commonplace cliché than the 'abundance of people, scarcity of land' concept – and none more necessary. To be sure, there are places in eastern China (the mountainous south and much of the north east) where denser populations might well create more effective resource use; but in general labour is abundant and land resource scarce. Both are becoming more so. Under the Maoists, the fiction of a Chinese population still around 800 millions was maintained (Beijing Economic Institute: 104); and frequent accounts of arable land creation and land reconstruction invited belief that the arable area had been increased. After 1976 it became apparent (in accordance with informed Western belief – Aird) that the population had already risen to more than 900 million, and also that the arable area had fallen since 1958. Surplus labour began to be seriously discussed for the first time since 1956.

It has already been argued that the responsibility systems have profound implications for the working lives of individuals in rural China. In the media, more attention is given to the social consequences of these systems. It is argued that they have resulted in improved worker motivation and brought additional workers into active production (the old and young, who now contribute to the work effort of the households). These changes have led to valuable increases in productivity of labour and hence improvements in output and standards of living, but they have also brought into the open the previously concealed underemployment of working people in the countryside in many areas, especially the north China plain. It now appears that underemployment has long substituted for unemployment in densely settled Chinese countrysides, contrary to many flattering opinions published in Maoist times – for instance, by the FAO Study Mission (60) – 'work is found, not only for the able-bodied men and women of the labour force, but also for old people willing to work' and for schoolchildren. It is now reported that in general surplus labour in the countryside amounts to about one-third of total rural labour (CCP 1981), and that in some localities this figure rises to one-half (FBIS *Daily Report*, 22 Sept. 1981, P9, quoting a Wuhan broadcast of 20 Sept. 1981). In a group of cases where precise study has been reported (Ma Renping 1981a), in communes in Qi, Lankao and Tongxu counties in eastern Henan, the figure for surplus labour is given as 42.3%. Under the responsibility systems, it is reported in this area, more people are available for work than formerly, especially old people and youngsters under eighteen; and at the same time labour productivity has sharply increased, in many cases by 100% or even more. In fact, even before the responsibility systems were introduced, the problem of surplus rural labour was sometimes raised (Yang Xiqing). For instance, in Liling county in Hunan province, people were being allocated to farm-work in 1979 by rota, or drawing lots. Arable land was less than 1 *mou* per person and in some areas only 0.2 or 0.3 *mou* – less than 200 sq m. Pingshan brigade in Wangfang commune in Liling, with 0.5 *mou* of arable per person, at that time already had intensive cultivation conjoined with brigade enterprises – a coal-mine, machine-shop, pigs, ducks, silkworms, fish, woods and a restaurant, together occupying 46% of all labour-days. At that time total income per person was roughly 151 *yuan* per year, and all labour was occupied – indeed an idyllic condition, by the standards of many other units (Yang Xiqing). Similar conditions have already been reviewed at Dongqiao.

The two main solutions to the problem of surplus labour which are now usually proposed are those already in use in Pingshan and Dongqiao in 1979 – intensification and diversification of the rural production systems. Intensification includes such measures as pot-growing of cotton seedlings, multiple cropping, land reconstruction work and so forth. Diversification includes the widening of the arable crop base and the introduction or extension of many kinds of industry, handicrafts, animal, fish and orchard husbandry. It also includes diversification of production based on private plots, together with pig-keeping, poultry and eggs, and so forth, and

hopefully rises in living standards in such forms as new houses, better personal services and more entertainment (Ma Renping 1981a: 7).

Diversification leads towards other policies which are now being proposed in the context of surplus labour. One, necessarily, is increased local trade, and what are called 'new economic linkages', which include the processing of farm outputs including milling, trades related to farm mechanisation, haulage, manufacture of bricks and other building materials, handicrafts and various service trades as well as local commerce. Businesses of two kinds are envisaged – on the one hand, a majority of self-managing units of up to about fifteen households, particularly in handicrafts, but also in trade; on the other, a minority of bigger businesses, particularly in manufacturing (bricks, paper, flour or oilseed milling, breeding chickens) – the latter of course need more capital, which in the Henan examples under discussion is furnished by those householders participating, usually in equal shares (Ma Renping 1981a: 5). Obviously, this kind of enterprise could compete directly with collective enterprise at brigade or commune level; there seems to be no question but that the exclusive collective principle is being frankly abandoned in the search for means to supply the desperate shortage of enterprise in the countryside which that principle stood to perpetuate. All these linkages depend, it is said, upon three conditions which all arise from the responsibility systems – increased rural incomes and food supplies, surplus labour seeking work, and needs among the people for materials for both production and consumption. Paucity of collective enterprise is also specifically mentioned. Methods of income distribution in these enterprises are already proliferating. Distribution may be according to investment, where investment is unequal but work equal; according to work, in the opposite conditions; and according to both, where both are unequal. It is no longer claimed that distribution of incomes from such enterprises must be made through the production team or brigade. Here the Chinese rural system has surrendered an important point of collective principle, but has gained in return a potentially vast increase in the desperately small number of local entrepreneurs represented by the collective units alone (Ma Renping 1981a: 7–8). Another analysis of this experience lays stress not only on surplus labour and the problem of increased cash incomes but nothing to buy, but also upon the

Pl. 1. 'Reaping a bumper harvest from land wrested from the sea' – an official Maoist picture of 1970.

Pl. 2. Undiversified paddy landscape in Tonglu county, Zhejiang. Mountains occupied by poor, cut-over scrub in the background.

Pl. 3. Private plots. Commune members' vegetable gardens, Shaanxi.

Pl. 4. Transport by tractor in prosperous countryside, Zhejiang province, 1982. Paddy-fields and a good local road.

Pl. 5. Henan; the north-western periphery of the north China plain, bordering the loess. People turning up for collective work in the fields on a bright autumn morning in 1977.

Pl. 6. Tea-garden near Hangzhou.

Pl. 7. A rural free market – daily marketing in a quiet side-street in a small county town in Shaanxi, 1982.

Pl. 8. The rural building boom. New village houses in prosperous Zhejiang countryside, 1982. The structures are good but the houses will lack running water.

Pl. 9a, b. Old village houses now used as stores and sheds, in the Xian suburban belt, Shaanxi. This village is now (1982) being rebuilt – hence the piles of bricks.

problem of craft skills without outlet (Huang Yuejun). Here too, the implication is that the new household enterprises are filling gaps in the economic system left open by collective policy.

Management of suburban farm outputs, especially those involving animals, is of course a special case. Here household groups may well manage collective production more or less totally. An enthusiastic account of this kind of production has appeared for seven suburban communes at Lanzhou, Gansu province (Peng Xiaozhong). These households are responsible for poultry and animal farming, keeping stall-fed cattle and goats together with pigs, rabbits, poultry and bees. In return for feed there is a regular supply of manure. Surplus labour is absorbed, urban diets improved and income generated. Professional methods of stock management give high performance.

Discussion of new economic linkages leads to a topic which has attracted some interesting discussion – the stimulation of the rural towns. Some authors consider growth of these towns to represent a genuine and effective solution of the problem of surplus labour in the countryside or the big cities, or perhaps both (Jin Daqin: 33). There are said to be about 56,000 small towns in China, some 3,200 at county level and more than 53,000 at commune level. Typically (Kaifeng prefecture in Henan is taken as example) such towns have 3,000–5,000 people, and definite economic functions including manufacturing and trade. They may be considered in thousands of cases ripe for expansion as manufacturing, business and cultural centres, but at present they are often very run-down, with old property, narrow streets, quite elementary infrastructures (roads, water supply, drainage, sanitation), and very limited commercial networks. It is argued that if each small town finds work for 2,000 redundant rural workers, then 56,000 such towns could find such work for around 120 million such people – a reasonable notion, but one which must be considered in the context of a consequent need to expand each of these small-town economies by about 100%, to generate the additional work. To do this, it is argued, planning at a relevant scale must be adopted (the scale of the county or group of counties is proposed), with proper attention to local infrastructure and proper investment priorities. The successful example given is a town called Huazhong in Wuxi municipality in Jiangsu. Huazhong has grown from around 400 people in

1949 to 8,000. It has commune enterprises, a department store, travel agency, restaurants, teahouses, photographic studio, various facilities such as shops and clinic, a middle school and a cinema (Jin Daqin: 35). Huazhong suggests an agreeable picture which may well be realistic, but as always the identification and solution of problems in southern Jiangsu, especially problems which relate to social and economic sophistication, is a very different matter from the same process in the north China plain or in Hubei. Obviously in the field of small-town development, much will depend upon the success of the movement to encourage family and cooperative enterprises in the service trades, which has already been discussed. Even more is likely to depend upon policy for commerce.

Prosperity and polarisation

In the rural China of the present, unlike that of Mao's time, peasant household prosperity is a proclaimed first aim of the system. As a result, the distribution of prosperity has begun to assume a fresh interest. Klatt (31) lists a number of Western studies in this field, which as he points out is a particularly difficult one. Surveys of rural incomes are made from time to time in China, and results published, but these tend to lay their main emphasis, predictably, upon prosperous units, and the rationalisations by which they are accompanied show every sign of relating mainly to current official fashions in policy, rather than to a more rounded and critical outlook. These surveys have moved from those based on collective incomes alone to others in which income from family production is prominent (*People's Daily*, 31 July 1980, 29 June 1981; Yun Jing). It is not claimed in either type of survey that the units which are represented are a random sample; on the contrary, they are represented as places of sound, sometimes exceptional, achievement.

One measure often adopted in these reports is the number of brigades where income distributed collectively (including income in kind, such as food) exceeds 300 *yuan* per person. There were 1,622 such brigades in 1979 and 5,569 in 1980, of a total of brigades around 700,000. (Some allowance for inflation, probably around 5%, should be made in comparing these figures.) The 1,622 richest brigades of 1979 were distributed among

26 of the 29 province-level units and came from a variety of environments, but it is not surprising that 58% lay in suburban locations (Wang Hanzhi). In 1979 only five province-level units – Shanghai, Guangdong, Heilongjiang, Zhejiang and Liaoning – contributed more than a few of these brigades; but by 1980 this group of five provinces had grown to fifteen (*People's Daily*, 29 June 1981).

As early as 1980, the press commentaries on these reports laid emphasis on points such as management and enterprise, then newly in vogue.

The first of these points is the rejection of the small-scale and local-self-sufficiency model of development, and the acceptance of diversification involving trade. 'Although there are still obstacles in the way of communes and brigades which wish to organise trading links', nevertheless exchange of commodities 'can be managed' (Wang Hanzhi). For all China in 1979, the proportion of the output of basic rural accounting units which entered trade was 31%, but for these prosperous brigades the proportion was always above 50%, and rose in some cases as high as 80%.

The second point is the escape from the constraints of monoculture. In China as a whole in 1979, the average contribution of the farm economy to the incomes of rural local accounting units was 75%; and of that proportion grain (and potato) farming contributed 76%, forestry, herding and fishing 6% and other kinds of rural work 31%. But in the prosperous brigades, the figure for outputs other than agriculture is never less than 50%. Further points relate to continued land construction (for which only one example, in the north-west, is given), and to features of organisation and management, particularly the job responsibility and contract systems.

Since about 1981, information and commentary on this kind of topic from China has adopted a new perspective – that of income by families. This increasingly substitutes for the use of brigades. Since about the same time also, it is realistic to think of the income of prosperous rural families under two headings which may have rather little in common – income from the collective (usually through household responsibility systems) and income from family production. An average income of 63 *yuan* per person for family production has already been quoted for 1980, but in a field of this kind averages may be less significant than extremes. Specialist families with strong

family production schedules in such fields as poultry or pigs could earn as much as 5,000 *yuan* net (for the whole of a large household with six or seven workers) in 1981; but such families would be no more than 1% or 2% of all households (Yu Guoyao: 3–4). Poor families, even in reasonably prosperous areas, meanwhile might have cash incomes only one-tenth of this (Yun Jing: 56). Differences of this order are now rationalised in terms of differences in families' labour supplies and skills, the extent of family production, the availability of family capital, and other family circumstances such as illness (Yun Jing: 59). But however they are rationalised these figures obviously say something, however crudely, about local social relationships as they are now developing; and in addition, though less obviously, they relate to geographical relationships – most of the evidence for strong family production and other kinds of lucrative rural outputs is from localities close to towns which also lie in the prosperous regions. (The cases quoted by Yu Guoyao, for instance, are in suburban Qiqihar in Heilongjiang and Lishu county in Jilin province, on the railway between Shenyang and Changchun.) There is a good deal of evidence that in such limited areas a whole group of favourable pressures converge to generate rural prosperity on a scale now totally beyond the experience of any part of the Chinese countryside before 1980. These areas include much of the north-east, southern Jiangsu and the rest of the Yangzi delta area, the Pearl River delta and other favoured areas in the south, and suburban peripheries everywhere. From this point of view, accounts such as those of Liuzhuang (see pp. 88–9) and Xiashidang (see pp. 27–9) represent the bridge between the Maoist countrysides and these most prosperous areas. Broadly, the older rural prosperity indicates a sound bulk food supply, adequate in quantity and not too dependent on potatoes, varied alternative foods including vegetables, beancurd, fish, eggs and some pork, supplies of fuel, usually firewood, supplies of simple consumer goods such as thermos flasks and shoes, rising to more important items such as bicycles and radios; and some surplus in the local economy to provide for investment in the production system. To these, the newer rural prosperity now adds new or improved houses, improved services such as piped water and electric light, and much more consumer demand. Increasingly, as time goes on, there will be further social demands that rural prosperity should provide much more, such as better communications and transport, a still wider schedule of consumer items, entertainment, better diets, much better education, and much more social opportunity for rural people in both business and the bureaucracy.

Detail about poverty takes longer to go out of date. Poverty can still be illustrated from the case of Guyuan county on the Great Wall (see p. 149) or Tongzi village in mountain Hunan (see p. 124). Severe poverty in contemporary China indicates a basic food supply as little as one-half of need, generally supplied in part by the state, with very scanty supplies of fuel and virtually no cash in the local economy at all. It is units with low cash incomes which are also generally short of food, fuel and amenities (Du Runsheng). In neither prosperous nor poor rural communities is there much variety in life or opportunity to change one's individual or family condition, as those things are understood in urban China, among the bureaucrats, or in rural communities in western Europe – but in this respect rural experience in China differs little from that in other densely peopled parts of Asia, Japan apart.

For 1979–80, 23% of rural accounting units reported incomes per person (including incomes in kind) of more than 100 *yuan*; 50% incomes between 50 and 100 *yuan*; and 27% incomes less than 50 *yuan* (Wu Xiang). The 27% of units last named represent the heart of Chinese poverty. In China as a whole, some 200 counties have conditions little or no better than in the early days after Liberation, and some are worse off. Incomes remain very low at the weaker end of Chinese rural life, and among the poorest, there are many units which depend upon state-supplied grain for food, loans for production and official help for livelihood. Moreover, even among the 50% of units with cash incomes between 50 and 100 *yuan*, there are many which depend on state or other help and support in various ways. 'When the collective economy is badly managed, the people's motivation is low; when the people's motivation is low, the collective economy is badly managed' – as many as 100 million people live in units which are the victims of this vicious circle (Wu Xiang). Another author (Du Runsheng: 28) presses this point still harder – 'With little income and grain, they are bound to practise egalitarian distribution . . . the more they muddle along, the poorer they become; the poorer they become the more they practise egalitarianism; the more they

do so the poorer they become.'

Some specific claims have been made for increases in prosperity in poor regions – for instance in a group of areas including north-west Shandong and eastern Honan in the north China plain, north-west Shanxi, northern Shaanxi, central Gansu and western Ningxia in the north-west, and mountain peripheries in southern Shaanxi, western Honan, western Hubei, Guizhou, Yunnan and Sichuan (Feng Leshu 1982). Here it is claimed that increased farm diversification (for instance, in cotton and oilseeds) and family production have led to increased cash incomes, and that at the same time reductions in grain acreage have been accompanied by increases in grain production. It is not denied, however, that there is still a long way to go – and it should not escape notice that in the list of poor areas under discussion those in the north China plain have profited much more from the cotton boom than others.

Present policy will naturally suggest to outsiders that a process of economic polarisation is at work in rural China today – the poor households and poor villages remaining as they are, but the rich consolidating their position and accumulating productive assets, business relationships and profitable links with vested interests in the bureaucracy. Groups which have been able so to promote their own prosperity appear to be in part embryo class groups, in part local and regional groupings. Evidence for this kind of development is patchy and inadequate, partly no doubt because of inhibitions (and quite possibly confusions) of political principle; partly as a result of rigidity of thinking in the bureaucracy – developments which take place without benefit of bureaucratic

The cadre (presumably a Maoist) is cutting off the heads of the plants which grow better than the others – in a garden called 'commune members' incomes. *Source: People's Daily,* 10 Dec. 1979. The artist is Shi Bo.

introduction may well pass without bureaucratic comment, or even recognition. It also bears remembering that marked differences in levels of rural prosperity survived the whole Maoist experiment, and in extreme cases (such as the metropolitan south versus the isolated north-west) probably even continued to widen.

Howe (187–9) argues convincingly that in China since Liberation, rural incomes have throughout been substantially lower than urban; and he points out that it is much easier to raise the 15% of urban incomes than the 80% of rural. However, one result of the present phase of relative liberalisation in the countryside has been to redress the terms of trade to the advantage of the rural producers, through falling back upon free markets and negotiated official prices. There are some signs of a welcome surge of rural prosperity of which the increase and rebuilding of the rural housing stock is the most dramatic indication. It is officially estimated that 14% of rural households built new houses or improved their existing houses during the three years 1978–80 (*People's Daily*, 19 Mar. 1981 – reported without prominence on p. 2). This would be about 22 million houses. Average floor areas are given as 70 sq m in northern China and 90 sq m in the south – both very good figures by Chinese urban standards. A subsequent estimate suggests that 15 million households built new houses in the same period of time, representing a total of 900 million sq m of floor area, suggesting 60 sq m per house, still a good figure (*People's Daily*, 18 June 1981 – this time the lead story on the front page). In 1981, 8 million new rural houses were built (*People' Daily*, 23 Jan. 1982), and a similar number in 1982 (State Statistical Bureau. 1983: 12). In prosperous rural areas effective demand for new houses is thought to be about 30% of all households; in areas of average prosperity, about 10%. In many places the order of priority for family spending has changed from food–clothing–housing to housing–clothing–food. There is now abundant visible evidence of building on this kind of scale, and of impressive quality, in prosperous parts of the country. In some areas, supplies of construction materials such as concrete units, glass, cement, steel and timber are now being built into the state plan (*People's Daily*, 19 Mar. 1981); but there are many more indications in the literature that local materials are those mainly used, and that special items like glass are still very scarce.

There is also a mounting shortage of all kinds of building materials.

The building boom came very suddenly. It is worth calling to mind in this context that in Chinese rural communities, where basic subsistence is provided by the team or brigade without the intervention of cash, cash income is disposable income, though clothing, school fees and health insurance must be met from it. Hence a modest increase in total income which takes the form of cash is a much less modest increase in disposable income. In addition to this, in the Shanghai countryside, while income from collective sources increased by 57% between 1976 and 1980, income from family production, which is usually received in cash, increased for the families surveyed by 140% (*People's Daily*, 17 Mar. 1982). It is partly for this reason that moderately prosperous families have been able to take up rebuilding so freely. Thus, seven years' savings, most of it probably from family production, will be sufficient (about 3,000 *yuan*) for a peasant family to build a four-room house, of course on a site allocated by the production team (Shen Chenzhong and Wang Fugui: 54–5).

In addition to building houses, peasant households have used their new prosperity to marry their sons, to purchase the 'three big items' (sewing-machines, bicycles, wrist-watches), and to have new clothes made. All these kinds of spending have implications for national policy – for birth-control (of which late marriage is supposed to be a cornerstone), for industrial and consumer production, and for textile supplies. Rural prosperity as a whole also represents a formidable challenge to the commercial departments.

Under the Maoists, when evidence of rural prosperity was produced in the press, it often took the form of bank deposits by peasant households, inviting the suspicion that people deposited their money because there was nothing to buy. One of the strengths of the Maoist fixed procurement and low price system was that if a brigade or household did have cash, it was not easy to spend. The sudden and unexpected influx of cash into the Shandong countryside which resulted from the cotton boom of 1980 was predictably embarrassing to the commercial departments. There are now four big problems in this field in western Shandong – difficulty in selling cotton, difficulty in selling grain, difficulty in selling pigs, and difficulty in buying manufactured goods of all kinds (Ji Xueyi and Zhang Kaixuan). More generally, the total value of consumer goods purchased in China in 1981 showed an increase of 60% over 1978, or at constant prices, 43%. Rural purchasing power increased more than twice as rapidly as urban. Purchasing power increased between 1978 and 1981 more rapidly than supplies of consumer goods – 66% as against 54%; new money was spent not only upon durable consumer goods, but also upon improved housing and better diets (FBIS *Daily Report*, 31 Mar. 1982, K4, quoting a Beijing broadcast of 30 Mar. 1982: from the State Statistical Bureau).

Nolan and White (1979, 1982) have made a particular study of equality and inequality in rural China before 1976 and since. Their conclusions carry conviction – that in the early and mid-1970s 'a basic floor had been established under rural incomes' through collective grain distribution, collective welfare provision and social guarantees. Earnings from work-points had probably tended increasingly towards equality. The remnant private sector to which these authors draw attention in Shanghai and Beijing does not appear to have been strong except in just such prosperous localities (1979: 31–2), but of course incomes in cash have the special property of disposability to which attention has already been drawn. Nolan and White also argue (1982: 183–4) that the Maoist countryside in 1976 contained substantial inequalities, and that in some respects (such as insistence on self-reliance) Maoist policy stood to perpetuate them. They point to 'frustratingly slow growth and stagnation in some areas', and argue that broadly speaking 'policies such as restrictions on private economy and the free market, overly high rates of accumulation and excessive redistribution' were not so much the outcome of direct orders from above as of local bodies operating local systems of principle and interest (1982: 183).

All these views are realistic. Income and property disparities in the Chinese countryside in Mao's time and up to the present are first and foremost inter-regional and second, inter-sectoral. Maoist policy suppressed the inter-sectoral disparities in large degree by redistributive social policies (some much easier to defend than others), and at a pinch by suppressing the sectors (particularly trade) which might generate disparities. It did little to suppress inter-regional disparities,

though here too suppression (especially of urban growth) had its place. Post-Maoist policy aims to tolerate the disparities of inter-sectoral origin, believing that prosperity will spread from favoured sectors and the localities where they are strong, and secure in the conviction that poor families and poor communities are protected by entrenched public ownership of the land and the general prohibition against employment of labour (Zuo Mu 1979). For inter-regional disparities, it relies on the stimulation of economic growth of all kinds and the exploitation of comparative regional advantages. Optimists for the present regime will argue that in both kinds of situation prosperity differentials are likely to be greater than in the Maoist system; but that in both the levels of prosperity of both rich and poor are likely to be higher than under the Maoists. Pessimists will argue that while the new scheme is realistic and constructive for prosperous areas with plenty of advantages like Suzhou, it has much less to offer to very poor areas like the mountain backwoods or densely populated areas with little resource like some in the north China plain. The evidence so far is that there is less difference in results under the two schemes, at least in terms of regional and local disparities, than might have been expected. Various examples explored in the regional chapters of this book suggest continuity across the policy divide, based on sound or unsound management, favourable or unfavourable position in relation to the state plan, location especially in relation to cities, capacity to attract or make advantageous investment, farm costs and so forth. In particular, few places where prosperity was strong under the Maoists appear to have experienced serious difficulties since.

Protecting the collective system

The collective system in rural China has in present practice three principal features – collective ownership of the means of production, especially the land; collective management of most rural production, and distribution of most incomes, through basic accounting units within the commune system; and collective responsibility of the producing units (especially the production teams) to senior units in the communes and finally to the state, through the rural planning system. In considering the widespread, rapid and often fundamental changes which have been introduced in China since the end of 1978, it is salutary also to look at features of continuity.

Of the three main features of the collective system, collective ownership is the most strongly defended and the least openly attacked. Attacks upon it do take place, for instance through extensions of the practices of the responsibility systems, but they are wholly unorthodox. In some places where collective property has been illegally allocated, this has been the outcome of cadres' failure to operate the responsibility systems properly. In others the peasants are directly to blame, and in some there have been demolitions of collective property and discontinuation of collective productive installations such as pump-wells. All these and various other kinds of attack upon collective property are prohibited (FBIS *Daily Report*, 14 Dec. 1980, 06–08, quoting *Zhejiang Daily* 13 Jan. 1981; also *People's Daily* Editorial, 4 Oct. 1981, translated in FBIS *Daily Report*, 9 Oct. 1981, K15–K17). In this and many other discussions, such as those in which the break-up of the commune system is envisaged, collective ownership of the major means of production, especially the land, is not called into question. Nevertheless it seems reasonable to expect continued risk of erosion of the collective system along this vital front. Even though it is unlikely to be particularly vulnerable, it is surely particularly tempting.

The second point is continued collective allocation of rural resources, management of production and distribution of incomes (including those which represent social security) through basic accounting units. In these respects, responsibility and contract systems inside the agricultural system and beyond it, and also the growth of private and 'specialist' production are all obviously in some degree natural enemies of the collective system, particularly in respect of its distributive functions. They all enable naïve people, or those whose motivations are hostile, to use their production contracts as bases from which to erode the collective. Such tendencies are resisted partly by exhortation, partly by administrative action like insistence upon collective accounting (Liu Xumao). There are also other means. A Guangxi circular insists that administration of rural economic activities must continue to take place through the production teams, not directly to households. These include the issue of cloth

coupons, relief funding, farm loans, production funds, grain purchase and sale, management of natural fertiliser, production quotas and the obligations imposed by the state plan (FBIS *Daily Report*, 8 Apr. 1982, P4, quoting a Nanning broadcast of 5 Apr. 1982). The points mentioned are all important ones, and illustrate the necessity of maintaining the commune system as a system of organisation and control, as well as simply the guardian of public ownership of the means of production. Here too economic growth, and the management conditions necessary for it, are the enemy of stability in organisation and control.

The maintenance of the present commune structure, with its hierarchy of responsibility, is another matter. Various authors, no doubt with official encouragement, have discussed its demolition (FBIS *Daily Report* 26 Aug. 1981, K1–K3, quoting a Beijing broadcast of 25 Aug. 1981), and experiments with alternatives have been made in Fengyang county in Anhui province and elsewhere. The final decision in the Constitution of 1982 to separate local government from the other functions of the commune system is bound to strengthen the communes as economic and planning units, by removing one kind of grievance against them. Probably the principal function of the commune system at present and for the foreseeable future is the maintenance of a hierarchy not so much of responsibility, as of social and economic control. This notion obviously relates directly to the third function already mentioned – the maintenance of the rural planning system. There is still very little detail in the Chinese media about the functioning of the planning system, but its maintenance continues to attract powerful support. 'The planned economy gives expression to the superiority of our socialist system', and 'administrative intervention is necessary for the practice of the planned economy'. Furthermore, 'We must adhere to the principle of taking the planned economy as the key link, with regulation by the market mechanism playing a supplementary role.' (*People's Daily*, 24 Feb. 1982, Editorial, translated in FBIS *Daily Report*, 26 Feb. 1982, K1–K2). A good deal is often said on this subject early in the year, presumably at the stage of detailed discussions on spring planting (e.g. *Liaoning Daily*, 12 Feb. 1982, quoted in FBIS *Daily Report* 25 Feb. 1982, S1–S2). From time to time quite uncompromising positions are proclaimed in relation to the state plan in the countryside. It is argued that loyalty to the state plan does not compromise the rights of production teams to determine their own policy, that grain outputs must be maintained according to the plan, that procurement and supply must continue to take place within the plan, and (most strikingly) that pig production must be brought within the plan, by allocation of official quotas to households through the brigades (Wu Zhenkun). Here as at Nanzhuang in 1979, it is difficult to dismiss the rationale of the state planners' position.

Probably nobody in contemporary China would argue openly for a return to free property in land, such as existed prior to Liberation – though there are no doubt people who would like to see it. Some influential people do argue openly for a return to village cooperative ownership and management, with local cooperative companies set up to operate local commercial and industrial undertakings (Liu Zheng and Chen Wuyuan) – and this appears to be one direction in which official policy is moving. Others argue that specialist household production is the necessary spearhead of local prosperity based on diversification, and that these specialist households should be as free as possible of collective obligations (Yu Guoyao). At least in discussion, some people in China take up what may be considered extreme anti-collectivist positions on these and similar issues. Other people, no doubt, regret the abandonment of extreme Maoist positions on collective ownership and management, though their opinions do not now reach the media. Protecting the collective system appears to be a routine necessity for some people including those at present in power; for others a grievously neglected imperative for survival; for yet others a greatly overrated pastime of the bureaucracy. Each party calls upon its strengths in the management system, in ideology and in common experience however defined. The development of their struggle in the countryside (it can hardly be resolved) will be one of the principal determinants of the development of China during the forthcoming generation.

Environment, population and livelihood in the plain

The north China plain extends from Beijing almost to the Yangzi River, almost 1,000 km in the north – south direction. In width it varies between 300 and 600 km. Its total area is given as 510,000 sq km (197,000 sq miles; larger than California but a little smaller than France) representing 5.3% of China's total area. Its farm population was 182 million in 1971, 25.6% of China's total population; ten years later it must be around 250 millions. The arable area of the plain is 360 million *mou*, 24% of China's total (Geographical Research Institute: 353). These simple facts indicate that while the plain is not the most acute regional problem of livelihood and development in China, it is without question the biggest and it may well be the most permanent. The north China plain is the most important single geographical region in China, and on the global scale it is one of the largest and most important geographical regions on earth.

The plain has been formed by deposition from the west – the Shandong hill masses were originally islands. The greater part of it is quite level and quite featureless – itself a remarkable feature when extending over hundreds of kilometres. But it is not uniform, due in part to its great size. Change over distance on the face of the plain is gradual and often imperceptible, but in terms of a number of critical geographical parameters the experience of Beijing at the northern end of the plain differs quite significantly from that of Yangzhou or Bengbu at the southern end. The most important are the precipitation totals and the winter temperatures. Frost-free periods range from about 180 days at Beijing to about 230 days north of the Yangzi, and the January isotherm of 0 °C crosses the plain from west to east at about the latitude of Xuzhou. As a whole the plain is dry, but to the north of the Qinling–Xuzhou zone, which has already been identified as the zone separating northern China from southern, precipitation falls below 800 mm, and drought may be serious. Particularly in the northern half of the plain, spring drought is a grave problem in many years, with strong drying winds and duststorms.

There is every reason to believe that the population of the north China plain, in common with that of rural China in general, increased by some 66% in the thirty years following Liberation – an increase supported mainly (in common with the increases of preceding generations) by further intensification of the rural production systems. There have been continual struggles against drought, assisted in some areas by state-supported major waterworks. Extension of irrigation in the plain was a major achievement of the Maoist phase – from 79 million *mou* (5.3 million ha) in 1965 to 108 million *mou* (14 million ha), 47.3% of the arable area (Department of Agriculture: 28). (Otherwise defined, the irrigable area of 162 million *mou* – 11 million ha – represents 60% of the arable area of the plain – Zhang Tianzeng: 16). Nevertheless, grain supplies remain stretched. The arithmetic speaks for itself. Rural population density (to say nothing of small and large towns) is generally about 1 person to 1.5 *mou* of arable in the plain, about 10 persons per hectare of arable, or 1,000 persons per sq km. The official target figure for grain yield in northern China, set up in 1956, but still not achieved in much of the plain (see fig. 2.6) is 400 *jin* per *mou*. Annual grain needs may be reckoned conventionally at around 500 *jin* per person. Hence the farm surplus above subsistence cannot be large, particularly when allowance is made for crops other than grain, unless yields are unusually high. Maoist policy was centred on grain (or potatoes). Cotton is the traditional second crop of the plain, and is of course much in demand, but cotton planting was drastically squeezed in Maoist times in favour of cereal supplies. Other crops were squeezed still more, so that in 1978 basic food crops occupied 84% of the sown area, and all economic crops 12% (Department of Agriculture: 29). Hence land use in the plain emerged from the Maoist decade as basically duocultural in grain (or potatoes) and cotton. The Maoist insistence on grain and cotton production alone no doubt struck particularly hard at the possibility of radical change in the plain, because the resources of the plain were already so much committed to grain and cotton, and there was already so little room for manoeuvre. Few rural units in the north China plain are rich in mountain, lake or riverside resource to which they can turn for fresh means of livelihood, whether through mining, crafts, gathering or cultivation.

Under the Maoists, the central problem of the plain, that of subsistence with a rising population, was solved at least for the present generation, but the alternative problem of the creation of pros-perity above subsistence was shelved or suppressed. Subsistence continues, but prosperity remains an improbable ideal for the majority of localities. Some units, favoured by resource, locality or enterprise, may be able to break out of the cycle of poverty during the forthcoming generation, but better housing, improved diet and slow improvement of social opportunities appear to be the best that the bulk of the people of the plain can look forward to during the rest of this century. In Henan, perhaps the most nearly 'typical' province in the plain agriculturally, one-quarter of all counties receive supplies of grain from the state on account of low production, and only one-quarter of counties have high production records (FBIS *Daily Report*, 17 May 1979, P4–P5, quoting a Beijing broadcast of 15 May 1979). Otherwise expressed, more than one-half of the arable in the three north China plain provinces of Hebei, Henan and Shandong is reckoned to be 'low-output' land, a term which is not defined but appears to indicate grain output per *mou* below 200 *jin*. Some of this land produces less than 100 *jin* per *mou* (*People's Daily*, 5 Mar. 1971). It would appear that about one-half of the arable in the plain can now call upon irrigation water and one-half is reckoned to be of inferior quality, perhaps because it lacks irrigation but often for other more fundamental reasons, such as gravelly soil structure, high alkalinity, waterlogging and so forth.

The detail of the subsistence problem in the plain takes various forms – the problems of both recurrent and exceptional drought, and for this and other reasons, deficient harvests in two years out of three; the problems of soil alkalinity; the problems (from the point of view of the state and the planning system) of the competition of cotton and grain for land; the problems (from the stand-point of the people) of the poverty trap in many brigades and communes – and of course the problem of a stagnant economy with growing populations, limited and difficult land, inadequate fertiliser, little scope for diversification, poor diets without variety or much improvement, and no perspectives at all. The precarious status of self-sufficiency in food in the north China plain was illustrated, if illustration were needed, in an important *People's Daily* article of 1974 (29 Sept. 1974, translated as 'A historic turning-point' in *SCMP*, 74 (45), 189–96). Here it was claimed that self-sufficiency in food in the plain had finally been achieved, ending the historic dependence of the plain upon supplies of food from the south.

It was apparent that the achievement was precarious even without the subsequent demonstration by Walker that the claim in this article could be accepted only within quite specific limits – the exclusion of Beijing and Tianjin from the calculations of need for grain in the plain, together with the recognition that conditions were never more than marginal in Hebei and Shandong, and that consumption wants, as opposed to needs, were not really being satisfied (Walker 1977). There has been some further improvement since that time. (Walker 1981: 230–4).

These are the natural weaknesses of the plain under dense populations. These weaknesses were aggravated by policies under the Maoists which insisted upon grain monoculture or grain and cotton duoculture, and at the same time suppressed flexibility and diversity in resource use. In particular these policies were hostile to production for markets other than the state, partly because diversification competed with grain for scarce arable resources, partly because production for any free market implies business development and hence invited identification with resurgent capitalism. Intensification of the grain economy, including intensification through farm mechanisation, was politically acceptable, but required heavy investments which few local communities could afford.

In this way the rural successes of the Maoist phase in the plain – considerable increases in irrigation capacity, mechanisation, use of fertiliser, and reconstruction and improvement techniques – achieved less than they might have done, and generated much less peasant satisfaction, because of the limitation of their effort to increased intensification of the monocultural or duocultural system. Indeed, rising costs of intensification conjoined with static farm incomes are now one standard ground of criticism of the Maoist rural system. It is reasonable to expect that in the present phase of more relaxed social policies, encouragement of mixed resource use and mixed production, together with improved commercial networks, villages will find that the earlier investments made under the Maoists also begin to pay off more heavily.

As these remarks show, the north China plain has great and chronic problems, and these were not solved under the Maoists and are far from solution up to the present. All this means that the problems of the north China plain are the central problems of development in China. Other regions are either more than self-sufficient, or small enough in population or extent to represent only limited burdens. The burden of the north China plain, on the other hand, with one-quarter of the country's population, is sufficient to condition the progress of the whole Chinese community.

Major engineering projects

In 1949, the north China plain was more than ready for an extended and many-sided programme of major engineering works. The Yellow River changed course dramatically in 1857, but due to disturbance in the country and the weakness of the official systems it was never made secure. Its banks were opened deliberately to the south as a military manœuvre against the Japanese in 1938, and extensive flooding and destruction resulted. Because its course is embanked, the Yellow River receives no tributaries downstream from the Qin, which together with the Luo and some other rivers enters the Yellow River above Taohuayu near Zhengzhou. The northern half of the plain is drained by a series of rivers (such as the Wei which flows through Xinxiang, only 50 km from the Yellow River) which flow broadly parallel to the coast and find limited and congested natural egress to the sea only through the Hai River below Tianjin. The southern half is drained by a group of rivers tributary to the Huai, which flows into the Hongzi Lake which in turn had only congested and confused outflow channels. All three of these systems cried out for rational engineering management, and all have duly been tackled in various ways and with varying degrees of success by the People's Government.

The Yellow River

The Yellow River was so perpetual and so well-known a threat in old China that its quiescence since Liberation is bound to impress observers. Nevertheless, the problems of the Yellow River and its basin have by no means been solved. Figures quoted from Shaanxi and Shanxi show that the burden of silt carried in its middle course has not fallen since Liberation; and in fact the central problem of the river's course is the burden of silt which it continues to carry – Shandong and Henan are continuing to shoulder burdens which are laid upon them by Shanxi, Shaanxi and

Ningxia. Silt carried by the river from the loess plateau is still being deposited in the river-bed in the lowland part of its course, sufficient to raise the bed about 10 cm per annum (Chen Rinong: 5). The levees are still being raised, now often by the use of material dredged from the bed; in some places the river now flows 3–5 m above the surrounding level of the plain. In many areas, seepage remains very serious in time of flood-water (*People's Daily*, 12 Dec. 1979). Silting has also been the downfall of the great Sanmen project. In north-west Henan the Yellow River passes through a series of gorges. In 1955 an ambitious plan for the whole river was published which proposed an important dam complex at this point, to be built with Soviet help (Yellow River Conservancy Committee). This plan was reviewed enthusiastically in the West (Tregear: 60–5). The Sanmen dam was expected to form an extensive lake; it was intended to control flooding and assist navigation, to make irrigation water available, and to produce 1,000 MW of electrical generation capacity. The Sanmen project was part of a comprehensive plan for the control and development of the Yellow River which also involved some dozens of major and secondary projects in various parts of the course of the river and its main tributaries, and the construction of almost a million minor dams to control water and silt in the basin, mainly on the loess plateau (Yellow River Conservancy Committee).

The Sanmen part of the project was started in 1957 and completed in 1960, but the extent of silting was not reduced in the meantime, and the reservoir and waterworks proved quite incapable of managing the tremendous annual influx of silt. According to Xinhua (21 Dec. 1974), 'Sedimentary formations on the river-bed rapidly extended upstream to the Wei River, . . . elevating the bottom of its inlet channel. The reservoir was thus in danger of being abandoned and the Wei River basin and the city of Sian were seriously menaced.' Smil, basing his study on satellite pictures, concurs in essentials (Smil). Subsequent reconstruction occupied the years from 1965 to 1973. The first stage was the cutting of two new silt discharge channels through rock, and converting four of the original eight steel pipes intended for power generation to the same use. The second stage comprised the lowering of the four remaining generator pipes and the opening of the outlets at the base of the dam, resulting in the lowering of the water level in the dam. In effect, the Sanmen dam is now unable, except in emergency, to impound the muddy flood-water of summer. It is used mainly to maintain water flow during winter, the time of low water and low silting, to provide irrigation and urban water, and to generate electricity at a moderate rate – 200 MW planned capacity (Xinhua, 21 Dec. 1974).

Some writers have regarded the Sanmen project as a disaster. This is perhaps an exaggeration, but it has certainly been a profoundly disappointing failure, and the more serious since the failure results from lack of exactly that marriage of industrial with intermediate and low technology which the Maoists so loudly proclaimed as 'walking on two legs'. Some other important parts of the original plan have been completed, apparently successfully, such as the Liujia dam above Lanzhou in Gansu.

To judge from this account, conditions on the Yellow River are akin to others in the development experience of the north China plain during the past generation – the line is being held and disaster staved off; but the necessary conditions for radical improvement have not yet been assembled. To stave off disaster in these conditions is not a mean achievement; but as the authorities in China well know, it is not as much as is needed.

The Huai and Hai river systems

The Huai and Hai rivers and their tributaries drain the southern and northern halves of the north China plain respectively. In general terms their problems have much in common, though in detail they differ considerably. Each drains the mountain peripheries and flat surface of a delta plain of great extent, subject to occasional very heavy rain and resultant flooding. Each river system has been deeply influenced by previous courses of the Yellow River which flowed much further north and reached the sea through Tianjin in ancient times, and which has at various times taken a course through the present Huai basin, to reach the sea south of Shandong. Each has also been influenced by the cutting of the Grand Canal over a period of centuries ending in the thirteenth century AD. The canal follows a course close to or identical with former Yellow River courses from Xuzhou to Tianjin, which obviously lies across the natural slope of the land and the feeble natural course of the local drainage almost throughout its length (Shanghai Normal University: 114). In addition, allowance must be made for the vast extent of the Huai drainage – about 200,000 sq km, and for the topography of much of the basin, which is broadly flat but has an abundance of minor topographical irregularities. In the case of the Hai River, the main problem is the confluence near Tianjin of the drainage of several long and important north-flowing rivers, such as the Ziya and Daqing, with the Yongding and others from the local mountain region to north and west; the serpentine Hai River represents their joint course, through flat and marshy country, to the Yellow Sea.

Important improvements were made in both systems between 1949 and 1976. These are shown in Figs 6.1 and 6.2 for the Huai and Hai systems respectively. For the Huai, the key engineering works have been the North Jiangsu Canal which opens a fresh outlet to the sea for the whole system from the Hongze Lake; groups of local canals and sluices in the middle and lower sections of the basin which permit local control of water; a series of flood-retention basins in the upper and middle courses, which supplement the flood-retention capacity of the natural lakes; and a number of reservoirs in the mountain peripheries to the south-west, in Anhui and Henan (*Huai he xin pian*). For the Hai, the key engineering works have been the creation of six or more major new outlets to the sea for the river system, diverting drainage away from the narrow, twisting and congested Hai River through Tianjin. In addition, flood-retention basins have been built

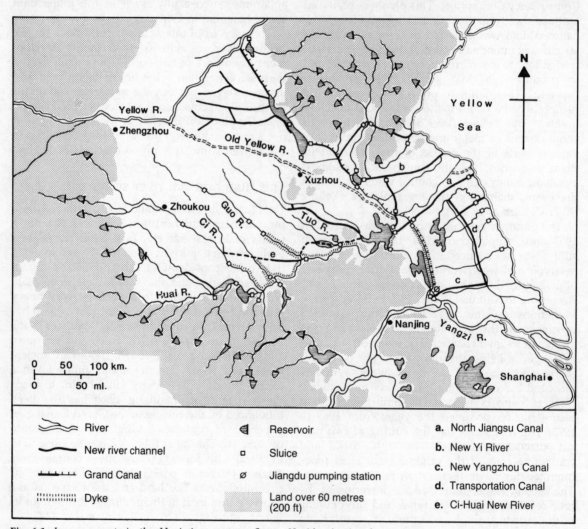

Fig. 6.1. Improvements in the Huai river system. *Source: Huai he xin pian*, frontispiece.

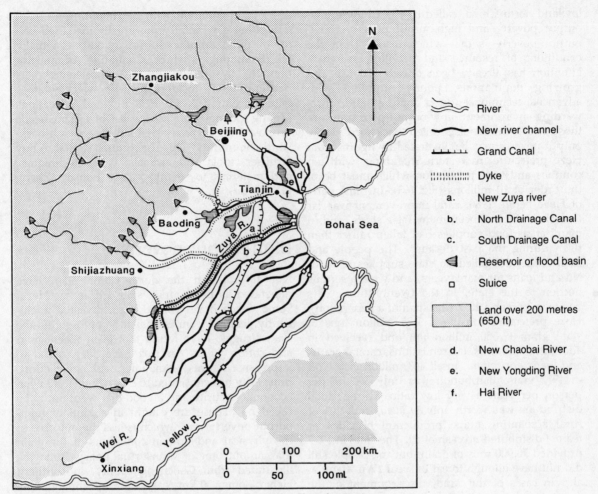

Fig. 6.2. Improvements in the Hai river system. *Source*: Ho Chin, frontispiece.

at various points in the system, together with reservoirs in the Taihang edge. The Hai system is less extensive and less complicated than the Huai, and the engineering works involved are rather less numerous but generally larger in scale (Ho Chin).

The map for the Huai system shows the Jiangdu pumping station, east-north-east of Nanjing (see Fig. 6.1). From this point it is already possible to divert water from the Yangzi northwards into the Huai system, though on a small scale only. If a large-scale scheme on the same lines ever materialises (it is discussed from time to time), it is likely to use the same point for the same purpose.

In both the Huai and the Hai basins, unlike that of the Yellow River, it seems reasonable to regard the fundamental engineering and environ-mental problems represented by the river systems as basically solved – although on the Huai at least, widespread flooding can still take place, as in 1982. Reconstruction policy must turn now to more detailed considerations such as local water supplies and drainage, soil improvement and so forth – and in the case of the Hai system, to making good the serious and persistent water shortage which has afflicted Tianjin as a result of the diversions (Deng Shulin), and whose reper-cussions are increasingly felt in Beijing (*People's Daily*, 14 June 1982).

Low-output poverty

There are two kinds of community poverty in

lowland north China, called by the Chinese low-output poverty and high-output poverty. Low-output poverty is that which results from the conditions of resource and peopling to which attention has already been drawn – dense and growing populations, poorly supplied with advanced techniques, in a limiting and unrewarding environment. Low-output-poor units are those which the Maoists called 'backward'. Low-output poverty may be illustrated by figures from Heze prefecture in western Shandong, with ten counties and total population which must be of the order of 10 millions (Fig. 6.3). In most parts of Heze before 1980, rural improvement was far to seek; there had been many false starts, and in many areas food supplies had fallen rather than risen during the past decades. The people and local authorities relied on state supplies of food, aid and loans for many years, and were a serious burden to the state. In the twenty-three years between 1955 and 1977 (the span of a generation), Heze prefecture consumed 1.25 million tons of state grain (2,500 million *jin*) and received in addition cash funds, tax remissions, capital grants and loans not repaid, in all 463 million *yuan*. Yet in 1977 grain distribution was only 300 *jin* per person per year, a very low ratio; average total distribution was worth only 39 *yuan*, and 70% of rural accounting units (production brigades or teams) distributed no cash at all. The state in 1977 provided 70,000 tons of grain, but the people still did not have enough to eat or wear (Wu Xiang et al.). In cases of this kind, the argument of the present regime is that improvement can be had from improvements in motivation among the people, and that improved motivation results from the introduction of responsibility and incentive systems and the abandonment of egalitarian distributive policies.

As to the results of these policies in terms of experience, information is still scanty; but there are signs that the underlying problems re-emerge without delay in the form of a labour surplus. The next step should be the creation of labour-intensive enterprises, which may be difficult if materials are scarce but which may take such forms as animals and poultry. Alternatively, economic crops such as cotton, oilseeds or peanuts may be useful. In fact, as will be seen, in the medium and long term there is much less difference between the needs of the various kinds of poor unit in the plain than might at first be imagined. Heze is particularly interesting because

in 1980, in common with neighbouring areas, it did gather a windfall from greatly increased cotton outputs; but other subsidiary outputs actually fell (Shandong province, Commune Administration: 16). In addition, by 1981, subsistence diets had improved considerably, with sweet potatoes falling from 40% to 10% of food allocations (Zhang Guangyou). But the list of urgent needs proposed for Heze in 1982 still suggests a backward community. This list features capital to buy fertiliser, tools and animals; better techniques; and materials to rebuild village houses (Zhang Guangyou).

High-output poverty

Not all units in the north China plain have depended as much upon state aid as has Heze. Some which have worked hard, invested intelligently, learned from Dazhai and not forgotten the class struggle have found that even when grain and cotton yields per *mou* have been raised to impressive figures, sometimes with great effort, prosperity has continued to elude them, and even economic security and a good diet were not to be relied on. These are caught in a kind of high-output poverty trap, which is less the outcome of the physical and human conditions of the plain than an outcome of Maoist rural policy. It may be illustrated from Gaocheng county, in southern Hebei some 30 km east of Shijiazhuang, the provincial capital (Wang Guihai and Hou Zhiyi).

In Gaocheng county, the average man–land ratio is 1.5 *mou* of arable per person. Since 1970, mainly through investment in land reconstruction, Gaocheng has become a major high-yield grain-supply county – though the figure for grain output per *mou* is not given. Gaocheng supplied an annual average of almost 100 million *jin* (50,000 tons) of grain to the state during the 1970s. Nevertheless, the county's community remains poor. Standards of living rise very slowly, and in some recent years have even fallen – figures for cash incomes are also not given.

The problem as seen from Gaocheng is the state's demands for grain. Gaocheng is a famous cotton county, and in 1970 cotton accounted for 36% of total farm incomes. But from 1970 onwards development was one-sided; the authorities insisted on expanding grain output at the expense of cotton, starving the cotton fields of fertiliser

Fig. 6.3. The north China plain – place-names.

and proper management, and transferring cotton cultivation progressively to poorer land, newly opened land and land which was difficult of access. As a result, average cotton yield fell from over 100 jin to 24 jin per mou. Outputs of oilseeds,

ginger, onions, garlic, chillis and even cabbages also fell drastically, so that even commune members found vegetable oil and vegetables scarce. In 1976 the county's output of grain fell to 10 million jin below that of 1975, but the county was forced to make the same deliveries to the state nevertheless, so that even foodgrain supplies in Gaocheng fell. The people felt themselves (to adopt the metaphor used in the Chinese text) driven desperate by the relentless climb up the state's grain mountain. Costs have also risen quite steeply – from 35% of gross output in 1971 to 47% in 1977; and net income as a proportion of gross has fallen correspondingly. Rising costs include the rising cost of fuel oil, but they also include the effects of ignorant and inadequate management. Needless to say, the Maoists interpreted all this experience rather differently. When grain output fell in 1971, this was attributed to revisionist wrecking, and political encouragement was supplied to restore the people's motivation. Output rose steeply in 1972 (*People's Daily*, 13 Nov. 1975).

Gaocheng lies in the heart of the plain, without mountain or sea or other wild resources to exploit. The best prospect for cash income is thought to be the gravelly land which follows ancient river-courses, plus river-banks, roadsides and other unused land – in all, about 40,000 *mou* in the county. Fruit-trees can be planted on this kind of land, and a successful start has been made with snow-pears. Baskets can also be made from local supplies of twigs. Some 15 *yuan* per year has already been added to commune members' incomes by this kind of enterprise (Wang Guihai and Hou Zhiyi).

Another case comes from Yanshan county, still in Hebei, but on the Shandong border, about 120 km due south of Tianjin (Lu Xiaoping and Xie Shiyan). At Liufan commune in Yanshan, as late as 1978, 94% of income originated in arable farming; subsidiary production of any kind was tiny. In communes of this kind under the Maoists, ponds and even lakes were not used to produce fish or aquatic vegetables; in some places there were not even vegetable gardens. In this commune in 1978, average annual income was only 58 *yuan*, and the teams owed a total of 8 million *yuan* to the state.

In Yanshan in 1979, impoverishment of this kind was still accompanied by management problems of various kinds. The first of these is that of private plots. All team members are now supposed to have access to land for private plots, but when this relaxation was proposed in Yanshan, cadres in many communes proposed to make available only land distant from the villages, poor land or land without access to water; conse-

quently the people voted against taking up private plots. A second is the problem of idle land close to villages. In many places, miscellaneous plots of land existed which were not used by the collective units, and households used them to keep pigs and chickens. After 1965, this kind of land use was denounced as capitalist, so the land went out of use altogether, and use is still to be revived. A third is the question of farm animals, which are one of the few practicable kinds of enterprise available to households in this highly cultivated plain. In 1979 on average, about one-half of farm households in the area had a pig, and there were signs of goat and cattle enterprises – but there is room for much more enterprise of this kind. During the Cultural Revolution, land for fodder was criticised and so given up; regeneration of enterprise is slow.

At Yanshan, it was argued in 1979 that here and elsewhere in Hebei (apart from Baoding), the great majority of local cadres were still basically supporters of the Cultural Revolution and watchmen for the Gang of Four. Throughout Yanshan county, the great majority of secretaries and other office-holders in the twenty-three communes were of this kind of thinking. Nor is this strange, it is pointed out; for many years these people's lives have been conditioned by routine reactions in the name of politics. It is for the higher authorities to put real energy into re-educating people of this sort – but this had not yet been done (Lu Xiaoping and Xie Shiyan).

The problem of high-output-poor units received extended treatment at county level in the *People's Daily* in November 1980, in a discussion which looked back explicitly to the Nanzhuang melon incident and which was evidently intended to be authoritative, at least for the time being. It relates specifically to Zhengding, the county of Nanzhuang (Hou Zhiyi and Zhao Deyun).

Zhengding itself has been a high-output-poor county. Zhengding provided an average of about 30,000 tons of grain to the state annually in the eight years from 1971 to 1978, but apart from 1974, average incomes remained below 80 *yuan*, and local grain supplies were always below 400 *jin* per person per year in practice. After 1974, the year when grain output per *mou* in Zhengding rose above 1,000 *jin* (a very creditable figure in the north China plain), net incomes fell steadily. In some units, cash incomes even fell below the value of food supplies. Cotton had formerly been important in Zhengding, but in the 1970s it was progressively squeezed out by the steadily increasing demands of the state, through the planning system, for grain. Other cash crops, especially peanuts, shared the same fate. Grain outputs rose, but costs rose much more and net incomes fell disastrously – by 5 million *yuan* for the county between 1975 and 1978, or by an average figure of 12.5 *yuan* per rural person, apparently about one-half of total cash incomes. Some illustrative figures are given in Table 6.1. These show the drastic rise in costs in the 1970s accompanied by an equally drastic fall in net outputs.

More detailed figures of the kind given in Table 6.1 are still scarce, but some have also been published for a county in Beijing municipality, Tong county. They tell much the same story, and are shown in Table 6.2. This table suggests interpretations which are now familiar. It may be summarised by the last two index figures given for 1979 upon 1970 – for costs, 208; for incomes, 136. Here (cf. Table 2.1) the technical inputs to agriculture such as fertiliser increased physically by factors of the order of three, and costs of physical inputs have also increased, though not by so much. At the same time, values of output increased by much less than costs. Since production teams are responsible for their losses in production, teams and team members naturally become anxious at trends of the kind revealed here.

Roads to prosperity

In terms of their origins high-output poverty and low-output poverty are two different things, but from the point of view of proposing policies which might be used to generate prosperity, they do not greatly differ. High-output units may be supposed to start with the advantage of business-like leadership and a well-motivated labour force, though even this cannot be taken entirely for granted. In practice experiences from both starting-points are quite varied and not always consistent, and of course many local histories are true to life in the intervention of unexpected constraints and opportunities. A series of reported cases will serve to illustrate various types of experience. They may be grouped under headings representing six types of policy – intensification, land reconstruction, improved terms of

Table 6.1. Zhengding county, Hebei – costs and outputs in 1970–78 (averages per *mou*)

	1972	1973	1974	1977	1978
Costs as % of gross outputs	36		41		53
	1970–73				
Net outputs *yuan*	64		—	27	27

Source: Hou Zhiyi and Zhao Deyun.

Table 6.2. Tong county, Beijing – costs and outputs in agriculture, 1970–79

	1970	1971	1979	Index of 1979 on 1970 or 1971
Total grain output (million *jin*)	—	365	467	128
Grain yield in *jin* per *mou*	—	505	724	143
Tractors per thousand *mou*	—	34	104	305
Fertiliser (*jin* per *mou*)	—	71	218	307
Electricity used in agriculture (kWh per *mou*)	—	30	2	303
Costs per *mou* of arable (*yuan*)	26.2	—	80.4	307
Costs per *jin* of grain (*yuan*)	0.06	—	0.08	156
Costs as % of gross income	34	—	52	153
Total farm costs	Not stated	—	Not stated	208
Total farm incomes	Not stated	—	Not stated	136

Source: Zhang Zhongwei and Liu Delun: 13.

trade, social reorganisation, diversification and industrialisation. Needless to say, these headings are in varying degrees overlapping, and should certainly not be regarded as mutually exclusive.

Intensification

The material on intensification does not all point in the same direction. At one level, the failure of technically successful intensification to produce prosperity on the ground – because of high costs or low prices or both – is the high-output-poor syndrome itself. Outputs are high but so are costs, with a tendency, as higher levels of both are reached, for costs to rise further and faster than outputs. Where the system requires local units to be responsible for their own subsistence and solvency, common prudence suggests caution in such conditions as these. Nevertheless, not all writers agree that costs must necessarily rise so disastrously. Yanshi county, Henan, is a case in point (Chen Kang). Yanshi lies in an area in north-western Henan (including Wen, Changge, Boai and Qiyang counties) where many units are now producing very good yields of winter wheat, in the 500–600 *jin* range. These high outputs depend on plentiful watering, heavy applications of fertiliser and high plant densities. At Yotan brigade in Yanshi, and elsewhere, it is argued that even higher yields (up to 950 *jin*) can be had, with more rational and exact regulation of inputs, and that costs can be brought down substantially – from 0.05 or 0.06 *yuan* per *jin* to 0.02, not including labour. It is also pointed out that pig manure is useful in reducing costs. Pigs now number between one and two per person in these counties, and natural fertiliser is available at the rate of 10,000–15,000 *jin* per *mou*, at a cost (not mentioned) in labour, and no doubt in motivation as well.

A similar case is argued for a brigade called Dongmagai, a Muslim village in Heze county, south-west Shandong. Here grain yields rose about 500 *jin* per *mou* in the 1970s, but costs were also high – as high as 0.11 *yuan* per *jin*. In 1978 a cattle enterprise was started which had 422 head in 1979 (280 head belonging to commune households; only 142 head belonging to the brigade collectively). As a direct result (it is argued) fertiliser has become plentiful, wheat yield per *mou* has risen to 660 *jin* and costs for growing grain have fallen to 0.045 *yuan* per *jin*. In addition, there are valuable sales of cattle, and a tanning business has been started (*People's Daily*, 11 Aug. 1979).

Technically, this experience at Dongmagai is close to Maoist ideals of arable intensification, but it depends (according to the account published) upon a condition which would have been anathema to the Maoists – the maintenance of animal herds which are preponderantly private in ownership. We are not told how the animals are fed; and this may very well depend upon another condition disliked by the Maoists – the diversion of land away from the collective arable. It may well be more realistic to think of Dongmagai as a case of diversification.

Full mechanisation on the land is the final goal to which notions of intensification lead, both in Mao's time and since. Mechanisation is expensive, however – according to one calculation, its capital cost must be reckoned at around 200 *yuan* per *mou* against present potential capital accumulation from the same land of around 5 or 6 *yuan* per *mou* (Huang Youjun). Obviously no such land will ever pay for its own mechanisation; realistically it is only units which have profit-making enterprises (so precariously tolerated under the Maoists) or other sources of income such as cotton sales to the state, which can afford to adopt the rural mechanisation policies favoured by Mao himself. It is obviously important in consideration of Maoist policies of land reconstruction and mechanisation, that these policies cost money at the same time as the Maoist planning system insisted that the land so improved or mechanised should be devoted to the production of grain at rock-bottom prices.

These points may be illustrated from the case of Luancheng county, which is the mechanisation model most used for the north China plain. Luancheng lies in central Hebei very close to Shijiazhuang. The county has 240,000 rural people and 118,000 rural workers, and 448,000 *mou* of collective arable which indicates 1.7 *mou* per person and 3.8 *mou* (0.25 ha) per worker. Most of the land is sown to grain (67%), and most of the rest to cotton (29%). In addition to electrical power, farm machinery is available in Luancheng to the extent of 0.2 hp per *mou* or 7.5 hp per ha – more than double the average degree of mechanisation in China (Yan Ruizhen and Liu Tianfu: 19, 21). Investment in mechanisation amounts to around 42 *yuan* per *mou* or 630 *yuan* per ha, and of this the state contributed about 6%, the communes, (including commune enterprises) about 5%, the brigades 19% and the production teams 70% (Tan Keliang and Tao Yuerui: 69, 70) – it is not explained how this was managed in the two latter cases. Costs, for instance of diesel fuel, are high. Pesticide and fertiliser use are high. Outputs apart from the arable are minute.

Unfortunately, the Luancheng case does not represent mechanisation as successful in reducing costs effectively. 'Because the prices of farm products are low, and costs high, commune members' income cannot be raised.' The average income was 83 *yuan* in 1971; 80 *yuan* in 1977. 'When farm prices were raised (in 1979), commune members enjoyed relatively large income increases.' (Tan Keliang and Tao Yuerui, 71) These authors go on to add that further finance may be hoped for from commune and brigade enterprise, 'whose prices are high and costs low'. It is agreed that where outputs are around 2,400 *jin* of grain per worker, accumulation rates can only be around 12 *yuan* per person or 7 *yuan* per *mou* per year, and progress cannot be rapid (Yan Ruizhen and Liu Tianfu, 20). Some of these relationships are made clear in Table 6.3.

Table 6.3. Luancheng county – costs and outputs in farming, 1965 and 1979

	Grain output per mou (jin)	Arable costs per mou (yuan)	Grain output per yuan of costs (jin)
1965	406	15.3	17.4
1979	1010	45.2	15.9

Source: He Guiting and Xu Xin: 16.

These figures indicate an impressive rise in grain yields, but also show at what cost it has been achieved. Grain output per unit of costs has actually fallen. On this showing, heavy expenditure on farm machinery has done very little to benefit Luancheng people; rather more to benefit the machinery manufacturers and the state. It is argued that mechanisation has particular relevance where workers are scarce and land plentiful, from the standpoint of the provision of grain to the state, and to save time especially where double cropping is practised – but as the case of Yushu in Jilin will show, even in such cases additional costs may be very high in relation to the value of additional output.

Qiliying – the Maoist model

The Maoist approach to the problems of the north China plain was essentially the approach through intensification – the improvement of the grain and cotton economy, especially in terms of yields per unit area, to the point where physical plenty could at last emerge – and if physical plenty did not produce much sense of prosperity, that was not a point which attracted much discussion under the Maoists. One of the best Maoist models

of rural development was Qiliying (Chiliying) commune, located in typical north China plain country in Xinxiang county, northern Henan, for which a book in English was produced (Chu Li and Tieh Chieh-yun). Qiliying, and more particularly Liuzhuang (Liuchuang), a village and brigade belonging to it, have also appeared from time to time in the Chinese press since Mao's death.

Qiliying is also of particular interest because the materials which exist are sufficient to construct a detailed topographical map of the commune. In this map (Fig. 6.4) detail taken from a recent sketch-map has been added to a pre-Liberation topographical map. The main feature of physical continuity in the two versions is the villages, all of which (apart from a few small ones situated on the boundaries) have become seats of the new brigades – and at the same time no brigades have been set up except at the old villages. Obviously in Qiliying the brigades, not the teams, represent the natural villages. The principal feature of change is of even greater importance – the three irrigation canals, branches of the People's Victory Canal which forms most of the north-western boundary of the commune, and which was built in 1951–52 along an old river-course to bring water for irrigation from the Yellow River to Xinxiang and other neighbouring counties.

Qiliying's economy belongs to the grain and cotton system which is typical of the plain. It is not claimed – and it is evidently not the case – that the arable economy has been radically changed since 1949 or 1958. But the traditional economy has been refashioned in a new mould. Irrigation water is now available to 90% of the arable, and over 90% of the land is 'worked' by tractors. (Chu Li and Tieh Chieh-yun: 17). Qiliying has been self-sufficient in food since 1965, and since that time has supplied grain as well as cotton to the state. This has been possible partly because of increased yields per unit area (from 167 *jin* of wheat and 62 *jin* of cotton per *mou* in 1967 to 1,100 *jin* of wheat and 155 *jin* of cotton in 1973); partly because of increased allocations of land for grain. Wheat, the principal grain crop, is still usually a winter crop, and cotton a summer crop; nevertheless, genuine double cropping with wheat and cotton in these latitudes is still not a practical possibility. Intercropping is the best that can be managed, together with possible catch crops (where fertiliser and labour are sufficient)

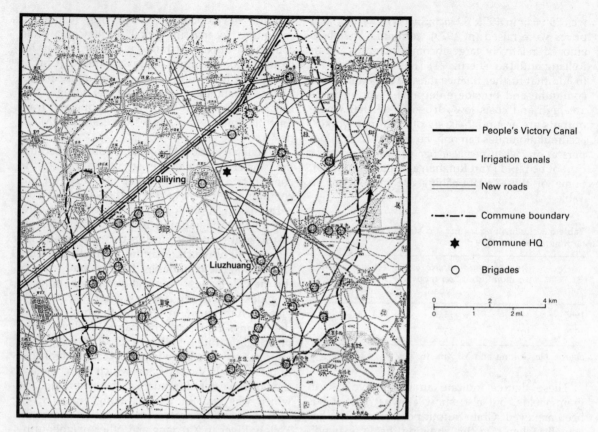

Fig. 6.4. Qiliying commune. In this map the detail shown in a recent sketch-map of Qiliying commune (Chu Li and Tieh Chieh-yun frontispiece) has been superimposed upon parts of a group of four pre-Liberation Japanese topographical maps of the same area. The original topographical maps were on the scale of 1/50,000. They show spot-heights numbered in Chinese or Japanese feet (very close in length to English feet, about 30 cm) to one place of decimals; villages; roads and footpaths; some earthworks; patches of wood and wasteland; and in two of the four sections a dot symbol indicating cultivated land. The detail from the recent map is that shown in the key.

on otherwise vacant land. Summer maize is one such crop reported in Maoist times, and there were probably others, such as potatoes.

Some aspects of the Maoist accounts of Qiliying in 1974 impress the reader more than others. Rises in yields are obviously impressive; but diversity on the land is still very limited, animals are still few, fertiliser makes only token appearances, and production other than directly from the land is quite scanty. Self-sufficiency conjoined with contributions to the state are the watchwords on the production side, and 'big and public' on the organisation side – accounting is at brigade level, and there is no sign of private plots. Nor is any indication given of income levels or consumption apart from grain. In the account of 1974, Liuzhuang attracted praise as a distinguished

producer of cotton and grain (with about one-quarter of its arable intercropped); as a place where subsidiary farm production was being successfully promoted (livestock including cattle and pigs, bees and poultry, together with household crafts such as dressmaking); and for its high level of farm mechanisation.

Since Mao's time, articles have continued to appear in praise of Xinxiang and Qiliying, but Liuzhuang brigade has attracted most attention. There are two kinds of divergence from the Maoist version of Liuzhuang – fresh developments since the middle 1970s, and reconsideration and revised reporting of the Maoist experience (*People's Daily*, 24 Jan. 1982; 21 March 1980).

Liuzhuang in 1981 has 207 households, against the 187 of 1973. Arable land is constant at 1,900 *mou*. Grain and cotton still dominate land use – 800 *mou* of wheat in winter, 1,000 *mou* of cotton in summer, plus 800 *mou* of summer crops other than cotton. Around 100 *mou* of land is used for fruit and vegetables. Intercropping is no longer reported. Instead, local industry has performed a sudden leap – there are ten factories and workshops, including paper, bricks and water-ices, as well as flour-milling and repair of farm tools. There are still about 200 animals. The pig population has fallen by more than half, but there are now more milk, cattle and goats. Building of new houses continues to be reported. Yields of grain and cotton rose again in 1981, to 1,700 *jin* and 175 *jin* per *mou*, after remaining around 1,600 *jin* and 150 *jin* respectively for six consecutive years – already high figures. Labour productivity on the land appears to have risen sharply. There are now said to be some 600 workers in Liuzhuang, against 800 in 1973, and now only one-third of this reduced total are occupied in field agriculture; the rest work in sideline production, industry and construction. No comparable figure is given for people working outside field agriculture in 1973, but there is every indication that they could not have been numerous – nor that industry and sidelines could contribute any figure remotely approaching 81% of all brigade income, as they did in 1981. The indications are that while maintaining basic farm production, self-sufficiency in food and standard contributions to the state, Liuzhuang has taken under employed labour (or labour formerly employed in interplanting) out of agriculture and found much more profitable opportunities for it, in the industries which have been mentioned. Brigade income from arable farming has fallen to only 19% of the total.

After Liberation, it is said, the Liuzhuang community occupied five years in reconstruction, ten years in raising farm yields and ten years achieving high and stable yields; now it is time to look ahead towards industry and subsidiary outputs, and the creation of a varied and integrated local economy (Feng Mingxin et al.). The land was physically reconstructed in 1964. At that time the seventy original irregular and uneven plots were rebuilt as four great irrigable fields (*People's Daily*, 21 Mar. 1980). At present, the farm-work is still considered hard, especially in the summer, but the social and physical conditions of life are quite good. Average total income is 600 *yuan* per worker per annum, representing 3.6 *yuan* for the working day. Total income per household was around 3,560 *yuan* in 1981, and cash income per household was 3,188 *yuan*, an increase of 31% over the previous year. Bulk food supplies are of course plentiful; but in addition Liuzhuang people are now eating 35 *jin* of meat per year, the same of eggs, 8 *jin* of sugar and so forth (*People's Daily*, 24 Jan. 1982). In 1979 such items as meat, bean-flour noodles and bean curd were represented as holiday fare. In 1979, it was reported that water-ices, melons and milk were available free or at low prices, and social benefits apparently free of charge included drinking water, domestic electricity, firewood, houses, clinic treatment, hot baths, films, burials and the kindergarten (Feng Mingxin et al.). Most of these amenities are not mentioned in 1982 (perhaps they are taken for granted; perhaps they represented an earlier, more consciously socialist phase); instead, new houses, television sets, radios, electric fans, record-players, bicycles and watches are reported (*People's Daily*, 24 Jan. 1982).

Even through the Cultural Revolution, it is now said, the leadership and people at Liuzhuang kept their heads and continued to reckon that the purpose of the revolution was to make the people prosperous, not to make them poor. Nevertheless, it is reported, net income fell between 1960 and 1969, because costs rose while gross income did not (*People's Daily*, 21 Mar. 1980).

How was Liuzhuang brigade (and to a lesser extent Qiliying commune) able to use intensification to become prosperous under the Maoists, when other units similarly placed environmentally such as Gaocheng found that prosperity continued to elude them year by year? Three possible lines of explanation arise. One is the fact that in Liuzhuang and Qiliying cotton cultivation continued at a healthy level throughout, bringing in a cash income from the state; the second, no doubt connected, is that grain production continued in the form of winter wheat, not summer maize; and the third is that what may have been possible for a brigade such as Liuzhuang, perhaps privileged in various ways, could hardly be possible for a county such as Gaocheng.. No claims resembling those for Qiliying or Liuzhuang were made for Xinxiang county as a whole.

Land reconstruction

During the two centuries before 1949, the human

population of the north China plain grew from a total of the order of 70 millions to one of 160 millions; but proportionate expansion of the farm economy and particularly of the rural environments did not take place. There was consequently room to expect that intelligent programmes of physical betterment of local land resources would produce significant improvements. The self-evident need for major works on the Yellow River and other natural drainage systems suggested the relevance of related minor schemes. The existence of important stretches of land encumbered by gravel- or sand-beds deposited by ancient floods or in former river-beds and the great extent of naturally alkaline surface soils argued in the same way. Land reconstruction (usually called 'fundamental rural construction') was a key element in most Maoist programmes for development. Land reconstruction also appealed to the Maoists from a social self-reliance point of view, as much of the Dazhai literature shows.

But it is one of the marks of the north China plain, that in spite of old-fashioned farm conditions which might be thought to invite physical reconstruction on the land as well as reorganisation of other aspects of the production system, nevertheless the plain does not occupy a prominent place in the literature on rural models of land construction. In a two-volume compilation of articles on this topic from Maoist times, containing thirty local models, none comes from the north China plain properly speaking, though there are a number from its peripheries (*Gaohao nongtian jiben jianshe*). Much the same may be said of the Dazhai literature – in spite of many points of relevance, little success in learning from Dazhai was reported from the heart of the plain. Apart from Qiliying, the models of development most used by the Maoists which came from Hebei, Henan and Shandong were all from the peripheries of the plain – Zunhua (Tsunhua) in the mountain periphery west of Beijing, Lin and Hui counties in mountainous north-west Henan and Yantai in peninsular Shandong.

This absence of genuine north China plain models of development is important, because it certainly indicates both paucity of development on the ground, and obstacles to the practice of development techniques which have not yet been overcome in this area. Most places in the north China plain lack resources other than farmland, and the farmland is already in use and does not offer easy or dramatic prospects for improvement.

Farmland improvement is necessarily limited because the land is flat, featureless and without fresh opportunities; water supplies are scanty but water logging and alkalinity are common dangers; improvement by mechanisation is expensive, and improvement by diversification was not, in Mao's time, a politically simple course of action. All in all, the Maoist literature in this field in the plain is not abundant or particularly impressive, and the post-Maoist literature is in places sharply critical.

In practice, in such areas as southern Hebei, western Shandong and eastern Henan, which are the heart of the plain, and apart from the major waterworks which have been discussed, success in land construction has lain mainly in improvements in water supplies based on both canals and wells, construction for irrigation and drainage, and some improvement of alkaline and gravel land. Something may be said about each of these topics in turn.

Water supplies and construction for irrigation

The north China plain is generally dry, and constructive enterprises naturally aim to improve water supplies. Sometimes, as with the People's Victory Canal which brings Yellow River water northwards into the Wei River in Hebei, providing irrigation water at Qiliying among other places, this appears to have been accomplished successfully on the medium scale. Elsewhere, similar works led to increases in water logging and progressive salination of the surface soil, as in Huimin prefecture in northern Shandong between 1957 and 1960. Nevertheless, solid progress has been made. In all three of Henan, Hebei and Shandong, irrigable areas have been raised to between 50% and 60% by 1978, from below 10% in 1949 and below 25% in 1957 (Geographical Research Institute: 79–80). In part this has been achieved by systems based on reservoirs and rivers or canals, in part upon well-sinking campaigns.

It is not surprising if success in such fields is sometimes less than complete. After 1978 a range of problems began to emerge. Details from Yishui county in southern Shandong show what these problems may amount to in practice (*People's Daily*, 26 Dec. 1979).

In Yishui, there have been various ambitious waterworks schemes since 1958, including 4 large or medium reservoirs and 149 others. Considerable progress has been made; 56,000 *mou* of land has been newly irrigated during the past twenty years, though this falls short of the area available for irrigation, about 1 million *mou*. Difficulties have taken various forms. One is that a great deal of construction work on the reservoirs remains unfinished, amounting to as much as one-third or more of the whole. Another is that many of the reservoirs are unsafe. Only 12 out of the 153 reservoirs of all kinds reach safety standards, and 75 are known to be faulty, including the 4 large and medium. A third problem is that the water distribution systems are incomplete and unsatisfactory – main channels without branches and branches without distributaries, so that the water cannot reach the fields. A fourth is that land construction has not always been adequate – where a field is not level, irrigation water does not reach the top, and may create a swamp at the bottom. A fifth problem is the poor quality of much of the engineering work, permitting extensive seepage from the dams and other kinds of water loss. Only about 20% of the water saved is actually available for use. As a result, charges for water are high. According to this analysis, proper finishing and management of the water schemes already undertaken could almost double the present irrigated area – though presumably the faulty reservoirs would still require remedial work. This kind of detailed local work has been neglected, however, because it is unambitious and unimpressive. Construction is admired; management neglected – 'horses but no saddles'. In 1979, all these problems were discussed at county level, and a start was to be made on tackling them.

There has also been sharp criticism of land construction methods and objectives from the southern end of the plain, in Anhui (Xu Zhongying). These criticisms relate to wells, to the reconstruction of whole landscapes on rectilinear lines, and to the reclamation of a lake.

On wells, it is argued that the state has pressurised local units in Anhui into building too many and too ambitious wells – a couple of pumping stations on the Wo River, it is argued, costing perhaps 500,000 *yuan*, would have done as much good as the 800 wells of the 1975–78 phase which cost in total about 1 million *yuan*, of which the state paid half. The officials insist upon wells like those of Hebei, 50 m deep, with motor-pumps, but wells in Anhui need be no more than 10 or 15 m deep. A shallow well is cheap and quick to build and can irrigate 20 *mou* of land – a realistic area where the ground surface is undulating.

On the reconstruction of whole landscapes, also in Anhui, criticism is sharper. Under the Gang of Four (no date is given), 5 million *yuan*, half of it local cash, half paid by the state, was spent, together with the labour of 30,000 people for three years, on diverting five rivers and constructing a rectilinear landscape – but in the end the new landscape, however impressive as a display of big square fields, was a failure, without satisfactory drainage or irrigation. Access from place to place was lost because of the new canals; and water and land are wasted because both roads and canals are too wide (Xu Zhongying). The geographical parameters of this particular affair are fairly clear – this part of Anhui has many small rivers flowing south-eastwards, across the grain of marked rectilinear land layouts, oriented north-south, inherited from historic land-allocation schemes. To reconstruct the rectilinear layouts on an ambitious scale must have been a tempting possibility to modern administrators.

One phase of Maoist land reconstruction policy for which nobody now has a good word to say is the reclamation of lakes. In Huoqiu county in western Anhui, Chengxi Lake was partly reclaimed, reducing its area by two-thirds and its capacity of 700 million cu m by nine-tenths. As a direct result, the lake could no longer accommodate the flood waters resulting from heavy rain, and flood danger in the whole area was sharply increased. (It is ironical that Chengxi is one of the lakes on the tributaries of the Huai, intended to help regulate the flow in times of flood.) In addition, fish and shellfish could no longer reach the lake to spawn, due to the sluice-gates, and fish output fell by nine-tenths. Aquatic vegetables such as lotus and water-chestnut were also lost. Previously as many as 1 million wild duck could be caught on the lake annually; now there are virtually none. Meanwhile, as much as one-third of the reclaimed fields are waterlogged and lying waste (Hou Xueyu 1981). Closely similar accounts are given of Baidang Lake in Congyang county in the same province, drained after 1958 (*People's Daily*, 10 June 1981), and of lakes drained in various southern provinces (*People's Daily*, 6 Aug. 1981). There are in addition signs of a contrary problem, where towards the southern edge of the plain in Anhui, many shallow valleys have been dammed to form local lakes which are presumably useful in water control but which in most cases must have drowned farmland, contributing no doubt to the aggregate loss of arable to which attention has been drawn.

Alkaline soil

In the field of land reconstruction in the north China plain, alkaline soil is a special problem. Around 50 million *mou* (3.3 million ha or 33,000 sq km) of land on the plain is affected by alkalinity – probably up to 10% of the total area. This land typically lies waste or, if cultivated, produces grain yields only of 100 or 200 *jin* per *mou* (*People's Daily*, 27 May 1980).

In broad terms, the causes of alkalinity are not at issue. Soils and soil materials virtually throughout the plain and further inland are alkaline; alkalinity represents deposits left on the surface by evaporation of water which is always alkaline. Water-tables are usually high, which means that alkali is difficult to wash out of the soil from the surface.

Methods of tackling alkalinity are in part physical, in part chemical. Physical methods include the traditional practice of gathering alkaline soil and surface deposits into mounds, and the deepening of ditches and rivers to lower local water-tables and so reduce seepage and improve drainage. Chemical methods include dressings of gypsum and animal manure. All these methods belong to standard practice, and were under discussion by scientists before Liberation (Thorp: 188; Russell: 764–9).

Progress appears to be patchy. Some places have claimed practical success – Guozhuang brigade in Xiao county in 1970 (Anhui province Revolutionary Committee et al.); Dongfeng brigade in Boye county in Hebei in 1973 (Baoding prefecture Revolutionary Committee et al.). Of these, the former used mainly physical methods, stripping off the worst-affected surface soil and replacing it by soil from hills and ditches; and building 'platform strip fields' by cutting fields into strips 20 m in breadth separated by ditches 1.5 m in depth. Here, rice cultivation, useful in helping to suppress alkalinity, was adopted in part; this too is an orthodox practice (Institute of Soil Science 1976: 256–9). Obviously the amount of work involved in this kind of operation is immense. The latter brigade used mainly animal manure with some deep ploughing – and almost

by accident found itself, even through the Cultural Revolution, with a strong animal-based economy, with feed-stuffs provided partly by direct cultivation, partly by grain wastes and sidelines, and partly by wild grass gathered in summer. Mengzhuang in Tungcheng (Xuzhou) county in Jiangsu, another brigade whose experience is quoted, lies in a former course of the Yellow River, with problems of waterlogging and sandy soils as well as alkalinity. Here drainage and irrigation ditches were dug, giving proper control of water, and green fertiliser was rotated with rice (Institute of Soil Science 1976: 259–60). It is revealing that these examples represent the experience of brigades – obviously they are small in scale, and surely local in significance. None of them is accompanied by parallel claims for much larger areas either locally or elsewhere; and none gives any suggestion of real breakthrough in this important field. The same goes for most recent discussion in the literature. Present policy looks for increased scientific understanding, especially of the behaviour of water in the soil. The claim of 1975 that half the alkali land in Shandong, Hebei and Henan had been de-alkalinised (Xinhua, 9 Sept. 1975), does not appear to have been repeated, but a recent writer (Zhang Tianzeng: 13) lays claim to 'change of condition' for about 12 million *mou* since Liberation, most of it in the 1960s.

Improved terms of trade

Any possibility of improvement based upon improved terms of trade with the state relates particularly to the high-output-poor units for whom these terms of trade are said to be critical. On this topic, it is difficult to gain any assurance that the full story can be elucidated, because this kind of material is reported in the press only very discontinuously. Examples show that lower costs and more predictable and rational business relationships, as well as higher prices, are involved in this field.

The central problem for high-output-poor units is the obligation (through the planning system) to allocate local resources to produce specified quantities of commodity food for delivery to the state at what are considered to be low prices. Hence either rises in price or relaxation of the system of obligation, or both, would represent improvement in the terms of trade. In 1979 and since, both have taken place.

On a local scale, an article about a brigade in Jin county close to Shijiazhuang, Dongzhaozhuang, gives an indication of the effects of the farm price rises late in 1979 (Wang Yunming et al.). Official prices for quota production of grain and cotton then rose by 20%; official prices for production above quota of cotton rose by 30%, and of grain by 50%. Prices for pork and eggs also rose. The effect in Dongzhaozhuang was to raise individual incomes in the brigade by an average of 25 *yuan* for the year. According to the argument now used, these price increases came none too soon. Jin county had been a specialist cotton county, but in recent years the people were very reluctant to grow cotton at all, fearing to make a loss. The situation in grain was little better. In 1971 the brigade delivered 162,000 *jin* of grain and 50,000 *jin* of cotton to the state. During the 1970s outputs and deliveries increased every year, but the value of the labour-day remained constant from 1971 to 1978 at approximately 0.55 *yuan* – in fact quite a good figure at that time, but not considered enough. Controlled prices of other outputs were also too low to create prosperity or to stimulate output. The price rises were a step in the right direction.

The relaxation of the system of obligation has taken the form of a package of interdependent policies – namely, the reduction of quotas, the toleration of production outside the plan, free marketing and the encouragement of subsidiary production whether at household level or collective level. All these measures operate in effect by enabling the state's terms for trade under quota to be improved upon by dealings outside the state quota system. Reduction of quotas both relaxes physical delivery obligations, and invites sales to the state at the higher prices paid (by arrangement) for supplies above quota. Production outside the plan and subsidiary production are both available for sale through the free market system, either at higher free prices or at least at prices which are directly negotiable.

A recent review of conditions at provincial level in Shandong gives a broad perspective on these changes (Shandong province, Commune Administration). Table 6.4 gives the relevant figures.

They show gross farm output by value rising by 185% between 1957 and 1977, but costs rising by 281% and total distribution by only 97%; given the effects of population growth in addition it is

Table 6.4. Outputs, costs and distribution in rural Shandong, 1957, 1977 and 1980

	1957		1977		1980	
	(million yuan)	(%)	(million yuan)	(%)	(million yuan)	(%)
Total farm output (gross)	3,109	100	8,875	100	12,149	100
Total farm costs	1,007	32	3,839	43	3,881	32
Total collective accumulation funds	186	6	1,041	12	1,223	10
Total distribution to commune members	1,916	62	3,781	43	6,833	56
Average total value of distribution to commune members (per person) yuan	51.9		57.6		105.2	

Source: Shandong province, Commune Administration: 13.

not surprising that distribution per person rose by only 11% in almost a generation. The figures for 1977–80, even allowing for inflation now given as 4.4% annually in rural areas (Xinhua, 19 Apr. 1981) indicate much more rapid increases in total output and total distribution, fall in costs back to the 32% of 1957, and distribution per person which has risen by 83% in three years. Particularly as relating to as large an area and population as those of rural Shandong, these figures are impressive.

In the interpretation of these figures by the Shandong authorities, a quite wide range of points is made. One is improved worker motivation, based on increased incomes and social reorganisation under the responsibility systems. A second is the restructuring of the cropping system. Cotton output in Shandong fell from 222,000 tons in 1956 to 149,000 tons in 1977, but in 1979 and 1980 (and subsequently), cotton outputs have increased greatly, to 167,000 tons in 1979 and 537,000 tons in 1980. The return to commodity cotton has transformed conditions in some units, as will be shown in Chapter 11. Outputs of peanuts have also risen substantially. These changes appear to represent changes within the state plan. In addition diversified production has increased, and in an advanced unit like Yantai prefecture (advanced under the Maoists as well as subsequently) now contributes 42% of all rural outputs (Shandong province, Commune Administration: 15). Farm costs have been reduced by improved management including the responsibility systems. Problems are recognised, both continuing and newly emerging – in 1980–81, more than 93,000 basic-level accounting units (brigades or teams), that is 24%, still distribute annual incomes of less than 50 *yuan*, and 14% of units still have no cash at all to distribute; 25% of units still distribute less than 300 *jin* of grain annually. Broadly, diversified production enterprises (woodlands, herding, subsidiary outputs of all kinds, including industry) are not performing well. Some units have allowed public accumulation and public social provision to fall back. Accounting problems are emerging in the wake of the responsibility systems (Shandong province, Commune Administration: 15–16). Of the points raised the most serious is probably that of food supply, particularly since average supply per person in the province is still only 360 *jin*, and that figure apparently depends to some extent upon state supplies. There is also probably room for uneasiness about over-dependence on cotton. In general, however, the marked improvement in incomes over the past few years appears to have been achieved surprisingly painlessly, and abundantly illustrates the benefits to be gained from simple relaxations of the planning and procurement systems, with their powerful hold on resource use.

Social reorganisation and family production

In the present context, social reorganisation since 1978 may be considered to have two sides – the responsibility systems (improving efficiency in collective production and freeing in part the peasant's working day) and household production from private plots and other family enterprises. In fact in media reports at village level, rather less is said about the beneficial effects of contract and responsibility systems upon local production than might be expected – as in Shandong, they are credited less with stimulating enterprise than with raising motivation and reducing costs. Reports from Jin county in Hebei, some 50 km east of Shijiazhuang, neighbour to both Gaocheng and Luancheng, give some useful insights (Wang Junwei et al.; Liu Ruilong).

Here what is praised is a contract system for grain and cotton, where after very unhappy experience of authoritarian behaviour and misuse of administrative powers by the state organs before 1976, the responsible authorities at county level sign individual contracts with production teams specifying guaranteed conditions for output, supplies to the state, supplies to the people, and the marketing of local produce (Liu Ruilong). The county contracts with each local unit for specified total output and specified supplies for the state, on the basis of a six-year average. If the state agencies subsequently reduce or increase demand, the rise or fall in demand is spread proportionately among local units; advantage and disadvantage are equitably shared. Commune members' own entitlement to cotton from the cotton harvest is guaranteed. Certain production factors are also guaranteed – fertiliser, pesticides and diesel fuel. In addition, the county purchasing agencies have agreed to market specialist outputs from the communes and brigades (Wang Junwei et al.).

It is claimed that after this group of systems was introduced in 1979 and 1980, by 1981 grain output increased by 19% and cotton by 126%; total farm income by 23%, distribution to commune members by 46% and contributions to the state by 84% – though these last three figures surely include the farm price rises of 1979 (Liu Ruilong).

The media report on these arrangements is very favourable, and where economic bullying and official exploitation have been familiar and bitterly resented experiences in the Maoist countrysides, it is not surprising if the peasants take what advantage they can get when times improve. Moreover, prices for quota outputs are still low. It is argued (Wang Junwei et al.) that where China still has no fundamental legal code on economic relationships, no machinery for the supervision of contracts, and so forth, and while price relationships between industry and agriculture are still not realistic, local contracts are a useful way to get production moving and to encourage the proper fulfilment of the state plans. But some of these arguments bode ill for the future. If the stage agencies are involved in contractual deals which provide local privileges and immunities in return for guaranteed supplies pressure is bound to mount later for these privileges and immunities to be extended to other suppliers, to the disadvantage of the state purchasers and with the risk of bringing down the whole system.

One interesting and perhaps surprising feature of this account is the limitation of these optimistic claims in Jin to the effects of the contract systems – no additional claims are made for diversification or even family production. Hence the scheme relates directly to the state plan and to the relief of the high-output-poor syndrome. It is therefore no accident that if we try to look beyond present achievement in a scheme of this kind, we will find that future improvement must depend on improved terms of trade once again, whether with the state (mainly) or with private customers. Surplus labour problems may also be expected to emerge in this kind of case, but are not specifically mentioned in Jin county.

The development of family production appears increasingly to be regarded as the foundation of diversification in the plain – a view which must be favourable to family production but must limit the prospective scope of diversification, and must be ominous for the future of the collective economy. Three communes in Qi county, also in the heart of the plain in north-eastern Henan, have a total of 334 joint-household enterprises involving 1771 households, 6.6% of all households (Ma Renping 1981a). The list of twenty-one kinds of enterprise is revealing. Table 6.5 gives a summary. Two-fifths of the enterprises are concerned with processing of local produce – grain, cotton, oilseeds. Another two-fifths represent the building boom. Services, especially production and convenience services such as blacksmiths and repairers, are very few – most of those called 'services' are apparently in effect shops. In this list, it is local services which must

Table 6.5. Joint-household enterprises in three communes in Qi county, 1981

	Enterprises	Households
Processing rural produce (oil, grain, feed mills; cotton ginning)	135	460
Bricks and building	130	968
Services – blacksmiths, shops, hand porters	35	91
Woodwork, paper manufacture, weaving	26	192
Greenhouses	8	60

Source: Ma Renping 1981a: 4–5.

be most capable of rapid and socially valuable increase. But genuine production diversification is represented in this list only by the paper and wood enterprises, the weavers and the greenhouses – this last is also a small group, and one which no doubt includes a service element, for instance in producing seedlings. No doubt the scarcity of materials in this arable countryside is partly to blame for limited diversification.

Private plots worked by individual peasant families are obviously a different matter from joint-household enterprises. Material on private plot economies is scarce, perhaps because of the diffuse character of this kind of production, perhaps because given low media prominence for political or administrative reasons. In Qing county south-west of Tianjin, in a brigade called Wuxinzhuang, a private plot amounts to 1.47 *mou* (980 sq m), and bears three main crops successively (garlic, tobacco, Chinese cabbage), interplanted with maize, potatoes and tree seedlings (Lu Weiyang et al.). This list suggests a mixture of production for local markets with subsistence, and appears to be representative. Income from this particular plot does not fall below 1,000 *yuan* per year and may reach 2,600 *yuan* – a very good figure by comparison with incomes from the collective (including subsistence) of the order of 600 or 800 *yuan* per household. Qing is exceptionally well situated, only 30 km from Cangzhou city and on main road and rail routes.

Diversification

Diversification is the road to prosperity which offers most promise to the hard-pressed grain-producing county, especially in the long run. Its record in practice, however, at least to judge from reports in the media, rather falls behind its promise. Technically, the simplest method of diversification is to broaden the arable crop base. In Julu county in southern Hebei, also in the heart of the plain, the grain crops are being confined to the best land, and sandy and alkaline land turned over to peanuts, cotton and rapeseed. At the same time, strips of land alongside watercourses and some of the maize and potato land are being turned over to green beans, cowpeas and sesame. The grainland has been reduced by 20,000 *mou*, but grain output has risen by 35%, in addition to important outputs of peanuts, sesame oil, cotton and rapeseed. Meanwhile, the local 'free' price of grain has fallen, but the official price rises of late 1979 have resulted in significant improvements in local incomes, according to this account. So of course have sales of the new crops such as beans and sesame oil.

Some additional detail about Julu also emerges. The county's 'grainland' is planted to the extent of one-quarter with sweet potatoes, which yield heavily and produce 40% of basic food output. The state will not accept more than 20% of the grain quota in the form of sweet potato. Dried sweet potato is consequently rather too common a food in Julu, and the people have been looking for a change, particularly in the new phase of prosperity and more varied diets. The county secretary visited various potential outlets for the surplus sweet potatoes; finally a price was negotiated with the state grain purchasing corporation. At the same time, the same corporation agreed to support the establishment of potato flour noodle factories at team level, and a contract was signed for future purchases of noodles (*People's Daily*, 27 Jan. 1980).

In many communes and brigades a range of more varied kinds of production came under discussion in 1980, and some of these appear to have been put into operation successfully. In fact these outputs are welcomed for their contributions to the people's living standards, often in very humble terms – millet porridge is now once more to be had; so is beancurd, especially at holiday times; and bean-flour noodles, various kinds of buns, and food flavourings such as garlic and chillis have all reappeared. In part, however, these outputs also contribute to cash incomes, through rural free markets or direct contracts with urban restaurants or canteens. Wangfang commune in Shan county, in extreme western Shandong, is a good example. Wangfang was a notoriously backward commune, but from 1979 onwards has started mulberry and silkworms, reeds, edible chrysanthemum, melons, rapeseed and alfalfa, together with goats and rabbits – in all eighteen types of subsidiary production. Grain production increased by 40%, and income from miscellaneous outputs doubled apparently within a year. Another commune in the same county is now growing peanuts, sesame seeds, millet, buckwheat and beans, garlic, gourds and various kinds of melon. Riverside 'beach' land growing melons can produce a cash income of 200 *yuan* per *mou* in this area. This kind of land is of course not suited to grain, but in the same commune good grainland produces incomes of less than 200 *yuan* per *mou* (*People's Daily*, 1 Feb. 1980).

Some units have based diversification upon woodland. Juancheng county in south-western Shandong reports valuable plantations of trees on sandy and gravelly land, started soon after Liberation and distinguished by clear decisions about ownership taken early in the 1960s – at Juancheng, trees belong to those who planted them, including family ownership of trees planted before and behind family houses. During the Cultural Revolution various efforts were made to get this system overturned, but thanks partly to deeds of possession issued earlier, the system was never changed. Now there are on average seventy trees per person in the county, and 36% of miscellaneous income comes from the trees (*People's Daily*, 19 Mar. 1980).

At Yanling county in Henan, south of Kaifeng, diversification based on woodland is enthusiastically reported (Yang Hengshan and Zhao Guoxin). The planting policy was adopted in 1963, and included roadsides, the edges of watercourses, the gravelly former bed of the Yellow River, shelter-belts between fields, and plantations – in all 17% of the total area of the county now bears trees. Timber is now plentiful – for building, local workshop use and sale. Animal feed supplies have improved, firewood is plentiful (300 million *jin* per year) and charcoal worth 1.6 million *yuan* is supplied to the state; fertiliser material (leaves and miscellaneous vegetation) is more plentiful; and of course money is being made. The woodlands now supply 19% of all rural incomes in Yanling. Here as elsewhere in recent years the trees are owned by those who planted them, with the implied condition that an authority such as the state may plant only on its own land, and with the explicit rider that trees planted by families in front of and behind their own houses belong to the families, not to the production team or brigade which actually owns the land.

Similarly, Weishi county, also in eastern Henan, has 90,000 *mou* of such plantations, all sources of useful income in the several communes where they are located. Most of these woods, which may represent about one-tenth of the total area of the county, appear to have been planted in the early years of the Cultural Revolution (*People's Daily*, 7 Feb. 1982).

Animal-rearing represents another standard route to diversification. A case from Xiao county in northern Anhui, very close to Xuzhou, depends upon goats. Previously (we are not told when) Xiao was a famous poor county, and the brigade under discussion, Wangtun, was also well known as a poor brigade – low-output-poor, it should be added. Of the arable, 80% was affected by alkalinity. The place was in debt, and depended upon state grain. There was talk of starting pigs, but no enthusiasm – how could pigs be fed when there was not even enough food for the people? Some people said, 'Pigs are for those who can afford them. Goats are cheaper. Goats eat grass, sweet potato foliage, tree leaves – things that are not too difficult to find.'

The goats were successful, but mainly on a family basis. A strong family of nine people keep a herd of about ten goats which provide income of 800 or 900 *yuan* per year; but even a weak family, where the man was going blind, was able to keep goats and do well. Goat-rearing has led to improvement of the arable by fertiliser application and also to pig- and cattle-rearing. A few per cent of the arable has been converted to alfalfa, peas and other fodder crops. Improved land and better motivation now produce increased grain supplies from a smaller grainland area (*People's Daily*, 13 June 1980).

A much more adventurous case, at county level, comes from Jinhu county, which lies between the Hongze and Gaoyou lakes in northern Jiangsu, at the southern end of the plain. In 1978 Jinhu already had a distinguished record of diversification (*People's Daily*, 22 Dec. 1978).

In 1977, Jinhu had 276,000 head of pigs, amounting to 4.5 head per household or 1 pig per person. There were also 1.2 million poultry, amounting to 19 birds per household, producing an average of 61 *jin* of eggs per household – seven times the average for the province. Average subsidiary income in 1978 was 92 *yuan* per household, cash. Grain yield was then 909 *jin* per *mou*; and the county's annual grain contribution to the state was 102 million *jin*, equivalent to the county's total output in 1965.

This state of affairs is of recent origin. In 1974, poultry-rearing was still held back by political pressures, though the same is not claimed of pigs. In 1975 the county was designated as a pig-rearing base and from then development was rapid. The county insists upon the interconnection between collective and private pig-rearing in the clearest and most explicit terms, and upon the rights of commune members to keep their own

pigs, provided, at least at the end of 1978, that fertiliser was supplied to the collective and pork to the state – 'this is socialism, not capitalism' (*People's Daily*, 22 Dec. 1978).

The poultry business is already highly organised, in part by the consumer organisations. The marketing units and restaurants supply young geese to local collective units who feed them to maturity. For chickens, in part the consumer units rear their own; in part they have them reared by collective units in the same way as geese. To provide all the needs of the county, however, 200,000 *jin* of eggs for hatching have to be bought from other counties each year. There were seventeen poultry-roasting units in the county in 1978 against only five in 1974; the rearing of young chicks for these units (which produce cooked meat for restaurants and for retail sale) is a profitable source of income for poor teams. Disease prevention, including inoculation where necessary, is provided for. Food for pigs and poultry includes grain allocated for the purpose and some which is grown specially. Households use bran from their own grain supplies, grain supplied in return for sales or in return for fertiliser supplies, feed-grain from land allocated for that purpose or grain grown on private plots. Land allocated for green fodder amounted to 8,000 *mou* for the county in 1978. Improvement in a case of this kind obviously represents not only the diversification now under discussion, but also improved terms of trade gained mainly by taking production and marketing out of the state system.

Also at county level, Ganyu county in northeast Jiangsu reports upon achievements using the simplest industrial raw materials – rice straw and dried sweet potato. Rice straw goes half to fuel, half to animal feed. Dried sweet potatoes support potato flour and noodle manufacture, and a wine which sells as far afield as Zhejiang. Refuse from the wine, flour and noodle factories goes to feed pigs. In addition, a wide range of subsidiary farm and hillside outputs is now being promoted, including mushrooms, fruit, mulberry for silk-worms, rabbits, goats, bamboo and bees. Attention is also being given to the increase of outputs from the sea, particularly the cultivation of seaweed and prawns (Jiangsu province, Commune and Brigade Enterprise Department Research Unit: 70). Ganyu also has milling of farm products and substantial business activity. Much less is said now than formerly about the difficulty of marketing varied outputs – in the case of fishponds, it is said that output and income were both greater in 1980 than the totals for the preceding twenty years. Responsibility systems are in use in subsidiary enterprises here, but at least in 1981–82 they were regarded not as joint household ventures so much as directly collective enterprises (Jiangsu province, Commune and Brigade Enterprise Department Research Unit: 72).

Water-bodies represent important diversification possibilities, sadly neglected in many places. Yutai county in south-western Shandong claims that the resources of Chaoyang and other lakes, important in traditional times, have been neglected under the Maoists because aquatic products implied trading, and trading was thought to lead back to capitalism (Duan Xinqiang and An Zizhen). People even on the islands were forced to grow grain, and had not even a boat. In the hill margins to the east of the lake, it was the same story – no woods, fruit or animals. Since Liberation, there has been land construction and water control in Yutai; former waterlogged land has been brought into production; grain yield has risen to 800 *jin* per *mou* (on the basis of double cropping with rice and wheat at least in part); and the county delivers over 100 million *jin* of grain annually to the state. But prosperity eludes them – they work hard but working capital is scarce, and they consider themselves a 'high-output-poor' county – this was in 1979. Diversification will be the next step, they hope, and for this they expect to turn to the lakes.

Some exceptionally interesting material relates to a brigade, Jiujie, situated in a small rural town, Xinjizhen, in Shulu county some 65 km east-south-east of Shijiazhuang in Hebei (*People's Daily*, 25 Aug. 1980). This brigade comprises 246 households, with 590 *mou* of arable land and 20 kinds of subsidiary enterprise, and in addition some commercial functions. This brigade has done well. Grain yield has been 1,500 *jin* per *mou* for several years, the local grain allowance is 500 *jin*, and average income per commune member was 230 *yuan* in 1979. In fact 58% of all household incomes rose above 1,000 *yuan* in 1977 when bonuses and incomes in kind are reckoned in.

Jiujie has only 0.54 *mou* (360 sq m) of arable land per person, and of this only 0.42 *mou* is available for food production; for reasons which are not stated but presumably indicate a state cotton quota (*People's Daily*, 11 June 1980).

A positive programme of diversification

through industry and various other enterprises was started in 1961, and as a result (it is not stated exactly how) Jiujie became self-sufficient in grain by 1965, having increased grain output by some 80,000 *jin* (apparently an increase of at least 700 *jin* per *mou*). After 1968, milk, poultry, pig and fur-marten enterprises were started at various junctures, plus a number of small engineering and metal workshops. The fur-marten enterprise is particularly profitable, and depends on a specific local advantage – a neighbouring slaughterhouse and cold store dealing with rabbits, which supplies the martens with food. Income from such enterprises has been of critical importance in supporting the arable economy of Jiujie, where there is now 0.8 hp of mechanical power per *mou* of land. Farm mechanisation has resulted in fairly fundamental changes here. Before the arable was mechanised, 76% of the 340-strong labour force was employed on the land, but in 1978 the figure was only 22%. It is argued that this is one genuine way forward in Chinese rural policy; the re-employment, in a diverse and industrious countryside, of the labour necessarily set free from farm-work by necessary mechanisation. But one clear implication of the present evidence is that each local community will have its own way to make; there is no high road to prosperity (*People's Daily*, 11 June 1980; 25 Aug. 1980).

Industrialisation

As various examples suggest, one implication of diversification policies is local industrialisation. It has already been argued that rural industry is the aristocrat of the commune production system. Industry in the Shanghai area may well take the form of work taken in by rural units as clients of urban factories – a kind of industrial organisation familiar from Hong Kong, Taiwan and Japan, and one which answers to important east Asian stereotypes. It may well be argued that 'client' industrialisation promises better, in north China plain conditions of resource and energy scarcity, than 'free-standing' industrialism. Truth to tell, up to the present examples of progress through industrialisation in the plain are still relatively few.

One case is a brigade called Xixuying in Loudi commune, Luancheng county, Hebei (*People's*

Daily, 11 June 1979). Xixuying was a high-output-poor brigade. In 1968 the No. 6 production team began taking in bleaching and dyeing work and making designers' blueprints (the reasons and conditions for these two decisions are not explained). Net income rose at once by 15,000 *yuan* per year, and it became possible to give support to agricultural production; grain yield passed 1,000 *jin* per *mou* in 1972. In the years which followed, this unit started other enterprises – flour-milling and a foundry; and other neighbouring production teams took up glass-making, dyeing and painting pictures (also unexplained). By 1978, grain yield at Xixuying was 1,200 *jin* per *mou*, grain allocation was 535 *jin* per person and distribution per person was worth 158 *yuan*.

A second, also reported with very little explanation, comes from Aiguo commune in Ju county, south-east Shandong. Here the original seven blacksmiths' and carpenters' workshops are now nine factories employing 670 workpeople; the commune can produce 'Taishan' 26 hp tractors, electric motors, transformers and other electrical machinery; and they have ambitious plans for further extension into farm machinery. Emphasis is laid, in the Maoist fashion, upon the support which industrialism can give to agriculture. Sandy areas have been reclaimed, and wells and other installations for water control built. In Aiguo brigade, grain yield has risen to 1,500 *jin* per *mou* and distribution to 160 *yuan* per person per year, four times that of 1970. Industry and subsidiary occupations now produce 58% of total income in Aiguo (*People's Daily*, 12 Jan. 1980).

A more developed group of examples comes, perhaps appropriately, from Xinxiang county in Henan, and refers specifically to Qiliying. The Xinxiang county committee has summed up the experience of Qiliying and Liuzhuang, we read, and recognises that comparatively rapid development of the collective economy cannot be had from grain monoculture and simple agriculture. The way forward is through diversification and rural industry. In Xinxiang in 1979, accordingly, there were already 625 such enterprises. This works out as three per brigade on average – a start no doubt but not yet an impressive ratio. A number of local examples are given. At Hehe commune, Tianxiaoguo brigade has started a small cotton-mill, using mainly the workers' concessionary cotton, and is both spinning and weaving. Incomes in the brigade have shot ahead (*People's Daily*, 30 Oct. 1979).

In the same report, Dakuai commune is represented as a well-known failure in the county up to around 1970. Chenbao brigade in this commune, with about 4,000 people and 6,000 *mou* of arable land, depended year by year on state grain. It received some help from the county and started workshops making paper, bricks and machinery (presumably repairs). This brigade is now well equipped, has abundant cash in reserve, supplies 1 million *jin* of grain annually to the state, and distributed 143 *yuan* per worker in cash in 1978. Of the 70 former backward brigades in Xinxiang county, 46 are said to have become advanced brigades (like Chenbao) by 1979, and 24 to have risen to average levels. We are not informed about any tendency to backsliding, or about the behaviour of the average.

In Xinxiang on average, cash incomes work out at 115 *yuan*, the highest county figure in Henan. According to the report of 1979, it was always clear to the Xinxiang authorities that the main purposes of the revolution were contributions to the state, accumulation in the collectives, and prosperity for the peasants – hence they did not accept the ideas of the Gang of Four. The views of the people are not discussed.

Industrial resources, in common with resources of most other kinds, are scarce in the north China plain. It is no doubt not accidental that when the criticism is raised of commune and brigade industry that it absorbs valuable resources in inefficient production, examples are found in the plain. Henan has more than 100 locally run cotton-spinning workshops of which this criticism is made (Li Anding); and there has been particular criticism of the free-for-all destructive exploitation of minerals in the same province. Here it is claimed that 300 separate units are exploiting bauxite, 160 of them illegally. Similar exploitation affects gold and other minerals (Yang Yusheng and Hao Jian).

All in all, claims which are made in the field of rural industrialisation in the plain, even those which are quite local, remain very modest; and there is continued stress on the inevitable problems. In Shandong in 1982, commune and brigade enterprises were worth only 67% more than in 1978 before the modernisation policy was started; and problems of poor communications, low technical levels, poor marketing prospects and broken contracts remained significant (FBIS *Daily Report*, 13 Oct. 1983, quoting a Jinan broadcast of 10 Oct. 1983).

The north China plain in retrospect

At the start of this chapter it was argued that the north China plain is the heart of Chinese poverty – some other places are poorer, but no other poor part of China is so large or so important. For this reason, prominence has been given to the models of development which are available, and particularly to those which belong to the heart of the plain, rather than to the peripheries, which both in Maoist times and at the present tend to have special advantages. Some of these models promise well; but in this area more than most, the status of models should be borne in mind – by definition they are exceptional places worthy of study, and where feasible, imitation. There is no evidence of any real development breakthrough up to the present in the north China plain. It is worth bearing in mind also that the kind of windfall gained in the north China plain in 1980 and to some extent since, as a result of increased cotton acreages and good cotton harvests conjoined with favourable state prices for cotton, can easily outclass most kinds of diversification in bringing money to the people, at least in the short term. In 1980 the country people had so much money to spend that demand for bicycles in Shandong alone (with the biggest cotton boom) exceeded by 1 million the available supplies, and for sewing machines, by 550,000 (*People's Daily*, 29 Jan. 1981). (Presumably some of this demand represented duplication.) For the same and other reasons, there is now a widespread building boom. Cash windfalls of any kind are obviously welcome in themselves, but they contribute little to the movement for diversification or intensification or any other kind of more effective resource use, or to the prosperity of the plain in the long run. Ultimately the creation of a growing prosperity which is fundamentally stable is the central problem for policy in the north China plain, and one of the central problems for China as a whole.

A good deal of stress was laid in the media discussions of 1979 and 1980, in the first enthusiasm of relatively unrestricted reporting, upon the high-output-poor syndrome in the plain, and upon the contribution of Maoist official management to it. Maoist prejudice against local marketing of rural surpluses certainly created much dissatisfaction, but it must be realised that the fundamentals of the high-output-poor condition are those of dense rural populations in any

community and at any level of technological sophistication – increasing rural demand (and labour supply, both arising from continuing population increase) leads to continuing intensification of the subsistence system; whether or not an imperial or a Maoist government also tightens the screw by demanding produce at low prices affects the level at which the system operates year by year, but not its principles. By the same token, the loosening of the official screw will lead to evident relaxation within the system, but it will not lead to fundamental change. Fundamental change can only come through widening of the effective resource base or reduction of the population or both. Reduction of the population may be possible in the long term through more effective birth control, but must be distant; migration on a requisite scale and within a matter of years or even decades would have to be to the northeast, and is not really conceivable. Widening of the effective resource base is the goal of the various 'roads to prosperity' which have been discussed. About these various possibilities, it is easier to be optimistic. A wide range of varied opportunities exists in these countrysides, in terms of fresh production for both subsistence and trade. Few of these would have implications beyond the local county, but few would need to have. Even fewer would make any big money; but this is not the practical function of local enterprise in the north China plain, any more than in rural Japan or rural France. But there appear to be three kinds of problem on the horizon in this field.

The first problem, paradoxically, relates to the existence of the opportunities and the capacity of the community, even when released from outside constraints, to make use of them. At first sight such a 'problem' may appear non-existent, but its existence is suggested partly by the rather slow progress in this field in the years since 1978, and partly in the ambitious scale of claims for potential in this field, as measured by historic standards. It is possible that to some extent, Maoist policy may be being used now to conceal other kinds of inadequacy such as technical ignorance or management indifference. One crude indication of a deep-seated problem in this field may well be found in Fig. 6.3 itself. It is noteworthy that in Hebei, for example, the great majority of the places discussed in this chapter, which by definition are those with noteworthy achievements or those whose problems reach public discussion, lie within 100 km of the provincial capital, Shijiazhuang. The counties named in Hebei and in the plain as a whole represent much less than 10% of the total. The isolation of the other 90% may conceal interesting developments, but it is more likely to conceal stagnation, inertia and elementary bureaucratic management in sadly backward communities. The second problem relates to the collective system. The problem for the collective system, if prosperity begins to develop through local enterprise, will be to maintain the capacity of the collective units to practise unified distribution – the capacity of these units to bring the expanded incomes of the enterprise workers and managers within the collective distribution system. When grain is relatively scarce, this is likely to present less formidable difficulties than when it is more plentiful, since the collective will normally control food distribution; but here and elsewhere the collective system must beware the encroachment of privileges, exemptions and straight corruptions in its relations with the growing enterprise system. Unfortunately, this is probably a counsel of perfection. The third problem relates to a group of important needs at local level which promises grave difficulty in finding satisfaction without proper programmes of development at levels probably involving commune and county together. They include continued investment in land reconstruction, especially tackling of the alkalinity problem, local communications, the besetting problem of energy supplies for industry and domestic use, and of course the commercial system.

Finally, there is little room for optimism about the north China plain. It can hardly survive at all unless it remains broadly self-sufficient in food, or nearly so; and at the same time it can expect no worthwhile progress without the creation of production and trading networks of greatly increased diversity and complexity. In short, further intensification will necessarily have to be accompanied by widespread diversification; and the community will have to run quite hard in order to stand still.

'Fish and rice country'

Throughout the long history of northern Chinese penetration of the south and the growth of the southern regional economies, the area at the mouth of the Yangzi has been one of the most distinguished. It was called 'Jiangnan', 'south of the river', a name which means the southern parts of Anhui and Jiangsu together with northern Zhejiang, and which still has a connotation of prosperity in relaxed and rewarding environments – 'fish and rice country', as another traditional phrase has it. This has been for eight centuries or more one of the most advanced and most metropolitan areas in China, and it continues to be so. Partly for this reason no doubt, some of the information which is available for this area is exceptionally full and revealing.

This is true particularly of southern Jiangsu and Shanghai. Shanghai was formerly part of Jiangsu, but in the reorganisation of 1958 was erected (in common with Beijing and Tianjin) into a municipality covering a very large area, about 5,600 sq km in the case of Shanghai, much of it rural, and with the rank of a province. Shanghai has ten counties, of which Shanghai county itself is one. This chapter relates mainly to the ten counties of Shanghai and the eight counties of neighbouring Suzhou prefecture, the adjoining part of Jiangsu province. Taken together, Shanghai and Suzhou occupy the area between the Qiantang estuary, Lake Tai and the Yangzi estuary, which is beyond question the most advanced large area in rural China.

In view of its history and strong resource base, it is not surprising that rural population densities in this area are generally very high. Standard rural population densities (including the populations of local small towns) are of the order of one person per *mou* of arable (15 persons per ha, 1,500 persons per sq km of arable), but they vary by at least 50% on the county scale in Shanghai itself – from 1.3 *mou* per person in Jinshan county to 0.7 *mou* in Shanghai county. On the local scale, variations are of course still more marked. These populations must be at least 50% more densely settled than in 1949, given the known rates of population increase; and some are likely to have doubled. Under the Maoists these dense populations were not featured as problematical, and some forms of development, such as triple cropping which was brought in at that time, actually require abundant supplies of rural labour. In the present phase it is recognised that in these conditions some rural labour may well be surplus to the needs of the economy in its present form, but this is considered a reason for fresh stimulation of enterprise. Broadly, it does not appear that incomes are lowest where rural populations are most dense – rather the reverse.

Physical environments in the Shanghai–Suzhou area are good. The summers are subtropical, and may be reckoned to extend from May to October. The winters are short and (with January mean daily temperature minimum at Shanghai of 1 °C) not very cold; the frost-free period ranges from 240 days at Shanghai to 220 days further inland. Precipitation is about 1,100 mm, falling mainly in June–September but with a useful spring fall.

Topography is flat; creeks, rivers and canals ubiquitous. To the east of Lake Tai lies a large area of interconnected lakes scattered with islands and interdigitated with peninsulas and necks of land. Soils are of two kinds – on the Yangzi and sea margins, deep soils of sand or silt origins, generally permeable, and of less value for paddy; elsewhere, also deep soils, but muddy, water-retentive, suited to paddy and developed as paddy soils through generations of use.

The basic land use of the area predictably reflects these conditions (Fig. 7.1), together with the presence of Shanghai city with its demand for vegetables.

Rice and cotton are the principal summer crops, separated according to soil types as indicated. Either is usually rotated with a winter

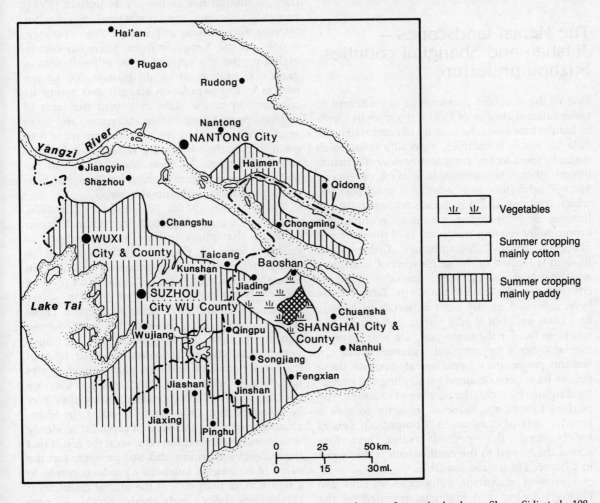

Fig. 7.1. Land use and place-names in Shanghai city and Suzhou prefecture. *Source*: for land use, Shang Sidi et al.: 108.

103

grain, oilseed or green fertiliser crop. In addition, as will be shown, the rice areas made important innovations in triple cropping in the 1970s, though these were and are controversial. Physically, very high levels of output per unit area can be obtained in this area – locally, as high as 1,100 *jin* per *mou* for early rice, 1,000 *jin* for late rice and 800 *jin* for winter wheat or barley – and for the three crops, 2,400 *jin* or more in the year, or 18 tons per ha (Shanghai Farm Science Institute: 66). This would involve a double-cropping index of about 260. In spite of its dense population, Suzhou is an important supplier to the state. In 1974 this prefecture supplied surplus grain sufficient to feed 5 million people, together with other important outputs.

The Maoist landscapes – Jinshan and Shanghai counties; Suzhou prefecture

One of the standard problems in any attempt to make rational studies of local economics in China in Maoist times was the scarcity of comprehensive data for whole economies, especially data which could be used in any comparative way. Particular interest therefore attaches to a book of essays, *Manage agriculture well; establish Dazhai counties*, which contains useful materials on agriculture in Jinshan and Shanghai counties in Shanghai municipality relating mainly to 1974 (Jinshan and Shanghai county Revolutionary Committees). Jinshan is located in the south-west of Shanghai, and Shanghai county, which includes Shanghai city, lies near the coast to the north. Table 7.1 has been compiled mainly from materials in *Manage agriculture well*, but in addition output details, less complete but for the same year, are also given in the table for a hypothetical 'average' county in Suzhou prefecture – hypothetical, because these figures have been obtained by dividing the prefectural figures by eight, the number of counties. The Suzhou figures are included in order to give a broader base of comparison. Comparable figures for Nantong, the specialist cotton prefecture across the Yangzi to the north which is discussed in Chapter 11, are not available.

The most important differences in land use between Jinshan and Shanghai revealed by the table are that while the latter had about 36% of its collective arable under cotton and 18% under vegetables or melons, Jinshan had only 12% under cotton, no mention of vegetables, and less than 2% under melons. Two factors appear to be jointly responsible for these differences – the importance of Shanghai county in supplying vegetables to the city (this county supplies one-third of the total which enters the city), and the differences in soils between the south-west (Jinshan) and north-east (Shanghai) of the municipality. Shanghai county is representative of important areas of light soils on both banks of the Yangzi which are important cotton producers, while Jinshan represents areas to the west and south, with grain-based economies. The parallel figures which are given in Table 7.1 for Suzhou show a countryside heavily committed to grain (77%) – though not as heavily as Jinshan (85%), probably because the prefectural figures for Suzhou also include important cotton counties, mainly on the Yangzi margin. Shanghai county excluding the city appears to be self-sufficient in grain (297 million *jin* would provide 561 *jin* per person to the population stated), and makes its contribution to the state mainly in the form of vegetables, and presumably also cotton and rapeseed. Jinshan makes its contribution mainly in grain, but Suzhou in cotton, rapeseed and silk as well as in grain. All three also sell pigs to the state, though no figure is given for Shanghai; here the contribution is presumably small.

These figures are for 1974, published in 1976, and they are accompanied by rationalisations suited to that phase in time, mainly political in content. Some of these rationalisations can be reinterpreted with the advantage of hindsight. In Shanghai county, it is argued in 1976, a variety of types of production all compete for scarce resources with collective grain production. These include private plots, fish-breeding and fisheries, handicrafts and short-distance haulage businesses. All these are represented as survivors of the former small-business economy – such things may help to raise living standards, but they are also the soil in which capitalism grows; they may be tolerated but only up to a point. In Shenzhuang commune, this kind of capitalist tendency was formerly allowed full rein, with the result that the collective economy did not prosper, but the value of household subsidiary production rose to a figure more than 40% of the official distribution ('collectives poor, individuals rich'). A new Dazhai movement was set afoot in consequence,

Table 7.1. Comparative details for farm outputs, 1974 – Jinshan and Shanghai counties, Shanghai, also county average, Suzhou prefecture

	Jinshan county	Shanghai county	Suzhou prefecture – an 'average' county
Rural population	Approaching 400,000	400,000	725,000
Farmworkers	200,000	n/a	394,000
Collective arable area (mou)	540,000	390,000	844,000
Area sown			
Grain (mou)	460,000	182,000	647,000
Cotton (mou)	63,000	138,000	197,000 (say)
Melons, vegetables (mou)	10,000	70,000	
Arable area per rural person (mou)	about 1.4	1.0	1.2
Yields			
Grain (jin per mou)	1,554	1,632	1353
Cotton (jin per mou)	141	119	n/a
Rapeseed (jin per mou)	283	269	n/a
Vegetables (jin per mou)	n/a	11,000	n/a
Pigs per mou	1.37	1.38	n/a
Outputs			
Grain (mill jin)	715	297	875
Cotton (mill jin)	8.9	16.4	n/a
Vegetables (mill jin)	n/a	597	n/a
Pigs (thousand head)	740	539	n/a
Annual supplies to the state, 1971–74			
Grain (mill jin)	100	Probably nil	316
Cotton (mill jin)	2.2	n/a	8.1
Rapeseed (mill jin)	7	n/a	9
Vegetables (mill jin)	n/a	597	n/a
Pigs (thousand head)	130	n/a	300
Silkworms (mill jin)	n/a	n/a	2.2

Sources: Materials in Jinshan and Shanghai county Revolutionary Committees: 1–21. For Suzhou: materials in People's Daily, 17 Sept. 1975.

and capitalist tendencies criticised. As a result, collective grain outputs rose by 15% and cotton by 25% (Jinshan and Shanghai county Revolutionary Committees: 17–18).

In Jinshan, a still more fundamental problem was uneasily tackled. In the present phase, we read (this is in 1974 or 1975) the commercial economy is unstable; the relative prices of commodities do not necessarily reflect their relative importance; and incomes per unit area from various crops are not the same. But for these reasons, it is all the more essential to take grain as the key link, to remain loyal to the state plan and resist creeping capitalism on the collective

arable, and also to resist the temptation to neglect collective grain in favour of economic crops grown on private plots and sold on the free market. In a brigade called Dongfanghong, appropriately located very close to the city, some cadres interested themselves more in production for cash than in the political line, encouraging diversification and economic crops at the expense of grain production; and some prosperous peasants neglected collective production in favour of private plots and the free market. Here too the deviants were criticised as 'heavy on cash, light on grain'. The collective economy was revitalised, and the poor and lower-middle peasants said,

'Take cash as the key link, and you lose your bearings; the people are poor and the land is barren. Take grain as the key link and grain is abundant and the animals thrive.' (Jinshan and Shanghai county Revolutionary Committees: 3–4) Trade outside the state system should be avoided, along with speculation and profiteering.

Both Jinshan and Shanghai lay emphasis on local industry as the servant of the farm economy – this means on the one hand the need to keep local industry closely tied to farm inputs such as tools and farm machinery, and on the other the need to devote industrial incomes to the improvement of agriculture. Elsewhere, in a discussion of the production plan for 1976 for Shanghai county, we read that the county expected to use up to 80% of its revenues in that year for the improvement of farm conditions, concentrating particularly on backward units (Shanghai county Revolutionary Committee: 6). Both counties lay heavy emphasis on continued land reconstruction – levelling, drainage and water-control works such as embankments, pumping stations and sluices (Jinshan and Shanghai county Revolutionary Committees: 6–12).

These considerations bring us close to the Maoist ideal of rural development, especially in prosperous areas. The Maoist ideal laid particular stress on high and rising yields of grain and cotton per unit area; on hand labour, fertiliser supplies (and hence pig-keeping), mechanisation where possible, and land reconstruction as the main means to these ends; and of course on political enthusiasm as the key to all. A simple calculation will serve to illustrate its rationale in terms of resources and management.

In the Shanghai–Suzhou area, 1 *mou* of land will easily produce, say, 1,000 *jin* of grain a year in two crops, if managed along reasonably intensive Chinese lines and kept supplied with natural fertiliser. (This 1,000 *jin* per *mou* is 7.5 tons per ha and was the Shanghai average in 1971 – Xinhua, 13 Dec. 1972). Five *mou* of land would normally support a family of (say) five people on average, including up to two workers plus some additional part-time labour, and would produce 5,000 *jin* of grain. Five people would consume between 2,000 and 2,500 *jin* of grain, leaving up to 3,000 *jin* for sale to the state, or some lesser amount if land is allocated to cotton or oilseeds or some other use, or if potatoes (grown in place of grain) are fed to pigs. At the rate of one person plus one pig to the *mou* of arable (normal figures in prosperous areas

in southern China), natural fertiliser will be available at the rate of 20,000 *jin* (10 tons) per *mou*, provided that labour is available to collect, compost, transport and spread it. Supplemented by limited amounts of chemical fertiliser, this is a rate more than adequate to maintain fertility. The labour requirement for fertiliser management on this scale can certainly be satisfied at the population density of one person per *mou* of arable (which is a density of 1,500 persons per sq km of arable); the principal constraint is shortage of time in the periods between harvesting and planting. Achievements in Suzhou under the Maoists serve to illustrate this rationale. In 1974, each of the 5.8 million rural people (not *workers*) of Suzhou supplied to the state, in addition to providing for their own subsistence, grain enough for one additional person, edible oil for two, meat for three and cotton for eight (*People's Daily*, 17 Sept. 1975). It is this kind of achievement which led the authorities to put out an exceptional leading article in the *People's Daily* on 23 July 1978, 'Looking at the south from Suzhou' – exceptional not only in the emphasis laid on progress in Suzhou, but in the use of a title which looked back unmistakably, and of course competitively, to that used for the report on the first national conference on learning from Dazhai in 1975 – 'Looking at the whole country from Dazhai' (*People's Daily*, 26 Sept. 1975).

This reasoning is quite persuasive until it is brought to mind that it is still more persuasive if applied to a countryside with more varied outputs; more intensive use of miscellaneous resources such as water-bodies and land not suited to grain crops, for instance to keep ducks and geese; more service trades such as building, transport, retail trade and repair; more commerce of all kinds; and more manufacturing. Some of these potential enterprises could be expected to contribute to the arable economy while taking nothing from it except labour – for instance, silkworms and ducks, which also contribute fertiliser. Others (milling, straw manufactures) would enable rural economies to charge higher prices for their products. Most would furnish increasing opportunities for the growing labour supply (strengthened by mobilisation of urban youngsters in Mao's time); and few would involve any reduction in grain output. This, broadly speaking, is the rationale of the changes brought in since 1978 in this kind of area. A variety of examples will illustrate the various forms taken by development, and isolate some characteristic successes and continuing problems.

The Maoist structure depended upon the identification of grain outputs as not only the first, but the absolute, priority in the Chinese countryside, and levels of grain supplies to the state as the most useful and effective indication of progress in that field. Costs were discussed only as an indicator of economy and effort; alternatives to the grain-based economy were not discussed at all, and the Dazhai model was held to be universally applicable. An interesting illustration from Shanghai, which looks forward to the comparative studies used after 1978, appeared in 1974 (Shanghai city, Maqiao commune: 173–4). In 1971 two brigades in closely comparable conditions produced respectively grain yields of 1,700 and 1,400 *jin* per *mou*, with ratios of costs to gross output of 28% (for high yield) and 23% (for low). On investigation at production team level, a number of extravagant and careless farm practices were identified in the high-cost team and (no doubt rightly) correlated with high costs. But after the chairman of the high-cost team recognised the problem, it was easily solved; costs fell to 26% of gross output and grain yield rose still higher, to 1,946 *jin* in 1973. In the economical team, gross output did not rise so high, and costs remained around 25%. This appears in retrospect to be an oblique attempt to tackle the problem of the association of high outputs with high costs, by showing that costs can be reduced while maintaining output. After the fall of the Gang of Four and the official relaxation of political pressure at the end of 1978, much more wide-ranging discussion of costs surfaced at once; also of excessive egalitarianism especially among units, and of policies designed to suit local conditions as an alternative to the universal model of Dazhai. In all these respects, Maoist priorities began to be stood on their heads, and not surprisingly, in that posture they were seen to be ridiculous.

An argument of a different kind, also very un-Maoist in implications, relates to land construction. It suggests that this important aspect of Maoist rural development policy depends on simplified – indeed simplistic – assumptions. These were expressed clearly by Chen Yonggui in 1972 (35), speaking of terracing work in northern China – 'The construction of one *mou* of terraced fields took at least over 200 work-days . . . seen alone, the amount of labour used in a particular year is really considerable. But taking the long-range view, since one *mou* of land generally yields 800 *jin* per annum, how much can it yield, say in 50 years?' The alternative view, which surfaced on behalf of Suzhou prefecture as early as mid-1978, takes cost into account – 'Land construction demands the revolutionary spirit of bitter struggle, but it cannot be done bare-handed. Capital is also needed. . . . ' (*People's Daily*, 23 July 1978) One *mou* of high- and stable-yielding 'one-ton land' (producing 2,000 *jin* to the *mou* and more) requires investment of the order of 120 *yuan*. The state is not likely to help; nor will egalitarian policies of redistribution of the proceeds of such investment. In Suzhou prefecture, in the three years 1975–78, 120 million *yuan* were spent on land reconstruction, and more than 50% of this came from commune or brigade resources – probably in large part from the profits of local industry. What increases in yield may be expected? A figure of 270 *jin* per *mou* increase in grain yield is explicitly quoted from Jiangyin county; other much higher figures appear to depend on the introduction of triple cropping in addition to land reconstruction – of course land reconstruction may be a prerequisite for triple cropping, but that is another story. The gross value of 270 *jin* of grain was about 40 *yuan* in 1978, but its net value would be only about 25 *yuan*. This has to be compared with investment of around 120 *yuan* per *mou*. Investment of the same money in industry, specialist farm outputs or pigs would probably all offer better prospects – indeed, in Wuxi county, which has a particularly distinguished record in land construction, it appears that this type of investment was undertaken in order to take up the very large revenues from local industry.

The post-Maoist critique

Through 1979 a literature built up in China on rural development issues which was not so much anti-Maoist as un-Maoist. In this literature, Maoist insights were usually treated quite seriously and even respectfully, but a wide range of arguments and materials was raised in which Maoist insights simply had no place. Many of the relevant points can be illustrated by a long investigative article from Shanghai city – 'How peasants can quickly become prosperous' (Shanghai city Revolutionary Committee). This study starts from the recognition that even in a prosperous part of rural China such as the Shanghai countryside, important differences in levels of income exist – average total income in the 204 communes, more than 2,800 brigades and more than 25,000 production teams of rural Shanghai was 230 *yuan* in 1978; but 312 production teams distributed more than 300 *yuan* and 1,485 teams distributed less than 120 *yuan*. The study analyses prosperity and poverty in rural Shanghai through two groups, each of ten brigades, one group poor and one rich. We are not told how these groups were selected, but this is not very important since what is at issue is the range of interpretative and policy points being made. We are assured that in terms of land and labour the two groups are similar (about 2 *mou* of arable per worker), and that cropping patterns, especially in relation to grain and cotton, are similar. Three kinds of difference are given prominence – incomes per person, productive investment per worker, and grain supplies to the state per worker. Broadly, the course of the argument is that these three indicators all depend upon a mixed group of relationships in production, illustrated in Tables 7.2 and 7.3, and that these relationships depend in turn upon various kinds of local conditions, problems, opportunities and achievements. The figures in Table 7.3 illustrate the widening of the spectrum of discussion which was then taking place. Emphasis is laid not upon physical outputs without consideration of costs, as in the Maoist scheme, but upon the value of each kind of enterprise to the community and individual. The Shanghai authorities are concerned to introduce a range of new indexes for the assess-

Table 7.3. Prosperous and poor brigades in Shanghai, various economic indicators. All values expressed in *yuan*, quantities in *jin*

	Ten prosperous brigades	Ten poor brigades	Difference (%)
Farm economy			
Average grain output per worker	3,160	2,370	33
Average cotton output per worker	154	113	36
Average rapeseed output per worker	143	116	23
Average value of output per *mou*	263	198	33
Average value of output per worker			
Gross	759	493	54
Net	541	322	68
Hence, costs per worker (and % of gross output)	218 (29%)	171 (35%)	27
Industrial economy			
percentage of labour employed in local industry	30	22	27
percentage of output contributed by local industry	43	33	23

Source: Material in Shanghai city Revolutionary Committee. Some figures have been deduced.

Table 7.2. Prosperous and poor brigades in Shanghai – principal economic indicators, 1978

	Ten prosperous brigades	Ten poor brigades	Difference (%)
Average incomes per person (*yuan*)	325	190	71
Average fixed investment per worker (*yuan*)	561	293	91
Average grain supplies to the state per worker (*jin*)	980 (rose from 556 in 1966)	472 (fell from 580 in 1966)	108

Source: Material in Shanghai city Revolutionary Committee.

ment of farm policy – or, to put it another way, to provide material which would help people to rationalise their experience that high unit-area outputs (in the Maoist style) did not necessarily create prosperity.

In the tables, physical outputs per worker are in general about one-third lower in poor brigades than rich, suggesting low productivity of labour on the land; but incomes are more than two-thirds lower, suggesting both high costs in agriculture (shown by much lower net output figures than gross) and also low performance in subsidiary production not governed by state prices. This is the essence of the interpretation in economic terms which is given in the official report. In technical terms, much more stress is laid upon water control and conservation, land reconstruction, fertiliser supplies, improved rotations and varieties, and scientific farm management. Examples are given which illustrate a wide range of problems and opportunities.

In Baoshan county, north of Shanghai city and on the Yangzi coast, the soil material is basically tidewater mud, prone to caking and poor in structure. Haixing brigade has undertaken an extended and ambitious programme of land reconstruction and improvement, including manuring at the rate of 12,000 *jin* (6 tons) of composted pig manure and pond mud to the *mou*. Yields are high in consequence – 2,637 *jin* of grain to the *mou*; 180 *jin* of cotton; net output per worker is 759 *yuan* for the year, and incomes are high in proportion, 240 *yuan* per person. At the neighbouring Qiangjia brigade, things have not gone so well. Grain and cotton yields are only 1,602 and 130 *jin* respectively, net output per worker only 376 *yuan*, and income per person only 140 *yuan*. At Haixing, people are very satisfied; incomes are little short of those enjoyed in the towns, and in some respects the people are better off than townsfolk.

Cases in Chuansha county, near the coast to the east of Shanghai city, illustrate the part played by subsidiary production and local industry, and the capacity for growth displayed by some units in recent years. In 1966, net income from these sources in Shanhuang and Dengyi brigades was the same, 20,000 *yuan*; but by 1978, Shanhuang had raised this figure to 223,000 *yuan*, an increase of more than ten times, while at Dengyi the same figure had only doubled. The explanation is many-sided, and relates to various enterprises at Shanhuang – a specialist pig unit employing 62 workers, eggs, 380,000 *jin* of milk produced annually by 166 cows fed for half the year with grass cut from the coastal embankments, and an embroidery business employing 140 women. At Dengyi, on the other hand, some enterprises have been given up. Washing nylon fabric (apparently for factories in the city) was not profitable, was given to the production teams, and has declined in value from 50,000 *yuan* to 20,000 *yuan*. Pigs and chickens have not been managed well, and have lost money. Industry has also done badly. Total income per person at Shanhuang in 1978 was 336 *yuan*, but at Dengyi only 173 *yuan*. Yet income from arable farming differs very little in the two brigades (Shanghai city Revolutionary Committee).

Discussion of these points lays stress on the role of the leaderships. Those in the prosperous brigades are praised for practical competence, realistic planning and businesslike management. Leadership in the weak brigades is criticised for disunity and quarrelsomeness, instability, and having too many young people with too little experience in leading positions. In the conditions of 1979, some of these expressions were no doubt code-words for Maoist and anti-Maoist.

Another pair of contrasted cases is quoted, this time from Qingpu county to the west of Shanghai, on the borders of Suzhou prefecture. In this contrast, the disparity of cash incomes is based on disparity of farm outputs. Luhua brigade has a moderate grain yield of 1,400 *jin*, cotton yield (a creditable figure) of 180 *jin*, net output per worker of 379 *yuan* and income per person of 150 *yuan*. Liujiazao brigade in the same county has a grain yield of more than 2,400 *jin* and cotton over 200 *jin*; net output per worker is 796 *yuan* and income per person 325 *yuan*. This difference is the outcome of a systematic programme of land reconstruction at Liujiazao. The brigade's land originally consisted of fifty-four embanked paddy-fields, but they were sloping and at various levels. After reconstruction there are six big level fields, all with irrigation ditches along the sides. Liujiazao has also planted willows and bamboos, started fishponds and planted (using retired people in part) 100,000 fruit-trees – worth 1 *yuan* per year each in fruit, and the trimmings are used for fuel. Meanwhile, Luhua has not improved its land or planted its roadsides, and its pig business, badly managed, loses 6,000 *yuan* a year on average.

In Shanghai county itself, Xinlong and Yuenong brigades have each gained about 270 workers between 1966 and 1978 (by natural increase, it would appear). Xinlong has provided work for the extra labour by starting pig, chicken, duck, fish and mushroom enterprises, growing willows and starting workshops. They have also started a short-distance haulage business which made 67,000 *yuan* in 1978. Meanwhile Yuenong has started various enterprises and lost money, and is now waiting for some big industrial opportunity. The additional workers are short of work, and incomes are 75% less than those at Xinlong (Shanghai city Revolutionary Committee).

A little like the Maoists, for whom the correct political line was the only, necessary and sufficient condition for economic progress, the publicists for the present regime are inclined to argue that economic acumen and sound business management are the indispensable conditions for the new kinds of progress. No doubt they are important; and no doubt in a crowded, intensively farmed and relatively sophisticated countryside like that of Shanghai, geographical diversities such as conditions of location, access, soil and water do not vary dramatically, and can to a significant degree be improved by human effort. Nevertheless, in the examples which have been quoted, diversities of various kinds do emerge – soil, location by the sea or on transport routes, availability of wild resource, ponds and rivers, and so forth. Among the 25,000 production teams of Shanghai, there must be as many local economic histories – and of these, half are no doubt histories of less than average success. Nevertheless, Shanghai's prosperity remains outstanding. In the Shanghai countryside as a whole, in 1978, average income per person was 230 *yuan*. In Jiangsu as a whole, it was only 85 *yuan* – little more than one-third of that figure (*People's Daily*, 17 July 1979).

Triple cropping – experience in Suzhou and Shanghai

One of the last major movements introduced under the Maoists was the widespread extension of triple-cropping practices in the Shanghai–Suzhou area. Triple cropping is in a sense the ultimate Maoist agricultural objective in the countryside – the expansion of the grain economy to occupy the whole yearly cycle, and the contraction of the rest of the rural economy to make this possible. In common with other forms of Maoist extremism, triple cropping was not popular, and it has been greatly reduced in extent since 1978; but it is nevertheless a topic of particular interest in both technical and economic terms.

As late as 1959, double cropping was by no means universal in Suzhou prefecture. By 1970 however, double cropping by summer paddy and winter wheat was already the rule throughout Suzhou, and between 15% and 30% of the arable was already being triple cropped. In 1971 triple cropping in Suzhou was increased abruptly to 70–80% of the arable (Huang Bingfu). Land used for cotton cannot be triple cropped, so it may be conjectured that practically all the land used for grain in the summer was then triple cropped.

Triple cropping, practised in various forms in many advanced parts of southern China, is a development of exceptional interest from the

standpoint of resource use. Triple cropping is always preceded in time by double cropping, a practice with a long history in both the Yangzi provinces and Guangdong, and now adopted in favoured areas virtually throughout southern China. Conventional double cropping in Guangdong is the taking of two summer crops of rice. The land is then fallowed for the winter. Conventional double cropping in Suzhou and the Shanghai area uses a summer crop of rice or cotton and a winter crop of wheat or another dry grain such as barley. In terms of these systems, triple cropping means in Guangdong the insertion of a third crop into the winter fallow season, and in Jiangsu the squeezing of a second crop into the summer season. Occasionally in the 1950s, triple cropping was already looked forward to as an ideal, though practical policy was more concerned at that time with the extension of double cropping in single-crop countrysides, as it is still in parts of Sichuan or the middle Yangzi provinces such as Jiangxi – or even further north in Jiangsu itself, for instance in the Huaiyin area (*People's Daily*, 15 Sept. 1979). Exceptionally, a few places, such as Songjiang county in Shanghai, do report practical triple cropping with three grain crops as early as 1956 (*People's Daily*, 30 Aug. 1979), but in 1965 only about 2% of Shanghai's grainland was triple cropped (Jiao Yuan: 4).

In traditional terms, the calendar year in Suzhou is too short by between one month and three months to permit triple cropping. Old-fashioned conventional double cropping in the Shanghai area provided for rice sown in April or May, transplanted in June and reaped in October, together with wheat or another winter crop sown in November and reaped in May or June. Occasional references in the 1950s suggest that first steps were taken towards triple cropping by the introduction of double-cropped rice in the Guangdong manner; but in Suzhou prefecture winter temperatures are lower by 10 °C or more than those at Guangzhou. The problem is the growing season for winter wheat, which at Guangzhou is 4 months, but at Shanghai must occupy $6\frac{1}{2}$ months, 200 days, from early November to the end of May. In this case, only 165 days are left for the two summer crops of rice. Rice requires a temperature of 10–12 °C to germinate, and at least 20 °C (early November at the latest in the Shanghai area) to pollinate successfully. It is possible to satisfy these requirements for two summer rice crops at Shanghai, bearing in mind

Table 7.4. Calendars for some triple-cropping plans – Brigade 88, Jinwei commune, Jinshan county, Shanghai

	Plan A	Plan B	Plan C
Previous winter crop			
Crop	Barley	Barley	Rapeseed
Date of harvest	20 May–2 June	20 May–2 June	3–5 June
Early rice crop			
Rice type	Early *xian*	Middle *xian*	Late *xian*
Date of sowing	20–30 April	24–26 April	17–18 April
Date of transplanting	21–31 May	2–4 June	5–6 June
Date of harvest	1–8 August	8–10 August	11–12 August
Late rice crop			
Rice type	Late *geng*	Early *xian*	Middle *geng*
Date of sowing	19–26 June	12–14 July	Late June–early July
Date of transplanting	2–6 August	7–8 August	9–13 August
Date of harvest	10–15 November	End of October–3 November	8–13 November
Subsequent winter crop			
Crop	Rapeseed or wheat not specified	Barley	Barley
Date of sowing		End of October–5 November	9–15 November

Source: Shanghai jiaoqu san shu zhi zaipei zhishu: 37.

that rice is transplanted, but there is practically no margin. As Table 7.4 shows, to grow two crops of rice at Shanghai requires 160–170 days' occupancy of the main fields, apart from the seedbeds, and that is exactly the time left after the needs of the winter wheat crop have been satisfied (Leeming 1979: 348). One way of relaxing the assumptions is obviously to grow a crop which is less demanding in the winter: in practice this means a green fertiliser, usually *Astralgus sinensis*, a kind of clover; and there is abundant evidence of the use of this crop as a half-way house between double and triple cropping. *Astralgus* fixes atmospheric nitrogen, and whether ploughed into the soil or fed to animals yields valuable fertiliser. It may also be used as one crop in a rotation occupying several years. Other devices may be used to promote flexibility. Rapeseed may be substituted for wheat in winter, and one of the most usual side-effects of triple cropping was the widespread substitution of barley for wheat as the standard winter crop – barley is less demanding, but also less esteemed.

From the point of view of the calendar, Chinese rice varieties are of two different genetic types which are also recognised elsewhere – early (*geng, japonica*) and late (*xian, indica*). Late varieties are the less highly bred and yield less highly, but they are better suited to hot and humid conditions and are photoperiod sensitive, so that their time of flowering is determined not by the age of the plant but by the diminution of the length of the daylight period after the summer solstice. Early varieties are more responsive to fertiliser and better resistant to cold, and their time of flowering depends on the age of the plant, not the length of the day. Early, middle and late varieties of both *xian* and *geng* types exist, so that according to need an early or late ripening early rice can be used for the early crop, and so forth. Varieties can be matched to produce a cropping plan which is economical of time, as Table 7.4 shows.

Even after 1970 and 1971, when triple cropping became standard in the Suzhou–Shanghai area and was being pushed forward in other areas as well, the movement received very little attention in the *People's Daily* or other popular media organs, especially bearing in mind its relevance to one of the main preoccupations of the media at that time, grain output. This general silence about triple cropping may hint at some embarrassment in official circles that this particular technical advance was not one which any local unit with proper political motivation could initiate – self-evidently it was a system only suited to advanced units in the southern half of China. The silence of the media on the subject also confirms that when triple cropping was brought in on a large scale, quite abruptly in the early 1970s, its introduction must have been entirely through the rural planning system, and without benefit of general publicity or, presumably, very much self-motivation on the part of the people. Until 1978, when criticism of the triple-cropping systems began to occupy a place of some prominence in the *People's Daily*, information in print about triple cropping in China came almost entirely from technical manuals on local self-improvement and rural development models, and exceptionally for that time, it generally had very low levels of political content.

A number of constraints obviously affect the practice of triple cropping in any locality. One is the extent to which output can be increased in practice.

In a production team in Jiading county, Shanghai, half the arable land is occupied by grains, mostly triple cropped, and most of the rest is under cotton. (Cotton is sown in April and may be transplanted in June, or it may spend up to forty days interplanted with the ripening wheat in the late spring; it cannot be united with a triple-cropping system except through interplanting.) There is a considerable pig population and some other production, such as mushrooms, which is not strictly agricultural (Jiading county, Writing Group: 133, 140–2). Under double cropping, grainland may therefore be reckoned to produce about 40% of the collective output of the team. When most of this land was converted from double to triple cropping, output from the grainland increased by less than 50% – probably no more than 40% even if organization was very successful, allowing for such features as rice seed-beds. An increase of this kind in the grain part of the team's economy represents an increase in the team's collective income as a whole of about 16%. Materials for Shanghai as a whole suggest a similar conclusion. Some 66% of the arable land in the Shanghai suburban area is sown to grain; and of this, 83% was 'basically' converted to triple cropping by 1974 – hence 55% of the total (Jiao Yuan: 1, 4). Allowances must be made for pigs, vegetables, services of various kinds, and other kinds of rural output; the output of the grainland is not likely to amount to more than 40% of total output – the same figure as that suggested for Jiading. If this output is increased by the suggested 40%, the same final figure, 16% is obtained. This 16% is a modest figure, bearing in mind the magnitude of the effort involved – effort in terms not only of additional labouring work, but also in terms of reorganisation of labour employment, fertiliser supplies and other agricultural inputs. Even more serious, as will be shown,

is the likelihood that if the increase in physical output is 16%, the increase in income to the team or brigade is much less.

A second problem is that of labour. Most reports of triple cropping relate to localities where arable is very scarce and labour plentiful. Around 1 *mou* (667 sq m) of arable per person is normal in lowland south China, and in most areas population growth has slowly but inexorably forced this figure downwards during the past generation – not all units have wild land which can be converted to new arable. At the same time, additional demand for labour in the new system is considerable – not less than the 16% by which output may be increased, and probably (bearing in mind additional fertiliser inputs) considerably more. There is also the problem of working against time to compress the three crops into the year. There is some indication that in these conditions scarcity of labour may easily supplant scarcity of land in the system. Under the triple-cropping system, during about twenty days of late July and early August, the 200,000 workers of Jinshan county, Shanghai (where collective arable works out at 1.3 *mou* per person) must harvest 375,000 *mou* of early rice and plant out 450,000 *mou* of late rice, and continue to care for the cotton fields. At this time workers might work an eighteen hour day and get no more than three hours' sleep. Yields can be impressive, however – 1,929 *jin* per *mou* (14.5 tons per ha) for the three grain crops at one brigade (Jinshan and Shanghai county Revolutionary Committees: 7). A very different (and of course much smaller) example comes from Hunan – the Shengli production team of Heping brigade and Dayao commune in Liuyang county. Shengli has less than 0.3 *mou* (191 sq m in fact) of arable per person, but all the arable is double cropped with rice and half also carries a winter crop of wheat. Average grain yield reaches the remarkable figure of 2,857 *jin* per *mou* (21.4 tons per ha). Shortage of labour is not complained of even at busy times, though at these times the Shengli workers who normally commute to work in factories at commune and brigade level all return to the land (*People's Daily*, 23 March 1979).

Most of the literature on triple cropping relates to the Shanghai–Suzhou area, rather than to areas further south such as Guangdong where triple cropping is also practised. Shanghai and Suzhou also originated the powerful current of criticism of triple cropping which appeared in the winter of 1978–79. (Xiong Yi; Huang Bingfu; Mu Jiajun and Li Jincheng). Apart from difficulties with the calendar and the pressures put upon labour (extending to overwork and complaints about health in some cases), these criticisms are of three main kinds: that soil fertility is hard to maintain under triple cropping and soil conditions are deteriorating in some areas; that triple cropping reduces fertiliser supplies at the same time as it demands additional fertiliser; and that the additional outputs available from triple cropping are not proportionate to the additional expenses involved. These are all serious criticisms.

Soil deterioration is said to occur because of the longer period the fields are under water, and the additional phase of tillage conjoined with inadequate coarse fertiliser. The topsoil layer tends to thin out, reducing food and water supplies to the crop by up to one-third. It also tends to become greasy and stiff, making tillage difficult and adversely affecting the growth of crops; and the impervious layer below the topsoil tends to become thicker. Fertiliser is scarce partly because the new varieties have short growing seasons and short straw; straw supplies are reduced per unit of grain output by about one-third under the new system. Straw, whether composted directly or fed to pigs, is one principal source of coarse fertiliser. The other is green fertiliser, also greatly reduced by triple cropping where three grain crops are grown.

The triple cropping system is expensive (Mu Jiajun and Li Jincheng; Xiong Yi). Table 7.5 shows labour inputs and costs of cultivation per *mou* of arable in Songjiang county, Shanghai, in 1966 and 1976. Both increased markedly as a result of the introduction of triple cropping; and surprisingly, the value of work-points actually fell in the same period, from 1.01 *yuan* in 1966 to 0.84 *yuan* in

Table 7.5. Labour and other costs of cultivation per *mou*, with value of the labour-day, in Songjiang county, Shanghai, 1966 and 1976

	1966	1976	Increase (%)
Labour input per *mou* of arable (man-days)	71.5	125.4	75.3
Costs (other than labour) per *mou* of arable (*yuan*)	21.2	33.5	58.0
Value of the labour day (*yuan*)	1.01	0.84	Decrease of 16.7

Source: Material in Mu Jiajun and Li Jincheng.

Table 7.6. Outputs and costs for an average 100 *mou* of arable land in Suzhou prefecture, under double and triple cropping

	Average before 1971 (under double cropping)	Average after 1971 (under triple cropping)
Grain yield (*jin* per *mou*)	798	1,020
Output of 100 *mou* (*jin*)	79,800	102,000
Grain eaten by 86 rural people (*jin*)	47,300	47,300
Grain for sale (*jin*)	32,500	54,700
Gross value of grain for sale (*yuan*)	4,648	7,822
Costs other than labour (*yuan*)	2,120	3,350
Net value of grain (*yuan*)	2,528	4,472
Labour-days used	7,150	12,540
Cash value of labour-day (*yuan*)	0.354	0.357

Source: People's Daily, 19 Sept. 1975 and 13 Mar. 1975. Costs per *mou* from Songjiang: Table 7.5; Grain prices from Peng Kuang-Hsi: 6.

1976. If these Songjiang figures for costs are applied to those available for the actual changes in output in Suzhou prefecture for roughly the same periods of time (1962–70 and 1971–78), the results for the cultivation of 100 *mou* of 'average' arable in Suzhou are those shown in Table 7.6. The implication of the figures is quite clear – it is that when conversion to triple cropping takes place, the state is able to purchase about 200 *jin* per *mou* more grain at standard prices, while the cash value of the labour-day remains unchanged. Rises in grain prices would make little difference to the relations between the values of the labour-day in the two cases. Rises in yields would generate higher values for the labour-day much more efficiently, but the yields in the triple-cropping system have to be roughly double those in the double-cropping system to create the same rise in the value of the labour-day.

It is easy to understand the argument that the extra physical effort for the people which triple cropping represents is not adequately rewarded in terms of cash at the end of the year. It is important to recall that the production team, the producing farm unit, is responsible for its own losses in production, unless subsidised by administrative decision. At Xiashidang in Sichuan, when triple cropping was introduced, labour demand was increased by 50%, but output by only 33%. No figure is given for other costs, but it is reported that a single crop of rice requires 30–40 *jin* of urea per *mou*; double cropping with rice and wheat requires 80 *jin*; and triple cropping with rice, rice and wheat requires upwards of 180 *jin*. In terms of grain yields, the last of these represents the least efficient use of fertiliser, and the first the most (Huang Yanjun and Yu Quanyu 1978a). In broad terms, Japanese experience in this field is that double cropping of rice, which is a necessary part of virtually all triple-cropping schemes, is worthwhile only if the output from the two rice crops is at least 150% of that from one crop alone (He Guiting et al.: 32). In China, a figure of 150 *jin* additional grain is accepted, representing 10–20% (Chen Lian: 23); but even an additional output of 200 *jin* would cost more than it would be worth at Chinese prices (Chen Lian: 26). Alternative schemes which do not involve double cropping of rice do exist, typically schemes using winter barley or rapeseed, early-summer rice and late-summer beans or maize; but all involve some degree of interplanting. Interplanting schemes (particularly if the rotation includes a green fertiliser) may well be better for the soil, but they involve still more work and do not, on average, yield higher outputs (*Zenyang zhong yumi*: 100–3).

All this means that when units do adopt triple cropping, the people find themselves not only with a considerably increased burden of work, particularly tedious labouring work such as spreading fertiliser, but also quite possibly with increased costs which reduce their money incomes. In these conditions of increased farm output but stagnant or falling incomes, the wages earned by commuters to local industries may well be a necessity to balance the books of the team. Any such experience must obviously be very bad for morale in the production teams. Even a commentator broadly sympathetic to triple cropping and prepared to take issue on some of the criticisms of it accepts that some units have found themselves seriously out of pocket through taking it on. He admits that some places are not really suited to triple cropping, even in Suzhou, and instances the Yangcheng Lake and other lake areas to the south-east of Suzhou city, because of their relative lack of labour – and he might have added, the real difficulties of access to the fields

in this watery landscape (Huang Bingfu). Other criticisms are accepted only in part. It is argued that experience with soil has been very mixed; some units have been imprudent, while others have successfully progressed beyond simple control of surface water to control of the water-table. Everyone agrees on the continued need for farmland reconstruction and rationalisation. As to coarse fertiliser, it is argued that the straw from the third crop makes up for that lost by use of short-straw varieties, and that pig populations have increased and can increase much faster.

Some units in southern China have made a success of triple cropping in technical terms, and if triple cropping leads to high or very high yields, of more than about 1,500 *jin* per *mou*, the labour-day is quite well paid (upwards of 1 *yuan* at 1971 prices). If mechanisation is possible, human effort will be much reduced and precious time saved, though costs may rise disproportionately. Conjoined with favourable physical conditions, dense human and pig populations, forceful management and successful industrial or subsidiary enterprises, and hopefully a fair degree of mechanisation on the land, an element of triple cropping in local rotations will raise output without laying unreasonable burdens on the working people. Examples appear in the press, though it is revealing that they tend to be at brigade level only (Gao Shangquan: 44–7). But it is hard to believe that this kind of scheme can offer much to a team which is already weak; and if as is now said, triple cropping was introduced 'across the board' in the time of the Gang of Four (1971 presumably), it must have been harmful to many units which already had problems of management, or cash shortage, or communications, or labour supply. The average yield of 1,020 *jin* per *mou* given for Suzhou in Table 7.6 is not a high figure, and must represent many weak local economies. It is a commonplace that Green Revolution technology benefits the rich and strong in peasant countrysides first and most. What is under discussion here is virtually an enforced Green Revolution movement, and here too the units with sound management, cash reserves and the best natural and technical resources necessarily profit disproportionately. In addition to this there is the question of alternative enterprises and investments. It does not appear that these were discussed officially when triple cropping was introduced, but comparison must inevitably have arisen.

Wuxi county – 'showplace of rural industrialisation'

Wuxi county, to the north of Lake Tai, is often taken as the most distinguished county in China in the field of rural industrialisation, and an interesting literature has accumulated. The widespread introduction of commune and brigade factories and workshops has been quite recent – it started in 1974, on the initiative of the county Communist Party authorities, and under the umbrella of the state plan. (Jiangsu province Revolutionary Committee). In all, 1,638 rural factories were started in 1974, 78% of them run by brigades, the rest by communes. These factories were praised for giving technical support to farm mechanisation, providing employment and raising the level of public ownership. Profits from local industry were required under the rules set up by the county party committee to be used mainly to support agriculture through mechanisation, land construction and so forth (60%), and to finance additional local industry (30%). Total output of rural industry in the thirty-five communes of Wuxi county in 1977 was 360 million *yuan* – more than industry in Wuxi city, and all achieved at much lower rates of capitalisation than would have been necessary in the city (Zhao Ming et al.).

Wuxi is an admirable locale for a policy of village industrialisation. Industrial markets are at hand in Shanghai and Wuxi, technical knowledge is relatively advanced, and many rural workers have had some experience of industrial jobs in the city at some time. Educated youngsters from the towns were also useful recruits to the factories. Local industrialisation was not new in 1974, but the scale of industrialisation does appear to have been drastically changed at that time. The figure given for local workshops and factories in 1978 is 1,900 (Xinhua, 10 Aug. 1978, 21) – only 262 more than the number set up in the programme of 1974. Many stories attest the simplicity and self-reliance of the workshops and factories in the early days – stories which do not differ in essentials from those to be heard elsewhere in developing countries, where industry is being started from scratch in rural communities. At Xingqiao in 1968 the commune started a plastics works making bags for food and fertiliser, with twelve women workers using flat-irons purchased for 60 *yuan*. In 1971, the commune used revenue accumulated from this enterprise to set up a farm machinery

works, using scrap-iron and the simplest equipment, in a bamboo shed with matting walls and tarpaulin roof. Turnover was 6 million *yuan* in all in 1978 (Yuan Qihe et al.). Anqi commune had industrial output worth 4.5 million *yuan* gross in 1978 from more than seventy workshops of various kinds, including farm machinery, chemicals, electroplating, and quarries producing stone, lime, cement and clay – an exceptional mineral endowment, as they point out. In this case, industry dates only from 1974. Much of what is reported from Wuxi appears to be genuine manufacturing industry, as opposed to craftsmen's work or farm processing. In exceptional cases, very big industrial jobs have been done – the county organised a group of communes to build gates for the floating dry-dock at Shanghai, and this organisation has since built gates of this kind for both Shanghai and Guangzhou, of up to 60 tons. Compared with urban factories, industry of this kind in the countryside is flexible and responds sensitively to demand. One way in which growth is expected to continue is through more large factories in the cities placing orders for components.

Conformably with Maoist – and even post-Maoist – thinking about rural industry, most commentators stress the marked rise in farm production in Wuxi since 1970, and claim for industry a large share of the credit. A further mark of the success of the rural industrialisation policy is the growth of the commune and brigade segment of rural output in Wuxi from 23% of the total for the three levels in 1970 to 64% in 1977 (Zhao Ming et al.) and further to 79% in 1980 (Chen Lian: 24). The strengthening of the brigades and communes within the three-tier structure is often regarded as one of the main achievements of rural industrialisation, together with technical support for agriculture and increases in rural incomes when profits from local industry are distributed, where that takes place. But in the case of the figures last quoted, it follows that the share of total output contributed by the teams (i.e. basically arable farming) has fallen from 77% to 21% in eleven years, in spite of heavy investment and rapid technical change on the land, and that the structure of the communes has undergone a sharp change as a result. Investment and technical change on the land, paid for in part by the profits of local industry, have resulted in very rapid increases in total output (7% per annum in commodity grain production, for

115

instance) and in a rate of growth in the farm sector of 6.3% per annum in 1970–76 (Zhao Ming et al.). In spite of this, agriculture in Wuxi has easily been overtaken as the leading sector by rural industry. As one tag has it, 'Better a little factory than even a ton of grain to the *mou*.' (Wang Gengjin and Zhu Rongji: 23) As a result, agriculture faces serious problems – the disparity between industrial and farm prices on the one hand, and the heavy burdens laid upon the farm system on the other, are bearing increasingly heavily upon the production teams, which are left with the unprofitable work of growing grain, including, at least until 1978, the onerous work of introducing the complex and labour-intensive change to triple cropping. Triple cropping raises output, but also raises costs in many cases more than proportionately; and these costs are borne by the production teams. To carry additional burdens for a reduced rate of reward is very bad for motivation. Local industry may subsidise agriculture by distributing high-productivity incomes through the teams, but this is not a way out for agriculture. This notion is one reason given by some critics for distrust of the present course of rural industrialisation (Wang Gengjin and Zhu Rongji: 22–3).

There are also other reasons. Rural industrialisation has proved profitable, and technically it presents few problems. Far too many communes have started such enterprises. As a result, in Wuxi and counties like it, there is now spare capacity in local industry, with machinery standing idle for 40% of the time (in Wuxi) or even more than 50% (in the neighbouring county of Jiading) (*People's Daily*, 10 July 1980). For this reason, prices of manufactures have tended to fall in Wuxi. Elsewhere, units which have started rural industrial enterprises have had all kinds of difficulties to face, according to the press, and success has eluded many, such as a commune in Shanxi which sent for people from Zhejiang to help in establishing an umbrella factory (*People's Daily*, 7 Oct. 1978), and Laishui county in Hebei where seven or eight printing-houses now compete for work, where formerly there was only one (*People's Daily*, 27 Apr. 1980) – there are many examples. Time and natural growth, in a county starved of industrial goods, may be expected to solve this kind of problem in due course, though not without discomfort and waste, and continued investments of enterprise and capital in communes which hope to keep ahead in the industrial

economy. A much more serious problem arises in relations between local industry and the state planning machinery.

Wuxi, called before Liberation 'little Shanghai' has a strong industrial and business tradition, especially in the engineering field. Many Wuxi men had contacts with factories in Shanghai and elsewhere in China. As a result, more than 70% of local industry in Wuxi works for big factories elsewhere, and more than 60% is in the engineering field. Furthermore, when local supplies of raw material or fuel have not been forthcoming, Wuxi local industry has often found it practical to come to reciprocal arrangements of various kinds with suppliers in other places, usually outside the provisions of the state plan. Wuxi local industry consumes 50,000 tons of steel annually, and most of this is procured other than through the state plan. Reciprocal arrangements have been made with mines in Shanxi for supply of coal which is often also scarce; and as a result of these arrangements, the villagers in Wuxi can also obtain coal. These practices at Wuxi are not necessarily representative of what happens in other counties, but they are important at Wuxi, and must cast serious doubt on the fitness of Wuxi to be considered a model. In these cases, the state plan is flouted by barter arrangements which have very far-reaching administrative implications (Wang Gengjin and Zhu Rongji: 21). They also have far-reaching implications for some of the familiar commonsense arguments for the encouragement of local industry, such as fortifying local self-sufficiency in a large country with poor communications (Perkins 1977: 5–6).

At Wuxi, it appears, industrial developments which are desirable – perhaps absolutely necessary – in themselves have created or compounded problems of two very different kinds. One set of these problems relate to the pauperisation of agriculture and the proletarianisation of farmworkers. This problem cannot be solved without raising the productivity of agriculture in money terms, and this notion, as has been pointed out, calls into question one of the most fundamental policies in the political economy of China – the policy of low farm prices. At Wuxi as elsewhere, free production and the free markets will reduce this problem, though not solve it. The other set of problems relates to the manipulation of commodity supply to obtain local advantage. Presumably in principle this kind of manipulation is to the disadvantage of other customers, though it may be achieved through production which would otherwise not take place at all. Clearly, any such manipulation, operating on a large scale in such vital commodities as coal and steel, and involving transport over vast distances, calls into question the capacity of the planning administration both to supply real need, and also to exercise the control over supplies which is supposed to be part of its function. The county party committee at Wuxi, whose judicious introduction of local industry in 1974 was so warmly praised by *Red Flag* in the following year, begin to look a little like Hong Kong businessmen operating a business network. At the same time, the industrial innovation which strengthened the central institutions of the communes and those directly under the hand of the party, and so won warm praise from the Maoists, has tended during its short life to move towards industrial bureaucracy and to proletarianise the peasants who were supposed to represent the heart and soul of Maoism, and whose interests lie elsewhere.

Is this inevitable if local industry is to be really successful? Critics of Wuxi argue for an industrial scheme of a much less ambitious kind, comprising manufacture based on local farm specialities (baskets), or on local minerals (bricks), or on local demand (farm tools) or on waste materials from the cities (Wang Gengjin and Zhu Rongji: 23). But this list does not convince – why stop there if more is feasible? Suppressing potential growth of the industrial sector in the communes will not make farming more profitable. The same critics themselves go on to accept rural industrialism for industrialism's sake provided it remains more or less within the state plan, on the grounds that it is economical and tends to reduce excessive urbanisation. Both of these criticisms seem to start from a basically Maoist position, and are internally consistent.

But there is no reason for discussion of rural industrialisation to begin and end with its function as support for agriculture. Many cases of diversification suggest that it may be fitted into a broad programme of economic and social revitalisation, whether tied in a client role to the main industrial centres, or dependent on local or regional suppliers and markets. In most parts of China agriculture is ready to shed labour on a considerable scale. From this point of view, the problems of rural industry are less those of technical competence or even material supplies than the availability and legitimacy of enterprise, and

problems of management including the accounting status and labour-supply arrangements of the rural factories.

Meanwhile development continues, and various kinds of dependency upon local industry emerge. At Wuxi, industry continues to subsidise triple cropping to the advantage of state grain procurements, and Wuxi county paid 90 million *yuan* in tax in 1980, amounting apparently to about two-thirds of the profits of rural industry. Distribution to rural families (about 17%), rural construction, social provision and special support for poor units also shared these profits. In Jiangsu as a whole at the end of 1979, rural industry contributed 43% of all income at the three levels in the commune (*People's Daily*, 11 Oct. 1979); in Suzhou prefecture at the end of 1980, 53% (*People's Daily*, 13 Nov. 1980).

There are signs of the extension of rural industry on the Wuxi model to areas far beyond Jiangsu. A case which is also presented as a model is Weihai in Shandong (Gu Shutang and Chang Xiuze). Shandong takes us beyond the confines of the lowland south, but the issues involved are akin to those at Wuxi.

At Weihai the discussion is centred on 'product diffusion' between town and country, based on 'factory-team links'. Product diffusion means the subcontracting of manufacturing work from town factories to rural collective units which enjoy these links. In 1979, 49 of the 83 enterprises belonging to Weihai city subcontracted work to a total of 160 rural brigades, some located within the city's rural limits and some beyond. The main kinds of production involved are carpets and embroidery. The merits of this kind of organisation are said to be the employment of surplus rural workers, the accommodation of workpeople and provision of space and equipment for manufacturing at costs only a fraction of those necessary in Weihai itself, and the growth of rural prosperity through the payment of labour employed and the additional stimulation of locally based commune and brigade enterprises. It is argued that labour in the countryside ought to be paid at the same rates as town labour for parallel work, and also that the town factories ought to pay more equitably for buildings, energy and so forth in the countryside – in these respects the rural subcontractors are obviously still disadvantaged, though we do not know to how great an extent. Problems of competition by brigades for phases of the work perceived as particularly advantageous are also mentioned. Technical support for rural production teams, quality control and stability in the allocation of work are also of great importance.

This account suggests that the course of development in this field remains basically that which has been identified for Wuxi – rural advantages of abundant space, low levels of social and physical capital provision and low levels of worker expectation are being exploited by urban factory managements which can expand production with the help of these advantages. In principle the system has more in common with the early stages of capitalist industrialisation than with Maoist egalitarianism; but it seems likely to continue to work to the satisfaction of both urban managements and rural client units for the foreseeable future.

Features of the rural system since 1980 – 'four wheels all turning together'

The rural economy of the Shanghai–Suzhou area now has, necessarily, two main features – the grain economy, still of the highest importance to local subsistence and to the state's commodity grain supplies, and still employing most of the labour; and the diversified economy, including commune and brigade industry, which now provides most of the income. Figures have appeared which make it possible to separate these for purposes of analysis (Table 7.7).

Commune and brigade industry, employing 26% of rural labour, now generates 70% of rural incomes in Suzhou prefecture, and field agriculture, employing 66% of labour, generates only 21%. A necessary concomitant of these relation-

Table 7.7. Suzhou prefecture – employment and value of output in various branches of production, 1980

	Employment		Net outputs	
	(thousand persons)	%	(million yuan)	%
Farming	2,230	66	995	21
Commune and brigade industry	880	26	3,424	70
Other subsidiary production	270	8	427	9

Source: Material in Xue Jinao: 24.

ships is that 72% of rural income is now generated at commune and brigade level, and only 28% at production team level (Xue Jinao). It is not surprising to learn that in Zhejiang province, at an earlier stage in the present scheme of development than Suzhou prefecture, diversified rural economy (including rural industry) contributes 60% of rural outputs by value, and that outputs at commune and brigade level constitute 40% of rural outputs (Tie Ying: 1981).

In 1947 Suzhou prefecture produced 2,300 million *jin* (1.15 million tons) of grain; in the 1950s around 3,900 million *jin*, in the 1960s around 4,800 million *jin* and in the 1970s around 6,900 million *jin* (3.45 million tons) (Xue Jinao: 23). Meanwhile (between 1949 and 1979) the arable area has fallen by 835,000 *mou* (55,700 ha, 11%), but of course the sown area has risen much more, by 163%, indicating a dramatic rise in the double-cropping index which was 238 in 1979 (Chen Lian: 22). Increases in double-cropping area, and in the 1970s triple cropping, are the most important features of these intensification movements. Rice was double cropped on 23% of the paddy-land in 1969 but on 86% in 1976 (both figures are almost certainly indicators of the extent of triple cropping); in 1981, after some years' relaxation of the triple-cropping policy, it occupied only 44% of the paddy (Chen Lian: 23). Triple cropping is expensive, and for this and other reasons which have been discussed, it is not popular. It is argued in addition that the effect of heavy state procurement obligations upon the local economy is necessarily a loss of incomes, due to low state prices, and also a loss of economic vitality due to the extraction of so high a proportion of output (Xue Jinao: 25). The unhappy experience of Yushu county in Jilin province (Ch. 11), the most important county supplier of commodity grain in China, but heavily in debt, is used in Suzhou to illustrate the evils of monoculture and the need for economic crops and diversified and industrial enterprises (Chen Lian: 26). Since 1978, Suzhou has gradually raised the proportion of the arable devoted to economic crops, though this has not yet been restored to the level of 1949. Since 1979, grain output in Suzhou has fallen drastically (by 44% of the 1976 figure), leading to proposals for stiffer definition of quota obligations in the state plan (Sun Ming et al.: 53, 55). Household responsibility systems do not appear to be dominant in Suzhou, understandably enough; but whether or not responsibility is devolved to households, the peasants have much wider interests than grain crops and are unwilling to plant grain, although industry now routinely subsidises grain (Sun Ming et al.: 55, 56). At the same time, prices and costs for crops of various kinds are a constant preoccupation (Jiading county, Agricultural Economics Investigation Unit). Because of free marketing, inflation and changing labour expectations, both are becoming much less predictable, and profitable industrial opportunities, particularly in the ten counties of Shanghai municipality, are increasingly intervening for both land and labour.

Surprisingly perhaps, subsidiary production other than rural industry has been slow to develop in this favoured part of China. This is partly no doubt because of the much more powerful thrust of industry, partly because resource of any kind is already being used in other phases of production, partly because commerce remains weak and supplies of all kinds, including those needed for production, are inadequate (Chen Lian: 28). The still under-used resources of mountains, water-bodies, road and river verges and so forth, are now represented not as opportunities for arable creation, as in Mao's time, but as opportunities for extending the diversified economy.

A few very successful diversification examples have reached the media. One is a brigade called Zhangzhuang, in Wu (Suzhou) county (*People's Daily*, 21 Feb. 1981). Here since 1973, fish-breeding has been gradually widened to include businesses breeding fish fry and freshwater mussels which are edible and also produce pearls. Green fodder is cultivated for both fish and pigs, and poultry flocks have multiplied. Meanwhile, contract work is being taken in from the urban factories – manufacture of fibreglass panels and cleaning and repairing of sacks. Incomes have risen, as might be expected (from 233 *yuan* per person to almost 300 in 1980), but stress is laid on the achievement of grain self-sufficiency after many years' marginal dependence on state supplies, with now a small grain surplus in addition, Zhangzhuang has only 0.5 *mou* or arable land per person, so these achievements are respectable. A similar sensitivity towards grain self-sufficiency appears in other recent favourable reports (*People's Daily*, 24 Dec. 1980; 19 Feb. 1981).

There is a saying among the masses in Suzhou, we read, which runs as follows: 'Better to plant cotton than rice; better melons than cotton; better

sugar than melons; but best of all to start a factory'. (Chen Lian: 26). Evidence for this kind of outlook has already been given in the context of Wuxi and elsewhere. In Suzhou, there is now no hesitation in recognising that profits from local industry are used to subsidise grain farming, including commodity grain (Sun Ming et al.: 56). In the communes in Suzhou prefecture, the average income per person is 164 *yuan*. Of this, 30% is created by field agriculture, 25% by subsidiary enterprises apart from industry, and 45% by local industry (Xue Jinao: 25). It may not be too cynical to suggest that the system of subsidy in this kind of area is tolerated by the people as a trade-off for the right to generate industrial and other income outside the state plan. Subsidy is said, however, to encourage extravagance on the land. Farm costs rose sharply in 1974–75 from 38% of gross output, and in 1980 reached 56% (Chen Lian: 27). In addition, the proportion of the profits of rural enterprise which is distributed to the people is usually only 15–20%, a modest figure with which not everyone is satisfied. However, we read quite openly, this kind of decision is made at high levels in the party; commune members and production teams have no right to take part in decisions of this kind (Chen Lian: 28). In some places, cooperation among different kinds of production within collective units (at brigade or commune level) has been objectified as 'agricultural–industrial–commercial complexes' (*People's Daily*, Editorial, 20 Aug. 1981, translated in FBIS *Daily Report*, 26 Aug. 1981, K6–K8); though this term seems to represent little more than official approval of schemes of this sort. Internal subsidy for grain outputs would probably be managed more readily in such complexes.

In an optimistic analysis, one writer praises 'four wheels all turning together' – that is, agriculture, industry, collective subsidiary production and family production (Jin Feng). This is from Wujiang county, on the shore of Lake Tai south of Suzhou, quintessential Jiangnan country. Physical and economic conditions are very favourable and the collective economy is stable. Average grain yield on the 85,000 *mou* of collective arable is around 1,200 *jin*, and between 33% and 40% of output (up to 20,000 tons) of grain is supplied to the state. We are not informed whether triple cropping is still practised, but it would appear likely. In 1981 Wujiang also supplied 400,000 pigs and 100,000 tons of vegetables specifically to the state, in addition to oilseeds, eggs and fish. This is the collective agriculture 'wheel'.

Labour is now deployed, and work done, mainly through specialist contract forms of the responsibility system; 55% of production teams are said to be now operating specialist contract groups in agriculture, industry and subsidiary production, under unified management within the collective system. Most of the remaining teams operate limited labour contracts, and a few have household contract systems.

It is not surprising to learn that 70% of rural income in Wujiang county is created in industry and subsidiary enterprises, and only 30% in agriculture. About 60% of collective income is now created at commune and brigade level; 40% at team level. It is reported that employment structure has changed greatly, presumably by releasing workers from agriculture into industry and sidelines; but no figures are given. Cash income from the collective is now attributed equally to agriculture, industry and subsidiary production, suggesting some improvement in the status of agriculture as a result of increased prices and the responsibility systems. Incomes in industry remain higher than in agriculture, and wherever farm outputs are high costs are also high – as much as 86 *yuan* per *mou* on average in 1980, possibly (the percentage is not given) around 36%. High costs and relatively low rewards continue to be bad for motivation on the land, and conditions have to be set up in the responsibility systems which are adequate to motivate people in each locality. Incomes are now comparable as between farm and factory jobs, but relations among teams doing different kinds of work are always a potential source of trouble. These are the industry and subsidiary 'wheels'.

Relative freedom at work, and (particularly in the farming sector) the dropping of the pretence of working when there was nothing to do, now encourages households to develop family production. Average income from family production was 120 *yuan* in 1981, 45% of the average total income per person of 267 *yuan*, and it was growing more rapidly than income in the other sectors. This is the 'wheel' of family production.

Outputs are high generally in Wujiang, but there are quite marked differences among the more than 6,000 teams in the county. Rich teams have total incomes in the 400–500 *yuan* per person range, while the poorest have only 50 *yuan* per person, or less. It is no doubt from teams of the latter kind that labour is most prone to leave the land. During 1978 and 1979, 121,000 (6%) of workers in rural Shanghai left their production teams, presumably to look for work in the city (Shi Zilu: 29). The factors involved are not difficult to recognise or illustrate, and not very different from those familiar from other developing countries – proximity to the city, the availability of urban jobs, the relatively burdensome and poorly paid character of farm-work, at least as perceived, the low prices for farm outputs. The consequences are also familiar. In some places labour is already scarce on the land, at least in terms of intensive cultivation; migrant labour from other provices may be employed (Shi Zilu: 29). Where labour is so scarce that crops are neglected and in some cases not harvested, commune authorities may well respond that the losses can be more than covered by income from rural industry; but particularly where there is no local industry, or not enough, workers may be hard to keep in the villages. Wages in industry, commerce and transport are double, or up to ten times, or even more, the income which can be had legitimately in the communes. Some communes are renting out land, for instance to state industry, at rents far beyond the potential farm income from the same land (Shi Zilu: 30). Both migration of labour and the renting of rural land are of doubtful legality. In these and many other respects it is proving difficult, in the Shanghai countryside, to reconcile economic growth, conjoined with marked differences in economic status between agriculture and industry, with stability. All four wheels are turning in the Shanghai countryside, and usually in the same direction, but they are certainly not all turning at the same speed.

Opportunity and prosperity

The area now under discussion, between Lake Tai and the sea, is by common consent the most advanced rural area in China. A number of features which represent this high level of advancement have been discussed – high grain yields dependent on double and triple cropping and heavy use of fertiliser, extensive adoption of industrial production in the villages, and relatively widespread diversification of farm production based on local urban markets with favourable communications and business links. A number of problems which arise within this system have also been discussed – the continuing poor profitability of grain outputs sold to the state and the low profitability of all rural activities, including rural industry, by urban standards. Paradoxically, the second of these is also the Shanghai countryside's main asset within the present system. Because most rural prices are low by urban standards, rural production for urban markets can readily be expanded in both market-gardening and industry. In so far as this can be done without serious loss of land by the grain agriculture still required by the state plan (and by the state's genuine need in an area of this kind), such development is to be welcomed, because in addition to generating income it provides jobs in labour-intensive types of production. If the collective income produced by this kind of development is used to mechanise or otherwise reduce the labour demands of grain agriculture, that is also to be welcomed, provided that the workers set free can be further employed in labour-intensive production. It has been argued that the liberation of the local production system from Maoist restrictions, which enables it to make sufficient money in workshops and subsidiary production to continue to subsidise the production of all-important grain, is a palliative rather than a curative approach to the fundamental problem of low profitability of grain. Rationally this must be so; but where opportunities for production other than grain are abundant, and cash incomes (both collective and household) potentially very high, a palliative approach may well have a long and rewarding life. The most important prospective casualty of long-term development of this kind must be, realistically, the collective system itself. It is hard to envisage the maintenance of genuine unified management and distribution at production team or brigade level beyond that which relates directly to the arable fields, the food-grain supply and the state plan, in conditions of proliferating opportunity and widespread adoption of family production schemes. Nevertheless, there would be much opportunity for collective enterprise, with superior levels of investment and bigger scales of operation, in the kinds of production under discussion – poultry, eggs, pigs, fruit and so forth.

Is the Shanghai–Suzhou scheme of production, opportunity and prosperity one which can be envisaged as an objective elsewhere in China? Here the answer must be no, except in very favoured localities – in the peripheries of the cities, in counties close to the new enterprise zones in Guangdong and Fujian, and generally where advantage can be taken, by production and marketing outside the state system, of high urban demand and relatively high prices. Up to the present, even in such favoured localities, the literature has more to say about rigidities in the field of rural–urban business interaction, than opportunities. For the great bulk of the countryside, development on the Shanghai model cannot be envisaged for the foreseeable future, though in any area there must be some limited scope for industrial and market-gardening enterprise, as standards of living slowly climb and schedules of demand widen even in backward inland counties distant from the cities. All this means that prosperity is likely to go on developing much more rapidly in the parts of China most favoured by nature and man. The Maoists limited this kind of polarisation mainly by penalising prosperity. Now that the Maoist scheme has been given up, favoured areas are bound to generate fresh prosperity.

Backward mountain communities

Among the more than 2,000 rural counties of China, 56% are reckoned to lie within the mountain regions. The mountain regions also include 90% of the country's forest area, 40% of its arable, one-third of its population and one-third of its grain production. At present almost one in four of Chinese production teams is considered to be impoverished, with low levels of production and low standards of living among the people and hence low levels of motivation which inevitably condition the outlook for progress. Of these poor units, the great majority are located in the mountain peripheries, many of them in old revolutionary bases to which the People's Republic owes a great deal (*People's Daily*, Editorial, 17 Jan. 1980). These units occur in the mountain areas in both north and south. Many of them have little in common with the high-output-poor units of the north China plain. They are typically isolated and backward, not necessarily short of grain (particularly in the south), but very poor in cash, and hence in investment and consumption. Real improvement in the backward mountain regions is an indispensable part of any policy for rural modernisation and development in China as a whole (Fig. 8.1).

Policy towards the mountain areas during the Maoist decade is something of a puzzle. Several of the most relentlessly publicised Maoist models of development – Dazhai, Lin, Hui, Zunhua – were mountain villages or counties (all from the north); and land construction, a central preoccupation of the media in Maoist times, is a topic specially relevant in the mountains. Yet on the whole the evidence both then and now suggests that the mountains were neglected in Mao's time – especially the mountains in the south. Yet the puzzle is perhaps not too difficult. The media and the planning system were and are two very different things. The media campaigned indefatigably for development, in the mountains as elsewhere. But from the point of view of the planners, a mountain commune which did not demand state grain supplies and displayed orthodox political thinking could reasonably be left alone. Mountain development cannot realistically take the road of greatly increased and intensified arable production; it must, broadly, depend on commercial surpluses. With transport stretched

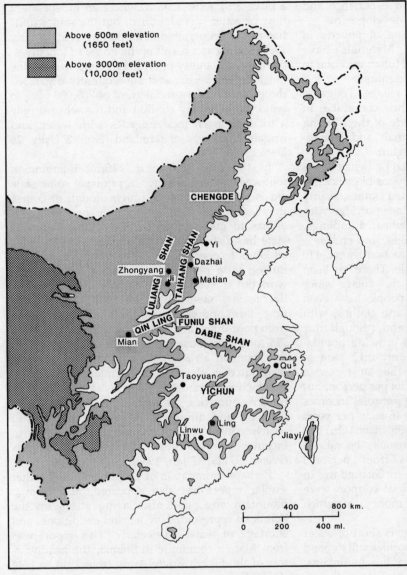

Above 500m elevation
(1650 feet)

Above 3000m elevation
(10,000 feet)

CHENGDE

Yi
Dazhai
Zhongyang
Matian

SHAN
LULIANG
TAIHANG SHAN

QIN LING
FUNIU SHAN
DABIE SHAN

Mian

Qu

Taoyuan
YICHUN

Linwu
Ling
Jiayi

0   400   800 km.

0   200   400 ml.

Fig. 8.1. Eastern China – mountain areas and some place-names.

and commercial mechanisms very weak, additional marketable surpluses in mountain areas would not necessarily be welcome to the state agencies, and in any case, the marketing of surpluses was already under political attack. In fact in many mountain communes, particularly in the south, the political campaigns of the Cultural Revolution had already struck heavy blows at the local capacity to produce such surpluses – as with mulberry orchards and tea-gardens in Zhejiang forcibly converted to paddy-fields, to the great

loss of local units (Lin Lixing). Partly for this reason no doubt, mountain development as an experience beyond that of the favoured models of the Maoists practically disappeared from discussion after 1966.

In the present phase, marketable surpluses are once more expected and encouraged, and mountain development has again become a prominent media topic, as it was before the Cultural Revolution. The state of the forests is a special issue and is discussed in Chapter 9. Here an attempt

123

will be made to review present experience and policy in the field of mountain development.

What is the practical meaning of poverty in Chinese mountain villages? Materials have appeared on two units, one in Hunan and one in Shanxi, which are worthy of attention.

The first of these is Tongzi village. Tongzi is part of Daping brigade, Xianghua commune, in Linwu county on the Hunan side of the Nanling mountain border between Hunan and Guangdong (Yan Shiguan and Ou Qinglin).

Those who investigated Tongzi on behalf of the *People's Daily* were impressed by visible evidence of poverty – no electricity, patched clothes, scanty heating, and evening meals of rice-porridge with only sweet potatoes and buckwheat dumplings, salted sweet potato or chilli leaves, and chillis.

Tongzi comprises three production teams, 110 households and about 500 people. There has been little change of any kind in the village since Liberation – year by year the people have been short of money, short of food and clothes, with the same production system and (though this point is not made) no doubt a growing population. The work-day is worth only 0.12 *yuan* in most years, or 0.5 *yuan* at the most. Grain supplies are usually at least 320 *jin* per person, but may fall as low as around 200 *jin*; total incomes per person are usually around 46 *yuan* per year, but they may fall as low as 35 *yuan*. On this showing, cash incomes must usually be nil. (A Chinese acquaintance reports from personal knowledge of one such village in Guangdong in 1980 that various kinds of official coupon were used to serve the function of money, of which there was none.)

Why this poverty? The village is short of water and prone to drought. Water supplies still depend on storage in natural pools in the mountains; when these dry up the people have to walk 2 or 3 km to neighbouring villages to fetch drinking water by hand. In 1979 there was an exceptional drought; the second crop of paddy dried out severely, outputs fell, and incomes fell to the low levels already mentioned.

There is a local river with a good flow, but it is polluted by a tin-mine some distance upstream, and the water cannot be used for drinking; even for irrigation it creates difficulties. The mine pumps out some 5,000 or 6,000 tons of polluted water daily, containing sulphur, arsenic, molybdenum, zinc and other poisonous materials. In 1974 the villagers planned to build a conduit from

a place 3 or 4 km distant, where an independent flow of water was identified, but the senior units had not given permission for this work up to early 1980. Mainly as a result of the *People's Daily* investigation, the county provided a pump to meet the most urgent needs, and subsequently organised the provision of a special grant of 700,000 *yuan* to build the necessary conduit and tunnel to supply a total of seven local brigades with water, and irrigate 3,000 *mou* of farmland (*People's Daily*, 26 Dec. 1980).

In the case of Tongzi, official intervention followed media publicity. In principle some state aid is available for such units, though of course they are advised to rely mainly on their own efforts to make progress. Since Liberation, the state has distributed 30,000 million *yuan* in aid of all kinds to poor units, and in recent years, 1,500 million *yuan* per year. (The latter figure would work out at 3,000 *yuan* for each of 500,000 production teams, one-tenth of the total.) At the same time, farm and enterprise taxes may be remitted from poor units, and so forth. In Zhejiang in 1979, 77% of the cash used to aid poor units came from the state, in all 8.7 million *yuan*, and this was distributed in eleven poor mountain counties, all of which then made investments in such fields as timber nurseries, mountain enclosures, land levelling and afforestation, and all but one of which subsequently registered increases in incomes from commune and brigade enterprises (*People's Daily*, 17 Jan. 1980).

Perhaps in imitation of Tongzi, a second rather similar report has also appeared, also from a mountain area, and also laying stress on the handicap represented by natural conditions, and shortage of water particularly. This report was from Matian commune in Shanxi, the headquarters of the Eighth Route Army from 1940 to 1944 (Duan Cunzhang).

The main natural problem is the Zhang River, which separates Matian from some of its arable land and cuts off its access to the outside world. A bridge is badly needed for the sake of practical convenience and because the river is dangerous when in flood; but no help is forthcoming to build it. There are other problems. Six of the brigades have no motorable road; some have no road at all, only footpaths. Fourteen brigades still have no electricity. Water is scarce and is often used several times over; in some places, people have to carry water as much as 10 km. Without water, houses cannot be repaired – and more important, pigs and poultry are not practicable. There is no capital to build a reservoir; subsistence is hand-to-mouth. In Xiamatian brigade food supplies recently rose to a satisfactory 600 *jin* per year from 358 *jin*, and the cash value of the working day from 0.5 *yuan* to 0.9 *yuan*, suggesting annual incomes per person of the order of 40–50 *yuan* at the latter date. Health care is backward; the local barefoot doctor is trained only to sell medicines and give injections. The twenty more isolated brigades never see a doctor or drugs. Predictably perhaps, the birth-rate is high, around 6%, and the population growth rate at present is nearly the same (Duan Cunzhang).

Although these two accounts show some signs of self-consciousness and were perhaps both written with an eye to public or official reaction, they contain sufficient realistic detail to carry conviction as representing one low level of village subsistence in mountain China.

Current policy for the mountains: diversification

A recent manual of mountain development policy from Zhejiang (Zhejiang province Agriculture Committee) represents current orthodoxy. In purely production terms, this is centred upon diversification – forestry and herding in addition to grain. In locality terms, the Zhejiang approach is both more adventurous and more specific than might be expected. One key section relates specifically to resources, drawing attention to the richness of native wild flora and fauna in China, the great diversity of habitats in the mountains according to slope, aspect, elevation and so forth, and the large extent of mountain land per person in most mountain areas, compared with the narrow limits to arable resources. (op. cit., 41–53). Here and elsewhere (op. cit., 17), examples are given of local units which have established prosperous economies based upon commercial specialities suited to their particular environments – seed potatoes in one brigade, quarrying in another, poultry in another, bamboo in another. In addition it is argued (op. cit., 62–9) that many mountain economies are stagnant and require sharp stimulus, which in turn will require marked improvement in commercial circulation (op. cit., 70–1). Realistically, it is not argued that the strengthening of commercial outputs can obviate

the need for self-sufficiency in food; but it is argued that types and varieties of grain and cultivation practices ought to be suited to mountain needs, and that by adaptation of appropriate practices cultivation on the limited arable land should be gradually intensified to increase food output (op. cit., 36–40).

Mountain diversification – the north

The much-repeated litany of Dazhai has made many of the environmental problems of the northern mountains familiar – gullies, droughts, the highly seasonal climate, and isolation. Gullies represent earlier deforestation conjoined with the effects of the dry winter and torrential rain at intervals in the summer; they destroy the arable and create acute local access problems. Winter is the season of main climatic stress, with drought, wind and a long season at risk of frost, usually around 220 days, giving around 140 days frost-free. Problems of isolation include both local problems and those represented by difficult journeys from major centres. The northern mountain environment is a hard one, and on the whole the literature since Dazhai has become less optimistic about it – less optimistic, certainly, about the possibility of changing the environment rather than adapting to it. Adaptation, broadly speaking, is the name of the approaches which are now being promoted. There is general hostility to the Maoist grain-at-all-costs policy, but otherwise little uniformity. Wide differences in environmental conditions contribute to wide differences in productivity, prosperity and policy, together with other factors such as local and provincial leadership.

Northern China, inland from the north China plain, is basically a plateau; hence a distinction of principle is not always made in the literature between the loess plateau and the mountains, particularly in Shanxi. Such a distinction must depend mainly upon topography (as distinct from elevation) and soils. The Taihang and Luliang mountains which represent the eastern and western edges of the Shanxi plateau block respectively are rugged and difficult country and in common with the rest of Shanxi have alkaline brown-earth soils of forest origin, rather than loess. These soils extend on to the Chengde plateau area to the north of Beijing, but are not widespread in the mountain ranges of the north-east, where soils are generally much more heavily leached, usually dark brown-earths (Institute of Soil Science 1978).

Forestry, herding and agriculture represent the three main kinds of livelihood open to the northern China mountain communities, and through the 1950s and early 1960s, when the mountain areas figured fairly frequently in the media, mixed development was promoted, usually involving some degree of commercial activity (Xinhua, 15 Oct. 1961, on Mian county, Shaanxi, for example). Under the Maoists, many afforestation claims were made (Xinhua, 8 Apr. 1972; 23 Nov. 1975); at the same time units every-where experienced pressure to make themselves self-sufficient in food-grain at whatever local cost (*People's Daily*, 18 Oct. 1972, translated in *SCMP*, 72(44),152–6 – from Shaanxi; 10 Apr. 1972, trans-lated in *SCMP*, 72 (17), 54–9 – from Fujian). Where production and investment continued which was oriented otherwise than towards grain production, it was insisted that these must be subsidiary to subsistence (Dao county party committee 1972). At the same time the Depart-ment of Commerce, to judge from its own mate-rials, abandoned interest in mountain produce in favour of the class struggle (Department of Commerce 1972: 70–4). By the standards of moun-tain reports from the early 1960s, with their low grain yields, diversity of outputs and relatively high levels of commercial activity, these pressures represented considerable changes among which the depression of cash production cannot have been welcome. Nevertheless the mountain communes must now contemplate the freer and more competitive future with mixed feelings. The mountain environments are not strong, and with few exceptions the communities are not well placed in any race towards prosperity.

Moreover the likelihood of practical change in the foreseeable future, especially in terms of the obligation to provide for local self-sufficiency, must not be exaggerated. The Luliang prefecture in western Shanxi is an isolated mountain area with 1.4 million people. If it had a deficit of, say, 150 *jin* of grain per person (about 30%) the phys-ical supply of grain would demand the provision of 100 trucks for 300 days per year to deliver food from central Shanxi to the communes in the mountains (Wang Guoying). Obviously this obli-gation is not one which the state or province would wish to shoulder. It is claimed that this argument leads directly to more specialised arable management with greatly increased yields on the best arable land in the mountains, and quite possibly to conversion of some of the present arable to grazing or trees. Where it does not lead, is to any possibility of production teams' using their self-management rights to step out of the obligations of the state plan, planting only what can be sold for cash, and expecting to consume state-supplied grain at home.

Grain yields which are quoted from various mountain areas in the north vary within a wide range. Figures close to or above 1,000 *jin* per *mou* represent the top of this range, and are obviously exceptional. Low figures may be very low. At a brigade in Ji county in south-eastern Shanxi, not really in mountain country, yields per *mou* were raised from 56 *jin* to 194 *jin* during the 1970s. Many yields in the low hundreds are quoted, and many places subsequently praised for improved yields started from levels of this kind ten or twenty years ago (Wang Guoying). Intensification in the sense in which that term may be under-stood in the lowlands offers rather little to many units in the mountains, where 'low-output-poor' is the watchword, rather than 'high-output-poor'. Intensification is a slow starter in the mountains.

The obvious alternative is diversification, or 'integrated development' as it is often called in media discussion of the mountains, presumably in order to retain the commitment to self-suffi-ciency in food within the model. Forestry, herding and agriculture itself may all provide foundations for a diversified local economy. In some cases diversification does represent a fresh start; but in others no more than the restoration of the tradi-tional economy.

In Yi county, north of Baoding in Hebei, at the edge of the Taihang escarpment, a brigade called Chuangjiao adopted such a programme in 1970 as a supplement to a grain economy which was not successful (Hu Yaobang). Under this programme, 4,200 *mou* of woodland has been planted and 3,000 *mou* of natural woodland fenced for protec-tion; at the same time 300 *mou* of land was improved to *sanbao* standard, and an animal economy started. By 1978, the woodland and animal enterprises were contributing 43% of cash income, and grain yields had been higher than 1,000 *jin* per *mou* for eight years. This is one of a number of cases where it is argued that the opportunities for profitable forestry in the mountains represent the way towards prosperity in this kind of environment. Some people argue that afforestation brings improvement in water management, grain output and opportunities for local industry as well. Many other units in Yi have followed this kind of rationale – it is reported that 97% of all brigades in the county now have at least one forestry team. The general principles suggested are that timber production should be encouraged in the high and distant mountain areas and tree crops such as oilseeds and fruit in the foothills. 'Private' mountain plots have been introduced in some places. At Dongguxian brigade in Dugang commune, an area of 250 *mou* of barren mountainside was distributed among households, and the whole area successfully planted to trees in three days (Hu Yaobang). Yi county has designated six communes and eighty-four brigades where forestry is to be the main field of production. These units are to receive the same food-grain allocations as in 1979 for three years; grain-surplus units will be allowed to keep any additional surplus, and grain-deficit units will not find their commodity grain supplies reduced if they increase grain output. Trees previously collectivised are being returned to their individual owners, or compensation paid.

Integrated development also features in an account from the Luliang mountains in western Shanxi (Wang Guoying). Two brigades, Wangjiagou in Lishi county and Gaojiagou in Zhongyang county, are constrasted. The former has an impressive record in engineering land construction and received a state grant for this kind of work twenty years ago, but the results in terms of output have been limited. Gaojiagou on the other hand has combined terracing and dams with afforestation and improved grazing; and the results are better.

The extensive mountain area north-east of Beijing, mostly drained by the Luan River, is Chengde prefecture (Zheng Qimin). It was formerly forest land, cut over earlier in the present century, and now has a mixed mountain economy with herding, farming and forestry. The Maoists depressed herding in favour of grain farming. At a date unspecified, a state grazing farm of 1.3 million *mou* (866 sq km) was converted to grain farming, for the sake of saving commodity grain and in the hope of creating a commodity grain base. But while the animal population fell, grain output did not rise, and the farm lost 470,000 *yuan* in 1978. In Weichang county in the same prefecture, with only sixty or seventy frost-free days, 22,600 *mou* of grassland were converted to arable in 1975–78, but for every 10 *mou* planted 9 gave no harvest. Everywhere in Chengde, it is argued, herding has been suppressed but grain output has not risen to take its place. What appears to be exceptional here is the extent to which Maoist policies were continued up to 1979 at least. Animal populations were still falling late in the 1970s, as they had been ever since 1966. Between 1975 and 1978 the cattle population fell by a further 8%, and the goat population, which is the most important, by 30%. Some counties in Chengde now have no more goats than in the early Liberation phase.

The only reason for this continued fall which is given is continued official hostility to the private rearing of goats. Because of political criticism, private goat populations in Chengde fell from 26,000 animals in 1957 to 1,765 animals in 1977. At least until 1977, private goat-rearing continued to be bitterly criticised at high levels in Hebei province. What is now argued is that if the people are not allowed to keep private goats, collective goat-rearing suffers severely and at once (Zheng Qimin).

In addition to diversification or rediversification, the orthodoxy of the present also offers another policy change to the mountain areas – responsibility systems. Explicitly, the household responsibility systems have been represented as appropriate to the needs of mountain areas (CCP 1981: K8). A good deal of discussion has been reported on points of principle and politics in connection with the northern mountains (FBIS *Daily Report*, 20 Aug. 1981, quoting *Shanxi Daily*, 22 July 1981), but rather little which relates directly to production or organisation on the ground. Satisfying increases in production are attributed to responsibility systems in Yuncheng prefecture in extreme south-west Shanxi – not mountainous country (*People's Daily*, 18 Jan. 1982); but no such claims are made for mountain areas in any of the several articles on the responsibility system from Shanxi which appeared in 1981. Claims are few also for mountain areas in other provinces. There is room here to suggest that the northern mountain communities, by and large, have settled down to a quiet, traditional and, if necessary, indigent life within the new philosophical systems.

Mountain diversification – the south

It is obvious that in any policy for increasing rural diversification, southern China has many advantages by comparison with the north – much longer growing seasons, much better water supplies, much more varied wild flora, and more extensive broken hill-and-valley topography. Nevertheless, rather less achievement has been reported in this field in recent years, even from the south, than might have been expected. The regional model in this field which is most prominent in recent literature is Yichun prefecture in western Jiangxi. Yichun has sixteen counties including Yichun county, and it lies in mixed foothills, plains and mountain topography, where conditions for diversification are good. In the thirty years up to 1978, the rural economy remained grain-orientated with very little development in terms of varied outputs. Average grain yield is around 840 *jin* per *mou* – a good but not distinguished figure. Grain output per person increased very little between 1952 and 1978. Farming remained old-fashioned, with very little mechanisation (Zhong Jiaming: 37); and incomes were necessarily low. Units here were caught in a high-output-poor

trap, it is said, until in 1979 policies were introduced which encouraged them to convert from grain monoculture to a mixed economy. In the first year of change, in the majority of cases grain outputs nevertheless rose by about 10% while cash incomes rose by 30% or more. Units have converted paddy-fields to economic crops, and have started pig, cattle, duck, chicken and other enterprises, many of which have experienced very rapid subsequent growth (*People's Daily*, 23 Feb. 1980). A number of examples illustrate the continued greater profitability of economic crops, woodland and animal or poultry enterprises, or manufacturing, than of grain crops – though the continuation of high grain outputs is stressed (Zhong Jiaming: 39). Table 8.1 presents an analysis of production data for one team, Tangbei, from the point of view of present policy, and indicates the greater profitability of various kinds of diversified outputs. (The two rows of figures at the end of the table relating to outputs net of costs other than labour, which have been added, make the same point still more forcibly.)

A number of further points arise. Diversification is being closely linked to specialist responsibility groups and related systems of supply and payment by contract. Groups of this kind were organised in 39% of production teams in 1980 and in almost 70% by 1981. Responsibility for production may be fixed at any one of a variety of levels – team, working-group, household, worker; and bonuses are adjusted to take account of these.

Table 8.1. Tangbei Production Team, Hongtang commune, Yichun county – costs and outputs in various activities, 1980

	Grain crops	Economic crops	Crafts	Brickworks	Woods	Oil and grain processing	Fishponds
Area (*mou*)	108	17	—	—	100	—	2
Output by weight (*jin*)	146,800	2,059	—	—	—	—	1,500
Gross output by value (*yuan*)	16,882	1,626	1,800	5,800	4,358	705	915
Labour employed (days)	11,394	877	832	1,768	1,401	94	112
Costs other than labour (*yuan*)	5,968	283	—	1,455	431	230	305
Gross output (*yuan*) per *yuan* of costs	2.82	5.74	—	3.98	10.1	3.06	3.0
Gross output per working day (*yuan*)	1.48	1.85	2.16	3.2	3.11	7.5	8.16
Net output (including labour) (*yuan*)	10,914	1,343	—	4,345	3,927	475	610
Net output per working day (*yuan*)	0.96	1.5	—	2.6	2.8	5.1	5.5

Source: Zhong Jiaming: 39–40.

Responsibility systems have been adopted in both grain farming and various kinds of subsidiary production (Chen Chuanyi et al. 1981).

In this way labour which is already surplus to need in the paddy-fields, sometimes to the extent of 40% or even more, is being progressively shifted from grain farming to specialist production, to the advantage of outputs, diets and incomes. In the wake of this shift, there is increasing talk of a second shift of equal potential importance – the reassessment and valorisation of the land resources of the rural communities other than the arable. At present 80% of rural labour, it is pointed out, uses only 20% of rural land resource (Zhong Jiaming; Chen Chuanyi et al. 1982). The argument is that in the new context of widened opportunity at both collective and household levels, a fresh start may be made upon the creation of new arable where economic crops can be grown, or fruit or tea-gardens planted.

A variety of other examples can be found in the literature. Broadly they tell the same story. Ling county in south-east Hunan (*People's Daily*, 17 Aug. 1979) raised farm outputs other than grain by 20% in 1976–78, and grain by 16% at the same time. Average net incomes rose from 74 *yuan* in the former year to 114 *yuan* in the latter. Left-wing interference, it is now argued, resulted in suppression of what had been a lively cash economy before the Cultural Revolution, so that average incomes fell from 84 *yuan* in 1971 to 74 *yuan* in 1976 – and even grain output did not rise in this phase. Now a fresh appraisal of the resources of the county's sixteen communes has been made. These include sites for hydroelectric stations, raw materials such as timber and bamboo, coal and cement minerals, and abundant opportunities for expansion in silk, fruit, herbs and tea. The nine-tenths of the county's area which is reckoned as mountain is to be seen as a place of opportunity, not of desolation. In 1978 commune and brigade enterprises were worth 9.6 million *yuan* gross income, against 4.2 million in 1976. Diversification pays, we are reminded, not least in terms of cash. A certain team planted 10 *mou* of unoccupied land with mulberry, and started silkworms in the same year, receiving 2,500 *yuan* income (gross apparently, but costs other than labour would not be high) as against only 600 *yuan* potential income from the same land had it been planted to paddy. No exodus from paddy is suggested, but the implications are obvious.

An oddity, but one which relates directly to the concept and practice of a diverse mountain economy, is dispersed settlement. Even in mountain areas, most people in rural China live in villages or hamlets, but some do not. In a number of counties in the Funiu Shan mountain countryside of western Henan, in the boundary zone between southern and northern China, such as Lushi, Luanchuan, Ruyang and Song counties, households to the total number of 10,000 or more live in scattered dwellings away from the villages. Under the Maoists, this way of life was thought to lead to spontaneous capitalism, and many families were removed to the villages, leading to neglect of mountain resources both arable and wild. In spring 1979, restrictions on living outside village communities were lifted in this area, allowing people to make an independent living in the mountains, with fixed production obligations and the right to keep surpluses according to the regulations for household responsibility systems. Encouragement was given to these migrants by many of the villages in such forms as work animals to take with them. At the same time, some of these families left their children in the villages (presumably with relatives) so that they could go to school. Most of the migrants became self-sufficient within a year, as well as planting trees and working in the woodlands (*People's Daily*, 23 July 1980). On a less optimistic note, it is presumably among such families that the authorities find some of those for whom household responsibility leads to neglect of birth-control and schooling.

Valorisation of mountain wasteland in southern China

Discussion of the northern mountains in the Chinese media tends to centre upon their hostility as environments and the limitations, as well as the problems, of development. This is not, however, the case with discussion of the mountains of the south. The southern mountains are treated much rather as favoured environments with abundant unfulfilled promise and unrealised opportunity – so much so, that sometimes even writers with a conservationist axe to grind find themselves falling into enthusiasm about the abundance of land and other actual and potential natural resources in the mountains, and the low prices at which many of them can be brought to the market. A recent long and imaginative article on mountain Zhejiang gives a broad conspectus on present thinking on mountain development in the south (Tie Ying 1980).

In Zhejiang as a whole there is about 100 million mou *of mountain country [67,000 sq km, about 70% of the land area]. If only one quarter of this area were properly developed for timber, bamboo, tea, silk, vegetable wax, oranges, spices and herbs, together with new arable land created in suitable locations, its output value must at the least amount to that of the province's present arable area of 27 million* mou.

Ambitious though this reasoning is, it is probably well founded in principle; but its realisation on the ground would obviously depend initially upon a long and complex process of colonisation, development, stabilisation and humanisation of the wild environment whose scale and implications are not yet being seriously discussed in China, and of which there is not much sign of real understanding. In this respect the Maoists' insistence on equating mountain development with efforts to grow grain on land little suited to it did a good deal of psychological as well as physical damage. Clearly, diversified production, much of it intended to enter commerce, is what will suit the mountain environments, but equally clearly, genuine mountain development will demand vast human effort and investment of many kinds.

Some writers are even more specific and more optimistic (Liu Houpei). Chestnut woods can yield 600–800 *jin* per *mou* of edible nuts, giving a marketable yield of nuts worth 200 *yuan* per *mou*, between three and five times the economic yield of paddy – but this possibility obviously depends not only upon environmental and farm conditions but also upon the potential market for chestnuts (usually sold dried as a specialist vegetable) and the existence of the necessary transport and marketing organisation. Similarly, land under natural grass in southern China typically yields about 800 *jin* per *mou* of grass per year – up to sixteen times the unit area yield of desert fringe areas in northern China, five times that of ordinary prairie grassland in the north, and three times that of marshy grassland in the north. But it is the north which specialises in animal husbandry. Taoyuan county in Hunan has 1.4 million *mou* of grassland, an area close to that of the arable. The present limited herds of cattle and

goats could be expanded by three times or more, and the state could be supplied annually with upwards of 6 million *jin* of meat. This calculation is surely realistic in itself, but what is less so is the unspoken assumption that the state would be able to handle 3,000 tons of meat annually, delivered by Taoyuan county.

Diversified production is now orthodox of course. 'Policies to suit local conditions' is the watchword – in the early 1960s before the Cultural Revolution, the same advice was given as 'treat a mountain farm like a general shop'. Soil, elevation, slope, aspect and accessibility all create important differences in land-use potential. For instance, mulberry is suited to river-banks and moderate slopes, where the soil is good and moisture reasonably plentiful. But further up the mountains, where the ground dries out severely in winter, mulberry will not thrive, and the tallow-tree, which is tolerant of drought, is better suited. Management ought to provide for some longer-term investments, it is now argued, such as tea or oranges, which take three years or more to produce any return and also some crops such as melons which produce results the same year (Tie Ying 1980).

Timber, fruit and silk are not the only way forward in the mountains. A very wide range of possible outputs can be suggested – for instance milk, edible fungus, animals other than pigs, nuts and fruit. Marketing is often a problem, however. In Qu county, Zhejiang, beekeeping is particularly profitable – annual gross output per worker can be 3,200 *yuan*, against average gross farm output of 432 *yuan*. But effective demand is inflexible; if output increases substantially, the price of honey falls to that of sugar (Tie Ying 1980). Many other examples illustrate the same point. Meat, milk and other perishables produced in mountain areas obviously present special marketing problems. Cold stores exist in China, but not usually in mountain areas. In many parts of China traditional methods of preserving meat exist, and there are traditional cheeses; but these cannot be taken for granted. Nor, up to the present, can constructive activity on the requisite scale on the part of the Department of Commerce. Rural free marketing is important now, but it cannot handle trade on the intercounty or interprovincial scale; and if it did do so, it could not but challenge important official prerogatives.

This discussion has already taken the Chinese

author some way beyond the low prices and limitless potential represented by the mountains. Low prices are no way to create prosperity, and limitless potential cannot be realised without near-limitless investment of which there is little sign at present. Other writers have tackled the same topic. According to the reports on the Fifth National People's Congress, a delegate pointed out that in the nineteen counties of southern Jiangxi alone, there is a total of about 5 million *mou* of red-earth land at present lying waste, virtually a 'red-earth desert' – an allusion to the ferralitic soils, poor in nutrients and weak in structure, which cover these hillsides (Institute of Soil Science 1978). In mountain areas throughout southern China, including all provinces from Jiangsu and Fujian to Sichuan and Yunnan, there is in aggregate as much as 100 million *mou* of waste hillside land available for development – an immense area by any standards, 7 million ha or 70,000 sq km; some 70% of the total area of a small Chinese province such as Zhejiang (*People's Daily*, 27 Sept. 1980). It is argued that most of this land could readily be planted to such commercial crops as oranges and other fruits, nuts, coffee, cocoa, tea, mulberry, oilseeds, lacquer, sisal, rubber, pepper, spices, medicinal herbs and bamboo, giving protection of the soil and preservation of ground-water as well as useful economic outputs. Here, too, there is little indication of the long-term local problems of settlement in these vast areas, though the obvious need for better commercial mechanisms is pointed out. To settle 70,000 sq km of hillsides effectively in Chinese terms would suggest population movement of not less than 14 million people – not an impossible enterprise, given suitable social organisation, but much more formidable than the planting of trees and the marketing of outputs, things which are already difficult for the community to manage. From the point of view of the development of the soils, a combination of orchards, bamboo, timber and dense mixed development is probably the best policy of all, but the social implications are vast.

These materials suggest that opportunities now exist for a major phase of fresh land colonisation in southern China, with all the necessary accompanying experiences of migration, village creation and so forth. Such a movement could not be based primarily upon paddy, for which irrigable land cannot be created in these areas on a large scale. It must be based upon dryfield agriculture like the comparable and very successful colonisation of farmland in mid-elevation western Taiwan in such counties as Jiayi, admittedly generally upon much better soils; and to a great extent it must be based upon marketable outputs such as fruit, vegetables, ginger, maize, poultry and animals, together with compensating local purchases of food-grain, especially rice (Williams: 95–103).

It is sometimes argued that while this kind of economy is possible for the smaller communities and smaller areas of mid-elevation Taiwan, it is out of the question on the scale requisite in Zhejiang, Hubei, Jiangxi or mountain Guangdong, with populations numbered in the tens of millions. To this it must be replied that where Taiwan has one Jiayi county, Guangdong has ten; but the problems and attendant possibilities of their solution, on the ground, are basically parallel. In Taiwan, settlement is usually by peasant families with land grants from the government; the people make their own farms over the period of a lifetime. In China it is hard to imagine that any communist government could accept a scheme of settlement based on premises of this kind, though there are signs of a continued movement of opinion in this direction (*Economic Daily*, 29 Mar. 1983, translated in FBIS *Daily Report*, 12 Apr. 1983), and it might well attract settlers if it were proposed. Even more to the point perhaps, Chinese official policy has been so unstable since 1949 that it is hard to believe that such a scheme could last a lifetime and more, as it should. In the absence of individual settlement, colonisation of these vast areas at the levels now envisaged cannot but be through official enterprise, presumably at provincial and county level. But there is little reason to believe that Chinese official enterprise at any level at present is capable of initiating, managing and sustaining any such ambitious and sensitive schemes. The same must apply to the scheme proposed by another author (Xiong Deshao), who suggests the widespread adoption of an animal husbandry economy, to occupy an available mountain grassland area which he estimates at 400 million *mou* (26.6 million ha or 270,000 sq km). Physical capacity to produce is one thing; practical social organisation on both the administrative and economic levels is another. Meanwhile, in these extensive mountain areas potential resources are neglected, and in many areas environmental conditions are deteriorating steadily (*People's Daily*, 16 Oct. 1979).

The mountain hinterlands

This discussion sets out from the recognition that on the whole the mountain communities in China are poor and backward for good environmental and traditional reasons – because of isolation, poor levels of resource use in relation to population, immobility in the production or trading systems or both, continued population growth conjoined with social indifference or resistance to change, and so on. Nevertheless, more than one-half of China's counties and one-third of its population belong to the mountains. They represent a burden to the state which (given generally very high levels of local and regional self-sufficiency) is not intolerable; and they also represent a wide range of fresh opportunities and generally under-capitalised resources. Particularly in southern China and as far north as the Qinling, and also to a lesser extent in the north-east, the mountain areas could maintain more people at better standards, and make more contribution to national outputs, than they do. To do so they would need to move more closely into the mainstream of the Chinese community. They would require more investment in agriculture to strengthen the subsistence side of local economies – irrigation schemes, small farm machines, better techniques, more animals and poultry and more local marketing, etc. In addition, very extensive areas await colonisation which can certainly not be undertaken at any level below county. They would also need more, and more reliable, trading links for commercial outputs – tea, nuts, dried fungi, fruit and herbs, bamboo and timber, animal products.

There is no doubt that more progress has been made in the subsistence economy than in the commercial economy during the past generation – Fig. 2.8 shows that the overwhelming majority of mountain areas in eastern China, apart from those on the Great Wall and desert frontier, are basically self-sufficient in food; and of course the majority of the 60,000 small hydroelectric stations must be in or near mountain areas – there was said to be an electricity supply in 70% of all communes in 1975 (Howe: 88), though obviously brigades and teams are another matter. In these environments, as far as subsistence is concerned, the responsibility systems, like the class struggle before them, seem likely to contribute more to immobilism than to change. To the commercial economy the present regime is likely to give more political and ideological encouragement than its predecessors, but there are so far only limited indications that it can give much more practical help or many incentives. Practical help would have to include better transport and storage systems; incentives must include regular business contacts and much more business trust. All these things will take time and good will to build. The special case of the boom conditions of parts of the forests, where capital is being squandered by one group or another while provincial or county authorities remain indifferent or powerless or both, does not augur well for rational and properly controlled commercial enterprise in the mountains in other fields. The Department of Commerce no doubt has more pressing and equally vital obligations in, for instance, the cotton counties of Shandong.

Self-help over a period of years (which is the traditional method) is likely to go far to supply the development needs of the subsistence side of the economies, given continued official stability and broad political encouragement as at present. But for fresh colonisation in the mountain countrysides, and even more for effective commercial development, positive activity above the level of the local units is essential.

Pl. 10. Traditional village houses in an old-fashioned alley in a suburban commune near Guangzhou.

Pl. 11. Landscape on the western periphery of the north China plain. Some signs of drought – a poor maize crop. But vegetable plots may have received special care.

Pl. 12. Carrying fertiliser to collective fields in the Shanghai countryside. This is an official Maoist picture from 1975.

Pl. 13. Mountain scenery at Badaling, some 70 km north-west of Beijing city but still within the bounds of the municipality.

Pl. 14. Jiangnan countryside – lowland Zhejiang near Hangzhou, 1982. Sparsely wooded hillsides form the background to low terraces which support the second crop of rice. Closer to the camera, a patch of tea-bushes where geese are being grazed in charge of a herdsman – both tea and geese are likely to be collective. The concrete pylons carry the electricity supply. In the foreground a film crew are making part of a feature film.

Pl. 15. Loess landscape – gullies and terraces in the loess landscape, in prosperous countryside with adequate rainfall close to Xian, central Shaanxi. Late summer; the fields have been cleared, probably of a maize crop.

Pl. 16. Qidong county, Jiangsu, a major cotton-producing county in the Nantong peninsula. Deliveries of cotton for the state.

Pl. 17. In the foothills of the Qinling Shan in central Shaanxi, south of Xian. Beyond this spot the valley narrows and the road ends, as the slopes become precipitous.

Pl. 18. Hillslope farming on land settled within the past generation in Nantou county, Taiwan. Paddy with garden crops and orchards; dispersed settlement; access by footpaths usable by motor-bikes.

9

Afforestation and the forest area

The past generation has not been a good one for Asia's forests, but China has often been excluded from the general Western criticisms of rapacious over-exploitation. We read in the Brandt report (Brandt et al.: 84) that 'Experience in China has shown that the combination of a strong political commitment at the top with broad public participation and shared benefits at the bottom can provide a basis for rapid reforestation' – but this optimism is not shared by the Chinese press in recent years. In fact, it emerges that the forests of China are and have long been under great pressure of exploitation, and that protection and conservation are on the defensive. A provisional forestry law, China's first, was published in 1979, with emphasis on protection and controlled development of the forests, but many evidences indicate that this can be no more than a first step. In fact, it was preceded by a number of quasi-legal directives issued in the period 1961–63; but these were swept away in the Maoist enthusiasm of the Cultural Revolution in 1966 and subsequently (Li Shiqiao: 7–9).

At present about 12.7% of the land area of China is under forest or woodland, a modest proportion which represents a total forested area of the order of 1.2 million sq km or 1,800 million *mou* (Zhang Jianguo: 44; Fig. 9.1). This figure includes orchards and other plantations. An alternative figure of 1,470 *mou* for timber forests has been proposed by the responsible minister (FBIS *Daily Report*, 9 Nov. 1981, 12, quoting a Beijing broadcast of 6 Nov. 1981). The minister added that 66% of this timber forest area represented immature forests. Of the whole forest area, 52% is owned and managed by the state. A generally rather conservative directive from the State Council (1980) proposes the increase of the forests finally to 30% of the total area of China, and as a first step to 20% of total area by the year 2,000. This aim may well be possible of attainment in principle, but it seems unlikely to be attained in the face of the many alternative preoccupations of the community. At present, forest renewal is barely keeping pace with cutting, and 1,000 million *mou* (67 million ha or 670,000 sq km) of suitable land await afforestation (Forestry Policy Research Unit 1980). Some light is thrown on the limitations of Western notions of extensive reforestation in Chi-

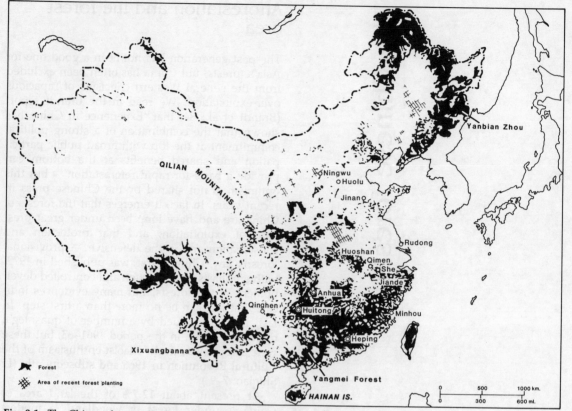

Fig. 9.1. The Chinese forests. *Source*: Forestry Department.

na by the information that one-third of state forest units are not served by roads, and two-thirds have no lorries (Zhang Jianguo: 44). Afforestation in such areas must be very difficult, but by the same token the protection to such areas afforded by their isolation must be one of the main supports of the survival of forest to the present.

Afforestation since Liberation has not been negligible, though its extent is not clear (Ross). The extent of forest cover in China is said to have been raised from 8% at Liberation to 12.7% in 1979, suggesting afforestation in that period of 675 million *mou* (45 million ha). But over the same period of time, the specific afforestation claim is only 420 million *mou* (28 million ha) (Zhang Jianguo: 44). According to *Ten Great Years* (133), 236 million *mou* was afforested between 1950 and 1957. It is common ground among Chinese commentators that the first years after Liberation were good years for afforestation, and that matters fell back subsequently. According to the official figures, the former rate of afforestation has now been more than restored. The present accelerated

rate of afforestation is around 4.5 million ha (68 million *mou*) per year (State Statistical Bureau, 1980, 1981, 1982, 1983). The present annual rate of consumption (including destruction) of timber in China in 1980 was estimated at around 200 million cu m (Forestry Policy Research Unit 1981: 41), which probably represents 50–70 million *mou* (3.5 –4.5 million ha) of forest. Forests have been vulnerable to destruction during phases of policy at both ends of the political spectrum – in 1958– 60 as a result of the 'backyard' iron and steel campaign and the collectivisation of resources, in 1966–76 during the Cultural Revolution, and since the latter half of 1979 as a result of economic liberalisation, with widespread over-exploitation by organisations of many diferent kinds (Forestry Policy Research Unit 1981).

In prehistoric times the eastern half of China had widespread forest cover, but there has been an extended historic process of deforestation of which the present is only the latest phase. Forest is now rare, apart from poorly developed and relatively inaccessible areas such as the south-west, the north-east, the Qinling and parts of the south-east. Floristically, the Chinese forests are remarkable for their extreme richness and diversity. The species count of around 35,000 is one of the richest on earth, and in addition the Chinese flora displays an exceptional degree (40–50%) of endemism – regional individuality (Grubov: 268–9). The natural fauna of China, both vertebrate and invertebrate, is also exceptionally rich (Bannikov et al.: 366–7), and of course is closely allied in ecological relationships with the forests. The richness of Chinese natural environments in living species is one foundation for the pharmacy of traditional medicine, and makes a noteworthy contribution to traditional diets among both rich and poor. This floristic richness also supports an exceptionally wide range of forest uses, as well as suggesting an exceptional need for conservation in modern times. Neither of these aims has been served by the widespread forest clearance which is now reported for most phases of policy since 1957.

Problems of deforestation

At the time of the land reform (1950–52), we read in a strongly worded anti-Maoist article from Fujian (*People's Daily*, 20 Sept. 1980), there were four classes of registered ownership of the forests – by individuals, by villages, by *xiangs* (rural districts) and by the state. After the 'big and public' movement of 1958, the woodlands were concentrated in the hands of the state, the communes (usually at the level previously represented by the *xiangs*) and the brigades; the production teams (i.e. the villages) were squeezed out along with the individuals, and the people lost interest in woodland maintenance or improvement.

Destruction of forest has since become a gross evil in China. According to one informed opinion, taking China as a whole, one-third of all standing timber is now being cut annually for firewood – and this is the most that can be taken from total resources. If demand continues to increase, there will be risk of total deforestation by the end of the present century (Luo Yuchuan). Some writers blame the Maoists – 'Take grain as the key link, and chop everything down' as one writer says (*People's Daily*, 2 Mar. 1979). Where the media in Maoist times often laid great stress on afforesta-

tion drives (*People's Daily*, 9 Apr. 1971, translated in SCMP 72–17; 17–19, and many others), this is puzzling. A 'letter' from Hunan gives an explanation (*People's Daily*, 17 Oct. 1979). In a certain brigade in Anhua county, we read, stands of Chinese fir were planted in response to pressure from senior units in 1964, with the help of a state grant. Later the young trees had to be cut down according to new instructions, and crops planted. Still later, the senior units called again for trees, and trees were planted once more; but later again contradictory instructions were given, and the trees were again removed and grain planted. Finally in 1974, instructions were again received for tree planting. During these fifteen years, which include the Maoist decade, trees were planted on this land on three separate occasions.

A less bizarre but even more relevant case is that of the Qilian mountain range in the environmentally sensitive Hexi corridor in Gansu (*People's Daily*, 27 July 1980). Here local factories, army units, and farming, herding and other collective units, were all involved in forest clearances which took place in the Maoist period. In all, some 300,000 *mou* of land were cleared in this area, representing 20,000 ha or 200 sq km. There were many cases of theft of timber. As a result, destruction was widespread, water conservation potential was reduced, some springs dried up and rivers lost volume, grain output fell in some areas and grazing grounds were reduced. In some places the clearance of woodland was still in progress in 1980; conjoined with expansion of grazing herds, this results in erosion-prone pastures and the thinning of the vegetation cover to the point of approaching desertification.

The truth of the matter seems to be that while the Maoists talked about afforestation, in practice they insisted upon increases in grain production at all costs – if necessary at the cost of forest clearance. In some areas the rot set in at the time of the ill-fated Great Leap Forward in 1958, when woods were cut down to provide charcoal for the 'backyard' iron furnaces (*People's Daily*, 6 Mar. 1981). Land clearance to create new arable has had very serious effects on the forests. In all, we now read, some 700,000 ha of woodland was cleared 'in recent years' to create new arable (*People's Daily*, 13 Sept. 1979) – and this would represent 7,000 sq km. It is worth calling to mind, however, that any deforestation provides cheap or free firewood and timber for the people's use or for sale, to the amount (in southern China) of about

5 cu m per *mou* or 75 cu m per hectare (*People's Daily*, 13 Sep. 1979). In this respect the people are provided with a powerful motive to clear forest land.

This brings us to an issue which is even more important in the Chinese forests than Maoist prejudice. The critical point, now and into the future, is that deforestation provides timber which can be used, sold or burnt. Local collective units are not zealous in protecting their own timber, and may well be enterprising in exploiting that belonging to the state. There are estimated to be 80 million rural households (47% of all rural households) in which firewood supplies are inadequate for three to six months of the year; and in the north China plain as well as on the loess plateau there are many communes and brigades in which shortage of firewood is acute, and in which as much as 20% of labour is expended in cutting and carting of firewood from mountains near or far (*People's Daily*, 23 May 1981). (In the 52% of rural households in which firewood is less scarce, doubtless more firewood is used.) In Rudong county in Jiangsu, there has been serious destruction of the coastal shelter-belts which protect the land from high winds. Here, of the original 15,000 *mou* of state shelter-belts, about 3,800 *mou* have been cut down since 1973, some to provide arable land for grain or cotton, some to supply kilns and brick-works with fuel. This has had the connivance, and sometimes the active encouragement, of the county authorities, and no doubt owes something to relentless state pressure upon local units to increase grain and cotton outputs under the Maoists (*People's Daily*, 15 Aug. 1979).

In parts of China where timber is still plentiful, particularly the mountains of the south, over-exploitation is now a gross evil. Different authorities have different interests in planting, conservation or exploitation. 'For one man who picks up a spade to plant trees, there are a hundred who pick up axes to chop them down' (Tie Ying 1980) In each of the five provinces of Fujian, Guangdong, Hunan, Anhui and Guizhou, cutting is now running at more than 10 million cu m annually above production, and in Yunnan, at more than 14 million cu m above. In Yunnan, this means that annual cutting is now double annual growth, and in Sichuan the situation is also serious – cutting is now 1.6 times growth. Of course in smaller units, counties for example, much higher figures for forest destruction can be found (Chi Weiyun: 42).

Tropical timber is a special problem. There were some 13 million *mou* of first-growth tropical forest in China in 1949; but in 1977, owing to excessive cutting and clearance mainly in Hainan island, only 3.6 million *mou* (Luo Yuchuan; Chi Weiyun: 42) – in Hainan the whole environment is now under heavy pressure due to deforestation without proper protection or restoration of the deforested areas (Yu Dechang: 49–50).

Theft may be serious. In Guangdong in 1978–79, 1.6 million cu m of timber were stolen from forests, involving violence and injury to 560 forestry workers and 3 men killed (*People's Daily*, 8 Oct. 1980). In Fujian, the new forestry law is openly flouted. Exploitation of state forests in the Wuyi mountain range in the west of Fujian has reached such a stage that the road between Chongan and Shaowu is blocked by piled timber – but all this cutting is without proper authority. In this case, ownership is evidently uncertain; hence everyone comes to take what is to be had (*People's Daily*, 8 Dec. 1980). In these cases and many others, what is really at issue is not the traditional right of local people to gather firewood, grown excessive in a time of rising standards and increased population, though that problem does exist, but essentially business operators practising exploitation on a large scale for commercial purposes.

Here as in many other respects, the resurgence of economic activity since the early 1970s is something which the system finds hard to regulate. Much is claimed for the State Council's 'Emergency circular on firmly checking indiscriminate tree cutting' of 5 December 1980 (FBIS *Daily Report*, 24 Feb. 1981: L19–L20, quoting Beijing radio, 20 Feb. 1981). Since the issue of this circular, it is reported, large quantities of illicitly cut timber have been 'frozen', and free markets in timber have been closed. More than 4 million cu m of cut timber were involved, and some 50,000 people, apparently forest employees operating rackets, dismissed. But disastrous cases are still coming to light. One is the theft of 2,800 *mou* of timber, planted to protect sandy land and worth 1 million *yuan*, in Huolu county west of Shijiazhuang in Hebei in 1980–81 (*People's Daily*, 4 May 1981). Another is continuous over-exploitation in many parts of Huitong county in south-western Hunan. Here steps were taken in 1981 to reduce cutting, but the excuse was used of extensive snow damage to trees in the winter of 1981–82, and cutting has been resumed in some communes

(Wu Xinghua). In some cases responsibility for woodland has been devolved from brigades to teams, and sometimes to households. Some state woodlands have been distributed. In some cases communes have entered into deals with factories in towns. Some cadres have done illegal personal deals. In all these cases the forests have suffered further cutting, and are likely to go on doing so (Wu Xinghua).

A further regular problem is forest fires. The dry winter inevitably puts all forests at risk, but so does increased human access. In approximately two months in 1979 in Guangxi there were 110 forest fires, which burned through a total of 128,000 *mou* of forest – this would be nearly 8,533 ha, or 85 sq km. Similarly in Fujian at the same time, there were 190 forest fires affecting 100,000 *mou*; and in Guangdong more than 100 fires, with loss of 70,000 *mou* (*People's Daily*, 12 Dec. 1979). According to another calculation, the area of forest lost in China due to fire since 1949 represents about one-third of all the afforestation in China since that date, and is about the same as the area cut for use (Liu Yunshan 1979). Fire represents total waste, but its suppression must await better social discipline and better systems of local vigilance.

Finally, there are ecological problems to consider. These are often mentioned incidentally, but are brought up directly and in detail in the context of Qingzhen county in Guizhou which is the western neighbour of the provincial capital, Guiyang (Wang Ganmei). Forest cover in Qingzhen at the time of Liberation was about 30%, but by 1975 this figure had fallen to 5%, due in the first place to the 'backyard' iron-smelting movement of 1958, in the second, to clearances for new arable since 1960 – and in the third, no doubt, though this is not mentioned, to local depredations of all kinds. Erosion has increased dramatically, resulting directly in the loss of 54% of the dryfield arable in the county – 271,000 *mou*, 18,000 ha or 180 sq km. Irrigation capacity has also been lost. At the same time, the newly created arable, amounting to 140,000 *mou*, produces generally low yields, of the order of 300 *jin*. Grain yields for Qingzhen as a whole are still low – only 385 *jin* per rural person, three-fifths of the national average of 636 *jin*. Animal populations have also fallen between 1958 and 1978 – cattle by 12%, goats by 87%. Grain supplies for the people are stretched; 23% of production teams receive only 300 *jin* per person per year, which is not sufficient, and 31% of teams distribute cash incomes of less than 40 *yuan* per person.

A particular case is quoted of a brigade called Shanbao, which up to 1966 had 500 *mou* of forest and 600 *mou* of scrub, a woodland income of 8,000 *yuan* per year, and plenty of grain. Fresh opening of land for arable began in 1967. This resulted in the virtual disappearance of the woodland and the doubling of the arable area, but a fall in grain output of around 30%, as well as the loss of cash income (Wang Ganmei: 72).

Here it is argued that impoverishment results directly or indirectly from interference with the forests. Probably there are other factors intervening, such as (to judge from many parallel accounts) the suppression of the cash side of local economies under the Maoists. But in terms of ecology, a place like Qingzhen, its forests located only 20 or 30 km from the provincial capital, would be particularly likely to suffer from the kind of environmental onslaught which is described. We may begin to postulate an outer von Thunen ring of urban-based ecological devastation around some Chinese cities, to lie beyond the inner ring of urban-based prosperity to which Donnithorne (1967: 88) has drawn attention.

Underlying problems

The weaknesses which underlie these losses

'Rats stealing oil.' The rats, dressed suspiciously like cadres, are stealing from a pot labelled 'Property of the people'. *Source: People's Daily*, 20 Aug. 1981. The artist is Miao Di.

appear to be of two different kinds – problems of ownership and management of the forests, and problems of timber use in the community at large.

A number of writers have pointed out anomalies in rights to ownership and use of the forests. Most of these anomalies arise within orthodox socialist structures. Most forests and woodlands at present belong either to the state or to collective units, but among these are enterprises and organisations, departments, institutions and state farms. Some woodlands belong jointly to more than one authority. Rights among these various units are not always clearly defined, and boundaries are often undefined or in dispute. In addition, rights to ownership or use of the forests may or may not be distinguished from similar rights to mountain resources other than the forests. Failure by the state to stabilise ownership and other rights, and sometimes failure by state organs to obey state regulations, has led to much confusion and exploitation in recent years. In some places, forest assets have been stripped by cowboy operators. All this can only be stopped by widespread clarification and stabilisation of rights to ownership and use of forest resources (Lin Yanshi: 6–10; Li Shiqiao: 9). This is so even in terms of collective and state ownership alone. In addition, there is now a powerful body of opinion which would like to see the use and management (not necessarily ownership) of actual or potential forestland allocated to local people, to grow trees which should be their property (Lin Yanshi: 10–12).

The price of timber is low – in Anhui 30 *yuan* per cu m. Cut into firewood, its price is 10% or 20% higher on the spot; and transported to town, for instance by commune members in their free time, its price rises to 50 or 60 *yuan*. In Fujian, the price of cut timber is higher, around 200 *yuan* per cu m, but it is still three or four times the price of raw timber (Fujian province Forestry Bureau). According to one calculation, a timber crop produces only a few *yuan* profit per cubic metre and may easily make a loss; but the same cubic metre of timber after manufacture will be worth up to 100 *yuan*, and possibly even more. In Zhejiang in 1978, the 101 state forestry units employed more than 10,000 men and produced timber worth 15 million *yuan*; but the timber workshops of Hangzhou alone, employing 2,500 men, produced outputs worth 17.5 million *yuan* (Forestry Policy Research Unit: 30). Grain is cheap in China, but timber is still cheaper – in Zhejiang, the price of timber in relation to grain has fallen

steadily from an equivalent of 600 *jin* of rice to 1 cu m of timber in the 1950s to 400 *jin* in the 1960s and 200 *jin* at the end of the 1970s (*People's Daily*, 8 Oct. 1979).

At the same time, use of timber in China is often extravagant, due to its low price, to ineptitude and inexperience in the community, and to rigidities in the supply system. Too many agencies are separately involved in supplying timber to the cities. Timber is not always properly seasoned before use, cutting is often extravagant, and unused timber is usually left with the consumer, and at least in Beijing, generally burned. A number of writers have pointed out the need for blockboard mills to make use of offcuts at sawmills, which at present are usually wasted (Liu Songjiao). Charcoal manufacture is the traditional use for such timber, but it is not mentioned in recent reports. In addition, timber is often used for functions where less scarce materials such as cement or basketwork might be used – in all these cases and many others, timber is being wasted in spite of its scarcity. In some places, an attempt is being made to protect timber resources by prohibition on the sale of timber articles outside the county or province – but this does not please the rural units which formerly used bamboo or substandard timber [sic] to produce furniture for urban markets; such wood is now burned or left to rot, and furniture remains notoriously scarce in the cities (*People's Daily*, 31 Mar. 1981). In wooded areas rural people tend to use timber very extravagantly – in the Dabie mountains in Anhui a new house is reckoned to consume between 10 and 30 cu m of timber. When a team of eighteen households in Huoshan county in the same province built new houses in 1979–80, they used 1,300 trees (*People's Daily* 31 Mar. 1981).

A classic problem case is reported from Ningwu county in northern Shanxi (*People's Daily*, 23 Mar. 1980). In this area, a rural household uses 30 *jin* of firewood daily, of which one-half may be sound mature timber. Hence in a year, this household uses 5,400 *jin* of mature timber, representing 2.5 cu m. The 2,230 households of the four communes hence consume about 5,570 cu m of mature timber annually as firewood. This is about one-fourth of all timber cut in the county. There is coal in Ningwu. Each household might use about 4 tons of coal per year in place of timber. But coal, which is mined at three small pits in one of the communes, costs 4 *yuan* the ton at the pithead, suggesting 16 *yuan* per year for a household, plus the cost of transport. Transport of coal cannot be easy. The communes have 3 lorries and 5 tractors between them, but more than 20 of the 53 brigades have no road access. Meanwhile, wood can be cut and gathered free by commune members in the 18,000 *mou* of woodland, whose ownership is in fact in dispute with the state.

A parallel example comes from Huizhou in south Anhui (Wang Lihuang and Zhou Yufu). Here, too, most households in the prefecture use firewood, and there is also heavy demand from tea-processing works, restaurants, brickworks and so forth. Timber replacement rates were 60% in the early years after Liberation; now only 30%. Erosion has resulted from wholesale clearance of woods. Here, too, there is coal in the area. A contrast is drawn between She and Qimen counties in Huizhou. In She, brickworks, quarries, workshops, tea processing, rural mechanisation and the towns have been converted to coal, and the county is now burning up to 40,000 cu m of wood less a year. But in Qimen there has been little conversion; the county tea-processing plant alone burns 2,000 cu m of good timber to process its 2.5 million kg of tea annually.

Paraffin is often a valuable substitute for firewood in rural economies, but in China it appears to be very scarce, and must be used for lighting rather than cooking. Less than half a litre per household per month was available in Rudong county, Jiangsu, in 1979 (*People's Daily*, 15 Aug. 1979). Similarly, improved rural electricity supplies cannot readily be used for cooking. Even organic gas supplies require substantial investment in scarce commodities such as plastic pipes, if they are to reach individual households.

Problems in the state forests

The points which have so far been discussed relate mainly to forests in areas where forest is not the main resource, or forestry the main industry. In areas of the latter kind, there are signs that discussion takes rather different forms, usually related to tensions between the forestry authorities and the local people.

In the Changbai mountains on the Korean frontier, it is argued that the state forestry administration is too powerful and too strict (Tian Liu). In the Yanbian Korean autonomous *zhou*, all the state forestry bureaux have county rank, and 40

of the 110 communes in the *zhou* fall within their jurisdiction. This causes administrative difficulties. As much as 80% of the whole area is wooded, but the state restricts access to the forests by the people, who have need of forest resources in their narrow, agriculturally backward and disadvantaged environment, with only 100–120 frost-free days in the year. Some of the forest is already poor second growth. The state does not have the means to improve these areas, and the people are not allowed to do so, or even to collect herbs, fungus, undergrowth and firewood. Fires are too common – in 1978, 287 fires destroyed 440,000 cu m of timber. The people of the forest countryside are very poor, and can get little or no advantage from the forests which occupy the majority of their habitat. They are arguing for improved access to forests, partly in the name of need and natural right, partly using the claim that improved access would result in better maintenance – a claim which in the light of experience elsewhere may be treated with some reserve.

A different but related story comes from Xishuangbanna in the extreme south of Yunnan, bordering on Burma and Laos, a large and thinly populated area with the status of an autonomous *zhou* (Cong Linzhong and Jiang Shaogao).

Here the main conflict is between two state organs, the Forestry Department which is responsible for the forests, and the Agricultural Land Department which is trying to extend the rubber plantations and increase rubber output; but the interests of both are in conflict with those of the local people. Subsistence, conservation and development are at odds. Conservationists, especially the Forestry Department, point to the extreme richness of the wild flora and fauna of Yunnan, and also the extent to which it has suffered environmental pollution and direct destruction since Liberation. Developmentalists, particularly the Agricultural Land Department, have very different interests – 'We have worked and fought to build rubber plantations for the state for twenty years; now suddenly we are branded as criminals' (Cong Linzhong and Jiang Shaogao)

The main preoccupation of the local administration is food supplies. Xishuangbanna is not self-sufficient in food. Both the arable area and food output have roughly doubled since Liberation, but so has population, now around 600,000. Arable yields are still low, and little changed since Liberation – 300 *jin* for paddy, 100 *jin* for dryfields. The local minority people still practise slash-and-burn agriculture, which naturally involves land clearance. Most forest fires originate in land clearance. There is great antagonism between agriculture and forestry. This applies particularly to expansion of agriculture in any form. When in 1980 grain output was increased by 60 million *jin* (30,000 tons), 80% of this increase was at the cost of forest clearances on the steep hillsides; grain output in the valley bottoms actually fell. To expand grain output in conditions of low yield must require fresh arable land.

There is also antagonism between official agricultural colonisation and the local administration. The Agricultural Land Department has 8 state farms and 74 settlements, involving in all 140,000 people, mostly producing rubber. The local authorities find this powerful organisation a burden, not least because of the need to find food supplies for the workers. The state supplies maize, but the workers want rice. Conflict between the state farms and the local farming people arises over farmland, the mountain forests, grazing land, potential rubber land, and water supplies; relations are often strained, both locally and at various administrative levels. Much the same is true, even at provincial level, between the Agricultural Land Department and the Forestry Department. As the state farm people say, 'We are all sleeping together in the big bed of socialism, but each has his own dream' (Cong Linzhong and Jiang Shaogao)

Ownership of much of the forest is far from clear. The province has proposed that some of the state-owned forest land should be transferred to the communes, to improve management through improved motivation on the part of the local people. In some cases, collective–state proportions of forest have been changed in this way from 3 : 7 to 7 : 3. Some local units have totally prevented access to the woods, even to the point of blowing up bridges and obstructing roads – to keep out trucks and power saws, they say; and they claim that they have been forced into this position by outside pressures upon the forests. The forestry professionals say that to distribute state-owned forests to collective units is a clear recipe for disaster – the brigades and communes would not hesitate to cut down everything for sale. This is what is said to have happened in the first years after Liberation – local units sold off their forest resources in exchange for grain, until the state monopoly in grain was started, breaking

off this trade. But local cutting for firewood is now not less than 1 million cu m per year in Xishuangbanna, representing the annual loss of 100,000 *mou* of forest. Forest cover in Xishuangbanna amounted to 70% or 80% at Liberation, a total of around 20 million *mou*; but half or more of this has been cut down since 1949, leaving a forest cover which amounts to only about 30%. Only about 1 million *mou* of first-growth forest remains (Cong Linzhong and Jiang Shaogao).

In Yunnan province in 1980, as these pressures work through, destruction of woodland for all kinds of reasons (gathering firewood, clearance for new arable, forest fires, timber cutting) amounts to 27 million cu m per year, while growth is around 14 million cu m per year – little more than one-half of destruction. Apart from the loss of woodland resources, much of it grossly wasteful, soil erosion has been greatly stimulated in some areas by forest clearance.

Rules and money are in conflict; but more than that, rules are in conflict with rules and money with money. One authority's rational measure is another's loss and a trespass upon the authority of a third. Responsible solutions, which would include more positive and constructive forest management by both the state and local units, more intensive agriculture, and less departmentalist jealousy among state organs, can be envisaged, but lamentably are far to seek in practice (Cong Linzhong and Jiang Shaogao).

Some constructive developments

Amid so much gloom on the forestry front, it is satisfying to read some success stories, Zhenshan and Dayi, two brigades in Minhou county, Fujian, have very satisfactory forestry policy and practice (*People's Daily*, 15 Sept. 1980). Both occupy valley locations near Fuzhou with good communications. Dayi has 12,000 *mou* of mountain land, Zhenshan 5,000 *mou*, and virtually all has been reafforested, apparently since Liberation. In both, afforestation has reduced erosion, improved water supplies and strengthened arable farming. In Zhenshan, about 59% of the brigade's total income comes from woodland; in Dayi 27%. Local measures have been put into operation against theft of timber and forest fires – heavy fines and other kinds of official measures against delinquents, and (perhaps more important) patrols to find them out. Arrangements are also made to allow commune households taking part in the forest production programme to receive allowances of wood – in Zhenshan, 150 kg of bamboo and 1 cu m of pinewood loppings and gatherings per year, and every two years 0.25 cu m of China fir. Dayi has redistributed about one-quarter of its woodland to the production teams. The rest is divided into twenty-one woodland districts, averaging about 430 *mou* (29 ha or 0.29 sq km), each with its forest caretaker. Payment is arranged to compensate for the isolation and responsibility of this job for those who undertake it.

Another case which has been mentioned more than once in the literature comes from Jiande county in mountain Zhejiang, about 120 km south-west of Hangzhou. This is Chunli brigade in Qianyuan commune. Here the planting of woods is managed according to a job responsibility system introduced in 1978, which prescribes quotas for fixed areas to be planted to fixed standards in fixed periods of time, against fixed remuneration. In addition the workers are entitled to perquisites during the first three years – grass and twigs for firewood, and 70% of the crops which can be interplanted with the trees in the first years; the remaining 30% goes to the production teams. At the end of three years the job responsibility group hands over the trees to the brigades and teams. A survival rate of 95% is assumed; for each additional sapling which survives, a bonus of 0.2 *yuan* is payable; but for each sapling which dies above the 5% allowed, the responsible worker loses 0.1 *yuan*. Under this system, in the winter and spring of 1978–79, 1,200 *mou* of China fir, much used in building, were planted, with a survival rate of 98%.

Elsewhere in Jiande there are 16 forest areas managed at commune level, and more than 200 belonging to brigades or teams. Most are run on some kind of partnership with commune members, with typically 10% of yield paid to the unit owning the land, 20% to further investment and 70% to the workers, to be distributed through the teams (*People's Daily*, 4 Aug. 1980).

Policies of practical cooperation between a state forest estate and local commune units, arrived at after a long period of contentiousness over boundaries and rights, have attracted praise in Guangdong. The Yangmei state forest occupies watershed land between the Sui and Liang rivers north-west of Guangzhou, stretching through parts of Quinguan, Huaiji, Yangshan and Guangming counties. Afforestation is to be extended on both state and village lands, using capital and expertise provided by the communes. Five small reservoirs are also to be built for joint use, Yangmei to provide 60% of capital, the communes 40% plus labour (*People's Daily*, 10 Oct. 1980).

Elsewhere in a similar context it is argued that effective management must rest upon clear and stable systems of ownership. In Heping county, Guangdong province, the responsibility system depends upon clear distinctions among forests owned by the state, by the commune, by the brigade, by the production team collectively and by individuals as 'private plot' copses; and also between rights of ownership, rights of management and rights of cutting. On this kind of basis, it is argued, individuals and the collective units know where they stand, and can and do behave constructively (*People's Daily*, 13 Mar. 1981).

Encouraging news about the planting of firewood copses comes from Heilongjiang province (*People's Daily*, 31 Mar. 1981). Heilongjiang is of course rich in forest in the mountains, but in the populated plains firewood is already very scarce; of 3.6 million rural households, 2 million are short of fuel and 1 million very seriously short. In some places people eat only one hot meal a day in summer, and in the bitter winter cannot keep their houses warm, so that frost forms inside the walls. In units of this kind, between 10% and 20% of all work may be occupied in collecting and transporting fuel. When grass is used as fuel, a household may burn as much grass as would feed eight goats or two cows. In these conditions firewood copses are a necessity, ideally at the level of about 3 *mou* per household – in Heilongjiang about 10% of land. Copses on this scale not only provide firewood, but make a valuable contribution to ecological stability in populated countrysides. Many kinds of area are suitable – roadsides, steep slopes, river-banks, etc. In this report, only a few brigades are mentioned as having established these copses, and the scheme is still at an early stage of development, but it obviously promises well.

By 1981 or 1982 the need for forest creation and protection throughout China was firmly established in the media, and publicity was being given to many regional and local afforestation drives – in Sichuan, Gansu and Guangdong, among other provinces, in the spring of 1982, for example

141

(*People's Daily*, 9 Feb., 13 Mar., 14 Mar. 1982). Newly planted areas were then being quoted which do bear significant relationships to planting need – in Guangxi, 15,000 ha; in Gansu, 100,000 ha; in Guangdong, 260,000 ha sown from the air.

The same was true also of 'private' copses to provide fuel. The State Council's directive (1980) specifically authorised this. 'In communes and brigades where there is mountain or other waste-land, and where firewood supplies are scarce, the provincial-level authorities should issue instructions that commune members should be allowed to use a certain limited area of open mountain, sandy or other wasteland to plant trees for themselves – provided that the interests of collective woodland development are not affected.' Individuals are also to be encouraged to plant trees outside their houses and elsewhere on land allocated by production teams, and trees planted by communal units and individuals are to be protected. In this and other respects priority is now being given to the creation of woodland, at some cost to the principle of collective ownership. The inhabitants of state-owned mountain or wasteland, where there is no prospect of state afforestation, are also invited to create woodland – in such a case, the woods will belong to the communal units, but the ownership of the land will not be affected. Alternatively, the state may cooperate with local units in afforestation projects, but opening of land of this kind for farming will not be allowed. Units such as workshops or mines may plant trees for their own use on land (such as roadsides) made available by production teams or other units, or may make cooperative arrangements and share the value of the timber (State Council 1980).

A *People's Daily* Editorial (17 Apr. 1982) lists trees suitable for planting in such copses in various regions, and suggests allocations of land at the rate of 1 or 2 *mou* per person (hence up to around 12 *mou* per household) for this purpose. Of course, not all localities have land to spare on this scale, and of course there are implicit long-term problems for continued collective ownership of land in all these schemes.

The forests under siege

The problems which have been discussed in this chapter, taken together, suggest a somewhat depressive view of forest and woodland prospects in contemporary China. It should be added that they represent a very fair selection from materials appearing in the Chinese press since 1978. There seems no doubt that the combination of a rural population which has almost doubled since Liberation, with a move to local community control of resources, somewhat better access in the mountains, and greatly increased demand for timber in the towns and rural industries, now puts exceptional pressure upon all forest resources except the most remote. Formerly, in China as elsewhere in east and south Asia, wild resource tended to be protected in some degree by poverty, lack of social organisation, inaccessibility and low levels of technique. At present, as a result of developments operating cumulatively during the past thirty years, China has a serious backlog of loss by forest clearance (and a backlog of cleared land which has not been redeveloped); a high present rate of deforestation (encouraged in many cases by disputes about the ownership of the forests, whether by the collective units or by the state); and a number of regional problems which relate either to resources of special value, as in Hainan or Yunnan, or to particularly vulnerable areas, such as mountain Fujian. Of the forest which is not at present under threat, much appears to be either too inaccessible (as in mountain Sichuan) or too distant from densely populated areas (as in the north-east). Neither of these kinds of protection is likely to endure for ever unless strengthened by human authority. The most encouraging feature of the present situation is the favourable global rate of afforestation, which to judge from the official figures (which do not suggest any rate for unsuccessful afforestation) is probably about the same as the present rate of cutting. Even so, a rate of afforestation which is parallel to that of clearance offers nothing at all to areas previously deforested. Details are not given, but presumably what is implied here, at least in some degree, is a greatly accelerated rate of cropping of trees in the most accessible forest areas.

Obviously there is a good deal here to distress conservationists; but in most Chinese countrysides a thoroughgoing conservationism of principle would be too distant from human need to be practicable. This is no doubt the case in the Chinese forests; but in these forests the present danger of final destruction of very much barely replaceable resource is acute. From the material which has been presented a number of priorities can be deduced, which taken together represent a rational approach to these great problems.

The first of these is indeed ecological protection. There is a powerful case for the total protection of all the natural forests which remain in China, though such a policy would necessarily be conditional upon the capacity of the provincial and county authorities to enforce it. It would also be conditional upon a series of measures intended to divert pressure of all kinds away from the forests. Some of these measures depend upon direct control and policing, or official sanctions, or both. They include rationalisation and stabilisation of ownership of the forest resources, suppression of theft, and limitation of free use. Suppression of forest fires may arise partly from these, but must also involve direct and effective policing. One central problem is that of supplies of firewood, both for domestic use and for local enterprises both rural and urban. The policy of allocation of land locally for firewood copses must be welcomed where this is feasible, as on the loess plateau, but in many problem areas such as the north China plain land is too scarce for such a policy to be generally viable. There is also no reason to think that such copses could supply local industries with fuel. For such areas, mostly densely peopled, and for industries and enterprises everywhere, policy must look towards the widespread and rapid substitution of alternative kinds of fuel, particularly paraffin (involving investment in suitable stoves) and coal. Local coal supplies which could generate income through commune enterprises promise particularly well in many areas. The present phase of rapidly growing rural prosperity and widening opportunity for rural workers is a relatively favourable time for such a change. It would involve heavy transport commitments, but there have been many indications that increased rural transport capacity might well be created by local collective units as part of the development of commune and brigade enterprises.

The reverse of the coin of forest protection is forest restoration. Two standards may be adopted for afforestation policy – the rate of deforestation and the extent of afforestable land. Of these, the second is obviously the more prudent standard to adopt, and the one which best makes use of available resources of land and labour. In this respect the Chinese concept which considers plantations of bamboo, orchards cropped for nuts, fruit or oilseeds, and mulberry and tea-gardens as akin to forests is realistic. In the 'red-earth deserts' of the central southern provinces the restoration of forests or plantations or both is an urgent priority. Here what is at issue is high-yield possibilities on poor land which is bound to deteriorate in a deforested condition. On the Great Wall frontier, there is an unanswerable case for as much afforestation as the local communities and provincial and county governments can manage to achieve. Successful large-scale achievements in fields of this kind are likely to be conditional upon resettlement ventures and also upon rationalisation of ownership and management.

Finally, there is a case for increased imports of softwood to supply demand in the cities. Such imports would cost the state hard currency, but would be consistent with the present reorientation of priorities between heavy industry and the countryside.

10

Problems of environment and livelihood

The loess plateau is the weakest major region of homeland China, and the one whose experience of development since 1949, and prospects for the future, offer least grounds for optimism. Broadly defined, it comprises the northern half of Shaanxi, most of Shanxi, eastern Gansu and parts of Qinghai and Ningxia – in all about 220 counties and cities, and a vast total area around 3 million sq km. To the north it abuts against the Great Wall, and beyond it the edges of the Gobi desert where moving sand presents the continuing threat of desert encroachment. This extended zone may be called the Great Wall frontier, in Lattimore's sense of a frontier of settlement (Lattimore 1940). Beyond the Great Wall lies Inner Mongolia.

To the east the limit of the plateau is the scarp of the Taihang Shan, rising abruptly 1,000 m above the north China plain, though in Shanxi many soils also have mountain and woodland characteristics. To the south it extends as far as the edge of the Guanzhong plain and Wei valley in middle Shaanxi. It includes most of the middle course of the Yellow River and most of its tributaries, including some of the most important such as the Fen in Shanxi. The loess has not always been a backward periphery; on the contrary, together with the Guanzhong plain and its city of Xian, its south-eastern half was for centuries up to Tang times part of the metropolitan heart of China. Xian lies at about 380 m elevation; the bulk of the plateau lies between 600 m and 2,000 m, and the mountains, especially in Shanxi and Gansu, rise up to about 3,000 m. Loess covers this vast area like a blanket, ranging in thickness from 30 m or less up to 100 m or even 200 m, forming the largest loess deposit on earth. Above 2,000 m elevation, the mountains rise through the loess covering like islands in a loess sea (Jiang Dehua). During historic times, progressive deforestation, erosion, desiccation and isolation have reduced the plateau to persistent poverty and placed it under constant threat of disaster and famine.

As Table 10.1 shows, the loess plateau is far from uniform. Dramatic differences in natural conditions arise between Xian, in the plain, and a place such as Yinchuan, 500 km away to the north-west. Topography becomes gradually more rugged, and vegetation conditions approach

Table 10.1. The loess plateau – types of landscape; types of problem and policy

Elevation (m)	Type of landscape	Localities	Problems	Policies now favoured
400–1,000	Arable valleys	Wei valley (Guanzhong) Fen valley, and tributaries	Threat of mountain sheetwash, sedimentation; topographical irregularities; soil alkalinity in places; resources still not completely used	Land reconstruction to improve farmland; improvement in water installations; intensification on the arable
Around 1,000	Plateau fringes – usually arable	Central Shaanxi, Shanxi	Erosion resulting in loss of farmland and increasing scarcity of ground-water	Land reconstruction aimed at conservation of resources. Shelter-belts and rationalisation of water use
1,000–2,000	Desert and semi-desert areas in pastoral use	Great Wall	Serious sand movement due to overgrazing and ploughing-up. Water scarce; agriculture backward	Protection and replanting of grassland and woods. Creation of *caokulun*, farm and pastoral local bases
1,000–1,500	Loess ridges. Mixed arable, pastoral, woodland	Northern Shaanxi, western Shanxi, Ningxia, eastern Gansu	Level land scarce, serious erosion; food, clothing and fuel scarce; arable, animal and woodland economies all weak	Organise broad-based local economies; restrict arable use of slopes; plant shelter-belts; promote *caokulun*; improve arable
1,500–2,500	Mountain areas, usually forested	Taihang, Luliang, Lupan and other mountain ranges	Poor environments with loss of forest and grassland resources; economies backward	Protect forest and grassland; eradicate insect pests; improve woodland; promote rational use of forests

Source: Adapted from Jiang Dehua: 3.

gradually towards desert, from south-east to north-west. Plains and shallow valleys give way north-westwards to pediment features, ridges, gullies and desert wastes. Soil changes from black and chestnut loams to sand. Conditions which seem difficult in, say, middle Shaanxi are already easy by comparison with the far north of the same province. In the course of the 400 km journey north from Xian to the provincial boundary at Jingbian, on the Great Wall, elevations rise from 380 m to around 1,500 m; precipitation falls from around 700 mm distributed among about 100 days of the year, to around 450 mm distributed among only about 70 days; and the frost-free period falls from about 210 days to about 140 days. Winter temperature minima fall from −15 °C to −21 °C, to −28 °C to −33 °C; summer maxima fall from 39 °C–42 °C to 36 °C–39 °C (Shaanxi Province, Agriculture and Forestry Bureau; 2–5). These conditions on the Great Wall in Shaanxi are already approaching those of the central Asian deserts. There is little effective difference between the edges of the southernmost salients of moving sand in northern Shaanxi, and those much further inland in Gansu or Xinjiang; in northern Shaanxi the north-west wind may blow for eleven months out of twelve. But population density is relatively high at 20 per sq km or less in most of northern Shaanxi and southern Ningxia. The figure is much lower than the 200 per sq km of the Guanzhong plain, but still much higher than the levels typical of Inner Mongolia or Xinjiang, 1 or 2 persons per sq km over vast areas. Inevitably, on the Great Wall frontier, pressures upon the environments remain lively (Huang Yongshi: 43–4).

Of the various natural weaknesses of the environments of the plateau, drought is by far the most fundamental; and drought and the threat of drought dominate the region. But the most urgent, and in human terms the most serious, of the plateau's environmental problems is the disastrous capacity for erosion of the soft loess surface by the rain which does fall. Erosion is considered to affect 90% of the surface of the plateau, and to be serious over 60% of the area. At present, between 5,000 and 15,000 tons of soil is lost on average every year from each square kilometre of the plateau, and in the areas most gravely affected this figure rises to 30,000 tons, or 30 kg per sq m per year (Jiang Dehua: 2). The figure for loss of soil in 1959 was much lower – 3,700 tons per sq km (Li Hsueh-tseng: 46). More than 1,600 million tons of material flows down the Yellow River every year, comprising between 30% and 60% of the river's flow (apparently by weight – Jiang Dehua: 2). This figure has increased in recent years from 1,300 million tons in the years immediately after Liberation (Tong Dalin and Bao Tong) – a disastrous increase in a figure already exceptionally high. Moreover, in addition to physical loss of soil, this erosion represents a grave loss of plant nutrients, on a scale estimated to be of the order of 11 kg of nitrates, phosphates and potash per ton of soil (*People's Daily*, 17 Nov. 1981).

Conditions on the desert frontier are varied, and not necessarily static. Figure 10.1 shows various kinds of desert surface, including moving dunes. On the Great Wall frontier in Shaanxi, the desert has advanced sharply in the past 150 years, with sand seas now extending about 70 km south of the Great Wall; and in the Yulin area, where encroachment is most serious, there has been loss of grazing land and even arable fields under moving sand. In Yulin county half the rural people are living in sand areas. In addition to the

threat represented by moving dunes, the loss of soil by gullying represents a constant deterioration of the environment in terms of depletion of ground-water. The effects of overgrazing and over-cultivation in recent centuries have been brought to a head, many Chinese commentators now insist, by extensive ill-considered conversion of unsuitable open hillside land to arable under the Maoists.

The disconcerting increase in the frequency of dust-storms in Beijing in recent years seems certain to be the direct result of accelerated clearance of forest and grassland on the Great Wall frontier in north-western Hebei and neighbouring areas of Inner Mongolia, where indiscriminate clearance of wood and pasture for arable has already led to extension of the sand seas. There has been planting of shelter-belts, but at Zhangbei in north-western Hebei, directly north-west of Beijing, the incidence of both high winds and sand-storms has increased during the 1970s (*People's Daily*, 6 Mar. 1979). The counter-argument, that the Beijing dust-storms are generated locally in the city and suburbs, does not carry

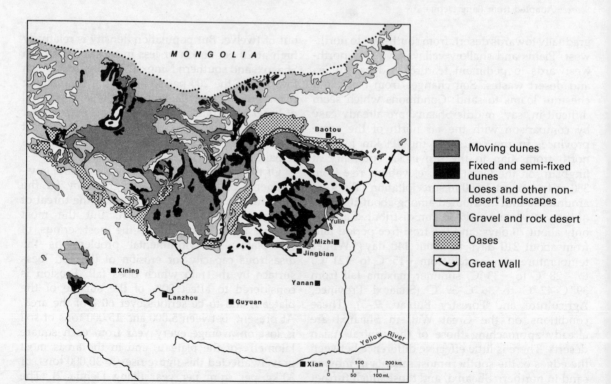

Fig. 10.1 Types of land surface in northern Shaanxi, Ningxia and Inner Mongolia. *Source*: Desert Research Institute.

much conviction (*Guangming Daily*, 4 Apr. 1979).

Nor is this the whole story. In addition to grave losses of soil on the loess plateau, there are obviously corresponding dangers for the north China plain in the burden of sediment carried by the Yellow River, since a great part of it is deposited in the bed of the lower river which is already embanked above the level of the plain, due to previous sedimentation.

Problems of very far-reaching kinds are now emerging. Thus, corresponding to an area where average grain output is less than 350 *jin* per *mou* of arable, thirty-nine counties on the loess plateau provide grain supplies of less than 300 *jin* per person per year – and this in a very severe winter climate, and an environment in which subsidiary food production is not easy. In some localities, as will be shown, conditions have reached a very low ebb in recent years, due to blown sand, erosion, scarcity of fuel and continuing low levels of subsistence production.

The heart of the problems of the loess plateau is northern Shaanxi, together with adjacent parts of Shanxi, Inner Mongolia, Ningxia, Gansu and Qinghai – some 200,000 sq km, 123 counties, about 24 million people. The definition excludes the mountainous south-eastern half of Shanxi and the relatively prosperous Guanzhong plain around Xian, and focuses attention upon the loess plateau proper, and what may be called the arid frontier or Great Wall frontier. Conditions here are very poor. Only about 10% of the land is in arable use, and more than 80% consists of bare slopes, generally without any use at all (*People's Daily*, 16 Oct. 1979). In this area, under the Maoists and up to the present, and in spite of the unfavourable conditions, agriculture is the mainstay of subsistence; but grain yields are low, on average 170 *jin* per *mou* – an average which takes into account local yields which are as low as 50, 40 or even 30 *jin*. This is the world of average annual grain allowances below 300 *jin* per person and average total incomes below 50 *yuan* – the last applies in 57% of the 123 counties of the area. In many localities, standards of living among the people are now lower than in the early years after Liberation or even during the Japanese War (Tong Dalin and Bao Tong).

It is problems of these kinds, arising within the environmental systems and also within the communities which depend upon them, in many areas more acute at the end of the 1970s than at the end of the 1950s, which constitute the foundation of contemporary discussion of development realities and policies, especially along the Great Wall. In most regions of China, the picture of regional and local development presented by the media since 1978 differs considerably from that presented during the Maoist decade, but for this Great Wall region the differences are exceptionally marked.

Land use and land policy

It is now usually argued that the loess plateau environment is basically unsuited to support arable farming, except in favoured special conditions in valleys and basins. A survey in 1973 showed that in that year, with rainfall of 340 mm, the loss of soil in woodland was 8 *jin* per *mou*; on grassland, 12 *jin* per *mou*; on arable with a crop, 476 *jin* per *mou*; and on arable in fallow, 900 *jin* per *mou*. Clearly, putting this land down to arable dramatically increases vulnerability to erosion (Tong Dalin and Bao Tong).

During the Maoist decade, however, there were powerful pressures upon all local units with access to wild land to construct farmland in its place. Limitless emphasis upon the Dazhai model, with its hillside terraces and reconstructed gullies and upon the slogan 'take grain as the key link', and no doubt pressure exerted by many senior units to follow these examples in the direction of grain self-sufficiency if not grain surplus, gave abundant licence to those who wished to transform by labour the semi-deserts of northern Shaanxi, Ningxia and Gansu. It is true that not all Maoist propaganda on the Great Wall frontier was agrarianist – Wushenzhao, the universal Maoist model of the Inner Mongolian fringe, was primarily a pastoral unit; but there can be no doubt that Maoist principle, reinforced strongly by administrative and economic necessity in a state system which could certainly not undertake to supply this vast area with commodity grain, led to much opening of arable, some it ill-considered. It is now said that the extent of productive grassland fell by between 30% and 50% in the ten years up to 1979 (*People's Daily*, Editorial, 2 Aug. 1979). A common traditional practice of farmers, obviously highly conducive to erosion, was the deliberate collapsing of loess cliffs in order to spread the fresh loess as fertiliser on the arable fields. Under the Maoists, the loess attracted particularly extensive terracing, in part no doubt because of the ease of working the soft soil (Leeming 1978: 37).

The Maoists were not the first Chinese authorities to encourage farmland creation in the desert fringes. Many colonisation and migration movements in Ming and Qing times adopted the same policies. Long before Liberation it was recognised that one cause of the southward extension of the desert was the removal of the natural grassland north of the Great Wall by Chinese farming settlers – first the loess particles were blown out, then the sand. Until Ming times, agriculture remained extremely limited north of the Great Wall. It is interesting that the historic record shows that floods on the Yellow River, disastrously frequent in recent centuries, were very few in the first six centuries AD, when these vast territories supported little except grazing. In the last centuries BC, many areas were richly forested.

From this background, in the first years after Liberation, writers were already proposing far-reaching measures like the planting of trees and sand-fixing ground plants in such areas as Yulin, which had suffered severely from the encroachment of blown sand. At that time, average grain output in northern Shaanxi was only 92 *jin* per person (Wang Chengjing: 20–2).

The fundamental problem at that time as always was the shortage of good land. Good land in the conditions of northern Shaanxi means bottom-land, or riversides or in hollows, with moist soil and sometimes permanent lakes. In these spots, there is little danger of serious erosion; and in many, reasonable grain yields, of over 100 *jin*, could be obtained even in the 1950s. Some of the hollows suffer from alkalinity, however, and the river fringes are always best; but this type of land is scarce. The main alternative type of development in the 1950s, with much more plentiful land but much more disastrous results, was a system of occasional farming which was essentially shifting cultivation – farming level stretches of sandy ground for three years in ten, the remaining seven years to be occupied in encouraging the wild vegetation cover, to rebuild the humus supply. Yields in this system were always low, but many households had no other land. The system was also destructive of the soil, because it broke up the natural vegetation cover, which was (and is) seriously destructive especially on slopes above 30°. Apart from this, the only alternative kind of livelihood

was the extension of the traditional trade with Inner Mongolia – timber, cloth and farm tools going inland, and salt and grain coming south, the latter from Baotou and the Yellow River. At that time this trade supplied the local grain deficiency – indeed it probably still does so (Wang Chengjing: 23–5). A 'commodity grain base' of at least regional significance is reported from the irrigated 'inland delta' area of the Bayannur Meng Banner, on the Yellow River west of Baotou, centred on Linhe and Wuyuan (*People's Daily*, 9 July 1979; Fig. 10.1).

An account of this kind throws some light upon the differences between traditional methods of exploitation and the land construction experiences of Dazhai, with obvious advantage to the latter. Eventually the plateau surface must be stabilised, and this must necessitate the stopping of the gullies already formed and the creation of conditions in which new gullies cannot start. The necessary work can only be done by local people – but local people's motivation cannot be expected to work miracles in the present phase. In the 1960s, it was esimated that opportunities existed for the construction of up to 1 *mou* per person of good land by embanking gullies in step form (Chia Chen-Lan), and at Dazhai it was argued that such land would produce up to quadruple normal hillside yields. But although such arguments are useful, they are not cardinal; what is cardinal is the suppression of erosion on the plateau, on the large scale and the small alike.

But it does not appear that either the local community, or opinion in China more broadly, is yet ready for this kind of approach. A recent article by an engineer (Gao Bowen 1981) who seeks solutions to the problem of continued deposition of sediment in the plains course of the Yellow River, argues for comprehensive local landscape management only after discussing such proposals as the diversion of Yangzi water northwards to carry the Yellow River silt away to the sea. According to this writer, only 30–60% of the surface of the loess plateau is at present in use of any kind. He argues finally for increased local physical control of erosion, linked with increased grass and forest cover (and increased grazing use), using management units such as local drainage basins of the order of 30–50 sq km in area. He estimates that such improved and reorientated landscape management will not only go far to suppress erosion and of course deposition downstream, but could raise local income on the loess plateau from the present standard figure of 3 or 4 *yuan* per year per *mou* to between 20 and 40 *yuan*. Sadly, the evidence so far is that the reconstruction of this whole vast region on such lines as these is simply beyond the physical capacity of the population. Sadly also, social and political motivation have already taken such hard knocks under the Maoists that they are bound to be very difficult to mobilise for fresh adventures in land construction. To a Western observer, however, there appears to be no alternative to some such approach in the long run. Realistically, what may best be hoped for is probably some gradual regeneration, based mainly on a return to pastoral farming, conjoined with the continued maintenance of the population partly through pastoralism but mainly through intensified arable farming on smaller arable areas. Afforestation must be specially welcomed, but is almost bound to remain limited in extent.

Some real progress is now being reported, notably erosion control measures on 75,000 sq km of the plateau, represented (perhaps optimistically) as 17.5% of the area in need of such control (*People's Daily*, 3 Dec. 1981). These measures include terracing of slopes, stabilisation of gullies and planting of grass and trees, and cannot in the nature of things represent more than a first beginning, over so vast an area. Measures of these kinds are certainly the right policy, but there is a very long way to go.

Arable farming

The loess soils are generally fertile and easily worked, and in these ways may be said to invite cultivation. The problem is lack of water. It is common to find that grain yields on newly created farmland are satisfactory in the first few years, although rarely spectacular, in the region of 200 or 300 *jin* per *mou*, but that yields tend to fall sharply in subsequent years to 100 *jin* and below. Land clearances for agriculture, together with natural variations from year to year in such climatic parameters as rainfall and the length of the frost-free period, encourage instability in the landscapes, and tends to set desert conditions once more in motion southwards. In these conditions, land construction works may well prove worse than useless. Moreover, land clearance for agriculture necessarily seeks out the land with the best natural conditions, and so almost always involves the loss of woodland and pasture. Where yields of grain from arable are small, this sacrifice may well be totally irrational. Yet shortage of food leads inevitably to creation of fresh arable, which itself impoverishes the environments.

Guyuan county in southern Ningxia, which is only 300 km from Xian city in the north-westerly direction and lies on the loess proper rather than on the arid frontier, is an important case in point, where development activity since Liberation has been basically destructive. At Guyuan in 1949, average grain output per person was 820 *jin*, but in 1977, only 380 *jin*; and cattle population and edible oil production had also fallen sharply. Up to about 1978 new arable to the extent of 1.23 million *mou* had been created in Guyuan, but the total grain output had increased by only 20 million *jin*. These figures suggest either an extremely low rate of yield (less than 20 *jin*) upon newly cleared land, or a fall in yields elsewhere in Guyuan. In fact, both seem to have taken place, and woodland was reduced by 20%. Grain consumption in Guyuan was only just over 200 *jin* per person for the year in 1977, and total income per person only 29 *yuan*. It is upon this kind of basis that Guyuan is specifically said to be one of the poorest areas on the loess plateau (*People's Daily*, 15 Jan. 1981).

Guyuan is subsequently reporting policies, also involving heavy investment of money and labour, which run directly counter to those of the Maoists. In 1979 the state furnished Guyuan county with 6 million *yuan* in capital, to restore the local economy. Almost 90% of this was spent at once on planting trees and grasses – in the same winter and spring 330,000 *mou* of grassland and 780,000 *mou* of woodland were planted. In 1980, a further 5.5 million *yuan* was supplied by the state, also to improve the animal and woodland sides of the economy (*People's Daily* 10 Oct. 1980). (Contrary to earlier, presumably Maoist, practice, the state's grants are not free grifts, but loans to be repaid in three or five years. In this way, we are told, spending will be responsible and economical.) No details are given yet of improvements in food supplies or incomes.

Zhenyuan county is adjacent to Guyuan, across the provincial boundary in Gansu, also in an area reputed for poverty, and still in loess country. Models here take a parallel form in terms of mixed development and reversal of Maoist priorities (Hu Guohua and He Maoji). The county party committee decided in late 1977 upon a reformulation of development policy based upon local models. Two brigades are particularly quoted – Shizui in Sancha commune, and Baijiachuang in Yinjiacheng commune. Both have poor mountain land resources, but both introduced schemes of mixed development conjoined with intensification on a reduced arable area during Maoist times – the former in the early 1970s, the latter in the middle 1960s. (We are not told in either case how this was politically feasible, but in both the reason given is the poverty of the previous extensive arable economy.) In both, arable has been turned over to grazing and woodland, to the extent of about 40% in each case. Animal populations have increased after a long period of stagnation, and grain yields per person have risen to 800 *jin* and upwards – more than 1,000 *jin* in good years. Yields per unit area, which are not quoted but which can be calculated to lie between 100 and 200 *jin* per *mou*, are of course still very low; to that extent the extensive arable economy has not been transformed. For the county as a whole the grain yield per *mou* must still be around 160 or 170 *jin*, according to the figures given (Hu Guohua and He Maoji). There is still a long way to go. A similar but more optimistic case is made for Liqu commune in Yan'an municipality, northern Shaanxi (*People's Daily*, 18 Aug. 1981). Here the arable area was reduced by 20,000 *mou*, or one-third, between 1978 and 1980, but grain output rose by 6%. Labour released from agriculture has been absorbed in woodland, grassland and workshop activities, and income has risen by 158% in three years. In these cases and others, policy since 1979 or 1980 has looked towards further conversion of arable to woodland and grazing, together with increased intensification of use of the remaining arable, including improved irrigation and more use of fertiliser, and the distribution of open hillside land to households to plant and maintain as 'private' wood and grazing lots.

But the allocation of wood and grazing lots to families is by no means the last word on rural policy in this area. This was one of the first areas to announce the use of responsibility systems in agricultural production. In Inner Mongolia, 30–40% of units rely on state-supplied grain from the important irrigated 'oasis' on the Yellow River west of Baotou; and some units have done so continuously for fifteen years, in spite of the low levels of supply from the state. It was already argued in 1980 that supplies elsewhere could only be increased by a self-responsibility system for

subsistence grain – the so-called *kouliang tian*, 'grain-supply land' system (Gu Lei and Tian Zongming). In Togtoh county on the Yellow River east of Baotou – good arable country by Mongolian standards – a commune called Zhongtan had drawn up regulations for this system which were regarded as realistic and satisfactory. The main points are the following. First, an amount of land based on long-term averages of productive capacity is made available to individual families for subsistence, together with an additional amount intended to produce grain for sale. Ownership of the land remains collective, and the holding cannot be sold or exchanged. Second, the households and the local units become responsible for their own subsistence, and (except in case of grave natural disaster) are no longer eligible to receive state grain. Third, large fields suitable for mechanical work must not be interfered with. Fourth, the state's quotas are to have priority in cases of labour allocation. Fifth, farm implements and work animals remain under collective ownership and management, and are to be allocated on a rotation basis. Sixth, allocation of surplus labour is to remain within the discretion of the production team. Seventh, commune members are to pay for mechanised ploughing, irrigation services and so forth, provided by the collective. Eighth, where the household is unable to cultivate the land allocated, the collective will supply not less than 320 *jin* of grain (per person presumably) for the year. The commercial and quota side of the system is discussed, but not so clearly. Contracts are dependent on the amount of labour a household (or a group of households) has available; and so presumably are the resultant cash incomes. Motivation towards grain production at state prices is apparently excellent, presumably because cash incomes in Inner Mongolia have been extremely low up to now. In 1980, 700,000 *jin* of grain was sold by Zhongtan commune to the state, three times the amount sold in the previous year.

It is clear that in late 1980 the official system was already preparing for contract and responsibility systems on the Great Wall frontier – in fact areas of this kind are those represented as particularly suited to household-based responsibility systems. Broadly, the weaknesses of public policy here are likely to be over-surrender to private interests of various sorts. Hence the continuing objectives of policy should be the maintenance of the regulations already specified for grain-supply land. When in 1981 the responsibility systems were discussed for this area, specifically in terms of Gansu province where 99% of rural units had adopted them, emphasis was laid upon household-based systems which were already in use in 73% of cases, upon rises in living standards due in part to diversification, in part to increase of farm outputs due to improved motivation, upon reduction of unproductive personnel in rural units, and upon the restoration of the rights of the rural household to take decisions and accept responsibility (Feng Jixin). Discussion is optimistic – perhaps too optimistic. Little or nothing is yet being said about the obvious weaknesses of household responsibility systems – short-term problems of management, and longer-term problems of the protection of the public ownership system, the status of the production plan, the likely emergence of wide differences in levels of prosperity both among families and among collective units, and so forth.

More broadly, policy on the arable land throughout the region appears now to have three main features. The first of these is represented by the introduction of the responsibility and contract systems. The second is the conversion of substantial areas of arable to grazing land and, where feasible, to forest. The third is the intensification of grain production, and the raising of yields per unit area, on the remaining arable.

The pastoral economy

Some contributions to discussion of the loess plateau give particular weight to the possibilities of pastoral farming, and envisage both subsistence and commerce much more dependent on animal products than at present. Some writers argue that 1 *mou* of land produces 2,500 *jin* of fodder, which can maintain 1 goat or 40–50 rabbits. The rabbits fed in pens would produce 80–100 *jin* of meat, plus 40–50 skins. The same *mou* of land, managed extensively, would produce less than 80 *jin* of grain – that is, less weight of grain than meat for the same area. Investment in pasture would be small and results rapid, it is argued; the environment would be protected because the grass sod would not be disturbed; in many ways this would be a return, with the help of science, to the historic pattern of land use (Shi Shan). The problem up to 1978 was that because the loess plateau had not been allocated animal-

herding responsibilities in the state plan, the state would not undertake to buy animal products nor to furnish commodity grain; hence conversion to animal-rearing was not feasible.

It is necessary here to sympathise with the state planners. Northern Shaanxi has no railways, and only two main roads link the Great Wall frontier in Shaanxi with the centre and south of the province. Xian itself lies 400 km south of the edge of the desert. There is no sign of cold storage or refrigerated transport. In principle meat could be preserved by labour-intensive traditional methods, but the obligation to purchase perishable and fairly bulky animal products in such areas as northern Shaanxi, and supply commodity grain in return, is not one which the state could afford to assume in 1978 or for the foreseeable future – the Department of Commerce is still unable to perform much less difficult tasks in much more accessible spots. (In 1979, from areas beyond the suburbs, the department was regularly suffering a loss of 20 *yuan* per head for pigs sold in Beijing – *People's Daily*, 2 Feb. 1979.) The northern frontier areas cannot hope to lay down any part of the burden of their own subsistence within the foreseeable future. To that extent, optimistic accounts of the possibilities of pastoral farming in these vast and remote areas must be considered a little unrealistic – proposals from the Hexi corridor in Gansu mention animals for food and work, wool, skins and dairy products (*People's Daily*, 29 Apr. 1979). But the state economic system has nothing to lose, and the environment has much to gain, by an increase in the contribution of pastoralism to human subsistence on the plateau. In terms of marketable surpluses of animal products, the state may within limits have something to gain, particularly supplies of relative imperishables such as wool. But subsistence must continue to be provided within the local communities.

Predictably, and in spite of the run-down of many animal populations under the Maoists, there are signs of a problem of overgrazing. In Inner Mongolia as a whole, overgrazing of the 800 million *mou* (53 million ha or 530,000 sq km) of grazing land in winter and spring amounts to 12 million goats or equivalent, or 50% above capacity (Liu Yunshan 1981: 14). Conditions in summer are better, but overgrazing still amounts to about 25%. Overgrazing and poor productivity in the animal economy are closely related, and of course both are related to environmental difficulties, such as the serious loss of grazing land to blown

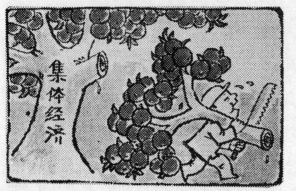

'We want our share' – cutting a branch from the tree called 'collective economy'. *Source: People's Daily*, 30 Jan. 1981. The artist is Liu Jingshui.

sand – as much as 30% since the 1960s. In the same space of time, the average live body-weight of a goat in Inner Mongolia has fallen from 28 *jin* to 18–20 *jin* (Liu Yunshan 1981: 14).

Low productivity and primitive management in the pastoral economy constitute a grave problem (Xu Peng). In China, say some Chinese critics, the authorities and the people still pay attention mainly to animal populations as an indicator of success, rather than the amount of their economic outputs. Output per unit area on the Chinese grasslands as a whole is only one-tenth of that in Australia – for instance, output of wool per sheep is only 1 kg per year in China, but 5 kg in Australia. Beef cattle in North America produce meat at an average rate of 85 kg per year, but Chinese cattle at only $3\frac{1}{2}$ kg per year (Xu Peng). Further insistence on increasing the size of herds can only lead to continued low quality and quantity of real outputs. The same factor, leading to undernourishment and weakness of the animals, leads to substantial losses in the severe winters. The standard animal death-rate in normal years in the northern plateaux is 6%; and in bad winters this figure rises to 24%. Even more serious is loss of weight by the animals in winter, representing four times the losses by deaths. All these losses amount to six or seven times the quantities of meat actually sold to the state. In Inner Mongolia in the thirty years since Liberation, there have been ten winters with heavy, drifting snow, each representing the loss of 1 million head of animals (Xu Peng).

These arguments lead in several rather different directions. One is towards *caokulun*, the local farm and pastoral bases, favoured spots

protected by walls, fences and shelter-belts, where pasture is improved and grass may be planted, and arable farming (presumably fortified by reasonable supplies of fertiliser) takes place (Inner Mongolia Investigation Team). *Caokulun* were introduced in Maoist times, but are still a recognised arm of rural policy (*People's Daily*, Editorial 2 Aug. 1979). Another is towards household livestock-rearing. 'Recently' (apparently in 1980), Shaanxi province abolished all restrictions on livestock breeding, and proposed that each animal raised should entitle its owner to the use of land for its maintenance (Ren Fengping: 29). Both of these ideas are essentially local in implications, and neither appears to offer very much to the solution of the major problems of the open ranges, but it is on the open ranges that the main problems of overgrazing, high animal death-rates and poor quality of animal outputs are to be found. Moreover, it is the open ranges which cannot be brought into effective use until much better transport is organised to bring their products to market.

Policies for the open ranges now under discussion include the control of animal populations, the improvement of physical condition of animals by better feeding and management, and increasing the rate of turnover of the animal populations and decreasing the rate of loss in winter, by a policy of slaughter within less than one year (Liu Yunshan 1981: 16; China Food Corporation: 56). Clearly, policies of this kind would involve the public authorities at various levels in a good deal of organising work, not least at the transport and marketing stage. Clearly also, progress in this field cannot be secure until means are found for the physical protection and improvement of the grassland resources themselves.

Afforestation and deforestation

The topic of afforestation on the Great Wall frontier is surrounded by some confusion. During the 1960s in the West some optimistic reports appeared (Richardson: 122–4, followed by more ambitious claims (Buchanan, 200–2); and even up to the present time substance has been lent to such reports and claims by the optimistic tone of various press releases from China – though in terms of hard facts the latter have generally been fairly modest. Since 1978, however, much more candid and realistic discussions have been taking place in the Chinese media on this topic; and it is now possible to gain a relatively clear idea not only of the actual extent of physical afforestation along the line of the 'Green Great Wall' which is planned as defence against the advancing desert, but also of the real problems and opportunities which arise in this formidable enterprise. It is also possible to gain a realistic idea of local needs, opportunities and problems in this field, particularly in relation to supplies of fuel.

Afforestation can reduce wind speeds, fix moving sand, protect arable land, and create favourable conditions for agriculture. It can also provide fuel and timber, and (in the form of foliage, it is said, though no doubt only to a very limited extent) fertiliser and fodder. The most frequently repeated precise claim in this field is that in Shaanxi, Gansu and Ningxia taken together, there were in 1975 '3,000 km of forest belts covering a total area of 533,000 ha', which had been 'built around deserts to break wind force and fix sand' (Xinhua, 30 Jan. 1975, 13; 8 Sept. 1975, 2).

In the northern parts of these three provinces, the linear extent of the 'frontier' zone which faces the deserts cannot be reckoned less than 1,200 km, and the real extent of the sandy areas in these three provinces which may be read from recent official maps is not less than 130,000 sq km or 13 million ha. The afforestation claim is hence only 4% of the area to which the need for afforestation relates. A similar conclusion is suggested by more detailed figures for northern Shaanxi. Afforestation in the Yulin prefecture is given as occupying 4.8 million *mou* in about 1971 (against 0.6 million *mou* before Liberation) (Shaanxi Province, Scientific Institute for Forestry and Agriculture: 15–16). This indicates a 1971 afforested area of about one-tenth of the whole prefecture. Of the three provinces, Shaanxi appears to be that in which progress in this field has been most rapid and most consistent, no doubt in part because of advantages of accessibility. Considered in terms of local effort and local achievement, afforestation is considerable, but considered in terms of need, it cannot be more than a first beginning. Media concentration on the success of a few units leads to a degree of admiration of particular local achievements, but lends support to the view that these are exceptional, and that as a whole the desert frontier remains open.

What are the problems? Probably the greatest is destruction by local people. 'If we plant 1 *mou* of woodland and cut down two or three the "Green Great Wall" will never be built.' (*People's Daily*, 15 June 1979) Yet at that time 'You need only go to the north, and travel about, to see for yourself on the roads the carts pulled by horses, oxen, camels, even the trains and tractors, all loaded with trunks, branches and roots of trees – the great majority cut down indiscriminately' (*People's Daily*, 15 June 1979). Timber and firewood are very scarce on the Great Wall frontier; if trees are grown, it is difficult to deny that they represent timber and firewood. Reduction in millet acreage over the years has resulted in shortage of millet stalks for use as fuel (Geographical Research Institute: 131). Some units have successfully planted firewood copses, and manage their woods accordingly, but this is still exceptional. Some units, on the other hand, are responsible for cutting down trees which do not belong to them; this was particularly prevalent during the Cultural Revolution. Maintenance of woods has been generally very poor in the same phase, unlike the earlier years after Liberation. Woodland has been destroyed both in order to create arable, notably in the Cultural Revolution phase of enthusiasm for increased grain production everywhere, and also in the search for firewood. There has been some recent improvement, but cadres in some units still connive at indiscriminate cutting (*People's Daily*, 15 June 1979). Shaanxi has vast coal reserves, but up to now they are barely mentioned in this kind of discussion, presumably because neither coal nor transport are available on a suitable scale at present. Units which do have local access to coal are urged to use it.

Other serious problems arise. Many trees are planted, but only about one-third survive – this is for the whole country, and it may be supposed that the survival rate is lower in the far north than elsewhere. Watering of tree saplings is a heavy burden on local labour supplies, since the most important plantings may well be distant from water supplies. The harsh winds of spring take heavy toll of new trees.

In one important case, attention is drawn to the function of woodland in reducing erosion (*People's Daily*, 20 Sept. 1981). In Ying county in northern Shanxi, the important Zhenziliang Reservoir, built in 1957, lost 36% of its capacity through silting in 1958–61, an additional 25% in 1962–73, and a further 19% in the single year 1976. It was enlarged by raising the dam in 1977, but 59% of the total capacity of the enlarged reservoir has already been lost. Zhenziliang lies among denuded hills. Similar reservoirs in south-eastern Shaanxi and eastern Hebei, surrounded by hills with good forest cover, have lost little capacity. However, there are dramatic differences in degrees of drought and cold between the latter areas and northern Shanxi, which indicate not that forest cover is less valuable in the control of erosion, but that it is much more difficult to maintain or re-establish.

A radical solution to these problems is now being adopted – the allocation of between 5 and 10 *mou* of land on an individual basis to families to plant trees, mainly for firewood, with private ownership of the trees when grown. In 1979 in Yulin county in northern Shaanxi, a decision had already been taken on these lines (*People's Daily*, 23 Sept. 1979). In Yulin since Liberation, more than 100,000 *mou* (70 sq km) of woods and shelter-belts have been planted, and in places the movement of sand has been stopped; but this achievement has to been seen in context. Loose sand still affects 3 million of the 3.6 million *mou* of land (2,400 sq km) which are suitable for afforestation. It is argued that collective planting of woodland especially for fuel is unsatisfactory because of the scanty population and its scattered distribution, but also underlying this proposal is the proven impossibility of getting sufficient woodland planted by collective effort, and the impossibility of organising adequate protection of collective woodland from private woodcutting enterprise. Positive advantages of the scheme are given some prominence – private plantings need not replace collective, but may supplement them; an important aggregate contribution to afforestation could be made; firewood needs could be satisfied and the use of animal dung as fuel stopped; private planting saves public money; fodder and grazing could also be provided within these plantations – through these points do not all carry equal conviction. What are not discussed are serious weaknesses and potential dangers of such a scheme – the prospect of legal status for private property on the land, boundary disputes between private and collective or state interests, disputes within and among families, the encroachment of private holdings on other parts of the region's land resources, the possible growth of large holdings of land and accumulation of private fortunes particularly by influential cadres, and so forth. The parallel is not suggested in the media, but these wood-lots must be thought of at present as a kind of private plot in permanent long-term production of firewood and timber. In the long term the danger is that (as happened in historic phases of the growth of estates and manors in China), reclamation of wasteland may turn out to be the key to the establishment of private fortunes. Against these considerations, however, must be arrayed the arguments from necessity – that in no other way can afforestation be accelerated or even adequate supplies of firewood be provided for.

Increasing emphasis has been given to the planting of copses in the arid north since 1979, but conditions vary in the examples which reach the media. In Qiaowan commune, in Jingbian county in northern Shaanxi, every household is entitled to a private plot, a fodder plot, and 4–6 *mou* of wood-lot (Ren Fengping). This is 'as a result of policy relaxation'. In a group of counties to the south-east of Lanzhou, in east Gansu, firewood copses to the extent of 1 *mou* per person are being grown, and are expected to represent a permanent solution to the firewood problem at local level. Such local plantations may be sited so as to discourage erosion, and may strengthen local environments in various ways. It appears, however, that in Gansu these copses represent collective rather than private enterprise (Zhang Wenbing).

Orthodoxy in this field is now laying emphasis on the interdependence of the well-being of the state, the collectives and the individual – a favourite media theme in recent years (Yan Xiao et al.). Private woodland copses obviously akin to private farm plots are proposed, alongside both state and collective afforestation – it is pointed out that in Yan'an prefecture since Liberation, of the 2.8 million *mou* of afforestation achieved, 29% has been done by the state, 68% by collective units and about 3% by individuals. Various subsidiary relaxations of policy are proposed, most of which are designed to bring idle state land into practical use, and most of which would tend to strengthen the resources of the collectives or families or both as against those of the state. For instance, the allocation of state-owned land for family wood-lots is suggested, rather than collective land. Here and elsewhere, proposals are being made which use rational local resource allocation as a weapon in an underlying struggle against state ownership of local resources.

Occasionally, achievements in the field of afforestation on the loess reach the press which do seem to relate adequately to the scale of need. One such achievement is that of Chunhua county in Shaanxi, about 75 km north-west of Xian, in loess country with relatively favourable climatic conditions but with serious problems of open loess surfaces with deep gullies (*People's Daily*, 2 Apr. 1982). Here work on reforestation began about 1973, and forest cover has been raised from 3% to 19% of total area, representing 70% of the area suitable for afforestation in the county. The new woodland comprises in part orchards, in part a network of shelter-belts to protect the arable and grazing land. Outputs have improved considerably as a result. Erosion has also been drastically reduced as a result of afforestation and some other measures. If the picture of Chunhua given in the press is realistic, these achievements are as much, perhaps, as may be hoped for; particularly since they appear to have been made within the collective system; but it must be remembered that Chunhua lies more than 200 km to the south even of Yan'an.

The Green Great Wall remains a live issue. The present plan proposes an eight-year programme (1978–85) for the afforestation of 80 million *mou* of land (5.3 million ha, or 53,000 sq km) in the north-west, the north and the north-eastern provinces of China, extending from Heilongjiang to Xinjiang (Guo Longchun et al.). This is an ambitious plan which proposes for these eight years double the planting which was achieved in the phase 1949–76. Planting began in 1979 (Xinhua, 20 June 1980). This is to be the first phase in the creation of a permanent barrier on a realistic scale. This is of course a state plan, but it is far beyond the capacity of the approximately 1,000 state forests and tree nurseries to bring it to reality alone; the greater part of the work is to be done by local collective units. The Huajialing forest belt in Dingxi prefecture, in Gansu province south of Lanzhou, is given prominence as a model. Huajialing was a joint state–local enterprise, producing forest at a cost to the state of only 225 *yuan* per ha, against 1155 *yuan* per ha in the local state forests. In so ambitious a programme, attempted in conditions which vary so much from place to place, it seems likely that gross anomalies will continue to persist in various fields. The state gives financial assistance for the Green Great Wall, but much is left to the collective units in spite of their poverty. Funds allocated by the state in 1982 and earlier years have been at rates such as 40 *yuan* per ha and 100 *yuan* per ha (Xinhua, 26 Mar. 1982; *People's Daily*, 23 Sept. 1979) – figures which cannot represent more than one-third, and may well be as low as one-tenth or less, of those quoted above for costs in state forest creation. It remains to be seen what achievements can be made, at whatever cost and however financed, in practical afforestation in these very difficult environments; but there do not appear to be many grounds for easy optimism.

Experience and policy on the loess plateau

Environments are very difficult on the loess plateau, particularly towards the north-west. Conservation, never strong, has taken some particularly nasty knocks under the Maoist system, partly as a result of populism and local workers' or cadres' control, partly as a direct result of official policy which required increases in grain and favoured their achievement by extensions of the arable area. Erosion by water is still very serious and erosion by wind has increased; loss of soil is a gross evil. Restoration of the grass sod, afforestation and the planting of shelter-belts, although impressive locally in some places, still fall far short of need; and in addition, firewood is still very scarce. There are signs of a crisis, in the sense of further advances by the desert and further withdrawals by the people.

Policy and policy discussion at present revolve around the three issues which have been discussed, all issues of resource use in various ways. Arable farming is the least favoured, but it is difficult to follow some critics who argue for a countryside radically less self-sufficient in grain than at present. There are said to be four grain-deficient regions (apparently province-level units) on the loess plateau – presumably Shaanxi, Gansu, Ningxia and Inner Mongolia. These regions are prominent in Fig. 2.7, which shows areas of very low grain yield, and also in Fig. 2.8 which shows the distribution of grain deficits. Obviously, neither the state nor the provincial authorities can be looking forward to increasing their commitment to supplying such areas with commodity grain, especially over long and expensive lines of communication. Much more intensive arable farming on much smaller areas of arable land appears to promise much better; it accords with the *caokulun* principle which will also allow for better care of animals and probably better social provision for the people especially in winter, and for more diversity in production, proper collection and use of fertiliser, and so forth. There have been some limited signs of continuing official enthusiasm for *caokulun* in Inner Mongolia (*People's Daily*, 20 Mar. 1982). In the loess itself a similar policy outlook underlies the call for 1 *mou* per person of stable and high-yielding arable land, 2 *mou* of woodland and more than 1 *mou* of productive grassland – all originally to have been achieved by 1980 (Xinhua, 5 July 1977).

'Policies to suit local resources' was taken up after 1978 as a key slogan for development. On the Great Wall frontier, it has generally been understood to indicate more grazing and less arable. From a conservationist point of view there is nothing to quarrel with in this argument. From an economic point of view, similar problems to those of commodity grain supply are likely to arise for local units in disposing of animal products other than wool and leather in the Great Wall region, due to poor means of communication and the expense and organisation necessary to set up an extended and varied trade in animal products. What should be the proper status, method of protection, and system of production for the great mass of the surface of the plateau remains unresolved. It seems unlikely that individual families operating within a responsibility system framework will be able to handle weak resources on the vast scale which is involved, still less set about the restoration of the 30% of the grasslands which are said to be in a degenerated condition; and current proposals of this kind do not appear realistic (*People's Daily*, 20 Mar. 1982; translated in FBIS *Daily Report*, 25 Mar. 1982, R2–R3).

Forestry on the Great Wall frontier is not looked to as a foundation of commerce, no doubt rightly. Trees are desirable locally to supply firewood and to protect villages and animal bases from wind; and on a grand scale, to build the Green Great Wall to protect the grassland and arable from advancing desert conditons. Of these functions, the first is probably the most important and the easiest to supply; the last certainly the most difficult to supply and perhaps the least essential. Grass sod or other ground vegetation is probably at least as effective in fixing sand as shelter-belts; and it must be much easier to restore this sod than to plant trees and bring them to

maturity. Even if the plan for family wood-lots remains orthodox and produces satisfactory results, it is not likely to have functions beyond its present intentions – the supply of firewood for local use. The Green Great Wall cannot be a glorified wood-lot; but all the signs are that what real motivation the local people have towards planting and preservation of woodland arises from the need for timber and firewood for use. At the same time, the state does not have the capacity to build the Green Great Wall alone. All this means that when achievements are made in the construction of the Green Great Wall, that is so much ground gained, but that the enterprise as a whole is unlikely to be completed within this century. In addition, for the Green Great Wall, protection is likely to be as important as completion.

Much of the information available from China relates to models, which represent successful communities worthy of imitation. The less successful 80%, or even 50%, of the community makes little appearance in the official press – there are allusions, and much more information since 1978 than in Maoist times, but even now indications are limited. At Zichang in northern Shaanxi north of Yan'an, for the past years under the extreme Left, there was begging for food and people ate chaff and leaves (*People's Daily*, 1 Nov. 1981). In poor brigades in Zichang such as Sunjiahe, the people are said to have welcomed the new management methods, including distribution of food according to work-points and allowances of grazing and wood-lot land to families – but they are still afraid that these changes may be short-lived. Communities where water is particularly scarce, erosion particularly severe, access particularly difficult or aspect particularly exposed, must expect to find improvement particularly difficult. It is in such brigades that people who slipped off to town illegally under the Maoists (forty from Sunjiahe) have still not returned; where the labour-day is still worth only a few *fen* and the working year only 10 or 15 *yuan* cash, and where there is real food for only half the year and wild plants for the rest (He Jiazheng). Zichang county lies between Yan'an and the Great Wall; it is open range country with plenty of land but few people.

But even in poor counties it is now claimed, 'the machinery is beginning to move' (Feng Leshu 1980). A formidable diversity of types of rural organisation is already emerging, together with a wider range of public comment. Some people criticise the new contract systems on the grounds that they amount in effect to self-management by individual households, and hence rejection of the collective principle. Some authors accept this criticism as basically true, but argue that it was Maoism which dug its own grave in this context, by depriving the local people of any right to take decisions, and requiring them simply to accept orders. Others argue that self-management is a vital principle of the collective economy. Some units, even small ones such as the twenty-seven-household Mafulang brigade in Xing county on the Yellow River in north-east Shaanxi are now adopting very adventurous cropping systems which are strongly orientated towards commercial crops – in this case red beans, sunflower seeds, onions and caster oil; but we are not told how these crops came to be selected – or, more important, how these policies relate to the state plan. 'Is this chaos? Or vitality?' Certainly it is a struggle between methods of work, and between comparative advantages of localities and types of individuals (Feng Leshu 1980).

Yet there is a darker side to all this economic adventurism on the loess plateau. Three great problems remain – the shortage of food, the shortage of capital, and the inadequacy of the commercial network (He Jiazheng). It is pointed out that units cannot expect to find themselves bailed out by the state if they allowed their grain supplies to fall back for the sake of cash outputs. The state does help investment in Shaanxi, but not yet enough in forestry and the animal economy; junior units should be encouraged to exercise autonomy in investment. Commerce as always is the great sticking-point. Cases are cited of communes which could not arrange the sale of grain above quota at the preferential price; of a commune which could not get its 200 tons of apples taken up; of units which find that markets for surplus outputs are extremely fickle (He Jiazheng). It does not seem likely that the state commercial system will wish to make specially advantageous arrangements for those who flout the state planning system; they will have to make their own way, and the going cannot always be easy. To these three problems must be added the many-sided one of ecological instability, for which neither state, nor collective, nor individuals are at present able to propose any range of adequate solutions.

Supplies for the state

During the 1950s arrangements were devised for the handling of farm surpluses in China and their distribution to approved consumers. The heart of these arrangements at the production stage was and is the system of compulsory farm purchase quotas introduced in 1953, which requires collective units to deliver specified quantities of specified commodities year by year to the state purchasing organisations. Furthermore, in a group of very important commodities, including grain and cotton, trading was not permitted at all except through the state organs until 1980, and even since 1980 only on a small scale and at a local level. Quotas are fixed according to precedent and through negotiation within the planning machinery, as shown in Chapter 4. In this chapter the main intention is not to survey the basic management of the procurement and allocation systems at national level, which has been done by a number of authors (Perkins 1966: especially Chs 3 and 4; Donnithorne 1967: Chs 11 and 13; Eckstein: Ch. 4), but to explore the experience and development of the commodity supply system on the ground, together with that of some of the 'commodity bases' upon which it depends (Figure 11.1).

Within the procurement system, grain and cotton are by far the most important commodities, and at the same time those whose rural origins are most varied and widespread. Predictably, they are also those for which information is most diffuse and incomplete, and sometimes inconsistent. Sugar is the commodity for which production and procurement problems are most clearly documented in the literature. A review of experience in handling these three commodities illustrates many characteristic arrangements and problems. In particular, it serves to illustrate further the central role occupied in Chinese rural management by the state plan, which is the instrument through which commodities are produced for procurement.

Commodity grain bases

In his speech of March 1978, introducing the proposed ten-year plan for 1976–85, the then Chairman Hua Guofeng stressed the importance of twelve commodity grain bases in China, and

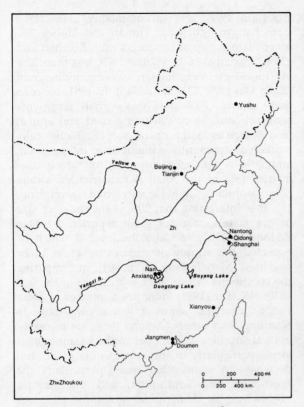

Fig. 11.1. Rural commodity bases – some place-names.

proposed the aim of a twofold or threefold [*sic*] increase in their output by 1985 (Xinhua, 10 March 1978); but he did not name any of these bases. An earlier Chinese source referred to eight commodity grain bases (Xinhua, 27 Dec. 1974), also without specifying areas. Six main sources of commodity grain in south China have been listed officially – northern Zhejiang, southern Jiangsu, the Pearl River delta in Guangdong, the Jianghan plain in Hubei, the Chengdu plain in Sichuan, and the Dongting and Boyang basins in Hunan and Jiangxi (*People's Daily*, 23 July 1978); and to these must certainly be added Jilin and Heilongjiang in the north-east, bringing the number up to eight.

A recent map published in China (Fig. 11.2) shows grain bases of various kinds, but does not indicate absolute or relative outputs or surpluses of grain. It differs more than might be expected from the map of local surpluses (see Fig. 2.8), no doubt at least in part because a local rural surplus (as in Liaoning) need not necessarily indicate a surplus available as commodity grain. Both maps agree that surplus grain in Sichuan comes mainly from the Yangzi plain around Chongqing, rather than from the Chengdu plain mentioned in the list above.

All the commodity grain bases have grain outputs substantially and (in principle) consistently higher than those necessary to feed the local people. In some, productivity per unit of land is very high, but in others it remains relatively low;

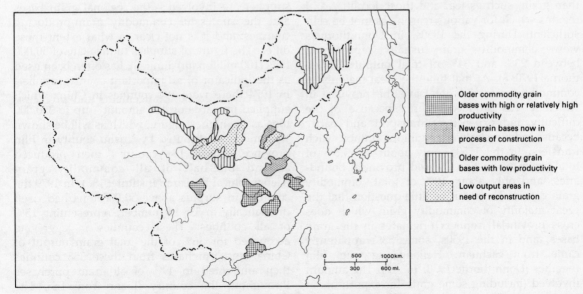

Fig. 11.2. Commodity grain bases. *Source*: Geographical Research Institute: 141.

159

the key feature in all appears to be high productivity per unit of labour, due in some cases to intensification, in others to relative abundance of land. It has already been shown that Suzhou prefecture, for example, produces a rice surplus through highly intensive methods; but the three grain bases in the central Yangzi region, the Dongting and Boyang basins in Hunan and Jiangxi, and the central Hubei basin around Wuhan and on the Han River, are all rich alluvial flats where flood risks have been greatly reduced by modern engineering works, and the cropping area has consequently been expanded rapidly and efficiently on excellent land; yields per unit area in these conditions are still not particularly high.

The commodity grain bases are of course not the government's only source of marketable grain; all local units with grain surplus contribute supplies to the state, and one of the commonest grounds for praise of local units in the media under the Maoists was their conversion from grain-deficient to grain-surplus status. Nevertheless, the large scale of the largest county surpluses reported, compared with those elsewhere, justifies a conclusion that the grain bases are probably the localities where the state obtains the bulk of its commodity grain.

Commodity grain is of the highest importance. It feeds the towns and industrial workers, most of those who work in transport, administration and so forth, in part the army, those rural communities which produce valuable crops other than grain, such as tea, and those localities and regions which for various reasons cannot be self-sufficient. During the 1950s, in Donnithorne's view, commodity grain usually represented between 23% and 34% of total output (Donnithorne 1970: 8). At that time the great majority of commodity grain did not leave the province in which it was produced, partly because of the difficulty and expense of transport and partly because administrative conditions inhibit such transfers. In the 1950s, only about 2.5–3.5% of total grain production crossed provincial boundaries, and only about 10% of total commodity grain did so. There can be little question that the great majority of commodity grain which does cross provincial frontiers originates in the grain bases, and in the 1950s, some 53% apparently came from Sichuan, Heilongjiang and Jilin together (Donnithorne 1970: 16, 17). The amount involved (including some grain for export, about 1% of production) was 6 or 7 million tons in the

1950s. In 1978, 57% of commodity grain came from Jiangsu, Zhejiang, Hunan and Hubei, the other main group of producers (Yan Ruizhen and Zhou Zhixiang: 9). In 1978 or 1979, less than 20% of Chinese grain production was commodity grain (Zhan Wu 1979: 13; Chinn: 746). In 1981, we read quite clearly, 75% of China's grain represents rural self-sufficiency (including seed and animal feed as well as food for rural people); 5% is locally marketed, apparently without state intervention; and 20% is taken by the state, of which one-quarter (5% of the total) is redistributed locally (Zhu Daohua: 3; Grain Department Research Unit: 15). It is interesting that 20% is the order of size of the state's 'take' of grain reported by Mao Zedong in 1957, and also the level at which he expected the supply of commodity grain to be stabilised (Mao Zedong 1977b: 401). In comparing the conditions of the 1950s with those of the late 1970s, Walker (1981) identifies a number of more specific changes, some of which owe more to planning than others. Among them are increases in local supplies of grain per capita in some provinces, particularly in the north China plain, and decreases in some other areas, particularly the north-west and south-west, and the increase everywhere in demand for grain for purposes other than direct consumption. Fundamentally, however, the system has experienced little change, and local grain surpluses still cross provincial boundaries only with some difficulty.

In the supply of commodity grain two kinds of supplier are involved – the regional grain bases and the successful commodity grain-producing counties; and it is not clear to what extent these differ. The figure of supplies to the state of 50,000 tons (100 million *jin*) annually has often been used as the indicator of an important county supplier. In 1974 there were 194 counties in China which supplied upwards of this amount – up to 350,000 tons as the highest figure, which as will be shown was and is contributed by Yushu county in Jilin province. These 194 counties then produced around one-half of all commodity grain (Geographical Research Institute: 136). In 1979 the counties in surplus above 50,000 tons had risen dramatically to 338 in number, representing 15% of all counties. These counties in aggregate accounted for 36% of the total grain output of China, and purchases from these 338 counties then amounted to 49% of all grain purchases throughout the country (Liang Yan: L8). The stability of the figure for the state's dependence upon large suppliers, of around one-half, implies a parallel stability for dependence upon smaller suppliers – presumably in many cases grain-surplus counties located in or near grain-deficient regions, whose importance in conditions of limited transport capacity must be one of the fixed points of the system.

Net grain imports rose from a few million tons per year through most of the 1970s to around 12 million tons (sufficient to maintain about 50 million people) after 1979. It is usual to envisage that imported grain is used mainly to provide food supplies for the three great cities, Beijing, Tianjin and Shanghai. For Beijing and Tianjin, situated in the weaker part of a densely populated plain which is at best self-sufficient in food, this is no doubt true (Walker 1977: 556) – but for Shanghai, situated near the mouth of the Yangzi which must carry nearly half of China's commodity grain, it is less convincing. Rather than Shanghai, the geographical realities suggest the likelihood of imported grain maintaining such northern cities as Shijiazhuang and Hantan in Hebei, Zhengzhou and Luoyang in Henan, and Jinan and Jining in Shandong. In broad terms, it appears, food imports are necessitated above all by the food-supply problems of the north China plain and its cities and towns, including Beijing and Tianjin. Particularly in the north China plain, they have also surely played a part in the relaxation of the earlier acute shortages of cotton.

The *Red Flag* article which has already been quoted provides an official account of the 'grain problem' which is worth review (Liang Yan).

This writer's view is optimistic, though he admits that grain production in 1980 (and 1981) did not rise to the level of the bumper harvest of 1979. (It rose beyond this level in 1982 – State Statistical Bureau 1983: 3). He points out that there has been a large increase in the non-agricultural population in 1979 and 1980, involving increased demand for commodity grain, while the area sown to grain has tended to fall due to the growth of diversified local economies in many areas. Total grain output in China, we are reminded, is still only about 600 *jin* per person; and the supply of commodity grain is still tightly stretched. In terms of policy, he proclaims the importance to the state of the output of the grain-surplus counties and acknowledges the importance of the people's motivation in these areas, insists upon the state monopoly of trade in grain (with some relaxation after state quotas are satis-fied) and urges economy in the use of grain (to the disadvantage of rural people using grain to make wine). Some points only implied in this article are quite as important as those around which discussion was actually conducted. These include the disparity in price between grain and various alternative crops; the weakness of the state at present in its dealings with the peasants, especially those in grain-surplus units; and the mounting demand for commodity grain together with a tendency for the state's disposable supply of commodity grain (after needs for local redistribution have been satisfied) to be dependent increasingly upon imports and upon major producing counties. In addition, there are evidences that of the established grain bases Guangdong, for one, may be losing capacity to produce a surplus – population in Guangdong increased by 32% between 1965 and 1978, but grain output by only 20%; and average grain output per person fell in the same period from 625 *jin* to 567 *jin* (Liang Zhao et al.: 39).

A topic which obviously relates to commodity grain supplies is the Chinese official announcement of famine risk in Hubei and Hebei provinces in spring 1981, with an appeal for help from abroad ('Quarterly chronicle and documentation', *China Quarterly*, 86, 1981, 390).

The announcement was not expected. The *People's Daily* (27 Dec. 1980) proclaimed in December 1980 that the 1980 harvest had been the 'second best since Liberation'. As late as April 1981, we read in a journal intended for circulation abroad that 'in agriculture, the situation is very good now . . . stability in the rural sector means basic stability in the whole country' (Xue Muqiao 1981c). The floods which affected Hubei until December and severe drought in Hebei were already on record, and Hebei and Hubei were among the provinces in which grain output was earlier said to have fallen in 1980 compared with 1979. Hubei and Hebei are, however, both cotton-producing provinces, and Hebei was one of those in which an outstanding cotton harvest was gained in 1980 (*People's Daily*, 22 Jan. 1981). For an explanation of the grain problem in these provinces, it may be necessary to look to cotton in part.

In order to reduce cotton imports and stimulate Chinese cotton output, the state decided from 1980 onwards to allow special supplies of grain and urea to the 15 provinces and province-level units most involved with cotton production . . . The responsibility systems, higher cotton prices and better land combined to solve the food supply problems of the cotton producers; and cotton output in 1980 rose to an unprecedented figure.

Within this scheme, the standard allowance of incentive grain was 2 *jin* of grain for each *jin* of ginned cotton above quota (Grain Department Research Unit: 44–5). These appear to have been the standard arrangements. It is interesting that the authorities in Shandong adopted rather different arrangements apparently intended to encourage specialist rather than casual producers. These arrangements were said to be specifically designed to protect food supplies at the same time as providing incentives for increased cotton output and allocating an additional 1 million *mou* of superior arable to cotton production. It begins to appear that Hubei or Hebei, or both, may have over-reacted to the state's need for cotton and willingness to permit conversion of land back to cotton, and probably also in other respects to the general relaxation of the state's insistence on grain cultivation through the planning system. One possible result of this relaxation is obviously underproduction of unprofitable but all-important grain, with consequent risk of famine unless imports of food are organised. The Vice-Governor of Hebei province gave some countenance to this view in his report on the economic plan for 1980 (FBIS *Daily Report*, 16 Nov. 1981, R1, quoting a Shijiazhuang broadcast of 25 Oct. 1981): 'In agriculture, despite the serious drought and the subsequent drop in grain output, we were able to break the prolonged state of sluggish agricultural growth because we reaped a bumper harvest of cotton and oil-bearing crops.' Hence it appears that the Chinese appeal for help may have been as much a tentative attempt to find an overseas supplementary source of funds to finance imports of food, as a direct response to an unforeseen disaster experience. The floods of Hubei and drought in Hebei were severe on a regional scale, but on the national scale they do not appear to have differed greatly from those of earlier years. Basically, it appears to be changes in the priorities of the government and people inside China, and the perceptions of the Chinese government in relation to the outside world, which led to the unexpected request for help.

These particular problems of grain scarcity raise by implication the whole question of total demand for commodity grain, the distribution of demand and the various forms which it may take. Some demand represents absolute scarcity of food, often in areas of dense population together with limited capitalisation, as in various areas in the north China plain. Some represents poverty in desperately difficult environments, such as some on the Great Wall frontier and in mountain or other difficult environments in either north or south. More than 100 million people in China still suffer from scarcity of grain (Grain Department Research Unit: 16). In such cases, the state adopts a posture which is essentially that of the guarantor of social security, usually at a quite low consumer level.

Cases where demand for commodity grain arises in very hostile environments may be logistically difficult, and there are apparently problems of chronic indebtedness in many of them, but they do not represent problems of principle. Problems of principle in this field are mainly represented by cases where there is an opportunity of choice between grain self-sufficiency and specialisation in another crop which may well be much more profitable. This appears to be the position of units in the north China plain which have been allowed to turn over to cotton, like Heze. There is little broad information in this field, but materials have appeared which give an idea of the complexities of this kind of demand. One many-sided problem is the system of incentive grain supplies for producers of commercial outputs, which dates back to 1962. Problems arise because of the proliferation of preferential supply arrangements of various kinds – as many as fifty different schemes in Sichuan; as many as five schemes for cotton in Mianyang prefecture in the same province. Such a complex system is obviously prone to contradictions – and no doubt to corruption, though this is not discussed. It may also be simply unworkable. In Sichuan, annual increase of grain output is about 2,000 million *jin*; but if annual output of pigs were to rise to 30 million, local units would be entitled to an additional (and impossible) 3,000 million *jin* of grain for that reason alone (Yi Ke).

As always, the central problem is the low official price of grain, which depresses supply but tends to inflate demand. It would be possible in these conditions to encourage higher prices for grain whose purchase represents the pursuit of alternative more profitable kinds of land use. This strikes at the principle of a state trading monopoly in grain, but is no doubt one reason why the state is now willing to accept some private trading in grain which is surplus to the official quotas.

Yushu county, Jilin province. 'From Dazhai county to debtors' hall'

Yushu county lies about 150 km north-east of Changchun, in Jilin province in north-eastern China. In recent years Yushu has been the single most important county supplier of commodity grain to the state. Since 1971 Yushu has supplied the state with an average of more than 350,000 tons (700 million *jin*) of grain annually. In 1979 total grain output was 1,850 million *jin*, and supplies to the state 810 million *jin* (405,000 tons). The people find the burden of these contributions a heavy one. The title used for this section is taken from an article in the *People's Daily* (Gao Xinqing 1981). The expression used depends on a Chinese pun, in which 'Dazhai' the model brigade is equated with *dazhai*, heavy debts.

In 1972 a 'double million' target was adopted – outputs of 1 million tons of grain and 1 million pigs per annum. These targets were not realistic, and in the effort to reach that for grain some ill-considered changes were made (the target for pigs is not now discussed, and appears to have sunk without trace). Maize, which yields heavily, has become the principal crop; from 7% of cropped area it came to occupy some 60% in 1980. Soya-bean area has correspondingly fallen, from 38% early in Liberation times to 30% in the 1960s and 18% in 1979. Intercropping and similar devices have been used to strengthen maize outputs, and beans have become no more than an adjunct to maize production. Technical improvements like mechanisation have all been adapted towards the same end. Rotations have been upset and soil fertility has suffered; plant pests have become much more common.

The financial cost of Yushu's grain supplies to the state has been heavy. In 1970 the county owed the state 13 million *yuan*, but by the end of 1979 this figure had risen to 97 million – with interest, over 100 million, amounting to 100 *yuan* for each of the 1 million people. Indebtedness arises not only at county level; it goes right through the rural system, with the most indebted of the thirty-nine communes owing as much as 3 million *yuan*. Living standards are correspondingly low. In 1979 average cash incomes were only about 35 *yuan* per person (incomes in kind, mainly food and fuel, averaged about 90 *yuan* in addition), and some families were overspending. Indebtedness at the various institutional levels seems to have arisen in part from over-ambitious projects undertaken in the past (a river diversion; an auditorium) and from the inevitable development of the high-output-poor syndrome in a county so heavily committed to grain, and progressively losing its economic crops such as sugar-beet. In some respects Yushu's circumstances are still deteriorating – in recent years 550,000 *mou* of collective arable (13% of the total, and representing about 200 million *jin* of grain) has been lost to state and local construction or to extensions to private plots. Intensification, an obvious way forward, is not an easy option for a unit already heavily in debt, because it raises costs much more rapidly than it raises incomes. Mechanisation is already widespread in Yushu – 176 million *yuan* was spent on farm machinery between 1965 and 1979, averaging nearly 12 million *yuan* per year, invested mainly by collective units. In fact the county has 2,400 large and medium tractors, but has real need of only 1,400 – over-investment in mechanisation is another cause of indebtedness. It is no longer argued, at least in the press, that further farm price rises can be expected to generate prosperity and restore motivation in places like Yushu. The pressure is now for more varied outputs all of which will be more profitable than maize – soya beans, sugar-beet, peanuts, sunflowers, sesame. The loss of the traditional millet crop (low-yielding but a prized item of diet) is particularly resented. Obviously changes in the cropping pattern relate to changes in the operation of the planning system in Yushu, and here the local units are looking for more autonomy as well as better opportunities to make money (Gao Xinqing).

Hunan: the Dongting Lake plain commodity grain base

At first sight, it is obvious that environmental and social conditions in Hunan are the antithesis of those in Jilin. Far from being a cool-temperate plain of recent settlement on the northern periphery of the country, the Dongting plains which are the heart of Hunan are subtropical in climate and part of the south China homeland. Nevertheless, parallels exist between the two in respect of man–land relationships and hence the capacity of each to produce food over and above

163

the needs of the local people; and the needs of the state for commodity grain have tended to lead to parallels between the two in terms of management, including both state farms and communal and county units, whose problems as now perceived have much in common.

It will be helpful first to outline the special environmental features which make a significant grain surplus possible in the Dongting plain.

The plain lies at a height generally below 100 m, and of course forms part of the whole lake plain of the middle Yangzi, of which the larger part lies in Hubei to the north. In its present state, the Dongting Lake is not a single stretch of water; much rather a complex of interconnected lakes and river channels in various stages of silting. Eastern, western and southern lakes are now distinguished by name, separated by a wedge of relatively recent alluvial land lying mainly in Nan, Anxiang and Huarong counties to the north. This disposition is the result of a long though discontinuous phase of policy in Ming and Qing times, of permitting the natural floods of the Yangzi in summer to extend over Hunan territory rather than Hubei. Floods still take place – 120 million cu m of silt is said to enter the lake annually – but are now diverted in part to the new (1952) Jing River flood-retention basin which lies to the south-west of the Yangzi course, in Hubei just upstream from the Hunan border. This basin is 1,000 sq km in extent and is said to have capacity of 5,400 million cu m. In addition, local dykes and waterworks have been consolidated since Liberation into an effective flood-defence and water-management system (*China Reconstructs*, 1973 (10), 3–6). Nevertheless heavy flooding may still take place on the Yangzi, as in 1983.

Silting is said to have reduced the extent of the lake by about one-half during the past 150 years. The plain has been increased by the same processes, but of course not in the same proportion – perhaps one-fifth in Hunan – but the newly reclaimed parts of the plain are of particular significance in the commodity grain base, being formed of deep rich soil and being relatively thinly (because newly) populated. Reclamation accelerated sharply after Liberation; between 1896 and 1949 the average annual extent of reclamation was 20 sq km, but between 1949 and 1976, 97 sq km annually (Lin Jingqian; 7) There is an obvious contradiction between continued extensive reclamation and the varied uses of the lake. Under the Maoists, with their enthusiasm for

grain and scorn for miscellaneous outputs, this problem was not discussed or even recognised, but naturally it has surfaced in the present climate of opinion. It is now said that under the Maoists many local units embanked peripheral shoals and closed local channels in the lake and its many tributary waterways, to the extent of 30% of its 1954 area of 3,915 sq km (Liu Zhengui and Li Yeying). This resulted in loss of fisheries, increase in flooding and the creation of poor, waterlogged fields. Much of this work is now being undone (*People's Daily*, 6 Aug. 1981). But these are not the only problems. During the Cultural Revolution, effective management of the lake as a whole was given up, and all the local communities, plus people from other provinces such as Jiangsu, Anhui and even Shandong, exploited the lake, fishing freely, building embankments and and dams to catch fish and interfering with the lake habitat, sometimes drastically. Industrial waste and farm spraying residues have also entered the lake in increasing quantities, introducing a new and serious problems of pollution (Liu Guilian). Obviously political pressures have been influential in some of these experiences, but equally obviously, the present is a phase when all the resources of both the plain and the lake are coming under increasing pressure. In these conditions, the environmental, social and economic conventions of resource management of the past generation are called inevitably into question, but those of the next generation are still in process of formulation – and still have a considerable way to go.

No comprehensive figure is given for the grain output of the Dongting basin, but a round figure of 10 million *mou* of farmland has appeared, together with average yield of 800 *jin*, suggesting up to 8,000 million *jin* or 4 million tons of grain per annum, of which about 1 million tons may be contributed to state commodity supplies. The ten counties of the lake plain are said to contribute one-third of Hunan's commodity grain and one-fifth of its total grain, and at the same time to contribute one-seventh of the province's arable and one-tenth of its population (Zhu Li: 20). Yields of grain are not high by the standards of Jiangsu or Guangdong, partly no doubt because of lack of labour and hence low levels of intensification, partly because the Hunan communities are much more backward technically. Double cropping is reported as generally feasible rather than generally practised, and triple cropping seems to be no more than an oddity. The history of yields in Nan county appears to be typical. At one place in Nan in 1960, a yield of 250 *jin* was considered satisfactory, but the previous year's yield of 88 *jin* was disastrous (*New Hunan Daily*, 11 Sept. 1950). In the early 1960s, in Nan county taken as a whole, average yields were 553 *jin* per *mou* in a bad year but around 740 *jin* in good years – at that time half of the land was producing a green fertiliser crop in the winter (*Dagong Daily*, 21 Mar. 1965). Average grain yield in Nan county was still below 800 *jin* in 1969 when its neighbour Anxiang became the first county in Hunan to reach the south China grain yield target of 800 *jin* in that year. It has probably since risen above that figure, but at Anxiang, the most advanced grain county in the area, average yields have still not risen far above 1,000 *jin* for the county, although most local units now practise double cropping and many are claiming grain yields of the order of 1,600 *jin* (Gao Guanmin: 9). Physical conditions on the plain are of course good, with around 260 frost-free days and generally reliable rainfall. The physical problems of the plain are those of flood in summer and waterlogging in winter, together with strong north winds in spring.

Literature on the Dongting area under the Maoists laid stress on grain production and grain yields, and Anxiang county was its model – in 1974 we read that when some brigades in Anxiang started a brickworks and began to keep ducks in order to make money, political steps were taken by the commune authorities to revive local interest in further increases in grain production (*People's Daily*, 21 Aug. 1975, reprinted later in *Quan guo nongye xue Dazhai*: 60). At that time, we can now read, profitable kinds of production were suppressed, even mechanisation was not discussed, and cash incomes were scanty or completely lacking. Ramie (a fibre crop) and oranges had to be abandoned in favour of more grain. The costs of farming rose to unprecedented levels (45% of gross output is quoted), and units ran into debt, but the only harvests were unprofitable grain crops; hence a fresh round of high-output-poor experiences emerged. As late as 1976 economic bush crops were still being cleared away to create fresh arable (Yu Xianming et al.). Here as elsewhere it is argued that extreme insistence on grain outputs was unrealistic and counter-productive, partly because of the damage to motivation, partly because realistically a high level of grain output can best be achieved when local cash production

is available to subsidise it. Since 1978, policy has been reversed, and local units are encouraged to diversify in aquatic crops, fish, ducks and a variety of alternatives such as poultry, rabbits and pigs, usually combined with systems of specialist job responsibility. Grain outputs, it is argued, have since tended to rise rather than fall, for instance in Huarong county (*People's Daily*, 3 Nov. 1979).

State farms are a special case in the Hunan grain base. Detail of particular interest has been published on Qianliang Lake state farm; the largest in Hunan, situated on Dongting Lake, with excellent local conditions and a history extending into the 1950s. Until 1978, it is said, this organisation suffered seriously from various features of bureaucratism and indifference. Its cadres are attacked at some length for exploiting the people by insisting on endless dinners at the public expense – one group of twelve local cadres spent more than 2,000 *yuan* in this way in three years – and groups of cadres were in the habit of visiting the villages in order to be entertained to meals (*People's Daily*, 3 Nov. 1979). No figure is given for total grain output, but in 1978 grain output rose by 49% compared with 1977, sugar by 46% and miscellaneous outputs by 67%; total production rose by 37%. Eleven of the previous years had registered losses. The inadequacies listed include lack of rational management and economic approach, poor management of money and stores, and systems of cash distribution which did not always honour work-points. Clearly this place is represented (though in restrained language) as a Maoist organisational slum. Four proposals for change in 1979 owe more, perhaps, to these problems and the current intellectual fashions, than to the original concept of the state farm. They are the following. First, to strengthen the mixed economy of the farm, with cotton, sugar and pigs as well as grain, together with food and drink industries (canning and wine) and such industries as bricks and soap. The mixed economy ought, it is argued, to furnish more than 50% of all outputs. Second, to improve marketing, which has previously been through the state system, but which has so far given little satisfaction. In recent months the farm had been selling tinned food at retail locally, very profitably. Third, management is to be improved, without so much dependence on state subsidy and with much more emphasis on making ends meet. Fourth, payment to workers is to be rationalised, with proper allowance for outputs created in the mixed economy sector and incentive payments for both workers and cadres (*People's Daily*, 12 May 1979).

Some of these proposals are surprising, applied to a state farm intended (apparently) to supply grain to the state and lying within a commodity grain base. They owe something to the post-1978 enthusiasm for self-management and self-responsibility; and something, assuredly, to low levels of motivation and consequently of achievement in this and other state farms. It now appears that, at least for a period of years, state farms may tend to approximate more closely to ordinary communes, both in terms of their internal organisation and in terms of their relations with the state and the state plan. In fact in terms of comment in the media this position is increasingly represented as orthodox, with the introduction of responsibility systems in production, talk of state farms' 'self-management rights', and moves towards a diversified (and profitable) economic structure (*People's Daily*, Editorial) 25 Nov. 1981).

Commodity cotton – demand and supply

Rationing of cotton cloth, which began in China in 1954, was terminated (technically, 'suspended') at the end of 1983. Price rises were also proposed at the same time (FBIS *Daily Report*, 23 Nov. 1983, K9, quoting a Xinhua release of 22 Nov. 1983). During the early 1980s, cotton cloth has been much more plentiful than a decade earlier, when Howe estimated consumption per person as 6–8 sq m in 1974 (Howe: 171). Consumption of cotton has risen in line with sharp rises in cotton outputs during the 1980s (Table 11.1). In addition pressure of demand upon cotton supplies has been greatly eased by rapid growth of synthetic fibre outputs since 1978; synthetic fibre accounted for 33% of textile output in 1982 as against 16% in 1978 (FBIS *Daily Report*, 25 Nov. 1983, quoting a Xinhua release of 24 Nov. 1983). About 4,300 sq m of cotton cloth is represented by 1 ton of ginned cotton (*People's Daily*, 22 Jan. 1981); hence the greatly expanded cotton production of 1982, of 3.6 million tons, might be expected to represent about 15,500 sq m of cloth – around 15 sq m per person for the whole Chinese population. To this must be added the rapidly rising,

Table 11.1. Cotton output (thousand tons)

	Cotton output	Source of figure
Pre-Liberation peak year	849	*Ten Great Years*: 119
1957	1,640	*Ten Great Years*: 119
1965	2,097	Geographical Research Institute: 192
1973	2,379	*People's Daily*, 22 Jan. 1981 (highest before 1980)
1977	2,049	Xinhua, 17 Feb. 1977
1978	2,167	Xinhua, 30 Apr. 1980
1979	2,207	Xinhua, 30 Apr. 1980
1980	2,707	Xinhua, 29 Apr. 1981
1981	2,968	Xinhua, 29 Apr. 1982
1982	3,598	Xinhua, 29 Apr. 1983
1983 (Estimate)	3,780	Xinhua, 24 Nov. 1983

and now substantial, contribution of synthetic textiles.

State raw cotton procurement appears to be fairly strongly localised in high-yield areas, and increasingly limited to specialist producing units. It is intended in the sections which follow to review relationships between policy and experience in cotton production, mainly from the standpoint of cotton-producing rural areas.

Cotton in China is the commodity second in importance only to grain. It is the usual clothing material for everyone in all parts of the country, with or without synthetic fibre mixture; and while in most of China the summer is hot and clothing need not be elaborate, in winter in most of the country thick clothing of some kind is a necessity. This usually takes the form of cotton padding. Cotton cloth is also exported, and there are of course additional demands for cotton in various fields of production and consumption apart from clothing.

Table 11.1 shows total output of ginned cotton in China during recent years, with some earlier figures for comparison.

As these figures show, output of cotton rose before 1957, and continued to rise, but much more slowly and with marked fluctuations, thereafter. Chao considers that 'acreage expansion accounted for most of the output increase in the 1950s whereas factors other than the land input lay under the rising production after 1963' (Chao; 245). These alternative factors were improved varieties and more fertiliser, leading to higher yields; in fact cotton acreage was reduced slightly during the Cultural Revolution.

A cotton yield of 100 *jin* per *mou* (750 kg per ha) is a good yield by international standards; 1973 was a year of good yields, with average of 69 *jin* per *mou* (518 kg per ha) (Geographical Research Institute: 193). Average yields previously rose from 21 *jin* per *mou* (160 kg per ha) in 1949 to 38 *jin* (287 kg per ha) in 1957 (*Ten Great Years*: 119, 129). Average yield is now probably around 60 *jin* per *mou* (1978, 59 *jin* per *mou* – Geographical Research Institute: 193), and this suggests a total Chinese cotton area of about 85 million *mou* – practically the same as in 1957.

Since 1977, after a long interval, official figures for cotton output are again published, but there is still no regular regional breakdown. Table 11.2 summarises the breakdown which is available for 1973, a peak year which experienced much discussion in its time (*Mianhua shengchan*). In this table, regional production by acreage is headed by the north China plain, but in terms of specialisation by the Yangzi delta area (southern Jiangsu, Shanghai and northern Zhejiang) and the Jianghan plain in Hubei. These two areas contributed 34% of all China's cotton output in 1973, and probably contributed as much as one-half of the commodity cotton which was available for state purchase. These conditions appear to have

prevailed at least until 1979, when the proportion of commodity cotton contributed by Jiangsu alone was 23%–500,000 tons, 60% of it contributed by six important cotton counties (*People's Daily*, 20 Dec. 1979), probably the six counties of Nantong prefecture, which occupy the northern shore of the estuary of the Yangzi. During the 1980s, however, the north China plain appears to have reasserted its primacy, no doubt with the help of government and the planning system. By 1983 Shandong and Hebei were the two leading cotton provinces, producing together some 40% of the greatly increased total output. (FBIS *Daily Report*, 23 Nov. 1983, K19, quoting a Xinhua release of 22 Nov. 1983). The return of important parts of the land resource of the north China plain to its traditional cash crop of cotton appears to have been sufficient to transform many local economies in the plain, and at the same time to strengthen cotton supply dramatically.

Comparisons with conditions before Liberation are difficult, because the figures available for that time take no account at all of local production which did not enter trade. Cotton which did enter internal or international trade was mainly grown in Jiangsu (about 30%), Hubei (27%), Hebei and Shandong (about 13% each). Total commercial output at that time usually ranged between 600 million and 800 million *jin*, grown on about 28 million *mou* of land, with output around 25 *jin* per *mou* (Fong: 26, Tables 62, 66). Allowing for cotton which did not enter trade, the distribution of production before 1930 does not display marked discrepancies with that of the present.

Table 11.2. Regional breakdown of cotton production (1973)

	Cotton acreage as % of total Chinese cotton acreage	Average cotton yield (*jin* per mou)	Production as % of total Chinese cotton production
Yangzi delta	12	109	18
Hubei	10	115	16
Sichuan	6	74	6
Other Yangzi producing areas	7	62	5
North China plain – Hebei, Henan, Shandong, Anhui	22	57	20
Shaanxi; Shanxi	8	54	8
Producers not named	35	54	27

Source: Geographical Research Institute: 206–8.

Cotton supply – the technical side. 'Contradictions' between cotton and grain

Cotton can be grown in summer in most parts of China, though it is happiest on lighter soils in the north and centre; summer conditions in the south are rather too wet for the best results. A twofold problem arises, however – first, the competition between cotton and grain for land, and second, the difficulty of fitting a cotton crop into a double-cropping system. Cotton in central China requires a total growing season of between 180 and 210 days, and of course this period must span the summer. The remaining 150–180 days of winter weather, generally cold but sunny, together with the demands of the local community for food and the reluctance of the state to assume the burden of providing it, suggest recourse to some form of food production in the winter season, broadly from December to April. The widespread, versatile and familiar tradition of double cropping suggests the same. The snag is that the winter crops also require as much as 200 days in the fields; and no simple way has yet been found to compress the cotton season into the remaining 160 days, as is done successfully, though precariously, with the two successive summer crops of rice in some triple-cropping systems. Green fertiliser, the obvious alternative winter crop in terms of the calendar, is valuable in raising cotton yields, but yields no grain.

A good deal has been written on this dilemma and on technical means of solving it, particularly during the Maoist decade when particular stress was laid upon local units' self-sufficiency in grain. Most solutions depend in some degree upon intercropping. A scheme from Qidong, a specialist producing county in Jiangsu (Qidong county Revolutionary Committee: 57) gave outputs which were reckoned at about 800 *jin* for grain and 100 *jin* for cotton. There were five crops in three years, but revealingly only one was cotton. In this scheme, wheat was planted at the end of October and interplanted with cotton at the end of the following April; then the cotton was interplanted with broad beans in early October, and the broad beans with maize in early April the following year; then after the maize harvest, late rice was planted in early August, followed by wheat in November. This scheme is illustrated in Fig. 11.3.

Like all double-cropping and triple-cropping systems, this and the various alternatives which involve cotton necessitate heavy applications of fertiliser, constant attention to the fields and to the calendar, and plenty of labour. Double cropping including cotton has tended to move into northern China from the south during the past two decades (*Mianhua shengchan*: 62) – but it has certainly continued to increase in the south at the same time. Scientific opinion is less single-minded about the advantages of intercropping than the media and the local units which produce materials for the media have been; it is pointed out that while intercropping enables full use to be made of land, time and natural energy, conflicts may still arise among the needs of the various crops, as for water and fertiliser; and there is inevitably some loss of cotton output compared with the

cultivation of cotton as a single crop. Successive crops of cotton are to be avoided, because they encourage pests and diseases. The alternation of a rice-based rotation with a cotton-based rotation, which takes place extensively in Jiangsu, is praised; or a two-year rotation such as rice–wheat–cotton–green fertiliser may be adopted, which requires no intercropping. Each alternative winter crop has its merits. Cotton interplanted with wheat is protected from unseasonable spring cold or heavy rain; beans increase soil nitrogen and have foliage which can be used as green fertiliser; rapeseed ripens earlier than either (Hunan province Agricultural College: 129–30). The simplest scheme is probably to intercrop with peas during the summer – the peas are sown (this is in Hunan) in late February and early March, before the cotton, and grow with it. The weakness of this system is that output of peas is low; it is most useful on poor land, where the pea crop may be thought of as a kind of green fertiliser as well (*People's Daily*, 20 Feb. 1970).

These interplanting schemes are interesting technically, and they occupy a prominent place in the Maoist literature on cotton areas in China. It is not clear, however, that in practical terms they are really very important. The literature itself gives no indication that they are in widespread practical use. For specialist cotton producers particularly, they seem certain to be a practical nuisance, involving unfamiliar techniques and disrupting normal field management for the sake of a food supply which ought to be available through trade in the usual way. In practice, it seems probable that green fertiliser occupies most cotton land in progressive areas in winter. Any loss in food crops might then be made up, hopefully, by cropping more land to grain in summer and expecting a proportionately higher yield of cotton as a result of the green fertiliser crop. Bean output can probably best be maintained, at least in the south, by winter cropping not on the cotton land, but on summer grainland. In the years between about 1958 and 1973, the 'contradictions' between grain and cotton were usually represented as tending to result in the squeezing out of grain, and policy was concerned to redress this balance. This was typical of the Maoist phase. But from about 1973, a fresh concern for cotton supplies became evident, cotton imports rose, and Mao's delphic slogan, 'take grain as the key link; ensure all-round development', began to be used to lay emphasis less on grain (as previously) than

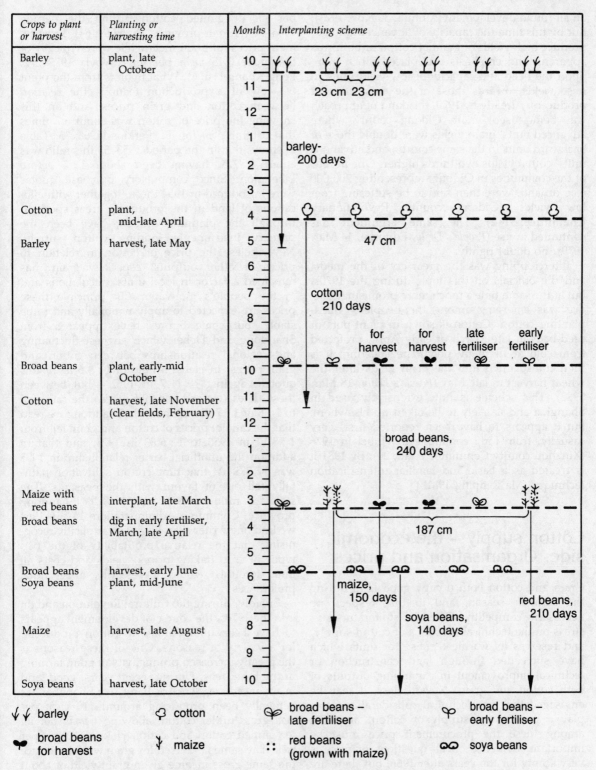

Fig. 11.3 Interplanting rotations in Qidong county, Jiangsu. *Source*: Qidong county Revolutionary Committee: 57.

on all-round development (Xinhua, 30 Nov. 1973). But by this time the capacity of advanced units to produce high yields of grain or cotton or both was apparent, and emphasis was placed much more upon the need and capacity of low-yield units to raise yields towards those of the most efficient producers. Already by 1970, this kind of approach was being used, as in Qidong county where advanced units' grain yields were double those of backward units in the same county, and advanced units' cotton yields two-thirds higher. One in four of the communes in Qidong, representing 200,000 *mou* of land, were then said to be suffering from low yields (Qidong county Revolutionary Committee: 31–2). The same argument has continued in use (*People's Daily*, Editorial, 14 Mar. 1979), no doubt rightly.

Intercropping was the great cry of the media and the officials on this topic during the 1970s, but at the same time a much more promising practice was emerging among the people – transplanting cotton. Cotton is sown in plant-pots or seed-beds in late March or early April, protected from cold at night by polythene sheeting; it is then transplanted into the main fields after the wheat harvest in late May (*People's Daily*, 18 Mar. 1982). This scheme is now extensively used in Shanghai and is likely to be taken up elsewhere; but it appears to have been reported first, very casually, from Liuji commune in Hubei in 1976 (Xinzhou county Committee et al.; 20). By 1981 it is treated as a basic and familiar intensification technique (Ma Renping 1981b).

Cotton supply – the economic side. Organisation and prices

Grain and cotton both occupy good land during the summer season, and in that respect are necessarily competitive. The Maoist literature lays stress on the technical problems of cotton supply, and reserves its warmest praise for units which have succeeded through land construction or technical improvement in expanding outputs of both cotton and grain. Nevertheless, it may be envisaged that non-technical considerations also play a part in the supply of cotton, and that among these the procurement price must be important. Evidence on all questions of price is very scanty for the years after 1966, but there are some indications that the state paid about 1 *yuan*

per *jin* of ginned cotton during the decade 1966–76 (Hunan province, *Accounts*: 64). Procurement prices for grain meanwhile were typically of the order 0.15 *yuan* per *jin* (Prybyla 1975: 272; Peng Kuang-Hsi: 6). What matters from the point of view of a production team is the relation between cotton and grain prices, and on this showing the price of cotton was about 6.7 times that of grain, *jin* for *jin*. Perkins (1966: 33, Table 2) shows that in the period 1953–55 this ratio was about 1 : 7.5, having been about 1 : 7 before Liberation. Since compulsory purchase quotas were introduced in 1954 these, together with allocations of land in the producing areas specified through the planning system, have been the primary instruments guiding cotton supply. Nevertheless the price of cotton in relation to prices of other outputs, especially grain, has remained a factor in local units' calculations and in the people's motivation. In principle these prices are expected to apply nationally and to be stable, but some figures have appeared from Shandong and Hebei which suggest fluctuating and regional relationships between cotton and grain prices. In Hebei a ratio of 1 : 8.6 in 1978 is quoted, against 1 : 11.7 in 1952 – but between these dates (we are not told when) the ratio fell to 1 : 6 or 1 : 7 (Jiang Shan). In Shandong we read that the ratio of prices of cotton and grain fell from 1 : 8.17 in 1950 to 1 : 6.83 in 1975, and that in addition the unofficial barter relationship in 1975 was 1 : 3.5. At that time cotton cultivation naturally fell out of favour with the peasants. The standard ratio in 1980 was 1 : 8.26 (Shandong province, Commune Administration: 14). In 1964 we find one writer (Pan Jingyuan) explicitly recognising that the relative profitability of the two types of crop (taking prices, yields and costs all into account) would necessarily affect total preferences.

Broadly, during the Cultural Revolution and on into the 1970s, the course of development appears to have been unfavourable to cotton producers, for a variety of reasons. One of these reasons is the greatly increased productivity of grain farming in the best areas. During recent years, good land in advanced areas such as Jiangsu or Shanghai has generally been producing around 110 *yuan* per *mou* gross under cotton, allowing 1 *yuan* per *jin* for ginned cotton and cotton yield of 110 *jin* per *mou*. The same land used for grain would produce the same gross income given grain yield of about 750 *jin* – a very moderate yield in this kind of area, under double cropping. With grain output of 1,400 *jin* (a typical good figure), gross income would be 210 *yuan* per *mou* – approaching double the figure for land under cotton, which of course cannot easily bear a second crop. We do not have comparative figures for costs, but they are surely higher for double cropping of grain, and labour inputs are also higher – but the monetary advantage probably still remained with grain farming in such areas. Under the Maoists, moreover, success in grain farming attracted favourable notice in the media and of course in the bureaucracy. In the 1950s cotton yields (previously very low) proved flexible; but in the 1970s cotton yields had already risen to good international levels in the best areas, and tended to stick while grain yields (partly because of extensions of double cropping) continued to rise in the same types of area. Changes in productivity threatened the old relationships with obsolescence. Meanwhile, pricing policy for cotton remained conservative. Hence, local units, in so far as they were able to exercise choice, might well settle for increasing grain production rather than cotton. In Nanhui county in the Shanghai municipality, some production teams found food supplies scanty and so preferred to plant more grain rather than more cotton; there have been misgivings about the best system of transplanting cotton in spring into land cleared of winter wheat; working capital for cotton has not always been available; and so forth. During the 1970s, units with problems of this kind have been guided, helped and pressurised in various ways to keep cotton production firmly in mind (*People's Daily*, 19 Mar. 1979). Concessionary cotton supplies are also allowed to producers – about 4% of output in Jiangsu in 1977 (*People's Daily*, 20 Dec. 1977).

The argument that units might find grain production more profitable than cotton applies to advanced areas in the south, where full double cropping is feasible. It does not apply generally in northern China, where grain yields cannot be so flexible. In northern China, particularly the north China plain, cotton production came under very different pressures in the 1970s – namely, sustained poor productivity, as Table 11.3 shows. Cotton yields per unit area in northern China were less than half those of the south, and total production (from roughly equal areas) more than double in the south. Yields in northern China had fallen since 1973. The reasons for these discouraging results are not far to seek. The Maoists,

Table 11.3. Cotton yields in *jin* per *mou* – northern and southern China

	1950	1973	1978
Southern China	20	—	83
Northern China	27	57 (peak year)	39

Source: Jiang Shan.

through the planning system, insisted increasingly on grain crops, and cotton was deprived of good land, water, fertiliser and labour. The state has not always been able or willing to furnish cotton producers with grain. Many units in the north China plain, such as Zhengding county, have specified the suppression of cotton cultivation as an aspect of the high-output-poverty upon which the Maoist authorities insisted. Even in northern China, moreover, it was argued that cotton prices were too low in relation to grain (Jiang Shan).

By 1977, the state authorities had become alarmed at the threat to already scanty supplies of cotton represented by these difficulties and introduced various incentives – increased prices, bonus payments and specialist producer groups in the villages (Ding Shourong; *People's Daily*, Editorial, 25 Dec. 1979). The new 'lumian' cotton variety was also popularised (Zhao Ziyang 1981: K4). These measures were dramatically successful, not in southern China where cotton production fell due to bad weather, but in the north, especially the north China plain. Attention has already been drawn, in the context of stable community enrichment in the plain, to the resultant late-1980 bonanza in terms of incomes. The fact is that surprisingly perhaps, Chinese cotton production still has a persistent boom-or-bust side which can be illustrated with materials from Zhoukou prefecture in eastern Honan. The following figures have been put together, relating to the good years of 1973 and 1980 and the two poor years which preceded them, for the ten counties of Zhoukou (Table 11.4).

Yields per *mou* in each of the two good years were 30% higher than in the previous year. Between 1979 and 1980, sales of cotton and incomes from cotton both doubled; but so apparently did the area planted to cotton, achieved presumably by a reduction in the area planted to grain. Sales to the state have probably increased little since 1973, however; there is no indication

171

Table 11.4. Experience with cotton in Zhoukou

	1972	1973	1979	1980
Area planted to cotton (thousand *mou*)	—	1,180	(Around 715)	1,400
Cotton yield (*jin* per *mou*)	(68)	88	(70)	Over 100
Total output of cotton (million *jin*)	—	104	—	(140)
Total cotton sales to the state (million *jin*)	—	—	Around 50	Over 100
Area planted to grain (thousand *mou*)	—	9,650	—	—
Grain yield (*jin* per *mou*)	353	442	—	—

Figures in parentheses have been deduced.
Sources: *Mianhua shengchan*: 13–17; *People's Daily*, 8 Jan. 1981

of the destination of the 28% of cotton output of 1980 which is not sold to the state, but this is presumably taken by the collective units as incentive cotton. In the 1973 and 1980 materials, very similar local accounts are given, each relating to an individual production team. In 1973 a team called Xiaoyang is said to have taken up cotton production from scratch in 1971–73, and achieved an income from cotton equivalent to 379 *yuan* per household in the good year 1973 (*Mianhua shengchan*: 15–6). In 1980 a brigade called Zhangpo, formerly poor, achieved cotton incomes of the order of 600 or 700 *yuan* per household (*People's Daily*, 8 Jan. 1981). In Zhoukou prefecture as a whole, after the bumper harvest of 1980, the state paid out 250 million *yuan* for cotton, amounting to 45 *yuan* per person, apparently at least double the cotton income of the prefecture in the previous year (*People's Daily*, 29 Jan. 1981). Cotton output in China as a whole increased again in 1981 and 1982, but apparently without such powerful regional dimensions.

Specialised cotton cultivation – the Nantong peninsula

A little more depth can be added to this analysis by reference to a single region – the Nantong peninsula which lies across the Yangzi from Shanghai. The peninsula comprises roughly the prefecture of the same name, with six counties,

7.12 million *mou* of arable land and population of 6.7 millions (Xinhua, 1 Oct. 1974). The six counties are Nantong, Qidong, Haian, Haimen, Rugao and Rudong. In Nantong much of the land is of relatively recent origin, representing deposition of silt by the river during the past two millennia. The soil is generally loose in texture and in places sandy. Cotton, admirably suited to local conditions, is the traditional local specialism, and up to the present the peninsula is one of the most important cotton-growing areas in China.

Until 1958, Nantong remained a specialised cotton area, depending on state supplies for grain, which of course replaced supplies previously provided by private business. In 1958–64, this situation was radically changed by cropping changes introduced through the planning system. Grain output rose from 1,600 million *jin* to 3,110 million jin in 1964 (Table 11.5), providing virtual self-sufficiency. During the same period, cotton output rose from 176 million *jin* to 284 million *jin* (Xinhua, 1 Oct. 1974), in spite of – presumably – a necessary shift in land allocation from cotton to grain. The scanty additional figures which are available support the supposition that a rapid rise in the previously very low cotton yield must have been the key to this achievement. Cotton yield rose to 119 *jin* per *mou* in the good year 1973 from 13 *jin*, an exceptionally low figure, in 1949 (Xinhua, 1 Oct. 1974). Grain yields also rose, to 1,066 *jin* per *mou* (indicating double cropping) in 1973, from a very ordinary 1949 figure of 248 *jin*. Indications here are that the authorities induced a rapid rise in both grain and cotton output by

Table 11.5 Cotton and grain production in Nantong prefecture

	Cotton production (*million* jin)	Grain production (*million* jin)	Area sown to cotton (*million* mou)	Jin of grain produced per jin of cotton
1958	176	1,600	—	9.1
1964	284	3,110	—	10.9
1973	290	3,920	2.9 (1972 figure)	13.5
1978	396	—	—	—
1979	probably 300	—	2.9	—

Source: Xinhua, 1 Oct. 1974; *People's Daily*, 15 Jan. 1973 (*SCMP*, 73 (5)), *People's Daily*, 19 Mar. 1979, 20 Dec. 1979.

cutting cotton acreage in favour of grain. In 1972, about 45% of the total arable was sown to cotton in Nantong prefecture, and this was also the figure for 1979. According to this reckoning, about 0.5 *mou* of land per person would be available for food crops; and if under double cropping this produced at a rate of, say, 1,000 *jin* per *mou*, the community could come close to self-sufficiency in food. This was the situation in 1973, to judge from the figures given in Table 11.5 – there would be about 580 *jin* of locally produced grain per person in that year. As Xinhua observed in the context of Nantong, in 1974, 'the development of grain production in the traditional industrial crop areas is one of China's important measures to develop farming on the basis of self-reliance' (Xinhua, 1 Oct. 1974).

No doubt there were differences, perhaps marked differences, among the six counties, and also locally among communes and brigades; land in some areas, especially loose soil near the coast, is quite unsuited to paddy, and most of the increase in grain output may well have taken the form of maize. There have also been complaints of low yields when cotton has been planted in paddy-fields (*People's Daily*, 15 Jan. 1973). It is interesting to observe, however, that in the same phase of policy, cotton-producing counties in Hubei, which is a grain-surplus province as well as an important cotton supplier, were apparently not put under the same pressure to become self-sufficient in grain (Tianmen county Revolutionary Committee: 5–11; Xinzhou county Revolutionary Committee et al,: 20). It may be envisaged that in such a case the state was content to trade off local surpluses of heavy and relatively perishable grain against alternative surpluses of light and relatively imperishable cotton, and to accept the consequent prosperity of cotton counties in eastern Hubei.

It is not stated how much grain is produced in Nantong since 1973, but it appears that by 1979 cotton producers had the whip-hand in policy. Cotton-producing units were guaranteed food supplies which would not fall below the level of those enjoyed by neighbouring grain-producing units, and once their state procurement quotas were satisfied, cotton-producing units were able to sell additional cotton to the state at a higher price, and also to ask for additional grain supplies as reward – typically, to the extent of 200 *jin* per person, perhaps one-third of consumption. Other privileges enjoyed by the cotton-producing units were rights to dispose of cottonseed oil and oilseed cake, by-products of cotton production, rights to preferential supplies of fertiliser, and rights to supplies of cotton for home use (*People's Daily*, 19 Mar. 1979). It is particularly interesting that these privileges were publicised as a matter of policy, suggesting that the government hoped to see other counties stimulated to emulation. If the heavy cotton harvests of 1980 and 1981 betoken some withdrawal of these privileges, that is likely to rank as an administrative matter and not to attract publicity.

Sugar bases – sugar and grain competing for land

Sugar production in China appears to represent a microcosm of the state's and the community's problems in establishing equitable, stable and economical systems for the procurement of agricultural commodities. Sugar in China comes in part from cane, grown in the south (especially but not only Guangdong and Fujian), and in part from beet, grown mainly in the north-east. Predictably, the state usually expects sugar-producing units to be self-sufficient in food, and hence sugar output is restricted; at the same time, the prices offered by the state for sugar are attacked by the producers as much too low. Meanwhile, the sugar-mills have their own problems.

As cotton and grain compete for land allocations in the north China plain and on the Yangzi, so sugar and grain compete in sugar areas. The foundation of the competition is the same – on the side of grain, the state's insistence on grain self-sufficiency in commodity producers, and on the side of sugar, the interest of potential specialist units in producing a crop of higher value than grain, which involves less work and, broadly, lower costs of production. The Maoists, of course, took the side of grain self-sufficiency, but in the present post-Maoist phase, little is heard in the press of the grain side of the argument; the pressure is all for specialisation.

The case for specialisation is based in large part upon such figures as those in Table 11.6.

These materials indicate that Chinese sugar yields are low by international standards, in spite of natural conditions for both beet and cane which are excellent, in north-eastern and south China respectively. They also indicate that gross dispar-

Table 11.6. Comparative yields of sugar (tons per ha)

	Cane	Beet
Queensland	9.0	
France	—	7.5
China	3.8	0.9
Guangdong, Fujian	8.0–10.0	—
Zhejiang, Yunnan	4.0	—
Sichuan, Guangxi	3.0	—
Hunan	2.0	—

Source: Materials in Zhao Hualing et al., and *People's Daily*, 4 May 1980.

ities exist in levels of productivity between Guangdong and Fujian on the one hand, and less favoured producers such as the north-east (producing beet) and Hunan on the other. The argument for regional and local specialisation is that China will not get the best out of her natural endowment or her investment in sugar-milling plant until these specialisms enjoy official recognition and encouragement.

But the case for specialisation also has another side, in which self-interest plays a larger part. Sugar production is very profitable. Table 11.7 indicates the scale of disparity in this respect between sugar and grain in Guangdong. Sugar is more profitable in terms of labour (using the Tianlu figures given) by a factor of almost six; and in terms of net output per unit area, by a factor of almost ten.

Within this framework, among the cane-producing provinces of the south, individual units argue their special cases – particularly those of the Pearl River delta in Guangdong (Liang Zhao et al.) and counties in southern Fujian such as Longxi, to which the arguments for specialisation in cane

Table 11.7. Rice and sugar in Guangdong – outputs and costs (*yuan*, 1979)

	Paddy rice	Sugar-cane
Gross output of 1 *mou*	112	126
Costs including labour	106	68
Net output of 1 *mou*	6	58
Return for one day's labour (Tianlu Brigade, Xinhua county, 1977)	0.8	4.6

Source: Materials in Liang Zhao et al.: 36–7.

sugar best relate. Some examples will illustrate the tenor of these arguments for individual counties.

Doumen lies at the maritime edge of the Pearl River delta. Here it is argued that for various reasons sugar-cane is a more realistic crop than paddy (Doumen county committee; 79–80). A good deal of the land is affected by marine salinity, of which sugar is much more tolerant than paddy; at the same time, labour is considered scarce in this county, and land plentiful. Transport in the delta is by water and hence very cheap, an important consideration for a bulky commodity like sugar-cane. Specifically, what is at stake at Doumen is 70,000 *mou* (4,667 ha) of land which was turned over to grain from sugar under the Maoists after 1966, and which the county and the people now wish to convert back to sugar. What is envisaged is commercial sugar monoculture on this land, preferably by mechanised means. The 70,000 *mou* of land, it is argued, will produce 280,000 tons of sugar cane, and this represents 33,600 tons of sugar, worth 21.3 million *yuan*, of which the state will receive 13.4 million. The same land in grain is worth only 0.4 million *yuan* to the state. The people would like to grow sugar-cane and to be assured of state rice supplies in return on a *jin*-for-*jin* basis – it is pointed out that *jin*-for-*jin* the world price of sugar is three times the world price of rice. The motives of the local people seem to be mixed – in part the lower labour demands of sugar, relating to scarcity of labour and the less need for land improvement with sugar; in part high incomes (the price of sugar is considered low, but of rice much lower); in part the access to raw materials for industry and subsidiary production represented by sugar and sugar-cane waste (alcohol or paper production; fodder for pigs). Fertiliser is not discussed, but would be a necessary input for grain – less so for sugar.

It is also argued that sugar prices are too low; the people are not satisfied in this respect. The state at present pays 1.69 *yuan* per 100 *jin* of cane. This 100 *jin* of cane can yield up to 13 *jin* of sugar and also by-products close to its own value. Moreover, 1.69 *yuan* is the price of only 3 *jin* of sugar. Hence the state gets 10 *jin* of sugar, plus the by-products, virtually for nothing – so the argument runs. Sugar-cane refuse can be used to make paper. Straw for the same purpose sells at 2.4 *yuan* per 100 *jin*, considerably more than the price of sugar-cane *before* crushing. Faced with this barrage of low prices for their outputs, it is argued, local motivation for increases in sugar output in Doumen is poor; but sugar is still preferred to grain.

Another view of the competition of grain and sugar for land in southern China comes from Fujian, the other main sugar-producing province. The author (Yu Jinman) is a member of the Fujian provincial planning committee.

In Fujian province as a whole, arable land now works out as only 0.8 *mou* per person (presumably of the rural population) – and in the sugar districts of the southern coastlands, 0.4 *mou*. In fact, arable land is now 11% less in extent than at Liberation, and the population has increased by 106%; arable land per person has fallen by upwards of one-half. Although average grain yield has risen from 287 *jin* per *mou* to 873 *jin* since Liberation, grain allowances are not high – average consumption in 1978 was only 116 *jin* above that of 1949 (the absolute figure is not given). Intensification with rising yields has taken place and still has a long way to go, but it will not necessarily release land for sugar, given present pressure of need upon grain outputs. There is sharp competition for land.

Localities vary, runs the argument; policy now is supposed to be adapted to local conditions. Compared with Zhejiang (no comparison with Guangdong is suggested), sugar output per unit area is double or treble in Fujian. At the same time, grain output per unit area is 30% or 40% higher in Zhejiang than in Fujian. It would be irrational (the argument runs) for Zhejiang to expand sugar output at the expense of grain, or Fujian to expand grain output by squeezing out the sugar crop. Each should depend on the other, the author argues. This, however, is certainly special pleading from the standpoint of Fujian; the author does not add that sugar outputs are much more profitable than grain (Yu Jinman).

Confirmation of the essence of this interpretation as far as grain equivalent is concerned comes from Xianyou county, Fujian province (*People's Daily*, 18 Oct. 1979). Under the Maoists, the authorities expected Xianyou to be self-sufficient in grain, and limited sugar acreage accordingly. After 1976, a more constructive sugar policy was adopted. Fertiliser was supplied in return for sugar at the rate of 1.5 *jin* (later 2 *jin*) per 100 *jin* of sugar-cane, and grain at the rate of 1 *jin* per 100 *jin* of cane, plus 12.5 *jin* of unprocessed grain per 100 *jin* of cane above quota. This system ran into difficulties when it transpired that the 'grain' supplied by the state included 80% of dried sweet potato; the people complained, and this proportion was later reduced to 20%. Trouble of a different kind arose in 1979, a year of bumper sugar harvest, in all 760,000 tons. The mills in Xianyou could not keep up with production. Although the county authorities set about increasing capacity in the mills, the senior authorities used the milling problem as an excuse to limit sugar growing in Xianyou to 790,000 tons, and to discontinue the incentives for production above quota. This of course was bad for the people's motivation, which had been raised very high during the previous three years, to a point where one-third of the arable in the county was being used for sugar, and sugar-cane was being grown on families' private plots.

It appears that an unscrupulously fought battle is in progress in southern China for designation for sugar production; and each area which has the power to do so presents itself in the media as best it can. What is at issue is both sugar acreage (representing income) and grain equivalent (representing other units' bearing the costs, hard labour and low incomes of grain production). It bears remembering that the obverse of high-output-poor units is other kinds of unit which profit from the subsidy represented by cheap grain. One way to handle this problem would be by imports of grain from abroad to set against exports of much more profitable sugar; even direct overseas trade authorised at provincial level is being proposed in Guangdong (Liang Zhao et al.). Bearing in mind the vast size and diversity of the Chinese subcontinent, it is not really surprising that these discussions suggest echoes of those within the European Economic Community on such subjects as production and marketing of vegetable oil and beef.

A similar argument arises in the north-east, but at county rather than provincial level. Output of sugar in the north-east remains low, and beet is usually scarce at the factories. Natural conditions are nevertheless excellent, especially in Heilongjiang, and for the people sugar is a profitable and popular crop. A number of institutional factors conspire to perpetuate weakness in the sugar business in the north-east (Zhao Hualing et al.).

The first of these is the grain quotas in the counties which could readily produce more sugar. These quotas remain high and in many cases are still tending to increase, no doubt in line with the state's perception of Jilin and Heilongjiang as the seat of a major commodity grain base. A second is the need to assure stability of grain output for local food supplies – a county which produces plenty of grain has plenty to eat, but the same is not necessarily the case for a county with a high sugar output. Third, encouragement and incentives (other than price) are high for grain, but not for sugar. Hence local specialisation in sugar production does not occur; the six big sugar-mills in Heilongjiang are used by thirty-eight counties. Transport costs are consequently heavy; and because production is scattered and incidental rather than specialised, yields tend to remain low.

Some glimpses have appeared in the literature of further problems created by or for the sugar-mills.

Sugar-cane is harvested in China in winter, but the date of harvest depends upon region and locality, according to the date when the sugar content of the cane reaches its maximum. In Qinzhou prefecture, Guangxi province, the sugar content of the cane delivered rises from 11% to 12% in November, through 13–14% in December to upwards of 15% in January and February; from March it begins to fall again. For many county administrations who have their own sugar-mills, this timing is inconvenient because the crop as a whole straddles the year's end, creating difficulties in the local accounts. As a result, many localities cut their sugar-cane in November and December, with consequent loss of sugar (*People's Daily*, 14 Nov. 1979).

In part this problem may be thought to depend upon counties managing their own sugar-mills, and in fact this is the implication of the argument. Further complaints about local sugar-mills have also reached the press (*People's Daily*, 21 Apr. 1980). In recent years many local authorities have started small sugar-mills, and a big mill like that at Jiangmen in the Pearl River delta, which formerly served four counties, now competes with no less than twenty local factories whose collective capacity is greater than Jiangmen's, so that plant is idle at Jiangmen while inferior sugar is produced elsewhere. This complaint falls into line with others which suggest that the proliferation of local enterprises, however profitable for individual rural units, may lead to over-investment and wasteful competition for supplies among these enterprises and those of the state.

Commodity bases and the Chinese countryside

'Commodity bases' are not limited to the kinds of production which have been discussed; many other localities lay claim to this status, in such fields as edible oil, silk, fish and many others. What has usually been at issue is a group of rights within the rural planning system – the right to allocate resources to a kind of production which enters the market, the right to call upon the state to guarantee purchase of at least part of the product, and where possible the right to call upon the state to furnish guaranteed supplies of cheap food in return. Obviously these aims relate directly to restrictions placed upon all rural units by the management of the rural planning system. Since 1979, with rural free marketing increasingly a reality, state purchase of outputs is less necessary and state food guarantees less probable; but the right to allocate resources is correspondingly more critical – with various implications for the rural production plans. Grain prices are still low, and for this reason among others units located in the commodity grain bases display as widespread interest in production other than grain as those anywhere else. In this and other ways the logic of recent developments would be a tendency for commodity bases, and dependence on them by the state, to wither away gradually, as production schedules widen and diversify in all parts of the country. Rural surpluses would then be produced and marketed (not necessarily through the state) wherever resources and demand could be united. Such developments would strengthen provincial and regional self-sufficiency, giving welcome relief to the transport system in its need to accommodate new trade representing economic growth. All this would suggest for state procurement of grain and other commodities sets of arrangements at provincial and local level not unlike those which are made at present for cotton – that is, with much less dependence upon 'bases' and more upon other surpluses.

But problems, some of them chronic, would still arise. Grain surpluses at low prices would surely become much more difficult to extract from rural communities on a satisfactory scale, suggesting growing imports of food and no reduction in the burden of movements of food upon the transport system. This alone may be considered sufficient reason to reject any such possibility, certainly as applying to grain. But at the same time, as in the present arrangements for cotton, it would be virtually impossible for bureaucrats to find the proper formulae for prices, incentives and constraints for production year by year in the counties, and problems of shortfall and surplus would inevitably arise, with which official organisation would be poorly equipped to deal. Here and elsewhere what is seriously at issue is the insistence of the state upon its own handling of the main commercial flows in China. Control (though by a variety of offices) is thereby assured; but flexibility is sacrificed. But while trade in rural surpluses (especially grain) remains so closely tied to price control and the rural production plans, it is hard to envisage the loosening of direct state control of this trade, for instance to independent commercial networks responsible to the state. Present indications, in a phase when local collective units are more nearly self-managing than at any time since 1955, are that physical constraints through the planning system have been considerably loosened but by no means given up; and that in the critical case of grain the state can afford to give up very little more of its apparatus of physical control, whether in the commodity grain bases or elsewhere.

The 'grain bases' from southern and north-eastern China which have been discussed in this chapter, although dissimilar in terms of environment, have in common that they represent the great bulk of rural areas in the eastern half of China – areas of moderate resource, moderate density of population, moderate degrees of accessibility and commercialisation, and low prosperity. They differ very much from the 'cotton bases' and 'sugar bases', which are also discussed here, in the extent to which their commerce with the state represents the opportunity to establish prosperity. The grain bases (southern Jiangsu apart) are up to the present areas where rural impoverishment is built into the system, because of low state prices for their main outputs. But low state prices for grain are not the only problem of such areas. Even if the state were willing to relax its demands upon the grain bases (as it may become willing and able to do), problems of isolation and lack of urban demand would remain. People in such counties as Yoyang in Hunan or Yushu in Jilin will be able to improve their diets by farm diversification, and it will not cost them much to rebuild their houses; but if they are to raise their living standards in other respects, they must sell to urban markets or the state. But urban markets (apart from rural towns dependent on the countryside) are distant; and sales to the state involve once more the whole apparatus of bureaucracy and monopoly. Even for trade with the state, moreover, problems of relative isolation from profitable markets still arise, especially where perishable commodities are involved. The message here, for grain bases which would like a share of the new prosperity, is that progress is bound to be relatively slow, depending upon networks of communications and business which (whether the state is involved in them or not) will have to be built up phase by phase over a matter of years. Much the same must be true for the bulk of rural eastern China. There cannot be many areas which can develop in the foreseeable future along the lines of Suzhou.

12

The official systems and the course of change

In common with other parts of the Chinese community, rural China has experienced dramatic changes since the death of Mao Zedong in 1976 and the reformulations of policy which followed in 1978. Many restrictions upon individual and collective behaviour have been given up, and fresh objectives have been adopted which include the active promotion of household prosperity. The people have responded promptly and energetically, especially where they stand to benefit directly in material terms, for instance in domestic production for the new rural and urban free markets and in new house construction. They have also responded in the same ways to the new freedoms in terms of organisation of farm production, represented by the various kinds of responsibility and contract systems. Taken together, these changes mean that the Chinese countryside now has powerful dynamic components which lie beyond the forms built up through the almost thirty years between Liberation in 1949 and the Third Plenum in 1978. It remains a moot point to what extent these changes and this dynamic represent positive official policy, and to what extent they represent compromises between the aspirations of the peasant communities ('spontaneous capitalist tendencies', as the Maoists would say) and the need and capacity for control of the countryside by the authorities and the Communist Party.

At the same time, the fundamentals of rural organisation in China remain basically unchanged since Mao's time. Their central morphological feature is the three-level hierarchy of the people's communes, but their central operational feature is the rural production plan. It is the plan which controls and manipulates the year's input of human and biological energy, which represents the demands made upon each local community by the state, and which constitutes a self-fulfilling forecast of the year's activity. By means of the production plan, the various imperatives of Chinese rural life are rationalised for each locality – some imperatives of subsistence, some of control, some of scarcity. It is witness to the importance of the plan in the official system that even now, when open discussion is applauded, rural communities are frequently reminded of their obligations to satisfy the plan, but are still seldom or never invited to analyse or comment upon the needs which it represents or the methods by which it is formulated. Needless to say, the same was true during the Maoist decade, in spite of the Maoists' proclaimed insistence upon consultation with the people. In the rural production plans, the Chinese Communist Party illustrates Marx's comment (in the Preface to the *Contribution to the critique of political economy*) that 'It is not the consciousness of men which determines their existence, but on the contrary their social existence which determines their consciousness.' The commune system supplies the structure of organisation by which the plan is made operational among 5 million subsistent and producing communities occupying a wide range of differing habitats. The decision of 1982 to separate rural administrative functions from the commune hierarchy is not likely to affect the fundamentals of rural organisation, which are not administrative but economic, and which relate much less to administrative management than to the production plan.

The remarkable stability of rural China during more than twenty years of rapid and sometimes irrational institutional and social change owes much to the commune and rural planning systems. Under the Maoists, economic growth was traded openly against stability – this was a feature which many Western critics, disenchanted with growth, particularly admired. But stability as a long-term aim raises long-term problems. Stability tends to generate economic linkages, local trade, fresh economic demand and production to satisfy it – in fact the very economic growth which has been renounced. Even more seriously, stability creates secure family life, and secure family life means bigger families, and bigger families, of course, represent population growth. As a result, population growth is now gravely threatening the whole fabric of Chinese society. According to the census of 1982, population in mainland China reached 1,008 millions in that year (Xinhua, 27 Oct. 1982, 3). Measures of various kinds have been taken by government to try to limit the further growth of population – a new marriage law prescribing later minimum ages for marriage, practical birth-control, social penalties against larger families, exhortation and so forth; but the Chinese population is likely to continue to grow, even if at a moderate rate, at least until the end of the present century. Policy cannot readily be found which will prevent the

further growth of a population in which people under twenty-one years of age now represent around one-half (*People's Daily*, Editorial, 11 Feb. 1980) – and numbers can hardly fail to rise to 1,200 millions by the year 2000. Even in present conditions, moreover, there is evidence of hostility to restrictions in family size, in the shape of a serious tendency towards female infanticide in rural areas which in extreme cases results in boys outnumbering girls by two to one or even more (*People's Daily* 7 Apr. 1983, translated in FBIS *Daily Report*, 7 Apr. 1983, K50). At the same time, there has been mounting impatience with a socialism which stood to perpetuate poverty rather than to generate growth – in this sense, Maoism is now decisively rejected. Since 1978, partly by reason of population growth, partly by reason of the realisation of China's growing backwardness by the standards of other east Asian communities, the present central authorities have opted for a policy of direct stimulation of economic growth. In this they certainly enjoy the support of a very substantial and widespread movement of public opinion, at the lowest assessment. As a result of growth, the rural systems inevitably come under strain in various respects.

One aspect of this strain arises in the operation of the production plans themselves. The production plan is the operational part of the rural system, but its dynamic potential is strictly limited in both time and scope. The plans are ill-adapted to accommodate growth, especially growth with popular, rather than official, forms and objectives. Another is the official trading system, which cannot possibly handle all the business which the countrysides could generate. Another is the problems within the rural bureaucracy itself. At the grass-roots level, according to one commentator, 'at present, around two-thirds of the basic-level cadres do not understand how to do management and control work' (FBIS *Daily Report*, 9 July 1981, R7, quoting *Hebei Daily*, 12 June 1981). Administration, moreover, is necessarily cumbersome – 'there are as many as 77 organs under the direct control of the province and some 50 to 60 organs under the direct control of every prefecture and county' (FBIS *Daily Report*, 30 Dec. 1981, 01, quoting the governor of Shandong province in a Jinan broadcast, 25 Dec. 1981). It may be argued that these numbers of official agencies are both too few and too many – too many for effective integration of policies; too few to handle the administration (and in many cases the direct

A bureaucrat thinks about the Four Modernisations . . . car, TV, drink . . . villa . . . children educated abroad . . . working the system. . . . *Source: People's Daily*, 20 Sept. 1980. The artist is Miao Di.

management) of the public and economic affairs of a Shandong population of the order of 75 millions and county populations of the order of 750,000. At the same time, enterprise is disastrously scarce, and must remain so even at the low technical levels relevant to most kinds of rural development, under present restrictions which limit the employment of labour to public authorities or, in the case of private employment to limited numbers of 'apprentices' and 'assistants'.

At a higher level, enterprise and the bureaucracy both work within an incomplete legal system (Gu Ming: K13) geared unharmoniously to an administrative system which has experienced marked changes in pace and direction; exploitation of all kinds is eased by anomalies in the system, which in turn invite corruption (Zhao Ziyang 1982: K32–33). Indeed, for most purposes the Chinese countryside has no system of law – that function has been neglected in many respects

and in others discharged since the 1950s by routine administrative procedures and the machinery of the production plans; and changes have been introduced mainly through quasi-legal official regulations of various kinds, such as the *Decisions on some agricultural questions* and various directives issued by the State Council. Even on such fundamental topics as the ownership of rural land and rights to employ labour, officials and people may hold inconsistent or erroneous views, as has been shown. Occasional official directives against specific abuses make a poor substitute for law as a framework for economic growth (CCP 1983b:, K13; Dong Likun; van der Sprenkel).

Most of these institutional difficulties join with self-interest and self-motivation to suggest economic growth outside the state plan rather than within it. Increasingly, this is what is reported, especially from the most advanced and prosperous areas. Most of the new growth is geared to local markets which pay in cash at market prices whether legally or not; while production within the plan continues to be geared to state quotas at low official prices or, at best, negotiated prices which the state tries hard to hold down, ever mindful of the rising cost of subsidised consumer prices (Zhao Ziyang, 1982: K11). Increasingly the official system offers little encouragement to rural units which wish to remain loyal to the state trading organisations upon which basic urban supplies and many exports depend, except where specially favourable official prices can be negotiated. The danger is that the official commodity system must depend increasingly upon less accessible and less sophisticated suppliers, especially for commodity grain, and hence upon backwardness and the exploitation of the rural poor.

Economic growth outside the plan may, however, be regarded as a problem or a desideratum according to policy preconceptions. The Maoists were right to treat the state plan as a fundamental instrument of both control and supply; and increasingly as the one is given up, so must be the other. But from the standpoint of the present authorities, the new freedom to trade is one central feature of a whole range of imaginative relaxations in the relations between organisation and production. Up to the present, these appear to have been remarkably successful in defusing peasant hostility to the state system, generating reasonably widespread prosperity, and stimulating production of grain as well as of varied outputs. This has been done partly by liberalisation of formal administration, partly by introduction of responsibility and contract systems which contain an incentive element, and partly by opening of a wide range of production opportunities outside the state plan. A rural building boom and unprecedented demand for consumer goods in the countryside is the happy result. Grain remains cheap and the planning system remains basically coercive, but the fact that the new system has already worked successfully for several years, in spite of its inconsistencies or because of them, is some indication that it may work for many more.

While it is working successfully, demands for higher standards of living in the countryside will continue, expressed in services and consumer goods – not Coca Cola whose political symbolism is often taken much too seriously, but valuable and important objects such as the 'five major items', bicycles, sewing-machines, wrist-watches, radios and television sets, together with furniture, clothing, improved diets, facilities for eating in restaurants, personal services like haircuts, repair services, transportation services, travel, better housing and so forth. Production of some of these things can easily be stimulated – vinegar, garlic, soy sauce, beancurd, ginger, snacks at cooked-food stalls, all scarce or unobtainable during the Maoist decade, demand only freedom for local rural enterprise and the toleration of one-family businesses like those which manage such production in Hong Kong, Taiwan and Japan. The same is true of repairs and personal services. This freedom is now part of official policy. The revelation that in densely populated parts of rural China upwards of one-third of the labour force is surplus to the work which has to be done in the present production systems suggests that people can readily be found to do these kinds of varied work. Most kinds of service industry relate to reasonable standards of living in Asian conditions (for instance, restaurants, tea-houses and noodle-stalls in rural towns), but some relate direct to productive capacity on the land, especially improved communications and improved stocks of investment goods in local retail outlets. There are now signs that the authorities recognise the gap between performance and need in rural commerce, but small indication of will or capacity to introduce reform of the fundamentals – that is, within the official part of the system – on the requisite scale. Some of the problems arise in the

industrial system, and as prosperity grows and demand extends, for instance to motor-bikes which are one of the fundamentals of rural transport elsewhere in east Asia, the countryside's demands upon the industrial system cannot but increase.

Problems and opportunities in the regions

In the various rural management schemes prior to 1978, no very important roles were assigned to the regions of China, apart from those which were designated as commodity production bases. Under the Maoists, a number of factors were put into operation which tended to reduce regional differentiation mainly by suppressing opportunities for favoured regions to develop favourably, particularly the depression of internal commerce and production for the market. Nevertheless, regional differences remained marked – those between north and south; those between areas of long settlement (like Shanxi) and areas of continued colonisation (like Jilin); those between accessible lowlands with long histories of prosperity (like Jiangnan) and the hinterlands (like mountain Zhejiang or Anhui); those between urban peripheries where profitable trade continued, though reduced drastically, and ordinary rural areas where opportunity for trade was strictly limited; those between specially backward areas, particularly the Great Wall frontier, and neighbouring areas which were less handicapped; and those between areas which fell directly into the state's 'high-output-poor' trap, and areas which through commodity sugar or cotton, or in other ways whether or not officially approved, found means to spring the trap to some degree. A number of authors have examined materials on these points (Nolan and White 1979; Paine; Vermeer; Klatt). But in principle and practice the schemes of development before 1978, and particularly that of the Maoists, were uniformitarian, because Communist Party policy did not admit deviations on matters of importance, because many kinds of growth potential were frozen due to inhibitions about their political and socio-economic implications in a socialist state, because of bureaucratic rigidities and positions of principle which tended to insist upon self-reliance in local units from province downwards, and because

181

official models of development (such as Dazhai) were promoted in the media with only minimal allowance, or none, for their implications for special regional opportunities or needs. It was not accidental that one of the first of the new development slogans after 1978 was 'policies to suit local conditions'.

The implications of the post-1978 scheme of development for regional differentiation are a different matter. A static model has been replaced by a model which, if not exactly dynamic, recognises social development over time and proposes measures to accommodate it. Of these the most important in the countryside are the growth of population on the one hand, and on the other the revitalisation of local commerce in its many forms. As a result areas with favourable location and favourable resource, skill and communications complexes are already showing indications of very rapid development – the Jiangnan countryside in southern Jiangsu, southern Liaoning, and the peripheries of the great cities everywhere. Here, in a kind of development familiar from many Third World countries, rural communities are tending to experience assimilation to the urban economies, labour is tending to migrate both to the cities and from more remote rural areas to those less remote, and there are signs of an urban scramble for rural land and other kinds of cheap rural opportunity. There are already evidences of the emergence of dramatic differences between these prosperous areas and the bulk of the countryside, powered by high urban prices based ultimately upon relatively very high levels of industrial and other kinds of urban productivity as measured in cash.

Meanwhile the growth of prosperity in areas more distant from the cities and industrial areas must be conditional upon prices offered by the state trading system for bulk surpluses such as grain and cotton, or upon limited opportunities for local trade in these and other surpluses, or the generation of local industry, hopefully with markets which are more than local. Alternatively, such prosperity may look towards the growth of much more complete local or provincial economies, with reasonable capacity to supply the industrial consumer and producer goods in terms of which prosperity is inevitably reckoned, and without serious shortages of grain or other simple foods, cotton and fuel. To list these requisites already invites corresponding lists of places where they are likely to be within reach, such as most lowland areas in southern China, and also areas where in the foreseeable future they are not, such as the Great Wall frontier and many poor mountain regions. In such lists, as ever, the north China plain occupies an anomalous position. It is likely to continue to do so, due to the burden represented by its own subsistence in a difficult and fragile environment. To propose any kind of provincial self-sufficiency scheme of development reminds us, moreover, that attempts to create local industrial self-sufficiency artificially have met with predictable official condemnation in strong language (State Council 1982). Provincial self-sufficiency in food, however, is presumably praiseworthy, unless it relates to satisfaction with self-sufficiency in a province from which the state expects to take a surplus.

For some aspects of official policy as now formulated, there can be nothing but welcome. Of those the broadest and most generally valuable is diversification, and with it the prospect of growth of local, regional and export trade. A policy tending towards grain monoculture wastes resources other than the arable, impoverishes diets, limits incomes and suppresses employment and enterprise. Whatever the scale and degree of Maoist preference for grain as the key link rather than the promotion of all-round development, there is no doubt that under the Maoists the potential of many localities for production of subsidiary outputs was neglected, with the results already mentioned. Everything is to be gained, particularly perhaps in mountain peripheries and other backward areas, from diversification into animal, poultry, woodland, aquatic and orchard specialisms. Sadly, the north China plain, with its shortage of varied or under-used resources, or both, seems the least likely of all the regions of China to profit from this kind of opportunity.

These remarks relate mainly to the regional opportunities which are offered by the new schemes of rural development. Regional problems have changed much less, though some, especially ecological problems, have surfaced only since 1978. Now many writers in China report ecological problems, and some an ecological crisis (Economics of Environment Forum; Weng Yongxi et al: 14). Realistically, experience and outlook are mixed. Examples have been given, especially from the forest and the edge of the desert, where the effort of the state or the local people, legal or not, has cut deep wounds in environmental stability. Of course these are not the first such wounds in the long history of Chinese land management; but the wounds of the present have less chance of healing than those of earlier centuries, and represent blows to a much weaker ecological body. In most parts of China, the wild environments which exist are now under heavy pressure. Some of this pressure is the inevitable result of rural populations now much more than double those of a century ago. Some results from better communications and better social organisation in remote areas; some from cumulative over-exploitation of wild resource for several or many generations; some from rising standards of living, expanded social needs and local self-management since Liberation. Some represents social construction which in other contexts must be considered praiseworthy. In many crucial areas the state itself, through building of railways and maintenance of airlines, through planned extension of the cultivated area as in the north-east, through rubber planting in Yunnan and Hainan and in many other ways, is the prime mover in the advance of humanity into the remaining Chinese wild corners of Asia which has close parallels in India and Indonesia.

Where the rural communities are most seriously at odds with the rural environments is in their need for fuel. Some 85% of the energy used in rural China comes from organic sources – indeed by the same token China as a whole depends to the extent of around 32% upon organic supplies of fuel, mostly firewood (Gao Shangquan: 124). Indications have already been given of the effects of this search for fuel upon the forests; and in addition it represents serious losses of fertiliser material such as straw and dung. Firewood copses and rural electrification are both sound policies at opposite ends of the technological scale, but neither can hope to furnish the average rural household with all the fuel which it needs year by year for cooking and for warmth in winter. Nor can either seriously expect to supply rapidly expanding rural industry with energy. Only the state and such state agencies as the provinces can hope to tackle this problem; and only fossil fuel, particularly coal, is likely to offer a realistic solution. But 'few rural areas can expect to get coal from major pits supplied through the state' (Gao Shangquan: 135), though local pits may be able to produce supplies. Coal supplies remain inadequate everywhere in rural China due in part to transportation problems analogous to those facing commodity grain, in part to the

priority accorded to state industry, and in part due to extravagance in use – even in the countryside, where coal is very scarce, it is often used extravagantly (Xu Junzhang and Huang Zhijie). Diesel supplies in the countryside have fallen steadily since 1978 (Gao Shangquan: 125) – which may be one reason why in advanced countrysides small tractors are more often seen in use for transport purposes than on the land.

But the environments do not begin and end with the remnant forests and open hillsides. Most of the people live, and most outputs are produced, in environments which have been humanised for hundreds of years. Here experience since Liberation and indications for the future are both much better – contrary to what is sometimes said in the West, Chinese communities are happier with humanised, productive landscapes than in communing with Nature. Many major construction jobs have been tackled and brought to some degree of success, such as the Hai and Huai schemes. The irrigated area has been increased by three times, multiple-cropping indexes have been steadily raised, plant and animal diseases have been successfully attacked, and fertiliser application has shot ahead. Chinese farming is now more scientific, better organised and more productive than at any previous time in history, and there is every reason to expect increasingly diversified farm economies to be increasingly supportive of rural environments. In all these ways, the human communities continue to display an impressive capacity to cooperate with the environment, once it has entered the world of human responsibility. Pollution has sharply increased, it is true, and it includes some serious pollution by pesticides as well as much which is of industrial origin (Yi Zhi 1980). Sadly, further rises in rural living standards seem almost certain to lead to further rises in pollution levels. But as production diversification develops there is likely to be increasingly successful ecological diversification in the landscape in such forms as bamboo groves, particularly in the south.

Consumer prosperity and producer sophistication go hand in hand, as the Maoists well knew. At a distance of 60 or 80 km from the great cities, even in good environments, the forms of rural life are already different from those in the suburban belt in terms of supplies of manufactures, extent of commercial circulation, variety of opportunity, quality of institutional provision and so forth; in terms of a regional developmental time-scale, such counties' experience may be as much as a generation behind that of the urban peripheries. Behind these counties lie others more isolated, separated by a similar or even longer notional space of time from those which are most advanced. It is these counties, the great majority, in which the fundamentals of China's development future must be decided. Beyond these counties lie others, usually separated by much longer spaces of time still – the most isolated counties in provinces peripheral to the Chinese heartland, such as Yunnan, Sichuan and Shaanxi. In areas of this kind, in terms of opportunities whether as producers, consumers or citizens, the position of households and individuals has changed only marginally since Liberation or during the present century, and population growth and ecological stability are probably the most important considerations in society and economy. At the opposite end of the scale, rural communities and households in the Jiangnan countrysides around Shanghai and Hangzhou, in Liaoning, and in the close city fringes everywhere, can now look forward to a course of development during the forthcoming generation which will begin to close the gap with similar communities and households in Taiwan and Hong Kong, if not with those of Japan.

A stable state

What is argued for here, ideally, is a long phase of institutional stability, uninterrupted construction, and steady economic growth. Given the present rate of demographic growth, as well as present demand for improvement in living standards, development without powerful cumulative change cannot be envisaged; but the community may nevertheless hope for change which leads increasingly towards a new stability. This would require broad regional, and wherever possible local, self-sufficiency in basic food supplies (not only grain but reasonable supplies of protein), together with continuing administrative control of food production and distribution; new houses; domestic amenities such as running water and electric light; rises in consumer standards which in terms of articles must inevitably be slow but which in terms of services could be rapid; rises in standards of entertainment and culture which (by the revival of traditional working-class culture) could also be rapid; the maintenance of the village

as a self-managing and responsible business accounting unit and the strengthening of the collective contribution to the new diversification systems, particularly at the village level; the maintenance and encouragement of the new committee system of management of local units, of successful contract and responsibility systems in farm production, and of collective accounting and distribution; the encouragement of effective business networks in the countryside commensurate with the acute need for increased trade of all kinds; and the establishment of improved legal processes for regulating conflicts in economic matters. What must not be looked towards is encroachment by junior units (up to provincial level) upon the prerogatives of units senior to them – this is one main reason why proper legal frameworks are so much needed. Nor should countenance be given to private organisations at any level, however lowly or however influential, which may seek to build up power sufficient to challenge or corrupt the official systems which relate to them. In return for continued entrenchment of the official system, the community might expect a more effective, lively and purposeful bureaucracy at all levels including the local level, and much more sensitivity within the official systems.

These are easy suggestions – or relatively easy. Most of them owe something to observation in other parts of east Asia, where Chinese or kindred traditions have developed in various individual ways. In a number of other fields, proposals even in principle are much more difficult to formulate – the effective control of family size in the countryside over successive generations; the control of individual migration, especially to the cities; supplies of fuel especially in densely settled rural areas; social class in the countryside and the creation of means to enable people of peasant origin to serve the community in high places; the supply of industrial goods and (more broadly) some widening of the pyramid of productivity; the stimulation of enterprise on the scale necessary for effective economic growth and diversification beyond the simple marketing of rural surpluses; the improvement of inter-provincial and intra-provincial transport networks to encourage a worth-while growth of internal business; and so forth.

What all these proposals tend towards, is a revival in modern terms of the Chinese state of the powerful phases of the greatest dynasties of traditional times – Qing in the eighteenth century, the earlier phases of Ming and Tang; even Han. Chinese society in these phases was distinguished by a powerful state and authoritarian government at the centre, with arms reaching into every county; but below county level, a host of self-managing community cells, self-sufficient in broad terms but not debarred from trade, traditionally at the level now occupied by the commune. What now seems to be almost within grasp in China, with all the weaknesses of the present, is a system of this kind without the landlords and gentry, or the ignorance, debt and disease of former centuries – and sustained by committee management, broader community trust, effective state support in case of need, science on the land, and some approach towards prosperity.

Further reading

Atlas: *Zhonghua renmin gongheguo fen sheng dituji (Hanyu pinyinban)* (*Atlas of China in pinyin*), Ditu chubanshe, Beijing, 1977. Place-names in *pinyin* spelling, useful physical maps, excellent indexes.

Buchanan, Keith, *The transformation of the Chinese earth*, Bell, London, 1970. Lively and varied work by a geographer. Covers the first two decades after Liberation

Donnithorne, Audrey, *China's economic system*, Allen and Unwin, London, 1967. The best book on the Chinese system up to the Cultural Revolution

Eckstein, Alexander, *China's economic revolution*, Cambridge Univ. Press, London and New York, 1977. Review of the Chinese system extending through the Cultural Revolution; particularly strong on development strategies

Feuchtwang, Stephan and Hussain, Athar (eds), *The Chinese economic reforms*, Croom Helm, London, 1983. Up-to-date review of Chinese economic reorganisation since the death of Mao which takes account of both practice and theory

Gray, Jack and White, Gordon (eds), *China's new development strategy*, Academic Press, London, 1982. Studies by various authors on recent developments in politics, industry, rural development and education

Howe, Christopher, *China's economy: a basic guide*, Paul Elek, London, 1978. Review of Chinese economic experience from Liberation until 1977; particularly strong on physical production and on sources.

Pannell, Clifton W and Ma, Laurence J C, *China, the geography of development and modernisation*, Edward Arnold, London, 1983. Up-to-date review of various geographical backgrounds to development problems.

Prybyla, Jan S, *The Chinese economy, problems and policies*, 2nd edn, Univ. of South Carolina Press, Colombia, S.C., 1981. Broad and perceptive review

Xu, Dixin et al., *China's search for economic growth*, New World Press, Beijing, 1982. A series of articles mainly on economic institutions

Xue, Muqiao, *China's socialist economy*, Foreign Languages Press, Beijing, 1981. New thinking in Chinese economics, by China's foremost economist

References

The following abbreviations are used in this list.

CC	Chinese Communist Party
CQ	*The China Quarterly*, London
EM	*Economic Management (Jingji Guanli)*, monthly, Beijing
ER	*Economic Research (Jingji Yanjiu)*, monthly, Beijing
FBIS	Foreign Broadcast Information Service, *Daily Report, China*. Springfield, Va. Translations of Chinese texts, five days weekly
JPRS	Joint Publications Research Service, a United States government translation agency
PAE	*Problems of Agricultural Economics (Nongye jingji wenti)*, monthly, Beijing
PD	*People's Daily (Renmin Ribao)*, Beijing
PPH	People's Publishing House
SCMM	*Selections from China Mainland Magazines*, a translation series (United States Consulate, Hong Kong). Title changed in 1973 to *Selections from People's Republic of China Magazines (SPRCM)*; series discontinued in 1977
SCMP	*Selections from China Mainland Press*, a translation series akin to the above. Title changed in 1973 to *Selections from People's Republic of China Press (SPRCP)*; discontinued in 1977
SPRCM	see above, *SCMM*
SPRCP	see above, *SCMP*
SWB	*Summary of World Broadcasts (Far East)*, London. Translations of monitored broadcasts, six days weekly
tr	translated
Xinhua	*News from Xinhua (Hsinhua, New China) News agency*. Daily official Chinese news bulletin, published in London

Agricultural Bureau, *Guoying nongchang nongye jishu shouce (Handbook of Agricultural Techniques for State Farms*, PPH, Shanghai, 1975

Aird, John S, 'Recent provincial population figures', *CQ*, 73, 1978, 1–44

Alley, Rewi, *Travels in China, 1966–71*, New World Press, Beijing, 1973

Anhui province Revolutionary Committee et al., 'Great changes in five years', *Red Flag*, 1970 (3), tr in *SCMM*, 70 (3), 124–8

Aziz, Sartaj, *Rural development – learning from China*, Macmillan, London, 1978

Bannikov, A G et al. 'The animal world', in Institute of Geography, USSR Academy of Sciences, *The physical geography of China*, vol i, 365–436

Baoding prefecture Revolutionary Committee et al., 'Combine agriculture with animal husbandry, and promote agriculture with animal husbandry', *Red Flag*, 1973 (4), tr in *SCMM*, 73 (4), 65–7

Beijing city, Rural Science Institute, *Kexue zhongtian shouce (Scientific farming handbook)*, PPH, Beijing, 1975

Beijing Economic Institute, Population Study Bureau, *Renkou lilun (Population theory)*, Shangwu, Beijing, 1977

Beijing radio lectures. *SWB*, Apr.–May 1979. A series of seventeen lectures on the people's communes on Beijing radio.

Brandt, W et al., *North–south; a programme for survival*, Pan, London, 1980

Buchanan, Keith, *The transformation of the Chinese earth*, Bell, London, 1970

Buck, John Lossing, *Land utilisation in China*, Commercial Press, Nanjing, 1938

Burchett, Wilfred with Alley, Rewi, *China, the quality of life*, Pelican, Harmondsworth, 1976

Burns, John P, 'Rural Guangdong's "second economy", 1962–74', *CQ*, 88, 1981, 629–44

Burton, Neil G and Bettelheim, Charles, *China since Mao*, Monthly Review Press, New York and London, 1978

CCP 1956, High tide of socialism. CCP, Administrative office of the Central Committee, *Zhongguo nongcun de shehuizhuyi gaochao* (*The high tide of socialism in rural China*), 3 vols, PPH, Beijing, 1956. Introduction and notes were by Mao Zedong (see *Selected Works*, vol 5, 1977, 242–76; see also *Socialist Upsurge*).

CCP 1958, Beidaihe Declaration. 'Resolution of the Central Committee of the Chinese Communist Party on the establishment of people's communes in the rural areas', 29 Aug, 1958, tr in Albert P Blaustein, *Fundamental legal documents of communist China*, Rothman, South Hackensack, N.J. 1962, 442–9

CCP 1962, New Sixty Articles. CCP Central Committee, 'Regulations on the work of the rural people's communes' (revised draft), September 1962. Tr in *Documents of the Chinese Communist Party Central Committee*, vol i, Union Research Institute, Hong Kong, 1969, 695–725, and reprinted in Domes 1980: 128–58

CCP 1978, Decisions. CCP Central Committee, 'Decisions on some agricultural questions'. FBIS–PRC–75–208, Supplement 032, quoting a Beijing broadcast of 5 Oct. 1979. An alternative translation appears in *Issues and Studies*, 15 (7), 102–19, 15 (8), 92–112, 15 (9), 104–15 (1979).

CCP 1981, Responsibility systems. CCP, Administrative Office and Central Party School, 'An investigation of, and views about, several present rural systems whereby responsibility is linked to output', *PD* 1 Sept. 1981, tr in *FBIS*, 9 Sept. 1981, K7–K15

CCP 1983a, Rural work. CCP Central Committee, 'Minutes of 1981 Rural Work Conference'. FBIS, 7 Apr. 1982, K1–K13, quoting a Beijing broadcast of 5 Apr. 1982

CCP 1983b, Rural economic policies. Communist Party of China (CPC) Central Committee, Document No. 1 of 1983, 'Some questions concerning the current rural economic policies'. Excerpts published by *Zhongguo nongmin bao*, 10 Apr. 1983, tr in *FBIS*, 13 Apr. 1983, K1–K13

Chao, K, *The development of cotton textile production in China*, Harvard Univ. Press, Cambridge, Mass., 1977

Chen Bijiang, 'These six commune households illustrate the value of private plots', *PD*, 5 July 1981

Chen Chuanyi et al., 1981, 'Progress with the "four specialist units with unified management" responsibility system in Yichun prefecture', *PD*, 14 Nov. 1981

Chen Chuanyi et al. 1982, ' "Specialism and contract" promoting all-round development in agriculture', *PD*, 2 Mar. 1982

Chen Kang, 'Henen promotes the experience of Yotan brigade in producing high yields of wheat at low cost', *PD*, 8 Aug. 1979

Chen Lian, 'A survey of changes in rural economic structures in Suzhou prefecture', *PAE*, 1981 (8), 22–8

Chen Po-Wen, 'Agriculture in mainland China as revealed in CCP documents: an analysis', *Issues and Studies*, 15 (11), 1979, 46–58

Chen Rinong, 'Survey of the Huanghe river', *China Reconstructs*, 1980 (3), 2–7

Chen Yingci, 'How are we to evaluate farmland capital construction in Xiyang?', *Guangming Daily*, 19 Jan. 1981, tr in *FBIS* 10 Feb. 1981, L15

Chen Yizi, 'Rural responsibility systems linking output to remuneration', *PD*, 5 Oct. 1982

Chen Yonggui 1972, 'On scientific farming', *Red Flag*, 1972 (2), tr in *SCMM*, 72 (2), 32–43

Chen Yonggui 1973, 'Speech at the Gansu meeting for exchange of experience in the mass movement of "In agriculture, learn from Tachai"', *Union Research Service*, 73 (7), 23 Oct. 1973, 86–106

Cheng, Joseph, 'Strategy for economic development', in Bill Brugger (ed.), *China, the impact of the Cultural Revolution*, Croom Helm, London, 1978, 126–52

Chi Weiyun, 'Strengthen subtropical forest construction in the mountain regions with ecological balance as the foundation', *PAE*, 1981 (4), 41–4

Chia Chen-Lan, 'Build steady-and-high-yield farmland on the north-western loess plateau', *PD*, 19 Mar. 1964, tr in *SCMP*, 16 June 1964, 9–16

Chiang Wei-Ch'ing, 'Further strengthen the dictatorship of the proletariat in the rural areas', *Red Flag*, 1975 (5), tr in *SPRCM*, 75 (16), 13–19

China Food Corporation, *Tantan rou qin dan gouxiao zhengci* (*Commercial policy for meat, poultry and eggs*), China Finance and Economics Press, Beijing, 1981

Chinn, D V, 'Basic commodity distribution in the People's Republic of China', *CQ* 84, 1980, 744–54

Chu Li and Tieh Chieh-Yun, *Inside a people's commune*, Foreign Languages Press, Beijing, 1974

Committee of Concerned Asian Scholars, *China! Inside the People's Republic*, Bantam, New York, 1972

Cong Linzhong and Jiang Shaogao, 'It is necessary to settle these contradictions between money and rules', *PD*, 6 Oct. 1980

Constitution, 1982, *The constitution of the People's Republic of China*, Foreign Languages Press, Beijing, 1983

Croll, Elizabeth, 'The promotion of domestic sideline production in rural China, 1978–79', in Gray and White: 235–54

Crook, Frederick W, 'The commune system in the People's Republic of China!, in United States Congress Joint Economic Committee, *China, a reassessment of the economy*, 366–410

Dai Qingqi and Yu Zhan, 'Study Comrade Deng Zihui's viewpoint on the agricultural production responsibility system', *PD*, 23 Feb. 1982, tr in *FBIS* 5 Mar. 1982, K16–K20

Dao county party committee, 'Strengthen leadership, make rational arrangements and energetically develop multiple undertakings', *PD*, 17 Apr. 1972, tr in *SCMP*, 72 (18), 1–8

Deng Shulin, 'Tianjin – the city that needed water', *China Reconstructs*, 1982 (2), 6–11

Deng Zhaoxiang and Li Heihu, 'Raising economic effectiveness, a fundamental principle for rural prosperity', *ER*, 1981 (5), 27–30

Department of Agriculture, 'Review of changes in the arable system in the northern region', *PAE*, 1981 (5), 27–30

Department of Commerce, 1971. 'Experiences in enterprise management of commerce in new industrial and mining areas', *Red Flag*, 1971 (11), tr in *SCMM*, 71 (10), 39–45

Department of Commerce 1972, *Banhao shehuizhuyi shangye* (*Make a good job of socialist commerce*), PPH, Beijing

Department of Commerce 1977, *Banhao changuan shangye* (*Local commerce under local enterprise management*), China Finance and Economics Press, Beijing

Desert Research Institute, Chinese Academy of Sciences, *Zhonghua renmin gongheguo shamo ditu* (*Map of the deserts of China*), 1 : 4 million, Cartographic Publishing House, Beijing, 1979

Ding Shourong (of the Shandong Cotton and Fibre Company), 'Incentive schemes in cotton production are good', *EM*, *1980 (4), 38–9*

Domes, Jurgen 1976, *China after the Cultural Revolution*, Hurst, London

Domes, Jurgen 1980, *Socialism in the Chinese countryside*, Hurst, London

Dong Likun, 'Nobody is above the law', *Shehui Kexue* (*Social science*), 1980 (1), 7–12

Donnithorne, Audrey 1967, *China's economic system*, Allen and Unwin, London

Donnithorne, Audrey 1970, *China's grain: output, procurement, transfers and trade*, Chinese University Press, Hong Kong

Doumen county committee, Propaganda Department, 'Taking the advantages to the state, the collective and the individual jointly into account in the sugar areas', *EM*, 1979 (6), 79–80

Du Runsheng 'The agricultural responsibility system and the reform of the rural economic system, *Red Flag*, 1981 (9), tr in *China Report*, *Red Flag*, 81 (9), 24–39, under Dun Runsheng. Du Runsheng is Director of the China Rural Development Research Centre, and this article is a revised version of a report given to the Central Party School

Duan Cunzhang, 'What the people need at Matian', *PD*, 29 Apr. 1980

Duan Xinqiang and An, Zizhen, 'The outlook of "mountain people depend on the mountains; lake people depend on the lakes"' *PD*, 21 May 1979

Dun Runsheng, see Du Runsheng

Economics of Environment Forum, 'Strengthen the study of eco-economic problems', *ER*, 1981 (11), 3–13

Eckstein, Alexander, *China's economic revolution*, Cambridge Univ. Press, Cambridge, 1977

Fang Jianzhong et al., 'Present status and future development of specialist grain households in the rural economy', *PAE*, 1983 (8), 48–51

Feng Daozhong, 'Make suburban areas into commodity bases for subsidiary food outputs', *PD*, 2 Feb. 1979

FAO Study Mission, *Learning from China. A report on agriculture and the Chinese people's communes*, FAO, Rome, 1978

Feng Jixin, 'What is necessary', *PD*, 11 July 1981, tr in *FBIS*, 29 July 1981

Feng Leshu 1980, 'Get the ideas moving; stimulate the rural economies', *PD*, 29 Nov. 1980

Feng Leshu 1982, 'Twelve poor prefectures raise commune members' living standards year by year', *PD*, 9 Aug. 1982

Feng Mingxin et al., 'The more they do, the more they are able to do', *PD*, 10 July 1979

Feng Zibao, 'The system of responsibility for output in agriculture and production relations must suit the nature of the productive forces', *ER*, 1981 (4), 60–4

Feuchtwang, Stephan and Hussain, Athar, *The Chinese economic reforms*, Croom Helm, London, 1983

Fong, H D, *Cotton industry and trade in China*, Nankai Institute of Economics, Tianjin, 1932

Fontana, Dorothy Grouse, 'Background to the fall of Hua Guofeng', *Asian Survey*, 22 (3), 1982, 237–60

Forestry Department, Research and Planning Unit, *Zhongguo shandi senlin* (*China's mountain forests*), Forestry Press, Beijing, 1981

Forestry Policy Research Unit 1980, 'Current questions on the forestry management system', *EM*, 1980 (7), 29–31

Forestry Policy Research Unit 1981, 'Run forestry work according to law', *Red Flag*, 1981 (5), tr in *China Report*, *Red Flag*, 1981 (5)

Fujian province Forestry Bureau, 'No time to sit back. Protect the forests', *PD*, 23 Mar. 1980

Gao Bowen 1981, 'Establish comprehensive control of small drainage basins in the middle Yellow River catchment', *PD*, 15 Jan. 1981

Gao Bowen 1982, 'Conservation is the essential foundation for final control of the Yellow River and for modernisation of agriculture on the loess plateau', in Tong Dalin et al.: 56–64

Gao Guanmin, 'Anxiang, a watery Dazhai', *Dili Zhishi* (*Geographical knowledge*), 1977 (11), 9–10

Gao Shangquan, *Zuo woguo ziji nongye xiandaihua de daolu* (*China's own route to agricultural modernisation*), Agricultural Press, Beijing, 1981

Gao Xinqing, 'From Dazhai county to debtors' hall' *PD*, 14 Mar. 1981

Gao Zhiyu, 'Why was our country's national economy able to progress during the "Great Cultural Revolution"?', *Red Flag*, 1981 (19), tr in *FBIS*, 3 Nov. 1981, K22–K23

Gaohao nongtian jiben jianshe (*Success in fundamental rural construction*), 2 vols, Agricultural Press, Beijing, 1974, 1975

Geographical Research Institute, Chinese Academy of Sciences, *Zhongguo nongye dili zong lun* (*Agricultural geography of China*), Science Press, Beijing, 1980

Ginsberg, Norton 1958, *The pattern of Asia*, Constable, Englewood Cliffs, N.J.

Ginsberg, Norton 1966, An historical atlas of China, by Albert Herrmann, 1966 edition with additions, Edinburgh Univ. Press, Edinburgh

Grain Department Research Unit, *Tantan nongcun liang you gouxiao zhengci* (*The rural procurement and supply system for grain and edible oil*), China Financial and Economic Press, Beijing, 1981

Gray, Jack, 'Rural enterprise in China, 1977–79' in Gray and White: 211–33

Gray, Jack and Gray, Maisie, 'China's new agricultural revolution' in Feuchtwang and Hussain: 151–84

Gray, Jack and White, Gordon (eds), *China's new development strategy*, Academic Press, London, 1982

Grubov, V I, 'Flora and vegetation' in Institute of Geography, USSR Academy of Sciences, *The physical geography of China*, vol i, 267–364

Gu Dafen and Liang Zhenliang, 'A well-earned success', *PD*, 6 Nov. 1978

Gu Lei and Tian Zongming, 'From "grain-supply land" to "contract"', PD, 1 Dec. 1980

Gu Ming, 'Further strengthen economic legislative work', *PD*, 4 Dec. 1981, tr in *FBIS*, 11 Dec. 1981, K12–K14

Gu Shutang and Chang Xiuze, 'A good form of

town–country cooperation – an investigation of "factory-team links and the diffusion of products" in Weihai municipality, *Red Flag*, 1980 (23), tr in *China Report, Red Flag*, 1980 (23), 32–40

Guangdong province Propaganda Department, *Guangdong sheng nongye xue Dazhai jingyan xuanbian (Selected reports on the campaigns to learn from Dazhai in agriculture in Guangdong)* 2 vols, Guangdong PPH, Guangzhou, 1973

Guo Longchun et al., 'Pool wisdom and effort; make the wilderness green', *PD*, 10 Dec. 1980

Hai he shen bian (Great changes on the Hai River), PPH, Beijing, 1973

Han Jinduo, 'Pay attention to the problem of supplying manufactured goods to the countryside', *Red Flag*, 1981 (20), tr in *China Report, Red Flag*, 1981 (20), 75–6

He Cun, 'Changes in farming systems will guarantee consolidation and further development of the responsibility systems', *Jingjixue Dongtai (Economic Trends)*, 1982 (1), 28–31, reprinted in *Nongye Jingji (Agricultural Economics)*, 1982 (2), 72–4

He Guiting et al., 'Can the area of double-cropped paddy be stabilised?' *PAE*, 1981 (5), 31–7

He Guiting and Xu Xin, 'High-output counties need to restructure farm production', *EM*, 1981 (5), 15–17

He Jiazheng, 'Hope and confidence among the people in northern Shaanxi', *PD*, 10 Oct. 1980

He Jingbei, 'Promote the healthy development of rural trade fairs', *EM*, 1981 (5), 12–14

Henan province, *Nongye shengchan zerenzhi shixing banfa (Methods of operating agricultural responsibility systems)*, Agricultural Press, Beijing, 1981

Hengyang prefecture party committee, 'Develop agriculture to promote industry; develop industry to arm agriculture', *People's Daily*, 17 July 1972, tr in *SCMP*, 72 (31), 13–19

Ho Chin, *Harm into benefit: taming the Haiho River*, Foreign Languages Press, Beijing, 1975

Hou Xueyu 1979 (Editor-in-chief; Institute of Botany, Chinese Academy of Sciences), *Zhonghua renmin gongheguo zhibei ditu (Map of vegetation cover of the People's Republic of China)*, 1 : 4 million, Cartographic Publishing House, Beijing (For this map, an English translation of the original key is available.)

Hou Xueyu 1981, 'Approaches to problems of increasing grain output', *PD*, 6 Mar. 1981

Hou Zhiyi and Zhao Deyun, 'Escaping from the grasp of the extreme left', *PD*, 7 Nov. 1980

Howe, Christopher, *China's economy: a basic guide*, Paul Elek, London, 1978

Hsiang Hui, 'Penetratingly carry out the two-road struggle in the countryside', *Red Flag*, 1976 (1), 71–6, tr in *SPRCM*, 76 (3), 84–90

Hsiaohsiang production brigade, 'Be ambitious when you're poor; guard against revisionism when you're rich' *Red Flag*, 1975 (11), tr in *SPRCM*, 75 (35), 32–6

Hu Changnuan, 'Problems of the scissors differential and the general level of prices', *ER*, 1979 (6), 62–9

Hu Guohua and He Maoji, 'Fertiliser from the herds; water from the forests', *PD*, 9 Mar. 1980

Hu Yaobang, 'The best way out of poverty and into prosperity for the mountains is mountain management with afforestation', *Zhongguo Linye (Chinese Forestry)*, 1980 (6), reprinted in *PD*, 8 June 1980

Huai he xin pian (A new phase on the Huai River), PPH, Beijing, 1975

Huang Bingfu, 'Further discussion on the arable area in southern Jiangsu – outlook and proposals', *PD*, 15 Mar. 1979

Huang Jichang, 'The peasants are setting new tasks', *PD*, 24 July 1979

Huang Yanjun and Yu Quanyu 1978a, 'Break out of the strait-jacket of "false left, actual right"; then agriculture can pick up speed', *PD*, 14 Nov. 1978

Huang Yanjun and Yu Quanyu 1978b, 'Commune and brigade cadres need an economic outlook', *PD*, 21 Nov. 1978

Huang Yongshi, 'Develop forest resources; protect ecological balances', *ER*, 1981 (3), 41–5

Huang Youjun, 'Travel the road of comprehensive development', *PD*, 11 June 1979

Huang Yuejun, 'How shall we regard the new economic linkages among the peasants? *PD*, 26 Nov. 1981

Hunan province, *Accounts*. Hunan province Revolutionary Committee, Agriculture Section, *Nongcun renmin gongshe shengchandui huiji (Accounts for rural production teams)*, Hunan PPH, Changsha, 1973

Hunan province Agricultural College, Crop husbandry group, *Mianhua zaipei (Cotton husbandry)*, Hunan PPH, Changsha, 1974

Hunan province, No. 2 Light Industry Supply Corporation, 'What items does the rural market need at present?', *EM*, 1982 (7), 14

Hung Ch'iao, 'Correctly handle the relations with peasants and make a success of rural commercial work', *PD*, 3 Sept. 1972, tr in *SCMP*, 72 (37), 158–64

Inner Mongolia Investigation Team, 'Build up the pastoral areas by taking animal husbandry as the main occupation', *Red Flag*, 1973 (4), tr in *SCMM*, 73 (4), 62–4

Institute of Geography, USSR Academy of Sciences, *The physical geography of China*, 2 vols, Praeger, New York, 1969

Institute of Soil Science 1976. Institute of Soil Science, Chinese Academy of Sciences, *Turang zhishi (Understanding soils)*, PPH, Shanghai

Institute of Soil Science 1978. Institute of Soil Science, Chinese Academy of Sciences, *Zhonghua renmin gongheguo turang ditu (Soils map of China)*, with accompanying text; 1 : 4 million, Cartographic Publishing House, Shanghai

Ji Jianxin, 'How is Jiangsu to develop its commercial network?' *EM*, 1981 (9), 47–55

Ji Xijian, 'An important way to raise rural economic effectiveness', *PAE*, 1983 (9), 26–30

Ji Xueyi and Zhang Kaixuan, 'The exchange system faces the challenge of the rural market', *PD*, 12 Dec. 1981

Jiading county, Agricultural Economics Investigation Unit, 'Investigation report on agricultural prices in Jiading county', *PAE*, 1981 (1), 54–9

Jiading county, Party Investigation Group, 'How they strengthen the brigade-level collective economy', *Xuexi yu pipan (Study and criticism)* 10, 1975, tr is *SPRCM*, 75 (33), 6–11

Jiading county Writing Group, 'Maintain political leadership, implement policy conscientiously', in *Renmin gongshe zai yue jin*, 133–42

Jian Hua, 'Collective commercial units should not be turned

into department stores', *Beijing Daily*, 9 Sept. 1981, tr in *FBIS* 9 Oct. 1981, K17–L18

Jiang Dehua, 'The loess plateau', *Dili Zhishi (Geographical Knowledge)*, 1979 (8), 1–3

Jiang Junchen et al., 'Relations between production and livelihood', *ER*, 1980 (9), 53–8

Jiang Shan, 'The struggle to raise cotton yields is the most urgent responsibility for the northern cotton producing areas', *PD*, 5 June 1979

Jiang Xingwei, 'Problems of the "scissors" gap between prices of agricultural and industrial products', *ER*, 1980 (4), 73–6

Jiangsu province, Commune and Brigade Enterprise Department Research Unit, 'Developing commune and brigade enterprises according to local conditions in Ganyu county', *EM*, 1982 (3), 69–72

Jiangsu province Revolutionary Committee, Investigation Team, 'A promising new thing. Investigation report on the development of commune-run and brigade-run industry in Wuxi county, Jiangsu' *Red Flag*, 1975 (10), tr in *SPRCM*, 75 (32), 30–5

Jiao Yuan, 'Use the Dazhai spirit to make a good job of farm mechanisation', *Xuexi yu pipan (Study and criticism)*, 1975 (10), tr in *SPRCM*, 75 (33), 1–5

Jenner, W J F, '1979, a new start for literature in China?', *CQ*, 86, 1981, 274–303

Jin Daqin, 'Urbanisation and the establishment of small towns', *EM*, 1981 (5), 33–8

Jin Feng, 'Four wheels all turning together', *PD*, 16 Feb. 1982

Jinshan and Shanghai county Revolutionary Committees, *Daban nongye, jianshe Dazhai xian (Manage agriculture well; establish Dazhai counties)*, PPH, Shanghai, 1976

Kaifeng prefecture and Gong county Working Group, 'Reduce unproductive personnel in the communes and brigades; reduce the burdens of the people', *EM*, 1982 (1), 59–61

Klatt, W, 'The staff of life: living standards in China, 1977–81', *CQ*, 93, 1983, 17–50

Kuo, Leslie T C, *The technical transformation of agriculture in communist China*, Praeger, New York, 1972

Lardy, Nicholas, *Economic growth and distribution in China*, Cambridge Univ. Press, Cambridge, 1978

Lattimore, Owen, *Inner Asian frontiers of China*, Beacon, Boston, 1940

Leeming, Frank 1978, 'New farmland terracing in contemporary China', *China Geographer*, 10, 29–39

Leeming, Frank 1979, 'Progress towards triple cropping in China', *Asian Survey*, 19 (5), 450–67

Li Anding, 'Small should not squeeze big', *PD*, 17 Nov. 1980

Li Hsueh-tseng, *Huangtu gaoyuan (The loess plateau)*, Beijing, 1959, tr as *Communist China's loess plateau*, JPRS, Washington, 1961

Li Shiqiao, *Senlin fa (shixing) jianshe (Sketch of the draft forestry law)*, China Forestry Press, Beijing, 1982

Li Yun, 'Develop new style building materials according to local need', *EM*, 1982 (3), 37–40

Liang Wensen, 'Balanced development of industry and agriculture', in Xu Dixin et al.: 52–78.

Liang Yan, 'It is necessary to attach great importance to the grain problem', *Red Flag*, 1981 (5), tr in *FBIS*, 27 Mar. 1981, L5–L10

Liang Zhao et al. 'An investigation into developing the strong points of cane sugar production in Guangdong', *Red Flag*, 1981 (2), tr in *China Report, Red Flag*, 1981 (2), 36–41

Lin Jingqian, 'Lessons from history on enclosing lakes', *ER*, 1981 (2), 75–8

Lin Lixing, 'Does "take grain as the key link" mean destroying orchards to make arable?', *PD*, 5 Oct. 1978

Lin Tian, 'Enquiries into problems of the commune system', *EM*, 1981 (1), 10–13

Lin Yanshi, *Guanyu linye jingji zhengci ruogan wenti (Some problems of the economic system in the forests)*, China Forestry Press, Beijing, 1982

Liu Gang et al. *Shanghai chengshi jiti suoyouzhi gongye yanjiu (Studies on collectively owned industry in Shanghai)*, PPH, Shanghai, 1980

Liu Guilian, 'Great need of protection for the Dongting fisheries', *PD*, 25 July 1979

Liu Hongli and Wu Hai, *Nongye shengchan zerenzhi (Responsibility systems in agriculture)*, PPH, Shanghai, 1981

Liu Houpei (of the Natural Resources Committee, Chinese Academy of Sciences), 'The mountains of the south have great potential', *PD*, 13 Sept. 1979

Liu Ruilong, 'Jin county's experience with the "three systems" of contract', *PD*, 3 Nov. 1981

Liu Songjiao, 'A valuable approach to timber shortage', *PD*, 22 Feb. 1980

Liu Xingjie, '"Poverty and hardship" – a letter from Laomiao commune, Fuping county, Shaanxi province', *PD*, 4 Jan. 1979

Liu Xumao, 'Perfecting the responsibility systems in agriculture', *PAE*, 1982 (10), 12–15

Liu Yunshan 1979, 'Save the forests; prevent forest fires', *PD*, 29 Oct. 1979

Liu Yunshan 1981, 'Livestock rearing on the grasslands should be strictly limited to carrying capacity', *PAE*, 1981 (6), 41–6

Liu Zheng and Chen Wuyuan (of the Economic Research Unit, Sichuan province Academy of Sciences), 'First steps in the reform of the rural management system', *EM*, 1981 (4), 37–48

Liu Zhengui and Li Yeying, 'The dialectics of production from lakes', *PD*, 24 Jan. 1979

Liu Zhongchun, 'Put a stop to the evil practice of irregular occupation of vegetable land', *PD*, 6 March 1982; also accompanying Editorial on the same date

Lu Weiyang et al., 'Consolidate the success of the rural people', *PD*, 2 May 1981

Lu Xiaoping and Xie Shiyan, 'The ice is breaking up; the land has a new lease of life', *PD*, 4 Oct. 1979

Lu Xueyi and Zhang Kaixuan, 'The challenge of the rural market facing the exchange and trade systems', *PD*, 12 Dec. 1981

Lu Yan, 'Grasp grain production and diversified operations well', *Red Flag*, 1973 (2), tr in *SCMP*, 73 (2), 62–7

Luo Yuchuan (of the National Forestry Bureau), 'Creation and protection of forest is an urgent and critical problem', *PD*, 6 Nov. 1978

Ma Hong, 'The transformation of China's economic structure and the realisation of the four modernisations', *EM*, 1979 (9), 2–5

Ma Renping 1981a, 'New problems emerging since the

introduction of the rural responsibility systems', *EM*, 1981 (8), 3–8

Ma Renping 1981b, 'New developments in the responsibility system in agriculture', *PAE*, 1981 (7), 25–30

Mao Zedong 1977a, 'Request for opinions on the seventeen-article document concerning agriculture' dated 21 Dec. 1955, *Selected Works*, Foreign Languages Press, Beijing, vol v, 277–80

Mao Zedong 1977b, 'On the correct handling of contradictions among the people', dated 27 Feb. 1957, *Selected Works*, Foreign Languages Press, Beijing, vol v, 384–421

Maxwell, Neville, 'The Tachai way', in Neville Maxwell (ed), *China's road to development*, Pergamon, Oxford, 1979, 41–95

Mianhua shengchan. Mianhua shengchan dianxing jingji xuanbian (Selected experiences of models in cotton production), Agriculture Press, Beijing, 1974

Milton, David, Milton, Nancy and Schurman, Franz, *People's China*, Random House, New York, 1974; Penguin, Harmondsworth, 1977

Mu Jiajun and Li Jincheng, 'Three threes are nine but two fives are ten', *PD*, 16 Dec. 1978

Nanning and Yulin prefectures, Revolutionary Committees, *Xuexi 'Zhongguo nongcun de shehuizhuyi gaochao' de xuyan he anyu (Reading the prefaces and editor's notes to 'The high tide of socialism in rural China'*, 2 vols, Guangxi PPH, Nanning, 1977

Nolan, Peter and White, Gordon 1979, 'Socialist development and rural inequality. The Chinese countryside in the 1970s', *Journal of Peasant Studies*, 7 (1), 1979, 3–48

Nolan, Peter and White, Gordon 1982, 'The distributive implications of China's new agricultural policies', in Gray and White: 175–209

Paine, Suzanne, 'Spatial aspects of Chinese development – issues, outcomes and policies, 1949–79', *Journal of Development Studies*, 17 (2), 1981, 133–95

Pannell, Clifton W and Ma, Laurence J C, *China: the geography of development and modernisation*, Edward Arnold, London, 1983

Pan Jingyuan, 'The economic significance of increases in cotton output', *PD*, 12 May 1964

Peng Kuang-Hsi, *Why China has no inflation*, Foreign Languages Press, Beijing, 1976

Peng Xiaozhong, 'Good results for specialist households in farmyard production', *PD*, 10 Nov. 1980

People's Bank of China, Guangdong provincial branch, *Accounting in the production teams of the rural people's communes*, tr in *Chinese Economic Studies*, 10 (1), 1976–77

Perkins, Dwight 1966, *Market control and planning in communist China*, Harvard Univ. Press, Cambridge, Mass, 1966

Perkins, Dwight 1969, *Agricultural development in China, 1368–1968*, Edinburgh Univ. Press, Edinburgh

Perkins, Dwight 1975, 'Constraints influencing China's agricultural performance', in United States Congress, Joint Economic Committee: 350–66

Perkins, Dwight 1977 (ed), *Rural small-scale industry in the People's Republic of China*, Univ. of California Press, Berkeley and Los Angeles

Prybyla, Jan S 1975, 'A note on prices and incomes in China', *Asian Survey*, 15 (3), 262–78

Prybyla, Jan S 1981, *The Chinese economy, problems and policies*, 2nd edn, Univ. of South Carolina Press, Colombia, S.C.

Qian Huiming, 'Official decisions harmful to the masses' interests', *PD*, 7 Feb. 1979

Qidong county Revolutionary Committee, *Liang mian shuang gaochan de douzheng shijian (Struggle and practice in gaining high outputs in both grain and cotton)*, PPH, Shanghai, 1970

Qingnian dituce (Atlas for youth), Cartographic Publishing House, Xian, 1978

Quan guo nongye fazhan gangyao tu jie (Illustrated introduction to principles for agricultural development, Beijing, 1956

Quan guo nongye xue Dazhai. Quan guo nongye xue Dazhai xianjin dianxing jingyan xuanbian (Selected experiences of rural models in learning from Dazhai), PPH, Beijing, 1975

Ren Fengping, 'A visit to northern Shaanxi – preliminary survey on building livestock and forestry bases on the loess plateau', *Red Flag*, 1980 (15), translated in *China Report, Red Flag*, 7 Oct. 1980, 24–35

Renmin gongshe zai yue jin (The people's communes are surging ahead), PPH, Shanghai, 1974

Richardson, S D, *Forestry in communist China*, Johns Hopkins Press, Baltimore, 1964

Riskin, Carl, 'China's rural industries: self-reliant systems or independent kingdoms?', *CQ*, 73, 1978, 77–98

Robinson, Joan 1969, *The Cultural Revolution in China*, Penguin, Harmondsworth

Robinson, Joan 1976, *Economic management in China*, Anglo-Chinese Educational Institute, London, 1976

Ross, Lester, 'Forestry in the People's Republic of China – estimating the gains and losses', in Clifton W Pannell and Christopher L Salter (eds), *China Geographer*, 11, 'Agriculture', Westview Press, Boulder, Col., 1981, 113–27

Russell, E W, *Soil conditions and plant growth*, 10th edn, Longman, London, 1973

Shaanxi province, Agriculture and Forestry Bureau, *Nongye kexue jishu shouce (Handbook of scientific techniques in agriculture)*, Shaanxi PPH, Xian, 1975

Shaanxi province, Scientific Institute for Forestry and Agriculture, *Senlin yu nongye (Forestry and agriculture)*, Science Press, Beijing, 1975

Shandong province, Commune Administration, 'Increasing production and incomes. Three big steps in three years', *EM*, 1981 (8), 13–16

Shandong province Investigation Bureau, 'Why is Shandong able to reap a bumper cotton harvest?' *Red Flag*, 1981 (8), tr in *China Report, Red Flag*, 1981 (8), 21–9

Shang Sidi et al., *Shanghai dili qian hua (Outline geography of Shanghai)*, PPH, Shanghai, 1974

Shanghai city, Maqiao commune, Zixing brigade, 'Increase production, reduce costs', in *Renmin gongshe zai yue jin*: 167–75

Shanghai city Revolutionary Committee, Department of Agriculture, Investigation Unit, 'How peasants can quickly become prosperous', *PD* 9 Aug. 1979

Shanghai county Revolutionary Committee, 'A year of bitter struggle. Establishing a Dazhai county', *Xuexi yu pipan (Study and criticism)*, 1975 (11), tr in *SPRCM*, 75 (37), 1–7

Shanghai Farm Science Institute, Soil Unit, 'Characteristics and maintenance of high-yield paddy soils in the Shanghai suburban area', *Zhongguo nongye kexue (Scientia agricultura sinica)*, 1978 (2), 66–72

Shanghai jiaogu san shu zhi zaipei zhishu (Techniques for

managing the three-harvest system in the Shanghai suburban area), PPH, Shanghai, 1975

Shanghai Normal University, *Jianming zhongguo dili (Concise geography of China)*, Shanghai, 1974

Shen Chenzhong and Wang Fugui, 'An investigation into problems of rural housing in suburban Shanghai', *PAE*, 1981 (6), 54–5

Shi Changjiang, 'Sound financial management is necessary to rural prosperity', *EM*, 1981 (9), 36–9

Shi Shan (of the Chinese Academy of Sciences), 'Improvement of pasture and grazing land is the way to combat the backwardness of the plateau country of the middle Yellow River', *PD*, 26 Nov. 1978

Shi Zilu, 'We should take it seriously that rural labour is quitting the Shanghai rural areas', *PAE*, 1981 (1), 29–33

Shulu county, 'Develop local industries in a vigorous effort to support agriculture', *PD*, 22 Aug. 1973, tr in *SCMP*, 73 (27), 176–80

Sigurdson, Jon 1975, 'Rural industries in China', in United States Congress, Joint Economic Committee, *China, a reassessment of the economy*, 411–35

Sigurdson, Jon 1979, 'Rural industrialisation in China: approaches and results', in Neville Maxwell (ed), *China's road to development*, 2nd edn, Pergamon, Oxford, 137–154

Smil, Vaclav, 'San-men-hsia reservoir; a space view', *Issues and Studies*, 15 (3), 1979, 77–82

Socialist Upsurge. CCP, Central Committee, *Socialist upsurge in China's countryside*, Foreign Languages Press, Beijing, 1957. This work comprises selections from CCP 1956, tr into English

Song Dahan and Zhang Chunzheng, 'Important changes in the system of people's communes', *Beijing Review*, 1982 (29), 15–17

Songjiang county, Tianma commune, Commerce Department, 'A new world of rural commercial work', in *Renmin gongshe zai yue jin*, 183–91

State Council 1980, Afforestation. 'Directive on the importance of encouraging afforestation', 5 Mar. 1980, tr in *FBIS*, 11 Mar. 1980, L10–L15, quoting a Beijing broadcast of 8 Mar. 1980

State Council 1981a, Market controls. *FBIS*, 16 Jan. 1981, L7–L9, quoting a Beijing broadcast of 15 Jan. 1981

State Council 1981b, Taxation on enterprises. 'State Council's regulations on taxation of rural enterprises', *FBIS*, 17 Feb. 1981, L14–L15, quoting a Beijing broadcast of 14 Feb. 1981

State Council 1981c, Enterprises. 'Regulations concerning implementation of the national economic readjustment policy by commune- and brigade-run enterprises', 4 May 1981, tr in *FBIS*, 22 May 1981, K16–K21, quoting a Beijing broadcast of 15 May 1981

State Council 1981d, Unhealthy practices. 'Circular concerning the prohibition of unhealthy practices in commodity circulation', 15 July 1981, tr in *FBIS*, 22 July 1981 K21–K22, quoting a Beijing broadcast of 16 July 1981

State Council 1981e, Self-employment. 'Regulations of a policy nature on non-agricultural self-employment', 15 July 1981, tr in *FBIS*, 21 July 1981, K19–K20, quoting a Beijing broadcast of 15 July 1981. 'Supplementary provisions' were issued on 13 Apr. 1983, tr in *FBIS*, 27 Apr. 1983, K9–K11

State Council 1982, Prohibiting blockades. 'Ten-point regulations to prohibit blockades in purchasing and marketing industrial products', *FBIS*, 21 Apr. 1982, K9–K11, quoting a Beijing broadcast of 20 Apr. 1982

State Council 1983, Rural commerce. 'Regulations . . . concerning reforms of the commodity circulation system in rural areas', *FBIS*, 10 Mar. 1983, K13–K17, quoting a Beijing broadcast of 26 Feb. 1983

State Council and CCP 1981, Diversified economy. 'Circular on diversified economy', issued on 30 Mar. 1981, based on the 'Report on the active development of a diversified economy' by the State Agricultural Commission. Tr in *FBIS*, 1 Apr., K8–K11, quoting a Beijing broadcast of 5 Apr. 1981

State Statistical Bureau 1979. Communique on fulfilment of China's 1978 national economic plan, Xinhua, 27 June 1979, 26–31

State Statistical Bureau 1980. Communique on fulfilment of China's 1979 national economic plan, Xinhua, 30 Apr. 1980, 27–35

State Statistical Bureau 1981. Communique on fulfilment of China's 1980 national economic plan, Xinhua, 29 Apr. 1981, 3–11

State Statistical Bureau 1982. Communique on fulfilment of China's 1981 national economic plan, Xinhua, 29 Apr. 1982, 3–11

State Statistical Bureau 1983. Communique on fulfilment of China's 1982 national economic plan, Xinhua, 29 Apr. 1983, 3–12

Sun Ming et al., 'New questions which have cropped up in grain production in Suzhou prefecture', *Red Flag*, 1982 (15), tr in *China Report, Red Flag*, 1982 (15), 50–5

Sun Pu, 'Why do some rural units lack working capital?', *PD*, 10 March 1981

Tan Keliang and Tao Yuerui, 'The problem of capital for rural modernisation', *ER*, 1981 (4), 69–72

Tang Lunhui et al., *Tantan nongcun jishi maoyi (Rural market trade)*, China Finance and Economics Press, Beijing, 1981

Ten Great Years. State Statistical Bureau, *Ten Great Years*, Foreign Languages Press, Beijing, 1959. Tr from *Weida de shi nian*, PPH, Beijing, 1958

Thorp, J, *Geography of the soils of China*, National Geological Survey of China, Nanjing, 1936

Tian Liu, 'Difficulties in accelerating economic development in the forest areas', *PD*, 13 Nov. 1979

Tianmen county Revolutionary Committee, *Tianmen mian xiang zai qianjin (Cotton county – progress in Tianmen)*, PPH, Beijing, 1976

Tie Ying 1980 (First Secretary to the Zhejiang province party committee), 'Construction in the mountain regions is the critical problem for modernisation in Zhejiang', *PD*, 14 June 1980

Tie Ying 1981, 'Zhejiang's Tie Ying on responsibility systems', Hangzhou broadcast of 25 Nov. 1981, reported in *FBIS*, 3 Dec. 1981, 02–03

Tong Dalin and Bao Tong, 'Problems of construction policy in the north-western loess plateau', *PD*, 26 Nov. 1978

Travers, S Lee, 'Bias in Chinese economic statistics; the case of the typical example investigation', *CQ*, 91, 1982, 478–85

Tregear, T R, *Economic geography of China*, Butterworths, London, 1970

United States Congress, Joint Economic Committee, *China, a reassessment of the economy*, United States Government Printing Office, Washington, 1975

van der Sprenkel, Sybille, 'The role of law in the changing

society', in Jack Gray (ed), *Modern China's search for a political form* Oxford Univ. Press,. London and New York, 1969

Vermeer, E B, 'Income differentials in rural China', *CQ*, 89, 1982, 1–33

Walker, Kenneth 1965, *Planning in Chinese agriculture: socialisation and the private sector, 1956–1962*, Frank Cass, London

Walker, Kenneth 1977, 'Grain self-sufficiency in north China, 1953–75', *CQ*, 71, 555–90

Walker, Kenneth 1981, 'China's grain production 1975–80 and 1952–57: some basic statistics', *CQ*, 86, 215–47

Wang Chengjing, *Shaanxi tudi liyong wenti (Land use in Shaanxi)*, Xinzhishi Press, Shanghai, 1956

Wang Ganmei, 'The status of woodland ecosystems in mountain agriculture', *ER*, 1981 (4), 71–3

Wang Gengjin and Zhu Rongji, 'Whither brigade and commune industry?', *EM*, 1979 (3), 21–3

Wang Guichen and Wei Daonan (of the Agricultural Economics Research Unit, Chinese Academy of Social Sciences), 'On household contract systems', *ER*, 1981 (1), 64–7

Wang Guihai and Hou Zhiyi, 'How to change Gaocheng's "high-output-poor"condition', *PD*, 7 Aug. 1979

Wang Guihai et al., 'What is indicated by this destruction of melons?' *PD*, 27 July 1979

Wang Guoying (Luliang prefecture party secretary), 'Construction in the Luliang mountains and guiding principles in agriculture', *PD*, 8 Nov. 1979

Wang Hanzhi, 'The experience of prosperous brigades depending upon the strength of the collective economy', *PD*, 26 Oct. 1980

Wang Hongmo, 'Why is the third plenary session of the eleventh CCP Central Committee, and not the fall of the "Gang of Four", taken as a great turning-point in history?', *Red Flag*, 1981 (21), tr in *China Report, Red Flag*, 1981 (21), 60–3

Wang Junwei et al., 'An important change in agricultural management', *PD*, 15 Jan. 1980

Wang Lihuang and Zhou Yufu, 'Growing problems of firewood supply and forest protection', *PD*, 23 July 1979

Wang Yunming et al., 'The peasants perceive the advantages', *PD*, 26 Oct. 1979

Wang Xinyin, 'Transform the passive attitude to inadequate vegetable supplies at Wuhan', *EM*, 1981 (9), 49–52

Weiss, Udo, 'China's rural marketing structure', *World Development*, 6, 1978, 647–62

Weng Yongxi et al., 'Views on strategic problems in China's agricultural development', *ER*, 1981 (11), 13–22

Williams, Jack F, 'Agricultural use of slopeland in Taiwan', in Clifton W Pannell and Christopher L Salter (eds), *China Geographer*, 11, 'Agriculture', Westview Press, Boulder, Col., 1981, 89–111

Wu Chou, *Report from Tungting*, Foreign Languages Press, Beijing, 1975

Wu Xiang. 'The open road and the log bridge', *PD*, 5 Nov. 1980, tr in *FBIS*, 7 Nov. 1980, L21–L29

Wu Xiang and Zhang Guangyou, 'Output-related responsibility systems have many advantages', *PD*, 9 April 1980

Wu Xiang et al, 'A historic turning-point', *PD*, 22 Jan. 1981

Wu Xinghua, 'Why has indiscriminate forest cutting not been stopped?', *PD*, 24 April 1982

Wu Zhenkun, 'Some questions relating to the continued

primacy of planned economy in agriculture', *PD*, 27 May 1982

Xia Lin and Shi Bo, 'City housing ought to occupy as little arable land as possible', *PD*, 18 Oct. 1979

Xiangxiang report, 'Seek effective measures and workable policies; solve the problem of excessive burdens carried by the peasants', and Editorial, *PD*, 5 July 1978

Xie Shirong, 'Discussion on the problems of Chinese-style modernisation'. *ER*, 1980 (1), 38–45

Xinzhou county Committee et al. (Xinzhou county Revolutionary Committee, poor and lower-middle peasants of Liuji commune, workers, peasants and soldiers of the class of 1972, Economics Department, Wuhan University), *Liuji gongshe nongye jiqihua (Agricultural mechanisation in Liuji commune)*, PPH, Beijing, 1976. Tr in *Chinese Economic Studies*, 12 (4), 1978

Xiong Deshao, 'Wide opportunities to convert grass into meat' *PAE*, 1982 (11), 31–4

Xiong Yi, 'Discussion on the arable system of southern Jiangsu – outlook and proposals', *PD*, 13 Jan. 1979

Xiyang county, *Dazhai dili (Geography of Dazhai)*, Shangwu, Beijing, 1975

Xu Dixin et al., *China's search for economic growth*, New World Press, Beijing, 1982

Xu Junzhang and Huang Zhijie, 'Find a way to solve rural energy problems', *PD*, 27 Oct. 1980

Xu Peng, 'Productive enterprise on the prairie requires a clear policy', *PD*, 13 Dec. 1979

Xu Zhongying, 'There is need to bring order out of chaos in rural land reconstruction', *PD*, 10 Nov. 1978

Xue Jinao, 'Form and development of the structure of production in Suzhou prefecture – farming, subsidiary enterprises and industry', *PAE*, 1981 (9), 23–7

Xue Muqiao 1981a, *Shehuizhuyi jingji zhidu de youyuexing he woguo de shijian (China's achievements and the superiority of the socialist system)*, 'Red Flag' Publishing House, Beijing

Xue Muqiao 1981b, *China's socialist economy*, Foreign Languages Press, Beijing

Xue Muqiao 1981c, 'Economic readjustment; Xue Muqiao explains', *China Reconstructs*, 1981 (4), 7–10

Xunyi report, 'Bring into play the good traditions of the party; transform the cadres' work-style', and Editorial, *PD*, 3 Aug. 1978

Yan Ruizhen and Liu Tianfu, 'Economic conditions for mechanisation', *ER*, 1980 (2), 19–25

Yan Ruizhen and Zhou Zhixiang, 'The structure of rural production in China', *PAE*, 1981 (3), 3–10

Yan Shiguan and Ou Qinglin, 'A village hoping for water', *PD*, 11 Feb. 1980

Yan Xiao et al., 'Points on afforestation on northern Shaanxi', *PAE*, 1981 (8), 42–5

Yang Hengshan and Zhao Guoxin, 'Converting dust bowls to green islands', *PD*, 31 Oct. 1980

Yang Xiqing, 'We ought to allocate rural labour rationally', *PD*, 6 June 1979

Yang Yintong (of the Jilin province Supply and Marketing Corporation), 'Why is urban–rural commodity flow still not free?', *PD*, 18 Apr. 1982

Yang Yusheng and Hao Jian, 'Serious destruction of mineral resources in Henan', *PD*, 2 Apr. 1982

Yao Liwen and Xu Xiji, 'New vitality in rural collective economy', *PD*, 5 June 1982

Yearbook 1980. China agricultural yearbook, 1980, ed. by He Kang et al., Agriculture Press, Beijing, 1981

Yearbook 1981. China agricultural yearbook, 1981, ed. by He Kang et al., Agriculture Press, Beijing, 1982

Yellow River Conservancy Committee, *Report on the multipurpose plan for the Yellow River*, Foreign Languages Press, Beijing, 1955

Yi Ke (of the Sichuan province Grain Administration), 'There is need to modernise the system of providing grain supplies to encourage subsidiary outputs', *PD*, 17 Oct. 1979

Yi Zhi 1980, 'Protect the environment, enrich the people', *PD*, 10 Nov. 1980

Yi Zhi 1981, 'We must control the use of cultivated land as strictly as we do population growth', *Red Flag*, 1981 (20), tr in *China Report, Red Flag*, 1981 (20), 64–71

Yu Dechang, 'Checking the degradation of the ecological environment in Hainan by the establishment of new ecological systems', *PAE*, 1981 (9), 49–53

Yu Guoyao, 'Problems of specialist households in the countryside', *PAE*, 1982 (10), 3–7

Yu Jinman, 'Problems of rural modernisation from the point of view of competition for land between grain and sugar'. *PD*, 23 Nov. 1979

Yu Yunda, 'Serious cases of illegal dealing in cultivated land in the Hangzhou suburban area', *PD*, 13 May 1982

Yu Xianming et al., 'Even commodity grain bases cannot rely on monoculture alone', *PD*, 6 Nov. 1979

Yuan Ming, 'Important changes in rural economic structures', *PD*, 22 Feb. 1982

Yuan Qihe et al., 'The secret of progress', *PD*, 15 Nov. 1978

Yun Jing, 'A rural investigation report', *Guangxi University Review*, 1981 (2), 14–28, reprinted in *Nongye Jingji (Agricultural Economics)*, 1982 (2), 55–9

Zenyang zhong yumi (How to grow maize), PPH, Shanghai, 1976

Zhan Wu 1979, 'Travelling the Chinese road to rural modernisation (i)', *EM*, 1979 (9), 11–17

Zhan Wu 1982, *Zhongguo de nongye (Chinese agriculture)*, PPH, Beijing

Zhan Wu and Wang Guizhen (of the Agricultural Economics Research Unit of the Chinese Academy of Social Sciences), 'Aspects of the job responsibility system – specialist contract groups and payment by results', *PD*, 19 March 1981

Zhang Chunqiao, 'On the extension of dictatorship over the bourgeois classes', *Red Flag*, 1975 (4), tr in *SPRCM* 75 (13), 4–6

Zhang Guangyou, 'Stronger year by year', *PD*, 14 Jan. 1982

Zhang Guofan. 'Correctly assess the scissors gap between agricultural and industrial commodities', *ER*, 1981 (4), 78–9

Zhang Jianguo, 'Strengthen economic study of the forests; increase forest outputs rapidly', *ER*, 1979 (1), 42–6

Zhang Lijuan and Shi Zhanao, *Dazhai (Dazhai)*, Shanxi PPH, Taiyuan, 1965

Zhang Tianzeng, 'Construction for water resource use in the development of agriculture in the north China plain', *PAE*, 1981 (7), 11–18

Zhang Wenbing, 'An important contribution to solving the fuel problem in arid areas', *PAE*, 1981 (4), 48–9

Zhang Zhenming. 'It is time to sound a warning about economy in the use of land', *PD*, 29 Apr. 1980

Zhang Zhongwei and Liu Delun, 'Some economic problems relating to agricultural modernisation in Tong county', *PAE*, 1981 (4), 11–17

Zhao Hualing et al., 'Get the system right; develop sugar production', *PD*, 20 Aug. 1979

Zhao Ming et al., 'Advance, not retreat', *PD*, 7 Nov. 1978

Zhao Ziyang (Premier of the State Council) 1981, 'Report on the work of the government, 1981', Xinhua, 14 Dec. 1981; *FBIS*, 16 Dec. 1981, K1–K35

Zhao Ziyang (Premier of the State Council) 1982, 'Several questions on the current economic work', *Red Flag*, 1982 (7), tr in *FBIS* 1 Apr. 1982, K1–13

Zhejiang province Agriculture Committee, *Zenyang shi shan qu jin kuai fuqilai (How to create prosperity in the mountain areas without delay)*. Zhejiang PPH, Hangzhou, 1982

Zheng Qimin, 'Why has pastoral production been falling year by year in Chengde prefecture?', *PD*, 14 Aug. 1979

Zhi Cheng, 'Set trade free', *PD*, 1 Dec. 1981

Zhong Jiaming, 'An investigation unto labour productivity in a mountainous area', *PAE*, 1981 (11), 36–41

Zhongguo dituce (Atlas of China), Cartographic Publishing House, Shanghai, 1978

Zhu Daohua, 'On commodity economy in Chinese agriculture', *PAE*, 1981 (4), 3–8

Zhu Li, *Dongting Hu (Dongting Lake)*, Zhonghua Publishing House, Hong Kong, 1975

Zuo Mu 1979, 'On emerging prosperity', *ER*, 1979 (7), 14–17

Zuo Mu 1980, 'On the role of local planning and the relations between plans and markets', *ER*, 1980 (7), 33–6

Zuo Ping et al., 'Rural market trade in the present phase in China', *EM*, 1979 (8), 34–39

Index